Peak
CONDITION

Peak
CONDITION

Winning Strategies to Prevent, Treat, and Rehabilitate Sports Injuries

James G. Garrick, M.D., and Peter Radetsky

Illustrations by Valerie Kells and Karen Jacobsen

Crown Publishers, Inc., New York

For Chris and Nancy

Foreword copyright © 1986 by Jane Fonda

Copyright © 1986 by James G. Garrick and Peter Radetsky

Published by Crown Publishers, Inc , 225 Park Avenue South, New York, New York 10003, and represented in Canada by the Canadian MANDA Group

CROWN is a trademark of Crown Publishers, Inc.

Manufactured in the United States of America

Library of Congress Cataloging-in-Publication Data

Garrick, James G.
  Peak condition.

  Includes index.
  1. Sports—Accidents and injuries—Popular works.
I. Radetsky, Peter. II. Title. [DNLM: 1. Athletic
Injuries—popular works. QT 260 G241p]
RD97.G37   1986   617'.1027   86–8831
ISBN 0-517-56246-4

10 9 8 7 6 5 4 3 2 1
First Edition

Contents

Foreword by Jane Fonda

The fitness movement has changed people's lives. It's true, millions of us will never be the same since we became aware that we can take responsibility for our own health and physical well-being. To me, what is especially exciting is that whether it be in swimming, volleyball, running, hiking, or aerobic dance, most of the millions of women who participate in the fitness movement have never thought of themselves as athletic, never gone out much for high-school sports. The fitness movement has given us the opportunity to explore our physical potential and rise to challenges we never would have dreamed possible. We are filled with a new sense of well-being that radiates out into every area of our lives. We gain confidence; we have an improved self-image; we're more able to stand up to our boss or handle a stressful situation with calm and equilibrium.

Just to give you a sense of the degree to which this movement has permeated the American culture, aerobic dance alone has become the largest organized fitness effort in our country. At present, there are more adults taking part regularly in aerobic dance programs than there are high-school students participating in interscholastic athletics.

Naturally, when large numbers of people begin to become a lot more active, there are injuries, and for a variety of reasons the fitness movement and aerobic dance programs in particular have been criticized for a myriad of faults ranging from being scientifically unfounded to being inordinately dangerous. Research conducted by Dr. James Garrick and the Center for Sports Medicine in San Francisco, however, is showing that there are very few injuries in aerobic dance, fewer in fact than in high-school interscholastic sports programs. More and more people are discovering what those of us involved in the fitness movement have known for some time: the benefits of exercise far outweigh the risks.

Still, there are risks. As more people exercise, more people get hurt. Nothing comes for free—getting in shape can be painful, especially since up until now there have been few thorough and convenient sources of information about what's going on in our bodies. Many of us have had to endure aches and pains and mysterious ailments because we didn't want—or couldn't afford—to visit a doctor every time something went wrong. Women especially find themselves in this predicament. Men have traditionally been more athletic and have access to sports-related information. Our society promotes sports as a way of life for men, but for many women this is a new world. It's exhilarating and exciting, but it can also be a little scary. It would be wonderful to have a clear, accessible source we could turn to to find out what goes on in our bodies during exercise—what things can go wrong, how to deal with those problems ourselves, and, if we can't, how and when to find good medical help.

Jim Garrick and Peter Radetsky have provided such a source. This book provides practical, down-to-earth, no-frills answers to these questions. It's a handbook to keep nearby when you exercise—we use it as a resource in our fitness centers—and I especially like the book for another reason: the authors never talk down to you, never give you the feeling that this is privileged information. It's a good-natured, realistic book that implies it is our *right* to have this information. Our bodies belong to us, and the knowledge of how they work should belong to us as well. That's one of the things the fitness movement has helped all of us realize.

Introduction

T hird and 12. Richard Green, a twenty-year-old wide receiver for the University of Iowa, waits for the center to snap the football. He's about to run a cross pattern, one that requires him to speed downfield as though going for the long bomb, then cut sharply to the inside to receive the ball. If the timing is right—if Richard makes his cut at precisely the right moment and the quarterback, anticipating where he will end up, releases the ball at the right moment—the play should gain fifteen yards, enough for a first down. And there's always the possibility that Richard, with his great speed, will break it to the outside for much more.

The snap. Richard charges downfield, counting to himself all the while. Two ... three ... at the count of four he pivots, his entire weight on his right leg, and turns toward the middle of the field. Meanwhile, the quarterback drops back, also counting. Four ... five ... at the count of six he turns and throws the ball to the spot where, after countless hours of practicing, he knows Richard will be. He can taste it—first down for sure, maybe a long gainer.

It's not to be. At the same instant, the ball and Richard, a good five yards away, thud to the ground. When he planted his foot to cut, his cleats caught in a seam in the artificial turf, turning his ankle at a right angle beneath him. Rather than cutting to the inside, Richard continues his trajectory downfield in the air, before crunching onto the carpet. Now, his groans accompanying the trill of referees' whistles blowing around him, he lies on the artificial turf, clutching his ankle, wishing he could take back that instant when he slammed his foot into the invisible seam.

All that Marilyn Bernardi is wishing right now is that she could've pulled the racquet back earlier, thereby hitting the ball sooner, and so avoided the weak forehand she just dribbled into the net. How embarrassing—with the pro standing not ten feet away, and the rest of the women looking on, and the doubles party in the next court probably chuckling to themselves at her ineptness.

Marilyn is thirty-eight years old and took up tennis just a few months ago. She knew she had to do *something,* and it was either that or running or aerobics. Well, running just didn't appeal to her—too lonely and just plain boring. And besides, she didn't much care for the idea of traipsing all over the city by herself. She didn't much care for the idea of stuffing herself into a leotard and bouncing around in front of all those people in aerobics class, either. Tennis was just the best alternative, especially when she signed up for a series of clinics sponsored by the local rec district. She met some nice people, found she enjoyed getting out in the sun three times a week, and lo and behold, she *was* learning how to play tennis. Before this, the last time she had stepped onto a court had been during a required P.E. class in college, and heaven knows, what little she learned then had long since flown out the window. But now she can hit the ball back and forth with reasonable accuracy and reasonable frequency. Her backhand might be a little erratic, but give her a second to prepare for her forehand and you'd better look out—the ball will be back in your court before you know it. Marilyn had never been much of an athlete, and so she's delighted with the progress she's made and the just plain fun she's having. She has even lost a couple of pounds—or maybe that's only wishful thinking.

All the more reason to get to this next ball in plenty of time, swing the racquet back, and stroke a good one over the net. Bong! The ball slams off the racquet of the player in the opposite court, skims the net (that's even better; it gives her an extra second to pull the racquet back), and heads about seven feet to Marilyn's right. Marilyn rushes to the ball, all the time going over the things she must remember: swing racquet head back on a line—good. Keep wrist stiff—good. Keep knees bent—good. Now *hit* all the way through the ball, and ...

She never gets that far. While concentrating on the ball flying toward her, she fails to notice a stray ball slowly rolling at her feet. She steps directly on top of it, turning her ankle 90 degrees beneath her, and with a shriek, racquet flying, the approaching shot bouncing harmlessly by, falls to the court clutching her ankle, all the while thinking that if that netted shot was embarrassing, this is ridiculous—until the stabbing pain becomes so sharp that she can't think of anything else.

Richard Green and Marilyn Bernardi are not real people. But they might as well be. They've just experienced the most frequent injury in all sports—a sprained ankle—in a couple of typical ways. That much they have in common. What they don't have in common is what happens to them *after* the injury. And what happens after the injury is the motivation behind this book. Read on. What you'll find out may seem ludicrous, even pitiful—but it's real. Moreover, it's likely that the same thing, or something very nearly like it, has happened to you.

Within seconds Richard Green is no longer clutching his ankle. Now someone else has hold of it, and that someone is an orthopedic surgeon, with the team trainer looking on. The referee has called time, and most of the team, not eager to have to punt the ball away anyhow, clusters around Richard to find out what happened.

The beauty of it all is that already the doctor is close to 90 percent sure of what has happened. He has cut off Richard's shoe and sock, and as there's no swelling yet because the injury has been attended to so promptly, he's able to examine the ankle almost as readily as though it weren't injured at all. While Richard is still lying on the ground the doctor's virtually certain that nothing's broken and there's no muscle or tendon damage—it's a sprain. Once they pull Richard to his feet, the fact that he's willing to put weight on the ankle reinforces the doctor's diagnosis; if Richard had refused to walk on it the likelihood would increase that it may be fractured. As Richard limps off the field to the applause of the crowd, the doctor is already mapping out his strategy.

If there's still any doubt, it's about to be dispelled once and for all— the X-ray machine is just down the tunnel to the locker room. Most colleges can have X-ray equipment available within ten minutes. The pros are similarly attentive—it's an NFL rule that there must be an X-ray facility at any stadium where games are played. And so, just to be absolutely certain, the doctor escorts Richard into the X-ray room. Five minutes later the verdict is in: no broken bones. The doctor was right in the first place. A sprain it is, and a severe one at that.

And that's that, because as soon as the X-ray machine buzzed for the last time, even before the results were in, Richard's ankle was immediately put in a compression binding consisting of crushed ice with a firm wrap around the outside. Now he rests comfortably, with his leg elevated, in a cart that allows him to be wheeled to the mouth of the tunnel to watch the rest of the game, or into the locker room to catch up with the outcome on TV. Everything has been done that can be done for the first day; tomorrow Richard will start rehabilitation.

When Marilyn turns her ankle and falls to the court, she too is surrounded by people wondering what has happened. The difference is, none of these people know what to do about it. Oh, the tennis pro may have an idea of what happened—he's certainly suffered a sprained ankle or two in his time—but there are thirty people taking the clinic, spread out over five courts, each at six bucks a session, and he simply doesn't have time to take care of Marilyn. He makes sure she gets off the court, tells her to stay off her feet, assures her he'll check on her soon, and hurries back to the other backhands and forehands and tentative serves.

So there Marilyn sits on a chair on the side of the court, her ankle beginning to throb like crazy, terrified to put weight on it, not knowing what to do next. Maybe she should go to the emergency room. But it's her right foot, so she can't drive, and the tennis clinic still has an hour to go. She doesn't know anybody well enough so that she'd feel right about asking them to give up their practice time and take her, and even if she did, she doesn't want to be a burden. So she sits, the leg resting on the ground, waiting for the clinic to end. She does, however, manage to pull off her tennis shoe. Ah, that gives some relief.

Well, by the time the clinic ends, her ankle, deprived of even the modest compression her shoe would have provided, is ballooning to softball proportions. And even though it's throbbing like mad, Marilyn has decided that she doesn't want to go to the emergency room after all. She hates the thought of an emergency room—who doesn't? Besides, she left the house a mess, and the kids will be home soon, and then her husband, and there's dinner to prepare. There's probably nothing seriously wrong with the ankle. It'll get better.

After one of the women at the clinic drops her at home, Marilyn finds that she hurts too much to do anything around the house. She simply has got to do something about this ankle. Let's see, what is it that you do to a swollen ankle? It's either ice it or put heat on it—she can't remember which. When the kids hurt themselves in soccer the coach said to ice the injury, didn't he? So she hobbles to the refrigerator and takes out some ice cubes. Ouch! It couldn't be ice—that hurts too much. A hot bath would feel much better.

And so it does. But by the time the kids burst through the door and her husband comes home, a bit later, her ankle is beginning to resemble a purple cantaloupe. Soaking in all that hot water felt lovely, but by promoting blood supply to the ankle it caused it to swell even more. Marilyn's husband, who played high-school football for a year and so remembers a little something about how to treat injuries, says, "Why didn't you ice it? We've got to get you to a doctor." So they put a bag of ice on the ankle, leave the kids to scrounge dinner, and go off to the emergency room.

It's six-thirty in the evening. The emergency room is packed. The first question the registration clerk asks Marilyn is "When did this happen?"

"At one-thirty this afternoon," she replies.

Well, the clerk thinks, if it happened at one-thirty and it's almost seven now, it certainly isn't an emergency. And she puts Marilyn at the bottom of the list. So again Marilyn sits down in a chair to wait, again with her foot hanging below her, although this time it has a bag of ice on it.

Forty-five minutes later, the nurse leads her into the emergency room. Twenty minutes later the doctor walks in, throws away the bag of ice, because by now it's dripping all over the floor, takes one look at her Hebrew National salami of an ankle, and says, "We better take X-rays." It's about the only thing he can do, because by this time you can't even tell what the anatomy of the ankle is—it's nothing more than a giant, taut balloon.

Now Marilyn sits in a wheelchair, with her ankle—if no longer hanging, not yet elevated either—stretched out in front of her, waiting to go into the X-ray room. There's a line for the X-ray room, and only one technician on duty at night. An hour later, the X-ray taken, she's wheeled back to the emergency room, and there she sits for another half hour until someone has a second to peek at the X-rays.

Finally the doctor comes back. He has a big smile on his face. "Good news! Nothing's broken. You've just sprained your ankle."

Marilyn, who is by now very nearly numb with worry, fatigue, and hunger, heaves a sigh of relief.

Realizing that the ankle will probably swell more during the night, the doctor decides that a cast is not a good idea, wraps the ankle with an Ace bandage, fits Marilyn with crutches, writes out a prescription for codeine to help with the pain, and tells her to see her doctor in the morning.

"But what should I do in the meanwhile?" Marilyn asks.

"Keep it iced," the doctor says. "Good luck." And he's off to the next patient.

It's now ten at night, almost nine hours since the injury occurred, and Marilyn has finally found out what Richard knew within a few minutes: the ankle is sprained. But whereas Richard's ankle was compressed, iced, and elevated immediately, thereby keeping swelling and pain to a minimum, Marilyn's ankle was hardly treated at all. In fact, she did all the wrong things—simply because she didn't know any better—and so made the problem worse. She's in for a rough night, and when she wakes up in the morning—if, indeed, she gets any sleep at all—her ankle will most likely be swollen into a fat cylinder, stretching the confines of the Ace wrap, and hurt more, not less. And this is just the first day. The worst is yet to come.

To make a long—and painful—story short, Richard Green starts the game two weeks later. The day after the injury, as soon as the swelling stopped, he began rehabilitating the ankle. With a small army of doctors, trainers, physical therapists, and nurses to assist him, and a clinic full of rehab equipment to utilize, and with all the time in the world to work himself back into shape, Richard was jogging gingerly in a matter of days, sprinting soon thereafter, running noncontact drills with the team soon after that, and was back in full pads ten days after he hurt himself. Although he plays somewhat sparingly in his first game back, he catches a touchdown pass and doesn't reinjure his ankle. He goes on to finish the season, playing every game, and starts getting some nibbles from pro scouts even before his senior year begins.

Marilyn, on the other hand—and this is the painful part—still complains of a weak ankle three months after the injury. She walks with shortened steps, her foot twisted to the outside, won't go near rough ground, turns her ankle at least once a week, and, needless to say, has not stepped onto a tennis court since that fateful afternoon. And she doesn't even want to talk about what she has been through during that time. She had to wear a cast for days, had problems with her knee and hip and lower back because of the abnormal way she moved while struggling to walk on the ankle, spent almost $400 on the whole business from the emergency room on, and although she doesn't really *blame* anybody for what happened, she wonders why it has taken her so long when the athletes she saw on TV during her long enforced idleness seem to bounce back right away. After all, didn't Jimmy Connors sprain his ankle the morning of the U.S. Open and play that afternoon?

It was hard enough for Marilyn to make her initial foray into the world of sporting activities; it'll be a while before she makes another one. Still, she misses it. The fun, the good company, the gratification of zinging the ball over the net—and she did lose a few pounds. But she can miss it all she wants. Without better treatment than she has received so far, or better advice, it'll be a long, long time before she's able to zing the ball again.

Two people, identical injuries. Why are the results so different? Two reasons: number one, Richard simply has access to terrific medical care. Not everyone does. As a college football player at a good school, Richard has available some of the best sports medicine in the world. And he's not alone. Other college and professional athletes are similarly taken care of, and, fully as important, they have the time to devote themselves to getting well—a luxury that Marilyn and millions of others just can't afford. If you make your living with your body, and suddenly your body is unable to perform, all that time you used to spend at your trade you can now devote to rehabilitation—a great boon.

But it's not realistic to think that Marilyn and others like her will ever have access to such superlative care. Although things are getting better—largely because recreational athletes have noticed that people like Richard quickly come back from injuries that could sideline most people for months, and wondered why the same care wasn't available for them—there's still a huge gap between the medical care offered to top athletes and that available for everyone else, and probably there always will be. If nothing else, there are too many time considerations for it ever to be otherwise. But there's one area in which there's no reason for a gap of any kind. It's at the heart of the second reason why Marilyn's experience was so much more difficult than Richard's—that is, *knowledge of how to treat yourself.*

It doesn't have to be much. Had Marilyn known enough to wrap her ankle right away, and ice it and elevate it, many of the problems she experienced could have been avoided—even if she didn't go to a doctor until later on. Indeed, not much more than that was done for Richard during the first day. But Marilyn didn't know, and there's really no reason why she should have known. She simply never had experience with such things. And she's not alone. For many people—perhaps most of us—the workings of the body are a mystery best left to the experts, and many get away with that kind of ignorance all their lives. There are plenty of doctors to at least partially fill the gap.

But these days people are more active than ever before. The fitness boom keeps booming, and people like Marilyn, who never before dreamed of pulling on a pair of tennis or running shoes or a swimsuit or leotard, are doing just that and, what's more, enjoying themselves so much that they're wondering what took them so long. And these people find that things come up—things like sprained ankles and the rest of the wide world of sports-related injuries—that they never had to deal with before.

Perhaps it's worse for women. Like Marilyn's husband, most men at least have had *some* experience with sports. There's a male tradition of sporting competition that runs deep and usually imparts some knowledge of how to deal with injuries. Until very recently, women have had none of that. But once you get beyond the well-known problems like sprained ankles and charley horses, even more experienced men begin to wander into unknown territory. Most of us, men and women alike, just don't know what to do when we're hurt.

But we should. Marilyn may never be taken care of the way Richard was, but she sure can *know how to treat herself* as well as Richard can, maybe better. Why not? Why spend months gimping around as a result of ignorance when you might be back on the courts or the track, or in the pool or the studio or the gym, doing the things you love? Why waste time and money dealing with problems long after the fact? The consequences of so many injuries are determined by what you do *immediately* after they occur—why suffer needlessly?

So where do you go for such good advice? To a doctor? It's hard enough just to get in to *see* a doctor, much less *talk* to him. To a book? You turn to the section on ankle sprains, and the book tells you to ice it and wrap it—that's better than nothing, but it doesn't tell you *how* to wrap it; it doesn't tell you that ice cubes won't do much and it's crushed ice you want; it doesn't tell you lots of other good things. Besides, it's either so dull or so technical that you have trouble staying with it anyway. And when it gets beyond the obvious stuff it says, "see a doctor," and you're right back where you started.

But there's no reason why everyone shouldn't know about these things. Read on. There hasn't been a book like this before. It explains how the body works, what injuries commonly occur during sports (with special attention to aerobics and dance), how to recognize those injuries, how to treat them ourselves, and how to get good help if we can't—all in an accessible and lively manner that presents our bodies as just what they are: wondrous machines that work in very interesting ways. Beyond the athletic enjoyment that this knowledge might afford you, you may find yourself becoming fascinated with these inner workings and, like the person who discovers athletics late, wonder what took you so long.

1 Some Do's and Don'ts, Some Truths and Misconceptions

Lindy Harris loves to ski. Originally a gymnast, now she focuses her intense athletic energy on the slopes. This year she plans to race competitively for her ski club. The only fly in the ointment is that at the moment, after skiing the first weekend of the season, she finds herself stretched out on the examining table nursing a tender and swollen knee.

"You skied for a few days and your knee decided it wasn't keen about it?" asks orthopedic surgeon James Garrick, Director of the Center for Sports Medicine in San Francisco.

"It wasn't real thrilled," Lindy replies.

"What did you do to get ready for the season?"

"Nothing."

Garrick peers at her over his half glasses. "Oh."

"I get in and out of a lot of cars, though," Lindy says quickly. She laughs. She's been here before.

"You knew what lecture you were going to get, didn't you?"

"Yes, I knew."

The fact is that few people prepare for ski season, and perhaps most can get away with it. But people who have problems should prepare for ski season. In Lindy's case, her troubles are compounded by the fact that years ago she had knee surgery for a gymnastics injury. Whether it's as a result of the surgery or simply a function of aging, she's experiencing some wear and tear in her knee. Garrick can feel little ridges of bone along the edges of the joint that irritate the soft tissue around the knee as it moves.

"My problem is that I was a gymnast for five years, but I didn't do anything for ten years after that," Lindy says. "So I'm one of those athletes who hasn't been an athlete for years but still thinks she is. When I get involved, I go for it all the way. But I'm not in the shape I was at twenty-one. The extra pounds come on, the extra weight on the knee ... I keep expecting a miracle brace that I can just put on and forget everything."

No miracles, but Garrick suggests that Lindy build up the quadriceps muscles in her thigh to help her kneecap track effectively. He prescribes an anti-inflammatory drug to reduce the swelling and agrees that she should continue to wear an orthopedic sleeve—a tight pull-on neoprene bandage—over her knee to provide support and help reduce swelling. He advises her to have a tiny wedge put between her ski and boot to position more of her weight on the outside of her knee, the healthier side.

"It might make your turns a little squirrely for a while because even an eighth or a sixteenth of an inch will change the way you edge. But you should be able to live with that better than with an uncomfortable knee. And," he says, "you might not want to sneak off to the ski slopes before you see me again."

"Seriously?" Lindy's laughter is not joyous. "Don't go this weekend? Is that what you're telling me?"

"Well"—Garrick squints over his half glasses—"you're really into pain, are you?"

"No."

"Are you into discomfort?"

"No."

"You're not over this last bout yet, you know."

Lindy, in a very small voice: "Oh."

"And if you really get bad now, you may not get well in time for ..."

She laughs. "Okay. I get it."

Garrick shrugs apologetically. "What can I say?"

There's not much to say. It's all part of the game. Lindy is experiencing the last of the three levels of athletic injuries. The first involves *getting in shape*. Almost all the problems at this level come under the heading of muscle soreness. Usually they're magnified beyond their real impact because at this stage you've probably never hurt anything before. Part of becoming an athlete is learning to put up with being injured. But if you've never been hurt, probably because you've never stressed anything hard enough to injure it, you won't know what to be worried about and what to ignore. It's easy to make the wrong decisions. You may go to a doctor for a problem that means nothing and ignore something that a doctor really should see. You may wake up in the morning not able to get out of bed and think you're in real trouble, but it may be nothing more than the result of not stretching the day before. Or you may walk around for days with a ligament tear that needs attention. People at level one simply have no good frame of reference.

Stick with your athletic activity long enough and you'll find yourself at level two: *learning the activity.* Once you get in shape, once you learn to handle muscle soreness, shin splints, tendinitis, and the rest of the common initial injuries in sports, you'll find yourself facing a second constellation of injuries that occur while you're learning your activity. Each activity makes its own particular demands on the body, and now that you're in shape and have a general sense of what your body can and cannot do, you must learn how to deal with these specific demands. The process takes time. For example, 60 percent of all football injuries occur *before* the first game, while the players are trying to adapt to the particular needs of the sport. In time you'll learn how to do the things that work and not do the others that hurt. Figure skaters, for example, learn how to fall. Instead of stretching out an arm to break the fall and breaking a wrist instead, skaters learn to crumple onto the ice and take the shock on their rear ends, where they're well padded.

The last level involves the risks of actually *performing the activity.* Some injuries are simply inherent in particular movements. This is where Lindy Harris ran afoul of both her sports. Although there's no rule that says she had to dislocate her knee doing backflips in gymnastics years ago, doing just that is an occupational hazard of the sport. There's no rule that says her knee had to swell the first day on the slopes, but she wasn't the only skier with a sore knee, that's for sure. She certainly wasn't going to develop tennis elbow instead, or bunions, the scourge of dancers. By the same token, a male gymnast doing an iron cross on the rings can separate his shoulder as a result of the dynamic forces involved. The shoulder is a very strong joint. You couldn't pull it apart if you tried. Normally a shoulder separation must be the result of a direct blow, as when a football player is thrown onto the ground directly on his shoulder. But a ring specialist can accomplish the same thing unaided—a dubious distinction.

So the question is, as you pass through the various levels of injury, what can you do about them? Most people go to the doctor. If you do, you want to find a doctor who knows your activity almost as well as you do. If not, many of these injuries can be puzzling. If you're a right-handed person who throws things, for example—a quarterback, a pitcher—and you have a sore left knee, then you probably will begin to deliver the ball differently because you don't want to hurt the knee even more. You may release more quickly, start depending more on your arm, so you don't have to come down on the knee with any force. That can lead to other problems—a sore elbow, say, or an injured shoulder. And the new injury most likely won't go away until you return to your old delivery. Unless your doctor understands the dynamics of the sport, and so can see that treating the elbow injury involves clearing up the knee problem first, little will change. Sports medicine is a world unto itself.

This book provides an entrée into this world. It's arranged mostly by body part. If your ankle hurts you'll find the culprit in Chapter 2, "The

Ankle," followed by some suggestions as to what to do about it. If you can't lift your arm above your head, look in Chapter 8, "The Shoulder." Each chapter includes a "map" of the area involved, with arrows pointing to various likely trouble spots. So if the back of your ankle is sore and swollen, there's a pretty good chance that an arrow, labeled "Achilles tendinitis," points right to the spot. Simply turn to that section of the chapter and you're in business. It's easy, simple, and straightforward. Most people will be able to find most of their ailments this way. (And if you can't, turn to the "Cross-reference" at the back of the book. Injuries, and where they can be found in the text, are listed by sport. Under "Tennis," for example, you'll find tennis elbow and tennis leg, among others, along with page numbers so you can turn right to them and start doing those things that will make you feel better.)

Injury Tip-offs

There are some general tip-offs that are common to all these chapters, things to be aware of while you're doing whatever it is you like to do. The nice thing about sports injuries is that, with the exception of back problems, you always have another side to use for comparison. So for all the symptoms we're about to discuss, use your good uninjured side as a barometer. If your ankle just doesn't feel right, but there's nothing obviously wrong that you can point a finger at, compare it with the other ankle. Does it seem to be swollen? Does it feel weaker? Are you less able to bend it? If the answer to these questions is "yes," you may indeed have a problem.

Some injuries are evident immediately. You know when you've hurt yourself; you know what the consequences are. Other injuries—most of them, really—sneak up on you. They may be even more serious in the long run, but they can be harder to identify in the beginning. The subsequent chapters deal with both these kinds of injuries in detail. In general, though, there are six signs of injury that you shouldn't ignore, no matter where they appear:

1. *Joint pain.* Don't ignore joint pain, especially in those joints not covered by muscles—the knee, ankle, elbow, wrist. Muscle pain may not be a problem. If it doesn't come on rapidly, muscle pain may be no more than a bit of soreness from overdoing your activity. But joint pain can be another story. If it lasts more than a couple of days, do something about it.

2. *Tenderness at a specific point.* Does it hurt when you push your finger against a particular spot? If you push against a bone, a joint, or a

muscle and it really hurts, but the corresponding area on the other side doesn't, you may have a problem.

3. *Swelling*. Sometimes swelling is obvious—your ankle looks like a softball, or one wrist is twice as fat as the other one—but sometimes swelling is not obvious at all. Sometimes you *feel* swollen long before anything seems to show up. The knee can be that way. Often people have a tough time noticing swelling in the knee, even though the joint may feel funny. Here's where comparing it with the other side can be invaluable.

If the swelling is obvious, often other things will start to go wrong as well. Body parts don't slide over each other as well as they should. For example, your knee may develop some clicking, as the tendons start snapping over each other because they've been pushed into different places as a result of the swelling.

4. If you can't see or feel any swelling even after comparing it with the other side, check for reduced *range of motion*. If there's any significant swelling, probably you'll lose the extremes of motion. Can you straighten out your knee as far as on the other side? Can you bend it as far? Or, if you can, does it feel odd at the extreme of motion? And is it pain that keeps you from straightening or bending it all the way, or is there a definite block? If the latter, there may be something in the way.

5. Look for *weakness* compared to the other side. Sometimes weakness is hard to notice, a little more subtle than swelling or reduced range of motion. One way to identify weakness in the legs is by going up and down stairs. Do you go up as easily on both sides? And, of course, if you have access to a weight facility, you can test your strength by comparing your lifting on both sides.

6. Never ignore *numbness* and *tingling*. It's the kind of sensation you get when you hit your funny bone, or when you sleep on your arm and it feels as though it's dead when you wake up. If there's no ready explanation for such a sensation it's usually an indication that you have a problem.

With all these things, first look for some obvious external cause. A crease in a figure skater's boot can cause pain in the front of the ankle. Tying toe shoe ribbons too tightly can give a ballerina all the symptoms of Achilles tendinitis. Clothing that's too tight, a wrinkle in your sock, something in your ski boot, an ill-fitting handball glove—sometimes what may seem like the knottiest problem can have a simple solution.

But if there's no obvious cause for any of these symptoms, then you need to find out why they're there. It may be that a day or two of swelling or pain or weakness or reduced motion is not cause for alarm—sometimes unexplainable things go on in our bodies and soon disappear just as mysteriously—but if you're no better in a couple of days, or if things get worse, then you should do something about it.

What to do about it

At first it's simple: don't injure yourself any more seriously than you did already, and minimize the secondary effects. In other words, *don't let whatever it is get worse, and don't let it get any more swollen*. The goal of first aid, of any initial treatment of any problem no matter where it is, is just that.

So, to begin with, *if it hurts, don't use it*. It's really a matter of listening to your body, using your head, and acting accordingly. More often than not you know if you've been hurt badly; there's an innate sense that warns us when real damage has been done. (For example, a quick indication as to whether you've broken or sprained an ankle is whether you're willing to put weight on it—if you are, you've probably sprained it; if not, you may be looking at a fracture.) But sometimes people go against their best judgment and, for one reason or another, continue to use the injured part—the supposed virtue of gutting it through, playing even though hurt, and all that business. So listen to your body and do what it tells you. It doesn't lie.

And the rest involves *keeping swelling down*. Swelling is the enemy because it causes pain and loss of motion, which in turn make you lose the ability to use your muscles. When you don't use muscles, they waste away, and once gone, muscles resist returning. Anyone who works out knows how much longer it takes to build strength than it does to lose it. Miss working out a few days and it almost seems as though you never exercised before—a process that accelerates with age. It's important to keep muscles strong, especially after an injury.

Applying *compression* to the injured part, *icing* it, and *elevating* it are antiswelling tools available to just about everyone. All of them fight swelling—elevation by keeping blood from pooling at a low point, ice by causing blood vessels to contract, thereby decreasing circulation, and compression by physically maintaining the normal contour of the injured area.

For acute injuries, the ones that happen suddenly and tend to swell quickly, compression is the most important of these tools. Applied correctly (and we'll suggest how in the chapters to come), it can do more than anything else to keep swelling to a minimum. Ice certainly won't hurt, but people can more readily carry around a couple of Ace bandages in their tote bags than they can a bag of crushed ice (and you should always use *crushed* ice, rather than cubes or chemical ice or anything else—crushed ice will mold itself to the contours of your body). With compression so effective in preventing swelling, perhaps the best reason to suggest that people ice injuries is to keep away from heat. *Don't apply heat to injuries.* Promoting circulation by stretching in a hot shower or Jacuzzi or sauna before you exercise can help you warm up, as stretching applies internal heat, and a hot shower can feel mighty good afterward, but don't stick your injured part in the hot water. Increasing circulation is the last thing you want to do for an injury, not at first anyway. Stay away from heat.

Again, if you hurt, don't make it worse by continuing to use the injured part. Wrap the area in some kind of compression dressing, keep it cold with a bag of crushed ice, and elevate it. That's about all you or anyone else can do at first.

Some General Truths About Sports Injuries

Deconditioning occurs faster than conditioning. You lose it faster than you got it, probably at a bare minimum of twice as fast. Twice as fast, that is, if you just stop working out—if you're sick with the flu, say, or otherwise indisposed, the rate can increase to perhaps five times as fast. The moral of the story is, to stay in shape you have to keep it up. And if you hurt yourself, find a healthy way of continuing to exercise and strengthen the injured part. The longer you're out, the harder it is to get back.

If you don't exercise, you pay the price. And that's not just true for strength and endurance; it's true for range of motion, cardiovascular health, your muscles' ability to contract, and just about anything else you can think of. For example, if you have tennis elbow and somebody puts you in a sling for ten days, when you get back to using the arm you'll find that you've lost range of motion in your shoulder, even though there's nothing wrong with the joint. The same goes for the knee, ankle, toes, and so on. It's important to stay active.

Misuse is worse than disuse. When you misuse something, you have to use other parts of your body inappropriately. If you can't walk normally after an ankle sprain, for example, it's better to go on crutches than gimp around with your ankle stiff and foot turned out. That awkward motion puts unaccustomed strain on the knee, the hip, even the back, and sometimes the resulting problems are more difficult to deal with than the initial ankle sprain. Our bodies are meant to function as designed. They rebel against inappropriate demands.

Strength and motion coexist. You can't have one without the other. The body is so smart that it won't allow a range of motion that it can't control. A graphic illustration of just that can occur with shoulder injuries. If, after an injury, you don't use your shoulder for a long time, it will lose much of its range of motion. Sometimes the loss is so severe that it leads to a condition called frozen shoulder. On the operating table, however, under anesthesia, the same shoulder can be completely flexible. With the muscles deactivated, a surgeon can turn the shoulder through a full 360 degrees of motion. After the patient wakes up and the muscles return to action, the shoulder goes right back to where it was—frozen. It's not that there's anything wrong with the shoulder, just that the muscles need to be stronger to control its motion.

If you're not strong enough to handle a full range of motion, your body just won't let you have it. So regaining strength is as important to rehabilitating an injury as regaining range of motion—they go together.

Some Common Misconceptions

Tight- or loose-jointed people suffer more injuries. Not so. Just because you happen to have loose joints doesn't mean that you're prey to more ligament injuries; just because you have tight joints doesn't mean you should look out for more muscle injuries. You run no greater or lesser chance of injury than anybody else.

If you have tightness or looseness because of an injury, however, it's a different story. That kind of situation usually means that you've never completely rehabilitated the injury, and unrehabilitated injuries often lead to more injuries. Make sure you completely recover from any injury.

And there's one other time when tightness can cause problems: when we age. Aging usually means tightening, and anyone who persists in being involved in activities that require a great deal of flexibility may be in for problems. It's hard to be a competing gymnast at forty-five years old, say, or a professional dancer. Aging is the great equalizer; just to remain as flexible as you are now requires more and more effort.

Muscle pulls are forever. It can seem that way if you're a runner and you've pulled your hamstring every year for the last ten years. But recurrent muscle pulls like that are usually the result of never quite completely rehabilitating the original injury. It's the old story—flexibility won't come back without strength, and tight muscles, muscles that aren't flexible, are likely to be injured. No, muscle pulls aren't forever, but you must thoroughly rehabilitate them to give the statement the lie.

Rehabilitation programs come to an end. If you've had a major injury, then, no, your rehab program probably will never end—especially if you demand a lot from the injured part. It may be that you can discard some specific rehab exercises, but the likelihood is that while you were injured you developed habits that you're never going to lose, habits that compensated for the injury and so misused other parts of your body. It can be a good idea to continue to do general rehab exercises a few days a week. That's not a huge commitment, but it may compensate for those subtle misuses that you do all the time. Rehab programs are like comets in that way—the tails can stretch out forever—and the purpose of the tail end of a rehab program is to bring the injured part all the way back to handle the demands of everyday activity.

We can always become stronger, faster, more flexible. We know what we're about to say may not be popular, but there *are* limits. Most of us are never going to be Montanas, Navratilovas, or Nureyevs. Work though we may, sweat and suffer as we can, there's a point beyond which we won't be able to go.

So much for the bad news. The good news is that as a practical matter most of us *will* be able to better our own lowly performances, at least at first. But the better we get, the harder we work, the more nearly we approach our limits, the more difficult it is to reach them—and the more we get hurt. Injuries increase as we approach our limits. Top athletes live constantly on the edge. Push too hard and you fall off into injury. The trick is to walk the line without falling off—to find a level that strikes the balance between performance and injury, and stay there.

The element that constantly destroys the balance is, of course, aging. It's the melancholy serenade of athletics, the unknown variable that throws every equation out of whack and makes life interesting. The good news here is that getting older does not necessarily mean getting worse. Our bodies grow smarter as we grow older, and even if we can't maintain flat-out strength and speed through the years, we can introduce increasingly rich experience and so, in some activities, actually better our performance. So even though the clock may say that our abilities are decreasing, our minds and hearts can report increased pleasure in the doing. Such can be the enduring joy of athletics.

2 The Ankle

Sprains

A few years ago a group of doctors in Los Angeles attempted to determine once and for all who needed surgery to repair damage caused by ankle sprains. There has been a great deal of controversy through the years as to how best to manage ankle sprains. Should you wrap them in bandages, put them in casts, repair them surgically? The Los Angeles group was trying to come up with a foolproof method for deciding. Their approach was simple.

Sprains injure ligaments, those tough bands of fibers that connect bone to bone. The ankle is full of them. When a ligament is injured, the ankle bone, or *talus,* is likely to be knocked out of line. You can measure this angle — it's called talar tilt. The greater the degree of talar tilt, the more severe the sprain, and the more likely that surgery might be the only way to restore the joint to anything approaching its former strength. Ligaments are flexible but not elastic. Like Saran Wrap, ligaments will bounce back if stretched, but if stretched too far or too violently they remain stretched — lumpy Saran Wrap — or they tear. The greater the tilt the greater the likelihood of a severe tear. But how much tilt is too much?

To find out, the L.A. group proposed a survey. If they could determine how much talar tilt normal people had, then they could use that information as a standard against which to compare the ankles of people with problems. If 3 to 7 degrees of tilt was normal, then anything over 9 degrees, say, might indicate that surgery was necessary. The approach sounded reasonable; they set to work.

But soon they ran into a bit of a problem: *they couldn't find enough people who hadn't had a significant ankle sprain at some time in the past to be able to determine what was normal.* In other words, ankle sprains are so common that there aren't any "normal" people. Oh, well. Back to the old drawing board.

Breathes there a person who has not turned his ankle? It might have happened by stepping into a hole while running, coming down with a rebound in basketball, landing after a grand jeté in ballet. The quick starts and stops of tennis will do it—more tennis players sprain their ankles than develop tennis elbow—as will running in place in aerobic exercise, especially when you're tired. Gymnasts dismounting after a routine, soccer players dribbling on goal, running backs making quick cuts, even swimmers who slip on the deck—all are prey to ankle sprains. And you don't have to sweat to do it; simply pushing awkwardly out of your chair can produce an impressive sprain. The ankle is the ultimate egalitarian—almost anything will produce a sprain, sometimes, it seems, the more minor the better. Eighty-five percent of all ankle injuries in sports are sprains.

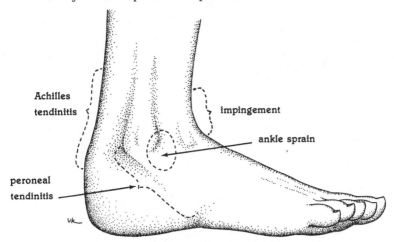

Lateral View of the Ankle

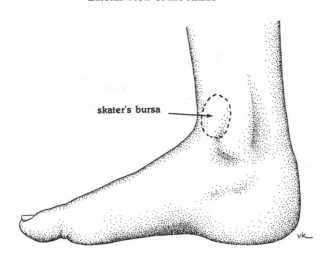

Medial View of the Ankle

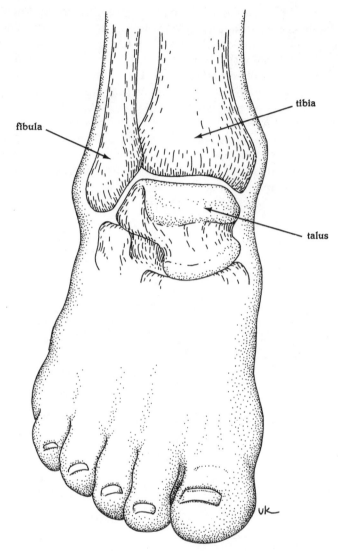

Cutaway View of the Ankle

To look at it, however, the ankle seems to portend better. It is a simple, straightforward structure, with none of the inherent instability of the knee or the complexity of the shoulder. Simply, the ankle is a kind of mortise and tenon, with the lower leg bones, the tibia and fibula, combining to form a concave, vaulted receptacle into which the ankle bone, the talus, fits. Dense tissue called cartilage cushions the meeting of those bony surfaces, and ligaments along the outsides of the bones hold the joint together. There is virtually no muscle at all around the joint.

It would seem a solid, stable structure, and so it is, with one important exception: the lip of the bowl formed by the tibia and fibula, the mortise half of the arrangement, is not uniform. On the outside of the ankle it protrudes farther down toward the foot than on the inside, and the outside lip is thicker than the inside, as well.

The result of this uneven construction is that the ankle bone is more easily able to roll toward the inside of the joint, where the bowl is shallower, than to the outside. When that natural inclination is encouraged by some outside agent—a pothole in the track, or an off-balance dismount—the upshot too often is that the ligaments on the outside of the ankle cannot take the stress of the violent roll inward, and they stretch, strain, or tear. The result, as virtually everyone knows who has ever taken a step, is the sharp pain, swelling, and drawn-out discomfort of an ankle sprain.

How to recognize an ankle sprain

People often find it surprising that an athlete they've watched hobble off the field in pain from an ankle sprain is back at work within days, while the amateur suffers for what seems like an eternity before being able to run, play, or dance again. The difference is largely the result of what's done in the first few minutes following the injury. The professional athlete's injury is diagnosed and treated instantly; the amateur may muck around for hours before hitting on an effective treatment, if then. With sprains, the first few minutes are critical. If you can diagnose and treat your sprain immediately, you'll save yourself untold time and discomfort later.

How do you know if you've suffered a sprain, rather than some more serious injury—a fracture, say, or some combination of problems? The ankle hurts like crazy, it's beginning to swell, you'll never walk again. The whole thing has probably disintegrated to dust, or so it seems. Some rules of thumb:

• Did you try it? The first thing that most people do when they sprain their ankle—after writhing around on the ground for a few minutes—is see if it works. Put a little weight on it; twist and turn it a little. It may hurt, but if you're able to do that, most likely you've "merely" sprained your ankle. Most people have an inherent sense that prevents them from even trying an ankle that is significantly fractured. If it's broken, the chances are nine to one that something will tell you to stay off it. If you're afraid to even try it, better go to the emergency room. Your instincts are probably right.

• If you're abnormally gutsy, and you try your ankle even though your better judgment advises against it, and you feel something grind in there or feel a strange gravelly sensation, then you'd better get off it and go to the emergency room. It's something other than a sprain.

- If your friends help you off the field by supporting you on either side while you hop on your good foot, and your injured ankle can't tolerate the jarring, better go to the emergency room.
- If the ankle feels numb or tingling, or if your foot feels initially cold, then you should go to the emergency room.

Otherwise, you almost certainly have a sprain. The above tests will indicate 95 percent of possible fractures.

What to do about it

So it's a sprain. Now what? The most important thing you can do is *apply compression* to the injured area—more important than getting off the ankle, more important than icing, more important than elevation; all these things can come later. Compressing the ankle *immediately* will prevent more discomfort than anything else you can do.

But not just any compression. To be effective it must constrict the site of the injury itself, rather than the surrounding area. It's easy to make the mistake of simply wrapping the ankle with an Ace bandage and letting it go at that. The ankle looks snug as a mummy, you can feel the comforting presence of the bandage—what more can you do? The problem with such a wrap is that it provides little pressure in the soft places, where the injury occurred. It provides pressure only over the ankle bones, which stick out farther than the rest of the ankle. Those soft hollows immediately surrounding the protruding ankle knobs are not affected by the wrap at all, with the result that they tend to swell out to the level of the wrap. Rather than keeping the swelling to a minimum, you actually encourage it. Upon removing the wrap you find an ankle beautifully swollen to precisely the contours determined by the bandage, as though it were formed in a mold.

Swelling is the body's natural reaction to the trauma of injury, but it hinders recovery. Almost all the initial swelling is from internal bleeding. When ligaments tear, so does the soft tissue capsule that surrounds the joint. The tissue is laced with tiny blood vessels, and they bleed. It is the swelling that makes the ankle stiff, and, once produced, it must dissipate before the ankle can regain its mobility. The pressure of the swelling itself is the cause of much of the lingering pain of an ankle sprain. It affects not only the injured parts but the surrounding ligaments, tendons, and other soft tissue, causing areas that previously had no contact to rub against each other, increasing the possibility of irritation and, consequently, more swelling—a vicious circle. And because swelling hinders movement, any muscles involved in the area tend to atrophy while they're immobilized. The recovery process then becomes needlessly complicated: you must work to reduce swelling to decrease pain and regain motion, then work to restrengthen the parts weakened by the swelling. Why not minimize the swelling in the first place? What you do during the first thirty minutes can cause a swing of six weeks one way or the other in getting over the injury.

A simple and effective way to counteract swelling right at the beginning is to take any soft pliable material—a pair of socks, an old T-shirt, disposable diapers (some Bay Area little league teams buy boxes of disposable diapers at the beginning of every season as part of their first aid kits)—and cut and fold it into the shape of a horseshoe. Place this impromptu horseshoe around the ankle knob, curved part down, then wrap the entire ankle, horseshoe and all, with the Ace bandage. The result is a snug bandage with roughly equal compression to all areas of the ankle, not just the ankle bones. Other, more elaborate devices are available—a sponge-rubber doughnut to be placed over the ankle knob, for example—but none will provide more effective treatment. It might be worthwhile for athletes to carry an Ace bandage and a couple of disposable diapers in their gym bags—instant medical care.

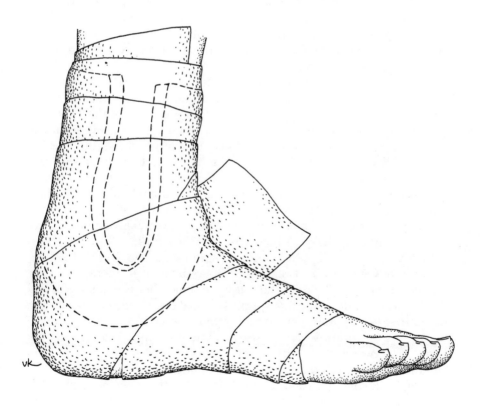

How to Wrap the Ankle

Compression does not have to be hard. You'll know if the wrap is too tight—if your foot gets warm and tingly, or starts to discolor, loosen the bandage. But it must be in the right place. Compression against the ankle knob will do nothing for the sprain. Be sure, by use of the horseshoe, to make the pressure firm and equal throughout the area. And keep it up for the first twenty-four hours.

So when in doubt, compress. And if *ice* is available, use that too, also the sooner the better. But not just any old ice. Crushed ice. The reason is obvious, once you think about it: just as the value of compression is reduced if it isn't constant over the entire area involved, so icing does little if the cold doesn't everywhere contact the injured parts. The ice must be contoured to the shape of the ankle, and it's pretty hard to contour a block of ice or a bag of ice cubes. Professional-team physical therapists carry crushed ice, no other.

Ice has much the same effect as compression. Cold is a natural condenser, constricting blood vessels and other soft tissue to keep swelling to a minimum. Don't ice directly against the skin but rather over a loose layer of Ace bandage. Icing hurts. After a while your ankle will ache as though it's sprained again; later it may go numb. Stay with the icing as long as you can stand it, then compress the ankle again. When alternated with compression, icing is especially effective—the two together are a dynamic duo.

As effective as icing can be, perhaps the primary reason for recommending its use is so people *will not* consider heat. *There is no acute athletic injury for which you should use heat*—at least not at first. No matter how good you think it might feel to take that freshly sprained ankle and soak it in a warm tub, don't. It may go in looking like an ankle—it'll come out looking like a salami. Heat has precisely the opposite effect as cold: it opens blood vessels, expands tissues. It is a great way to increase circulation, but increased circulation is the last thing a newly sprained ankle needs. Maybe later, after the bleeding and swelling have stopped, but certainly not now. If you expose the ankle to heat you will only delay its recovery. *Don't use heat*.

Not at first. Later, after you've compressed and iced, after the swelling has stabilized—twenty-four hours later, say—there are other things you can do. The important thing to remember is that none of the things you have done for this sprain will make any other injury worse in the first twenty-four hours. Even if you've misdiagnosed the injury, treated it as a sprain when it's really something else, you've done no harm. The worst thing that might happen is that the injury will continue to hurt like crazy, keep you up all night, fail to respond to any kind of treatment. In that case, see a doctor in the morning. But in 70 to 80 percent of such cases, the injury is not serious, and in two or three days it will be in pretty good shape.

Later treatments

Now, at least twenty-four hours after the initial injury, with swelling stabilized and pain no longer increasing, it may be time to increase the circulation around the joint. The increased blood flow will leach out some of the accumulated fluid and debris from the bleeding and promote healing, rather than delay it, as before. The timing is crucial here. As long as the ankle continues to swell, you don't want to increase circulation. The time to strike is when the swelling has stabilized.

One way to proceed is by the use of *contrast baths.* These baths, alternating warm and cold, can help to increase blood supply by first constricting the blood vessels with cold, then opening them with warmth, draining the area. The nice thing about contrast baths is that you can easily do them at home. Filling a plastic garbage pail with warm water and another with cold will do just fine. Or you might run the bathtub full of warm water and fill a wastebasket with cold. You can even use the toilet for the cold bath—the bowl stays cool if you flush it now and again. The secret to taking care of yourself at home is to use the things you already have on hand.

But the heat won't do much good unless it's active heat. You've got to do something with your ankle when it's in the warm water (and "warm" does not mean "hot"—100 degrees F, just above body temperature, will do just fine). You can keep your ankle active in the warm water just by moving it. One way is by writing the alphabet with your big toe, in letters as large as you can tolerate. The movement forces you to use all the motions of your ankle, up and down, side to side, in complex ways, which approximates what the ankle and its muscles do when running over rough ground. Any excuse to move the ankle in the warm water will do, but writing the alphabet may be less boring than simply moving up and down and side to side.

Try four minutes in the warm water to one minute in the cold (and the cold water should be *cold*—spike it with ice cubes), alternating cycles for twenty minutes every day. The regimen should help reduce swelling, but then if you've taken care of yourself properly from the beginning you shouldn't have much swelling to get rid of.

Another way to reduce swelling is by *movement.* Movement of the ankle is a form of internal massage, twisting and turning the tissue much as a masseur kneads it from the outside. This movement promotes circulation at the same time as it milks away the swelling. And besides the therapeutic effect of movement, the quicker you begin to move the ankle, the less muscle wasting you suffer and the sooner you recover. The old saw about staying off the ankle is just that, an old saw.

Let pain be your guide. If you can bear weight without hurting an hour after spraining it, then it's fine to walk on the ankle. You might have to take six-inch steps because it hurts to do more, but even with an extensive ankle injury you can walk—you just take teeny steps. Rehabilitation involves gradually taking longer and longer steps, increasing the ankle's range of motion. In this process you are your own therapist. Push, but not so much that it hurts. If you find you've done too much (the condition of your ankle the next morning will tell you), then back off some. So long as you're not in pain, you're not harming your ankle.

The longer you baby the ankle, the longer it will take to regain motion and strength. You won't be able to get back to your favorite activity until you regain them, and you won't get them back singly—strength accompanies range of motion and vice versa. As a general rule, your body won't allow you to have a range of motion that it can't control with strength. You may be able to stretch out the ankle, but it won't last if the muscles aren't up to controlling that motion. You have to bring strength and flexibility back simultaneously.

Flexing and walking are ways to do it. Bicycling, especially on a stationary bike (hard to fall off, no potholes to run into), is another. Soon after the injury, place the pedal directly under the ankle rather than the ball of your foot. That way, the ankle remains relatively stationary, but you keep your leg strong. As more and more ankle motion returns, move your foot farther back on the pedal. Bicycling provides an effective, relatively risk-free way of regaining strength. The motion is up and down, so there's little danger of turning the ankle again, and you're giving your calf muscles a good workout.

Conditioning the muscles near the ankle is more important than it may seem. Once you've stretched or torn ligaments, they will never again be as tight as they were. But everyone's ligaments are loose, sprained ankle or no. That's because ligaments are the second line of defense. Ligaments hold joints in alignment, but they don't provide strength. That is provided by the first line of defense, the muscles in the area. If the muscles are strong, you've got your own built-in splint. You don't need wood or plaster because the muscles will hold things together. So the best defense against reinjuring your ankle (or injuring it in the first place) is to build up the muscles in the lower leg.

Bicycling is a good way to do that. Another is to strap on a flotation vest and "run" in the deep end of a swimming pool. The vest provides buoyancy—you won't sink—and since the pull of gravity is greatly reduced in the pool, and the water itself provides resistance, it takes just about as much muscle to push a leg down as it does to pull it up. It is a terrific cardiovascular workout as well. Fifteen minutes of vigorous "running" will cause even the hardiest to gasp for breath. Just don't forget the flotation vest.

The peroneal muscles in the lower, outer calf are your first line of defense so far as ankle injuries are concerned. To strengthen them you can use a piece of bicycle inner tube or surgical tubing. Nail the ends of the tubing to a piece of board and stick your foot under the loop. Since the peroneal muscles allow you to pull your foot to the outside, exercise them by repeating that motion—lower the inside of your foot and pull up and out. As you develop strength, decrease the slack in the tubing to provide more tension. If you can't track down an old inner tube, you can use your other foot to provide resistance. Simply rest one foot on top of the other and pull against it. (You can even lift the family cat, depending on how calm, and fat, it is.) You'll notice a difference sooner than you think.

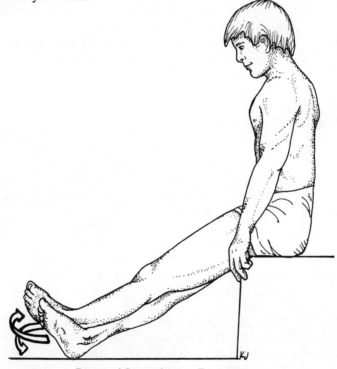

Peroneal Strengthening Exercise

Another way to strengthen the muscles around the ankle—and a test to see how the ankle is progressing—is to balance on your toes on the injured side. Push up onto your toes and, wobbly or no, hold the position as long as you can (*without,* sorry to say, clutching a chair, doorjamb, or friend to help you stay there). You'll feel it in your calf muscles as well as in the ankle. It's a good workout for all the muscles in the ankle and, if you're successful, an indication that your ankle may be strong enough to allow you to get back to your favorite activity.

Again, the steps in caring for a sprained ankle are simple:
1. Apply immediate compression.
2. Apply crushed ice, if available.
3. Move the ankle as much as comfort will allow.
4. Once the swelling has stabilized, use contrast baths to help prevent further swelling.
5. Exercise to regain motion and strength. Walk, bicycle, balance on your toes, and do exercises as comfort allows.

Professional athletes bear weight on their injured ankles the next day. They have lots of care lavished on them, of course, but they don't do much more than you can do at home. The secret to reducing the discomfort of a sprained ankle, and returning to your favorite activity as soon as possible, is caring for the injury immediately. *If* you know what to do.

MEDIAL ANKLE SPRAINS

We've been talking about the kind of ankle sprain in which you roll your foot in, toward the midline of the body. This type, called a lateral sprain, is by far the most common and is accompanied by pain and swelling on the outside of the ankle (roll foot in, tear ligaments on outside). The other kind of sprain, the medial sprain, is caused by rolling the foot out, away from the body, and involves pain on the inside of the ankle. It is relatively rare, because the way the ankle is constructed makes it difficult to roll the foot to the outside, as we've discussed. As a result of this anatomical prejudice, it takes some doing to accomplish a medial sprain—but when you do, it's likely that the injury is much worse.

In football or soccer a medial sprain may be the result of a runner cutting in one direction while his cleats catch in the ground and force the foot in the other. It may involve someone inadvertently stepping on the foot, or it may be caused by running into a hole. Because it requires so much force to roll the foot outward, medial sprains are often accompanied by other kinds of rotational injuries—a fracture, say. And because of the extra distance the foot has to travel to roll to the outside, the ligaments on the inside of the ankle often are completely torn off, rolling up like a window shade and sometimes lodging in the joint itself. These sprains may require surgical intervention.

So if the pain is on the inside of your ankle, you may want to pay particular attention to the warning signs discussed earlier. If any of them apply, see a doctor.

ACHILLES TENDINITIS

The Achilles tendon is the largest tendon in the body. Named for the Greek hero who was invulnerable everywhere except in his heel, the Achilles tendon is the taut cable that runs down the back of the leg from the lower calf to the heel. No other tendon is quite so obvious or exposed, and next to sprains, tendinitis, or inflammation of the Achilles tendon, is the most common ankle problem. Tendons connect muscle to bone; this tendon connects the calf muscles to the heel bone. Without the Achilles tendon, ballet dancers wouldn't be able to rise up on their toes, much less point them; the rest of us couldn't run or even walk up and down stairs.

Like ligaments, tendons are strong but not particularly elastic. They will stretch only so far—then something has to give. Usually what gives is not muscle, which is able to contract and expand, or bone, which is unyielding, but tendon, the weak link in the chain. In contrast to ankle sprains, however, the onset of tendinitis is usually not a dramatic event. Achilles tendinitis is an overuse injury. You notice that your tendon hurts a little bit in the morning after you've run too far the day before. Later in the day it loosens up, and you ignore it. A few days later you find that it hurts a bit at the end of your run, or after your tennis match, but you continue to ignore it. Three days later it's hurting in the middle of the run, and then it begins to hurt at the beginning as well. Pretty soon it hurts so much that you can't work out at all. By then you *are* aware: something is wrong with your Achilles tendon. This is the usual way people deal with Achilles tendinitis—ignore it until it starts compromising your activity so much that you can't ignore it anymore.

Although it might seem as though Achilles tendinitis is caused by overstretching, this is not usually the case (although it may be in women who are used to wearing high-heeled shoes and start doing a lot of hill climbing, for example; the Achilles tendon is shortened from the high heels and suddenly is asked to stretch as the ankle flexes in the opposite direction). Much of Achilles tendinitis is the result of weak calf muscles. The process works like this:

Muscles don't have many ways to tell you what's going on. If they're hurt or fatigued, they tighten up; and if they tighten up, they hurt more. That's why it's a good idea to stretch after doing an activity. Muscles that are fatigued tighten up and stay that way all night, and the next morning they don't work very well. But if you stretch them out at the end of the activity, the stretching lasts.

Muscles become fatigued from overuse. If you keep working the fatigued muscle, it continues to tighten, until finally it's significantly shorter than when you started. And then something gives. So Achilles tendinitis is not necessarily the result of *over*stretching, but of *normal* stretching that the tendon is unable to bear because the calf muscles are shorter and tighter than usual. It's a vicious circle: the more you use a muscle, the more tired it becomes. The more tired the muscle, the shorter it becomes, and tighter. The tighter the muscle, the greater the strain on the Achilles tendon.

Tendinitis probably starts as minute single-fiber tears. The tendon is made up of thousands of fibers; you're not going to miss a few. But when the fibers tear they also swell. As you continue to use the tendon, the swelling increases and begins to hurt. The Achilles tendon runs in a kind of loose sheath, and as it swells it can begin to rub against this sheath. That irritates the sheath, which can then swell, compounding the whole problem. In extreme cases the swollen tendon and sheath stick against each other; there simply isn't room for the tendon to slide in the sheath. It can lead to a condition called snowball crepitation, in which the tendon squeaks in the sheath, sounding much like the noise made by squeezing a handful of snow. Ballet dancers are prone to snowball crepitation. You can sometimes hear a dancer's Achilles tendon squeak from across the room, as though someone were pulling fingernails across a blackboard. That degree of severity is rare, however. If your Achilles tendon is squeaking, better see a doctor.

What to do about it

Since Achilles tendinitis usually starts insidiously and then feeds on itself, the thing to do is break the cycle before it has a chance to settle in. If you notice your tendon hurting after a workout, stretch well and ice the area to decrease the blood flow. To stretch, point your foot straight ahead, keep your heel on the ground, and slowly bend forward over your ankle. You'll feel the tug in your Achilles tendon. (Keeping your knee straight stretches the gastrocnemius, the large muscle in the calf, as well. Bending the knee stretches the smaller muscle, the soleus. More on that in Chapter 4, "The Lower Leg.")

Don't do your usual workout the next day. Do half as much, say, and then stretch and ice as before. Most likely the problem will go away by itself. As with ankle sprains, it's crucial to catch the problem immediately. As a general rule with overuse problems like Achilles tendinitis, it takes as long to get over the injury as it does to realize that it's there.

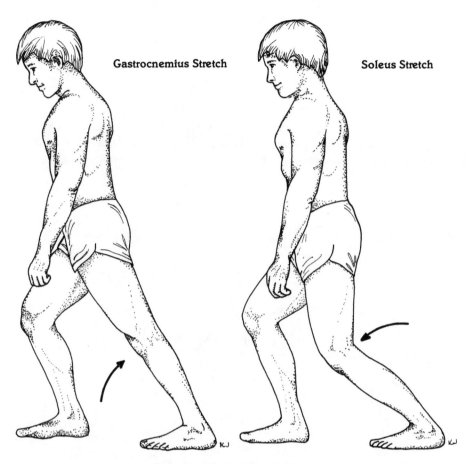

Gastrocnemius Stretch   Soleus Stretch

Stretching the Achilles Tendon

If you choose to ignore the pain for three weeks, it will take at least three weeks to get over it.

After the pain disappears, you can gradually go back to your usual workout schedule. Be sure to stretch well before and after the workout, however. And if the pain returns, break the cycle again by curtailing the activity, stretching as usual, and icing.

Strengthening the calf muscles is another way of reducing the impact of Achilles tendinitis, and reducing the risk that you might get it in the first place. Strong calf muscles can take more use and are less likely to tighten up at the end of a workout. To strengthen your calf muscles, do toe raises. With your foot pointing straight ahead, rise up on your toes with your knee straight to strengthen the gastrocnemius and with your knee bent to strengthen the soleus. Rise up, hold the position for a few seconds, then let down. Repeat the exercise until you get tired, then do it one more time. Gradually increase the number of toe raises until you're doing three sets of twenty each—that's a reasonable goal.

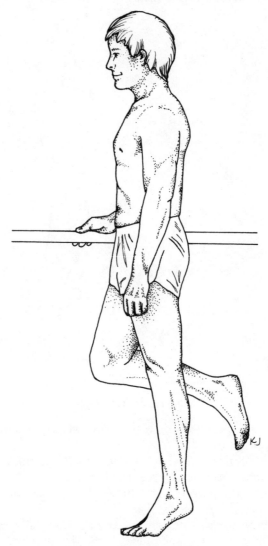

Calf-strengthening Exercise

And, as with ankle sprains, balancing on your toes is a good way to strengthen the calf muscles as well as provide a good workout for the muscles around the ankle. For this exercise it doesn't matter if your knee is straight or bent.

If, after all this, Achilles tendon pain persists, see a doctor.

ACHILLES TENDON RUPTURE

As the Achilles tendon is the largest and most exposed tendon in the body, it's also the most commonly ruptured tendon. But it doesn't happen often, and almost never in women. It's usually a man over thirty years old, usually someone who has been athletically active, usually someone who has had a previous bout with Achilles tendinitis. And often this person has had some kind of warning—pain or weakness in the tendon—and ignored it. The injury is usually the result of a sharp, quick movement: pushing off the ankle to return a serve in tennis, going for a rebound in basketball, even jumping from a boat onto a dock. The movement puts a sudden strain on the tendon that it simply cannot tolerate. As a result, the tendon rips.

Achilles tendon ruptures are strange injuries, in that the pain, or lack of it, is entirely out of proportion to the severity of the injury. The entire tendon may be severed, but often it doesn't hurt at all, at least not at first. The first response of someone who has ruptured his Achilles tendon is to look over his shoulder to see who hit his ankle. It's the primary diagnostic tip-off in the clinic—if someone immediately looked over his shoulder to see who threw something at him, usually he has ruptured his Achilles tendon. Tennis players swear that their partner hit them with the ball. Basketball players are ready to punch out the person who kicked them in the ankle. Dancers think someone threw something at them from the wings. There's no warning at all. You may hear a big pop (your friends may hear it, too) and feel as though someone's whacked you in the ankle. And that's it. No pain. No sense of being injured.

Except you can't push up on your toes any longer. You may be able to point your foot, as other tendons are involved in that movement, but you can't go up on your toes. For that reason, it's a devastating injury for ballet dancers.

Another way of checking for Achilles tendon ruptures is to run your finger down the back of your tendon. If your finger drops into a hole, you've ruptured the tendon. (Try that test immediately—the hole will soon fill up with blood.) And the ankle feels strange. It's hard to control your foot; it has a tendency to flop around.

What to do about it

See a doctor. There's really no home remedy for a ruptured Achilles tendon. You can make the diagnosis yourself (and probably as accurately as the doctor can—the injury is frequently misdiagnosed), but you'll need professional treatment. Until a doctor can see the injury, there are two things you can do: let your foot hang down, toes pointed to the ground, so as not to pull the ends of the torn tendon any farther apart from each other than they already are. Any treatment will be designed to facilitate those ends healing back together; you can begin to help the process along. And a firm compression wrap, much as with a sprained ankle, will help keep bleeding to a minimum.

A doctor will do one of two things: recommend surgery or put the ankle, in the toes-down position, in a cast for six weeks to two months. Both approaches rely on the tendon ends' growing back together. In surgery, the doctor can actually place the ends together, and, theoretically at least, you may end up with a tendon that more closely approximates its previous length and strength. Theoretically. Of course, you have to deal with potential surgical complications. Infection is a risk, because the blood supply to the area isn't particularly abundant.

Recent research has disputed the advisability of surgery. Studies have uncovered little if any difference in strength or range of motion between ruptured Achilles tendons treated surgically and those put in a cast to heal on their own. For years—perhaps centuries—doctors have treated children born with tight Achilles tendons (clubfoot) by actually severing the Achilles tendon during the first few months of the child's life, putting the ankle in a cast, and allowing the tendon to grow back together normally. There's no attempt to stitch or otherwise line up the severed ends—the tendon simply heals on its own. Today more and more people are treating Achilles tendon ruptures without surgery.

There is no right or wrong way, but so far as you're concerned the right thing to do is to make sure you see a doctor and get the injury treated professionally. And know that *there are options* as to the best way to go about it. Regardless of the approach, there's a nervous one-month period when the ankle comes out of the cast and begins to regain its strength and range of motion. That process can be assisted by effective rehabilitation. Stretching exercises such as those discussed with respect to Achilles tendinitis can help, as can use of therapy machines like the Cybex. But don't let your doctor simply remove the cast and tell you that you're on your own. Make sure that you're pointed in the direction of a good rehabilitation program. If treated effectively, Achilles tendon ruptures recover remarkably well.

Other Ankle Injuries
FRACTURES

You'll know it when you fracture an ankle. The pain is terrific. It doesn't *feel* like a sprain or Achilles tendon problem. But if you're just not sure, treat it as though it were an ankle sprain. You won't hurt the fracture that way and actually might help keep swelling and pain to a minimum. Keep movement to a minimum (you won't feel like moving it, anyway) and see a doctor.

IMPINGEMENT

A strange thing sometimes happens in the ankles of ballet dancers, gymnasts, and football linemen. The bone and soft tissue in the front of the ankle build up, making it hard to plié—that is, bend the knee over the front of the foot. It might seem odd that these three groups have anything in common, much less an unusual ankle problem. The common denominator is the fact that all these athletes rely on the plié as a basic technique. In ballet, of course, all jumps begin and end in plié, as do many turns. It is used at the barre to stretch the muscles and tendons and make them flexible. Gymnasts land in plié position after dismounting from an apparatus. And football linemen constantly plié when going into down position before the play (although one might think twice before complimenting a 250-pound lineman on his plié).

The plié position puts great pressure on the ankle. The skin and soft tissue over the bone must compress and wrinkle like an accordion. Sometimes, in reaction to this pressure, the bones grow ridges that lock against themselves, and the tissue swells, further reducing flexibility. When gymnasts miss a dismount and land short, the problem is intensified. The result of this impingement can be a great deal of pain and an actual inability to plié effectively—aesthetic death for the dancer, annoyance and discomfort for the others.

What to do about it

There is no cure for the problem, short of surgery. The operation involves removing the excess tissue and chipping away at the bone until it regains normal clearance and thickness. It can solve the problem for a time, but there is no assurance that the joint will not thicken all over again. Some people simply seem disposed that way. One well-known dancer has had the surgery four times in twenty-five years. (See Chapter 12, "Ballet," for more on impingement surgery.)

Before the extreme of surgery, though, there are some things you can do to mitigate the problem. Gymnasts can strengthen their calf muscles, so as to be able to use them as shock absorbers when they land from their dismounts. If the calf muscles are exceptionally strong, gymnasts can lean into the Achilles tendon before crunching the front of the ankle; the Achilles tendon is better equipped for that kind of shock. Dancers and football players can similarly strengthen their calf muscles. Dancers can learn to cheat a little—they can get away with lifting their heel in plié—and in football it doesn't matter how you look so long as you get the job done.

Ballet dancers also suffer impingement in the back of the ankle, making it hard for them to go up on their toes, much less on point. Again, surgery is the only real solution, but dancers can cheat to reduce the discomfort. They can sickle, or roll their feet, just enough to reduce the pressure on the back of the ankle. As little as 2 degrees will give some relief, and few people will notice the difference—but the dancer has to be very strong to be able to sustain the position. All such techniques are little more than stopgaps, however. Eventually the body is going to win the battle.

BURSITIS

Bursas (bursae, to be technical—one bursa, two or more bursae; from the Latin for "pouch") are small, moist envelopes that show up around joints wherever things slide over each other. They're the body's friction reducers, its ball bearings. The walls of the bursa slip back and forth, allowing things on top of the bursa—soft tissue—to slide easily over things beneath—bone. Sometimes the bursas can become irritated and inflamed. When that happens, they can swell and fill with fluid. The problem is called bursitis.

Bursitis is an occupational hazard for figure skaters. Champion figure skaters have inflamed bursas; so do ten-year-olds who are just cutting their teeth on the ice. These fluid-filled sacs along the front and sides of the ankle would be no problem for dancers—ballerinas can simply tie their ribbons around the bursas. Runners don't notice them, for their shoes don't reach high enough to make contact. But for skaters, who require a superb boot fit from side to side, inflamed bursas can be dangerous as well as simply an annoyance. The stability for taking off and landing comes from a snug, strong boot, as most skaters' ankles are not strong enough to absorb the pressure of jumps by themselves. If a boot cannot fit tightly because a swollen bursa is in the way, then the skater cannot take off and land technically correctly. The risk is an injury more serious than a pouch of fluid.

No one knows exactly what causes bursitis, but most likely the bursas become inflamed as a protective device. Football players get them on the elbow, perhaps to provide a cushion against the constant pounding on the ground (they're especially common on artificial turf). Figure skaters always get them in the same spot, the inside of the ankle, most likely to counter the pressure and rubbing of their boots and the stress of frequent push-offs and landings (see Chapter 14, "Figure Skating," for more on that). But the body works against itself. The fluid begets more fluid, which stretches and irritates the skin, producing more fluid. World men's figure skating champion Brian

Boitano's bursa was larger than an egg, so hard and swollen that it protruded like a giant Ping-Pong ball.

What to do about it

It may be that bursitis can be prevented (again, see Chapter 14), but once ensconced it's tough to get rid of. Bursas can be drained, but often they simply fill up again. The only remedy is surgery to remove the entire sac. Once gone, it's unlikely bursas will return.

OSTEOCHONDRITIS DISSECANS

The name alone is forbidding enough; the fact that no one knows just what causes the problem provides even less comfort. Osteochondritis dissecans (OD for short) describes a condition in which a piece of the ankle bone loses its blood supply and simply flakes away. The bone fragment may remain where it is, loose in its bed, or actually float away, leaving a crater behind. The diagnosis is very difficult; treatment should be professional.

OD sufferers are people with bizarre ankle complaints. You wake up one morning and your ankle just won't work. It's stiff and hurts like crazy. By midmorning it's fine, and it stays that way for the next five weeks. Then one day you get up from your desk and it feels as though somebody's stuck an ice pick in the ankle. It stays like that all day, even swells up a bit. But by the next morning it feels fine again.

You can't explain it. It isn't because you were running uphill, or breaking in new shoes, or lacing your boots too tightly. It's not your first week on point, and you haven't suddenly taken up racquetball. But the problem keeps coming back. Then it goes away, and by the time that you've forgotten you ever had it, it shows up yet again. Better go to a doctor.

Once in the examining room, you may find that the physician is as puzzled as you are. He'll probably take X-rays, but OD doesn't necessarily show up on X-rays. And even if he does suspect that the culprit is OD, he'll be hard pressed to tell you why it happens. It may be a consequence of ankle sprains, but it's hard to be sure. If you ask every person who has OD whether they've ever sprained an ankle, the answer will be yes. Everyone has sprained an ankle at some time. So the natural tendency is to conclude that OD is a fracture stemming from an ankle sprain, and indeed, occasionally it is. But it's difficult to tie all OD cases to ankle sprains. Osteochondritis dissecans may be the result of repeated pounding to the ankle joint, as few sports are easy on the ankle. Or it may arise spontaneously—no one is quite sure.

What to do about it

If the fragment of bone has come all the way loose, surgery is usually necessary. Occasionally the fragment can be pinned back in place; otherwise it simply has to be removed. And even if it hasn't come loose, it may require surgical removal in the hope that the crater will fill in on its own.

PERONEAL TENDON DISLOCATION AND TENDINITIS

It's almost impossible to sprain your ankle skiing—you can hardly twist your ankle in ski boots if your life depended on it. But if you go over the tops of your skis, you can dislocate or tear your peroneal tendons.

The peroneal tendons connect the peroneal muscles, which run along the outside of the lower calf, to the bones of the foot. These muscles enable you to pull your foot to the outside. The tendons run behind the outside ankle knob in a little groove with a gristly roof on it. You can easily find them with your fingers. They're primed to pop loose, but usually they don't. The best way to make them do so is to go straight forward over your skis. (Slipping backward off a stair can do it, also. The motion can cause the foot to flex up and forward—dorsiflexion, it's called—in a similar manner.) The muscles are particularly tight, and when the foot flexes forward they give very little. Something has to give, and the tendons simply pop out of their groove.

The tip-off to peroneal tendon dislocation is that it is *not* a result of twisting the ankle, as is a sprain. This is straight-ahead, over-the-top dorsiflexion. You usually feel something pop out of place. And you get a great deal of swelling that comes up very quickly just behind the ankle knob. In no time at all it looks as though a sausage has lodged beneath your skin.

What to do about it

At first you can treat peroneal tendinitis as you would Achilles tendinitis—compression, ice, rest. That will minimize discomfort, but any kind of lasting treatment should be offered by a doctor. It may be that a doctor will simply push the tendons back into their groove and put your ankle in a cast for four to six weeks, letting time and inactivity heal the injured area. Or he may do surgery to reconstruct the torn area. In either case, rehabilitation to regain motion and strength is a must.

CONSTRICTION TENDINITIS

If you lace your running shoes too tightly and then run for your usual few miles, you may wake up the next morning with a swollen and painful ankle and a roaring case of tendinitis. A number of small tendons run down the front of the ankle into the foot. They are very sensitive to pressure. These tendons move under the ridge of your shoelaces with every stride you take. An overly tight middle buckle of a ski boot can cause the same problem.

What to do about it

The remedy is obvious: loosen your footwear. And as with tendinitis elsewhere in the ankle, ice and rest will most likely take care of the problem.

Commonly Asked Questions About Ankle Injuries

When can I run again?

That's what everyone wants to know. After you've injured your ankle, when can you get back to training? There are three quick tests you can try on yourself at home:

1. You can run again when you can walk fast, without limping and without hurting, with a long stride. Almost as though you were race walking.

2. You can run again when you can balance on your toes on the injured side for as long as you can on the good side.

3. You can run again when you can hop up and down on your toes on the injured side ten times without dropping your heel and without hurting.

Then go ahead and try running. Go out on level ground and, after walking a bit to loosen up, jog for about a block. If it hurts after the third stride or so, then don't jog. You're not ready yet. Try again a couple of days later. A bit of discomfort is okay, but you really shouldn't hurt.

A good test is to have a friend run behind you to take a look at your gait. If you're limping at all, better not run. You tend to use the wrong muscles, and that can lead to other problems—tendinitis of the hip or knee, for example. And you're not training effectively anyway. You don't do yourself any favors by limping when you run.

You're better off doing other things: using a bicycle to strengthen your leg, rapid walking (walking rapidly over hilly terrain gives a strong aerobic workout), or "running" in the deep end of a swimming pool with a flotation vest on.

Can I walk or run while my ankle is still swollen?
Yes. If it doesn't hurt, you probably can. And if it doesn't continue to swell. Most ankle injuries remain a bit swollen even when you're back to full activity, at least for a little while. So if the injured ankle doesn't yet look identical to the other side, you're okay so long as it's comfortable and isn't getting worse. Remember to ice and stretch after you're done.

Why is my ankle stiff in the morning?
Generally, morning stiffness is nothing to worry about. With the night's inactivity, the ankle swells, causing stiffness. It will go down with the day's movement. Motion milks the fluid out of the ankle.

There aren't large tolerances in any joint; there isn't much space for extra baggage. If the soft tissue, the tendons and ligaments, and the surrounding capsules are swollen, then things don't slide the way they're supposed to, and motion depends on things sliding over each other. That's why the first few steps in the morning are short ones. Slowly they get longer and longer. Motion is like applying intermittent pressure—the circulation carries away the swelling.

Will ligaments heal so they're as tight as before the injury?
Probably not. But it really doesn't matter, *if* they don't bother you. The tightness of a joint is determined mainly by muscle strength, not ligament tightness. Everyone has loose ligaments, but usually we're not aware of it because the muscles take up the slack. That's why a good muscle-building rehab program is essential to recovering from any ligament injury (and a good bet to decrease the likelihood of being injured at all).

Why does a sprained ankle sometimes seem worse than a broken ankle?
The reason may be that when you break your ankle, most likely you'll go to a doctor to get it treated, take good care of it while it's healing, and then rehabilitate it carefully. When you sprain an ankle, you may not see anybody—indeed, may not do anything about it except

wait it out. So often sprained ankles can take forever to heal, if they ever do.

The moral of this story is that sprained ankles should be treated and rehabilitated as thoroughly as broken ankles. It's an injury that responds well to good treatment but can linger for what may seem a lifetime if neglected.

I sprained my ankle six months ago. Why does it still hurt?

Because you're not strong enough. Almost without exception, that's the answer.

A few years ago we planned to do a new surgical procedure for twelve people who complained of chronically weak ankles after suffering severe ankle sprains. They couldn't walk over rough ground without turning their ankles; stepping on a few pebbles was enough to cause pain; few could even balance on their toes. So that they would go into the surgery as strong as possible, we put these people on an ankle-strengthening program. We planned to compare the results afterward.

An interesting thing happened: all twelve came back saying that their ankles no longer bothered them. Simply building up strength had solved their problem. To this day we've never had to do that particular surgery.

The odds are about nineteen to one that if you strengthen the muscles around the ankle, you'll solve your ankle problem. If you're diligent, even two to three weeks of work is enough to make a difference. That's spending ten minutes a day—not a big investment in time, but all you need to show impressive results. Remember, peroneal muscles are the first line of defense against ankle sprains. Build them up as suggested in the section on sprains.

Do I need a cast for a sprain?

Probably not, so long as you're able to stay off the ankle when necessary. Some people have to go into casts because they just can't function without bearing weight. Climbing on and off the school bus, negotiating flights of stairs, getting to and from the subway—doing all this while wearing a cast for a few days might be easier than dealing with crutches for a few days. (Climbing stairs with crutches is one of life's more memorable experiences.)

The problem with walking with a cast is that because of the cast-induced limp you don't build up the strength to walk normally. We try to treat very few problems with casts. The odds are that you're not going to do anything castless that would cause you permanent damage, and you might do some good by beginning strengthening exercises. You can't do that in a cast.

Are taping, ankle supports, or braces any good?

Sometimes taping or using an ankle wrap will do some good, as, by providing a little external support, a hedge against disaster, it may nudge you into a higher level of activity than you might be ready for otherwise. There are a number of varieties available. None of them is bad.

Generally, the little elastic anklets don't help much. They may give you a sense of caution by reminding you that your ankle is not yet well, but they won't keep you from rolling over on it. If something is going to prevent you from respraining your ankle, and it's not your own strength, then it's going to have to be substantial and not terribly comfortable.

Braces fall in this category. A brace may help, and it won't harm you unless you wear it in lieu of exercise—that'll make you weak. But a brace is not a shortcut. It may help you back to doing the things you like to do a little quicker, but ultimately it won't solve the problem. What will is rehabilitation—good, diligent restrengthening work, with or without a brace.

3 The Foot

"Y ou're having foot problems?" Garrick asks.

"I know it's because of the boot," says world men's figure skating champion Brian Boitano. "And I know it's a muscle. I know it is. It's on the outside of the foot, on the bottom."

"Is your boot smooshing your foot?"

"It's just so tight. They pad it all the way around and underneath. They put in cork and stuff. I was there today. They took it all out. I go in there about once a week. They hate me."

"No, they don't," Garrick says. "Having you skate in their boots is not bad for business, my friend. They can tolerate a little grief."

"The funny thing is that they've gone narrower in my boot this time. They went to a point in the toe. But that gives me a problem with my third toe. If I lift it at all, the toe starts hitting. It jams right up there. It drives me crazy."

"Why did they make them narrower?"

"Because it was a nicer line. It looked better."

"God, you have long toes. I don't know if I've ever seen a human quite like this."

Brian laughs. There's always something. Before it was bursitis, then a knee, next an ankle, and now a foot.

"Well," Garrick says, "one thing you can do is make your foot narrower. Try putting a little pad under the front of your foot. It creates an arch across the foot, actually narrowing it a tiny bit. I'll give you an assortment of these things to fool with. If one of them solves the problem, that's great, the end of the story. If it doesn't, then you can have them widen the boot."

"I'm having trouble with my Achilles tendon, too," Brian says.

Garrick takes a look. "It's lumpy. How long have you had that lump?"

"I don't know. I might've strained it, because I did a show in Reno a couple of days ago, and my blade fell off while I was in the middle of something. So coming down I might have—"

Garrick laughs. "Run that by me again. Your blade fell off your boot? You mean the screws came loose?"

"I busted them out. The whole heel came off. In the middle of the show."

"Did you keep skating?"

"Well, I told the people that I couldn't do anything else that takes off or lands on my left foot, but when I got going it felt pretty good, so I did some things. The next day the heel hurt so bad I couldn't even walk when I got out of bed."

Isn't it always thus? The foot always takes it on the nose, so to speak. If it's not one thing, it's another, and the foot has to bear the brunt. Feet are mistreated and maligned, decried for being too large or too ugly, toes too long or too short, stuffed away into all manner of uncomfortable shoes, made the butt of jokes ("You sure put your foot in your mouth this time!"), taken for granted at best—in short, the foot don't get no respect.

But it should. It puts up with such abuse and works so well. We ask our feet to support over a hundred pounds, day after day, and we expect them to do so in grand style. Flexing, bending, turning, pitching and yawing, navigating changing and uneven terrain, gripping with the toes (and in the case of ballerinas actually balancing on the tip of them)— no wonder there are times when life offers no greater joy than being able to get off your feet.

But the foot is no passive bearer of weight. It's a flexible, ingeniously designed structure. It contains twenty-six separate bones and a complex web of ligaments to hold them together, muscles and tendons to animate them, and nerves to control them and give them feeling. Some of these muscles and tendons originate in the lower leg, some in the foot itself. Some are large, easily visible beneath the foot's thin skin; others are so tiny you'd never become aware of their existence— if they didn't go wrong. And all work together as part of a complicated scheme of guy wires and pulleys and levers that afford the foot its remarkable resilience and range of motion. All in all, quite a package to stuff inside a pair of 9½ C's.

So no wonder your feet get tired, and no wonder things go wrong. In aerobic dancing, foot problems account for almost a third of all complaints. In other sports they rank just behind the knee and ankle. But doctors don't see as many foot injuries as you might think. People simply put up with them. There are a lot of little overuse problems that are uncomfortable and irritating but that no one ever bothers to do anything about. People are always complaining about their feet, but rarely to the extent of actually doing anything, as though aching, painful feet were just our lot in life, especially when engaging in some kind of sports activity.

In some cases, perhaps so. In many others, not on your life. The following sections suggest ways to pinpoint and deal with these aches and pains. As might be expected, they are as many and varied as the complex structure of the foot itself. We'll start with the back part of the foot—the heel and vicinity—and work forward to the toes, which, as anyone who has ever stubbed a toe against a table leg in the middle of the night knows, may be last but certainly not least. And we'll end with suggestions on how to pick footwear. Believe it or not, it *is* possible to find shoes that are good for your feet—but it ain't easy.

A caution: *if you try the things suggested in this chapter and you continue to hurt, see a doctor.*

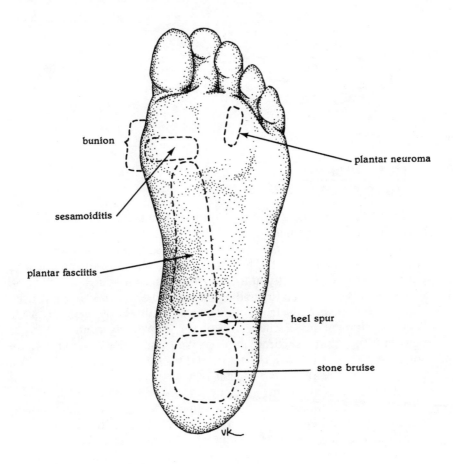

Bottom View of the Foot

Lateral View of the Foot

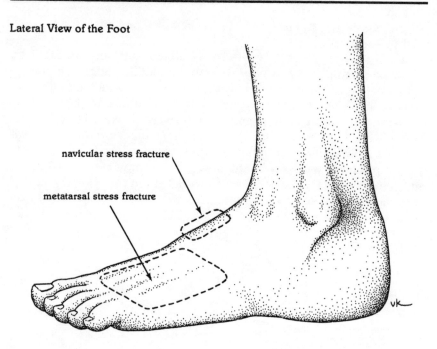

navicular stress fracture

metatarsal stress fracture

The Heel
STONE BRUISE

One of the most painful of foot injuries is a stone bruise—stepping with your heel onto something irregular, like a rock, pebble, or scrap of wood. It can even be the result of excessive pounding in aerobics class. A stone bruise can cause the heel to be so tender that you can't bear to put weight on it, forcing you to prance around on your toes for days.

The heel is cushioned to handle just such emergencies. It is suffused with fat, but differently from other places in the body. The fat in the heel is contained in a honeycomb of tiny, vertically running fibrous ligaments that hold it securely in place. You can't shift around the fat in your heel the way you can the fat on the back of your arm or leg. You don't see cellulite in heels. The fat in your heel can't go anyplace. It makes for a great cushion.

But as we get older these little ligaments stretch and break down, and the heel pad begins to lose some of its firmness. It then becomes more like the fat in the rest of your body, subject to being smooshed out of place. Your heel becomes less capable of cushioning you when you land on things—a sharp rock, for example. The result: on your toes.

What to do about it

The treatment for a stone bruise is simple and ingenious. If the bruise is painful because your heel pad has lost its original firmness, why not restore that firmness and let the body continue to use its own cushioning the way it's supposed to? The device that can do the job is a rigid plastic heel cup widely available in shoestores and running shops, costing only a buck or two. You might think that if it hurts to bear weight on your heel, the last thing in the world you'd want to do is put a rigid piece of plastic in your shoe. But the plastic cups the heel, and because it's rigid it constrains the fat, reforms it to its original shape. When you step down your heel no longer squirts out to the sides—it cushions your foot as it's supposed to.

The heel cup works very well, and you don't need to go to a doctor for it. It can be one of the most dramatic turnarounds you've ever seen: someone hobbles into the clinic, unable to put his heel down, climbs grimacing onto the examining table, slips a heel cup onto his foot, and slides off the table with a great smile on his face. Instant gratification. Just be sure to use a *rigid* cup. It's always tempting to buy the ones with padding, but it's the rigidity that does the job, reconfiguring the fat the way it was supposed to be in the first place.

BURSITIS

A bursa is a slim envelope with walls as thin as cigarette paper. The walls are moist, lubricated so that they can slide. Bursas show up in the body in areas where things move over each other—in and around joints, places where ligaments and tendons pass over bones. The bursas help reduce friction, making it possible for us to move.

There is a bursa in the heel, between the skin and the spot where the heel bone connects to the Achilles tendon. In some people the back of the shoe, the counter, can rub against this spot, irritating the bursa. If the irritation goes on long enough, the bursa walls can thicken and, like any part of the body that is inflamed, produce fluid. The fluid enlarges the bursal sac, further irritating the walls, which become thicker and produce more fluid—and so it goes, a vicious circle. The result can be a bump on the back of the heel, spongy at first, but gradually hardening to the consistency of a hard-boiled egg. And the larger and more rigid it becomes, the more it presses against the shoe counter, producing pressure that brings about pain and more irritation. The condition is called bursitis.

Bursitis can show up in a variety of locations in the foot besides the heel, and usually it's the result of a footwear problem—a shoe that's too narrow, too pointed, too tight in some way—that irritates the bursa. Some people have a tendency to roll in excessively when they walk or run (some dancers fall into this category), irritating bursas on the inside of the foot. And bursitis can be caused by a direct blow to the bursa. If the tiny blood vessels in the bursa rupture, they can bleed into the sac, enlarging the bursa and beginning the vicious circle. Unchecked, a bursa can become a real irritant.

What to do about it

The thing to do is stop the cycle as soon as possible. You treat a bursa as you treat anything that's inflamed: apply ice after activity, try aspirin (two with each meal), use contrast baths if it's really swollen. But the most important thing is to find out what caused the bursitis in the first place. The best medicine is always preventive.

Properly fitting shoes will go a long way to preventing inflamed bursas (see "Footwear," later in this chapter). A hint: if the counter of a new athletic shoe begins to rub against the back of your heel, there's an effective—and dramatic—way to remedy the situation. Take off the offending shoe. Place it on the floor, heel toward you. Then, with all the indignation you can muster, crush the counter of the shoe with the sole of your shod foot. The act is likely to elicit gasps from anyone looking on as you mutilate your $80 Nikes, but the shoe won't mind. It will spring back to something resembling its original form—now, however, more flexible in the back. Good news for your hardworking bursa, your Achilles tendon, and the rest of the area around your heel.

In extreme cases, the only remedy is surgery—actually cutting out the inflamed bursa. You and your doctor should view this as a last resort.

PLANTAR FASCIITIS

If you sit barefoot and relaxed, with one leg crossed over another, you might notice that the arch of your foot resembles a bow (more or less, depending on the state of your arch. A high-arched foot suggests a tensed bow, its arrow about to fly. A flat foot resembles more nearly a discarded bow—almost as straight as a piece of board). Pull back on your toes and you can see and feel the bowstring: the plantar fascia. It's a ligamentlike rope of fibrous tissue that starts at the heel of your foot and runs along the inside of the sole, where it fans out into little fingers and connects to the metatarsal bones at the base of the toes. It's really dense stuff, each strand about ⅛ inch thick. Its function, among other things, is to maintain the arch by not allowing the ends to pull too far apart—the same thing a bowstring does for a bow.

As you use the foot, the plantar fascia stretches and contracts. A great deal of pressure—for runners, a sudden stop, start, or turn; for dancers, prolonged periods on half-point—can overstretch the fascia. Normally, if the muscles in your foot are strong, they can absorb this pressure. The idea is that the muscles bear the brunt of such punishment. But if you're tired, or your muscles are wearing out, your foot tends to sag into the plantar fasciae. The fascia is a last line of defense. If it stretches enough that it loses its flexibility, it can actually tear. The condition is called plantar fasciitis.

Plantar fasciitis is not hard to recognize: the bottom of your foot hurts, anywhere from the heel forward. If you gently pull your toes back, making the fascia stand out, you can pinpoint the spot. Sometimes it will turn black and blue, sometimes become swollen. It's a common overuse problem, especially in runners and dancers. And it can be a particular problem for people with high arches. In such feet the fasciae tend to be tight, just as a bowstring is tightest when the bow is flexed. A tight fascia has less give and so can be more easily overstretched—it doesn't allow much shock absorption. People with flat feet, while susceptible to all sorts of other problems, do not as often suffer from plantar fasciitis—thank heaven for small blessings. Their fasciae are not tight enough to hold an arch in place, much less tear.

What to do about it

Treat plantar fasciitis as you would tendinitis or bursitis: stop doing what hurts, apply ice, take aspirin, give yourself contrast baths. And try to take some of the load off the bowstring. The idea is to artificially create an arch by bringing your heel and toes closer together, thereby easing the pressure on the fascia. One way to do it is to put an arch support in your shoe. But sometimes the arch support supports your arch in the very spot where it hurts—not a good idea. It may be that you have to see someone who can make you a customized arch support, an orthotic. Orthotics are not the answer for everything, but in this case they can make a huge difference, as the pain can be so severe that you can't even walk. So if rest, aspirin, contrast baths, and over-the-counter arch supports don't work, a visit to a podiatrist might be the ticket.

Plantar fasciitis can also feel just like a stone bruise in the heel. Sometimes the fascia can stretch and tear so violently that it actually pulls a piece of bone loose at the heel where the fascia connects, causing what's called a heel spur. Heel spurs can make spectacular X-rays—a nasty-looking spike of bone up to ¾ inch long floating in the heel—but in many instances removing the spike isn't going to solve the problem. What will help is removing the pressure on the fascia and getting rid of the inflammation.

Plantar fasciitis is not something to ignore. Like Achilles tendinitis, getting rid of it can be a long process once it becomes entrenched. But there is good news, for at least one segment of the athletic community: we don't see much plantar fasciitis in aerobic dancers. That's surprising, as aerobic dancers are up on their toes much of the time, testing the mettle of their plantar fasciae. But whatever the reason for such good news, we'll take it.

The Midfoot

TENDINITIS

Just as anywhere else in the body, the bulk of foot problems are overuse injuries. You try something new, or do more of your usual activity, overusing the muscles, which subsequently tighten up and pull against the tendons, which, being the most vulnerable in the chain of bone-muscle-tendon, cannot bear the strain and tear. It's an old story, repeated often in this book. The foot, however, offers a couple of unique wrinkles.

One is that you can get a kind of tendinitis that you don't see anywhere else: tendinitis that is the result of *external* pressure. Think about it. We really don't put constraining clothing around our arms, our legs, the rest of our body. But we wedge our feet into all sorts of confining footwear, sometimes for reasons that have little to do with comfort or protection. And this footwear can actually cause tendinitis in and of itself. When dealing with feet, therefore, we're in a world in which *clothing* can cause problems. (More on that later.)

The other thing about the foot is that it enables you to identify problems quickly and accurately, more so than elsewhere in the body. There's not a lot of fat in the foot, not a lot of muscle. You can see almost all the tendons. Anything that's kind of rigid, that feels like a little rope, is a tendon. When you move your feet, these little ropes move—you can't mistake them. So if one of them hurts when you move your foot, you probably have tendinitis. Sometimes you'll get the same thing that's possible with Achilles tendinitis: snowball crepitation—the tendon actually can squeak. And because there's little padding in the foot between the skin and tendons, the injured area may become red and swollen. So self-diagnosis in the foot is pretty easy.

Now, back to footwear. Because there's no padding in the foot, just lacing your shoes too tightly for a three- or four-mile run can cause so much irritation that you may be on the sidelines for three or four weeks. The tendons that run along the top of the foot are virtually on the surface. They're extremely sensitive to pressure. As you run, the tendons slide beneath the skin. Running puts the foot through a wide range of motion, and the tendons must move a long way. If there's outside pressure curtailing their ability to slide, the tendons can easily become inflamed. So, particularly when you're breaking in new shoes and haven't yet figured out how tightly or loosely to lace them, opt for loosely.

The same problem may arise in skiing. A too-tight center buckle on a ski boot is a common cause of tendinitis. Sometimes people have ill-designed or ill-fitting boots and find that they can't keep their heel down inside the boot. The first thing they do is tighten the center buckle over the instep of their foot. That probably won't keep the heel down either, but it will keep the tendons down—mash them, in fact. And sometimes it can squash one of the little nerves that run along the tendons to the foot. Like the tendons, the nerves in the foot are virtually unprotected. It's not uncommon in November and December to hear people complain that two or three of their toes are numb. They'll probably stay numb through the entire ski season and into the summer, all from one day of skiing. It's not a major problem, but it can be very annoying to have a constant tingling in your foot.

What to do about it

Treat tendinitis of the foot as you'd treat tendinitis anywhere: back off from doing what hurts. Also, you might try a shoe with a more rigid sole to block some of the motion of your foot. If there's swelling, give your foot contrast baths. Take aspirin. But the most important thing is to stop doing whatever it was that caused the problem in the first place. Then ease back slowly. Let pain be your guide. If it doesn't hurt, you're okay. If it hurts, you're doing too much. Back off for a while, and then push forward again.

STRESS FRACTURES

One of the most common foot problems, stress fractures occur more often than not in those small bones between the toes and the top of the foot called the metatarsals. (See Chapter 4, "The Lower Leg," for a thorough explanation of just what a stress fracture is.) You can easily feel the metatarsals. Some people think that if you have what's called "Morton's foot"—your second toe is longer than your big toe—you may have a tendency to suffer stress fractures, but this is a controversial point of view. You don't incur a stress fracture because there is something wrong with the mechanics of your foot, but rather because there is something wrong with the mechanics of your head—you went off and ran nine miles when you're used to running two, that sort of thing. Stress fractures are almost always the result of training mistakes like that.

You can get a stress fracture at the base of the fifth metatarsal, that area marked by a bump on the outside of your foot. Dancers, and basketball players even more, are susceptible to those. And jumping sports like basketball can cause a stress fracture of the navicular, the bony ridge on the top of the foot. They are horrible to deal with—difficult to see on X-rays, long to heal, sometimes even requiring surgery. It is the injury that basketball player Bill Walton has struggled with for years. Navicular stress fractures also are quite common in gymnasts. Some nationally prominent gymnasts have suffered this injury. They are nasty injuries. You just don't ignore things like this in the middle part or outside of your foot.

Fortunately, these bones are right there under the skin, visible and easy to keep track of. You'll see and feel swelling. And, like stress fractures of the shinbone, there will be a discrete area of tenderness. You can cover it with a dime or a nickel. In contrast to tendinitis, in which the painful area is more diffused, if you put your finger on a stress fracture it will *really* hurt. A caution: the commonest reason to hurt on the outside of the foot is that your shoes aren't wide enough. So the first thing to do if you suffer any of these symptoms is look to your shoes. If you hurt only when you wear one particular pair of shoes and are fine the rest of the time, you're in luck. It's much easier to replace a pair of shoes than it is to replace a foot.

What to do about it

If the symptoms persist no matter what shoes you wear, stop doing whatever it is that makes you hurt. Rest is the primary treatment for stress fractures. That and dealing with the swelling by icing and taking contrast baths. Getting into a stiff-soled shoe to reduce the movement of your foot can also help. Boots are very good in this regard. Hiking boots, cowboy boots—both can help. (The big problem with cowboy boots is getting them on and off. Once you're in them, they can solve a great many problems temporarily.)

If a few days of rest and reduced activity don't seem to be making headway, or if you stop your activity, the pain goes away, and then it comes back as soon as you begin again, it's a good idea to see a doctor. Because ...

FRACTURES

... if ignored, stress fractures can turn into overt fractures, actually severing and displacing the bone. The navicular bone, which occupies a position in the foot somewhat like the keystone of an arch, and is therefore particularly vulnerable, can be fractured this way, as can the base of the fifth metatarsal.

There are a couple of kinds of fracture that you can get at the base of this metatarsal (the bump on the outside of your foot, in front of and beneath the ankle knob). One is the result of a severe ankle sprain, which can pull off the peroneal tendon attached there. The peroneal tendon connects the peroneal muscles, which run along the outside of the lower calf, to the foot. You can easily see and feel the tendon coming down from the ankle knob. These muscles are part of your protection against ankle sprain, because they keep you from inverting your foot. If you step into a hole, say, and your foot begins to roll underneath you, the peroneal muscles tighten up strongly in an effort to hold back the foot and save you. But if your foot continues to roll in, something has to give. Sometimes that something is the tendon (see "Tendinitis," above), but sometimes it's not the tendon but a piece of the metatarsal bone itself. Here the bone isn't as strong as the tendon, so instead of the tendon peeling away from the bone, it takes a piece of the bone with it.

What to do about it

Usually the bone doesn't travel very far, just a couple of millimeters. In that case, it might heal by itself if you simply do the things that you'd normally do for an ankle sprain (see Chapter 2, "The Ankle"). In some activities, like basketball and dance, where there is a lot of side-to-side movement, it's especially crucial that these injuries heal perfectly, so you may have to endure a cast. The important thing, though, is that it's difficult to make this judgment on your own. So if you sprain your ankle, and the outside of your foot becomes sore and black and blue, better see somebody about it.

You can also suffer a regular fracture at the base of the fifth metatarsal. Dancers are plagued with these. Sometimes they start as stress fractures, are ignored, and turn into overt fractures. They can be nasty, difficult to deal with, with a horrible reputation for not healing together. It is a place in the foot where the likelihood of having to resort to surgery is very high. Another injury to see someone about.

The worst thing that can happen to the inside of the foot is the result of another ankle sprain, the less common medial sprain, which involves rolling the foot *out* away from the body. This motion can put strain on the posterior tibial muscles—one of the groups of muscles in the calf—and on the tendon that connects them to the foot. The tendon attaches to the foot at the navicular, that bony bump beneath and ahead of your inside ankle knob, and its major job is to support the arch of the foot. With some people, especially those with flat feet, this bump is very prominent. Frequently it protrudes just at the top level of shoes. (Sometimes ballet dancers roll the foot out so much in an attempt to increase turnout that their navicular area actually hits the floor. They form a callus over it.)

If your foot rolls out too severely, the tendon can tear, or it can pull so sharply that it pops a piece of bone loose, much as on the other side of the foot at the base of the fifth metatarsal. And, as in the metatarsal area, there's little padding around the navicular. This is usually an exquisitely tender injury. Fortunately, it's rare, not nearly so frequent as on the outside of the foot. It's another injury that should be seen by someone.

What to do about it

Other small bones in the midfoot can fracture as well—some the consequence of ankle sprains, most quite uncomfortable, some really awful. So a word to the wise: if you injure your foot anywhere from the midpart back to the ankle and it *really* hurts, with a lot of swelling (in the foot, not around the ankle itself) and black and blue discoloration, *then caution is very important. See a doctor and get an X-ray.*

CONTUSIONS

Dropping something on your foot or having somebody step on your foot in one sport or another can cause contusions, which are very common. Your foot is not well suited to being scrunched. We wear shoes to protect not only the bottom of the foot but the top as well. If you bruise the top of your foot badly, it isn't going to work very well. It can be as painful, and debilitating, as barking your shin. Remember that the black and blue of a bruise is really blood under the skin, and when there's bood under the skin in the foot, there's nowhere for it to go. It simply pools on top of the bone. All the bones in the foot are just under the skin, so the tendons on the top of your foot must slide directly over the bone. If there's a big sea of blood there, the tendons won't slide very well. Tendinitis can easily result from the obstruction.

What to do about it

Foot contusions should be treated the same way you treat contusions anywhere: apply a compression wrap as soon as possible. The more blood that pools under the skin, the longer it will take to get rid of it. Ice can help to prevent swelling; contrast baths can help to reduce it once it has formed.

DISLOCATIONS

The ultimate sprain is a dislocation, and there are some horrible dislocations that occur up in the foot. These are devastating injuries. There are so many bones in your foot, and so many things can go wrong with them. Again, if you *really* hurt your foot, and it swells and turns black and blue, don't even dream of not seeing somebody.

The Toes

FRACTURES

It's time to wince. We can no longer put off mentioning the bane of foot injuries: stubbing the toe. It hurts even to think about it. And more than just hurting, stubbing your toe can actually cause a fracture. If you're ambling along at 4 mph or so, your foot is actually swinging through at a speed more than twice that. If you're walking fast, your foot may be traveling 10 to 15 mph. And if you're running, forget it. Every once in a while we see an X-ray of a toe that looks as though somebody put a firecracker beneath it. You think, my God, how could anyone fracture a toe this badly? Then you remember that these are tiny bones, and if your foot is going 10 mph and it hits a coffee table in the middle of the night, or a doorjamb while you're setting off for your workout, or a wayward tree root in the middle of your cross-country run, you can do an incredible amount of damage.

What to do about it

The toe swells up, turns black and blue, looks horrible. But as a general rule, if it looks straight, you probably won't have to do anything more than tape it to the adjacent toe. Toes, like fingers, are different lengths, and the spaces between the joints in the toe are different lengths, too. Generally your toes fit against each other, like building blocks. If you want to stabilize a toe, just tape it to the next toe— presto, a built-in splint. Remember to put something absorbent between the toes—a little piece of lamb's wool, say, which is available at running stores—to absorb the perspiration. Otherwise you'll rot.

Tape the toes lightly enough so that you're still comfortable, and you may want to get into a stiffer-soled shoe to further protect the toe and reduce movement. Keep the toe in its ready-made splint for a couple of weeks, until the pain goes away. And that should be all that's necessary—until you stub it the next time.

You can give the same kind of homemade treatment to the big toe as well. You don't as often stub the big toe, but when you do it can be a beaut. It's particularly critical that there not be any deformity or displacement of the big toe, so if you really smash your big toe and you're reluctant to bear weight on it, it probably isn't a bad idea to get it X-rayed. It's a good-sized joint, and you must have good big toe motion for pushing off in virtually any sport, not to mention simply running and walking. It can't hurt to err on the side of caution when the big toe is involved.

DISLOCATIONS

Sports dislocations are most common in activities like gymnastics and dance, in which the footwear is soft. A gymnast's foot may have a tendency to stick to the mat. Especially if barefoot, in the midst of floor exercises, say, a gymnast can hang up on the big toe and go right over it. A ballet dancer on point can force the big toe to knuckle under with full weight on top of it. That kind of injury is not terribly common, but it can be devastating. There's so much weight on the big toe that sometimes the bone will actually pierce the skin. Needless to say, these injuries should be seen by someone. Fortunately, this kind of severe dislocation is not very common. In most sports the shoes have soles rigid enough to prevent the toe from going under.

Most of the time you could probably get away with putting a dislocated big toe into a stiff-soled shoe and a splint. If you can walk comfortably in a wood-soled clog, that's fine. But often people find it more convenient to have it put in a cast. And, again, as you need a completely healthy big toe to function well in so many activities, it can never hurt to get professional help.

You can stub the other toes and dislocate them, too. But we usually don't see these because people simply grab the toe and pop it back into place. And if it's not deformed, taping to the adjacent toe and going to a stiff-soled shoe can do the trick.

There's one more sport that is turning up dislocations these days: football. In the last few years football players have gone to lighter and lighter shoes, to make them "fast" (as though one ounce of shoe is going to make a difference to a guy who weighs 230 pounds). Football shoes are really quite flimsy now, and they contribute to football players getting something called turf toe. The shoe is so flimsy that when a lineman pushes off he's allowed a great deal of motion in the big toe, sometimes too much. He can overstretch the joint, like a ballet dancer going up on relevé and falling forward all the time. It turns into a chronic sprain, which is resprained every time the lineman pushes off (on artificial turf, that is—thus the name turf toe; on a grass surface the cleat can dig into the ground and make a little hole, allowing the toe to sink in and not overstretch every time). The toe can become hugely swollen and constantly tender. Even a little motion can hurt—not the ideal situation for a football player. This condition in turn can lead to a dislocation, the ultimate sprain.

If football players had stiffer-soled shoes, they couldn't get in an overstretched position in the first place. But you can't blame the footwear companies. They're just yielding to the demands of the customer.

BUNIONS

Bunions are *de rigueur* for dancers, a normal adaptation to the confining slippers dancers are always stuffing their feet into. In fact, most of the niggling problems to follow are simply a fact of life for dancers, whose feet resemble nothing less than a combat zone most of the time. But in the "normal" population, bunions can be a cause for comment, even embarrassment. Those big knobs at the outside of the big toe joint can seem unsightly and certainly can make fitting into shoes something of a trial. And as we age, our bunions tend to grow larger.

An overly tight shoe is a common cause; the other is that some people are simply born with bunions. The big toe drifts out at the joint, forming a mound that rubs against your footwear, overly tight or not. In response, the skin around the bunion thickens, increasing the pressure against the shoe, which then rubs more firmly, causing the skin to grow thicker—and so it goes. And compounding the problem is the fact that usually a large segment of the bunion is composed of a bursa between the skin and the bone. If the friction between foot and shoe occurs at the level of the skin, you get a thickening of the skin—a callus. But if the skin presses against the shoe so firmly that the skin actually slides over the bone, the result can be a bursa, which although filled with fluid, can feel as hard as bone. (See the discussion of bursitis earlier in this chapter.)

What to do about it

Most people simply learn to live with bunions. The important thing is not to let them get ahead of you. Wear shoes that are not too tight, and go barefoot as much as you can—bunions rarely hurt when there's nothing for them to chafe against. A crescent-shaped pad that goes *around* the bunion (in general never pad *over* the thing that hurts; pad around it, behind it, next to it, so that you can take the pressure in some other area) can help. There's also something called a bunion splint available; you can find it at the Dr. Scholl's counter in the drugstore. It pulls your toe out a little straighter, which helps take pressure off the bunion.

If your bunion becomes particularly sore and inflamed, ice the area after activity, try contrast baths, and take two aspirin with meals to reduce swelling. If the pain persists, you might see someone, but think more than twice if someone recommends surgery. Athletes should be *very* cautious about having any kind of surgery on their feet, certainly *not* bunion surgery. The hazards far outweigh the possible benefits.

And certainly people who are athletic should *never* have any kind of cosmetic surgery on their feet. Women tend to have bunions more often than men, and women sometimes want their bunions dealt with surgically just because they look so awful. It's not worth it. If you find yourself leaning in this direction, just think of dancers' feet. From an aesthetic point of view, they are a disaster. But dancers don't care. And, after all, who is more graceful and attractive than a dancer?

CALLUSES

Calluses, those thick, hard mounds of skin that show up on the bottom, or sometimes the side, of your foot, are caused by friction and pressure, and, like bunions and bursas, they can become self-perpetuating. As they grow bigger, they cause more friction and pressure; as there's more friction and pressure, they grow bigger.

There are some activities, like dance, in which calluses are desirable. They actually protect the feet against the constant pounding dancers put them through. When dancers have been off for a while, and their calluses have reduced or disappeared, they're at a real disadvantage. (Gymnasts want calluses on their hands, which they soak in all manner of potions—brine, for example—to make the calluses bigger.) Often dancers help soften calluses and corns—but do not remove them—by soaking their feet in tea. The acid in the tea helps control the calluses.

If calluses are allowed to become too thick they may crack. And they may crack all the way down through the callus, which is really only dead skin. Once you get a crack all the way through the callus, which may have taken you three years to build up to ⅛ inch thick, it will take you another three years to fill in the crack. The thicker the callus, the less resilient it becomes; the less resilient it becomes, the more likely it is to crack. And a cracked callus can actually bleed. Then infection can be a problem, because the crevices are so deep that they have a tendency to close over, trapping any infection within.

The other big problem with large calluses is that occasionally you can get blisters under the callus. That is one of life's less appealing experiences. We've seen people with fifty-cent-piece-sized blisters under a callus. They're horribly uncomfortable. The pressure caused by the blister's accumulation of fluid can't dissipate underneath a callus—there's no place for it to go. The upshot is pain. And if the blister breaks, the whole callus may come off. You can end up with a raw piece of meat the size of a fifty-cent piece. It may take months to heal. So there are some long-term reasons not to let calluses get ahead of you, even if you're just a recreational athlete.

What to do about it

There are surgical procedures that can make calluses less promi-nent, but it's much easier simply to spend ten minutes once a week sanding them down with a pumice stone, or even sandpaper. You may not solve the problem that way, but you can keep it from getting worse. Take a bath to soften the calluses, then sand them down. Let comfort be your guide—get them down to where they feel good. Since they will most likely form no matter what you do, keep them under control.

CORNS

Calluses and corns are the same thing in different places. Calluses occur on the bottom, or sometimes the side, of your foot. Corns occur in places where you're not bearing weight, most often on or between the toes. If you have a high arch and your toes tend to buckle up like claws, you may be particularly susceptible to corns.

What to do about it

Look to your footwear. If your shoes rub along the top of your toes, it's time to change styles. Corns can be a particular problem for women, because women's shoes rarely have a deep toe box—they make the foot look longer and so aren't very popular—and if your toes are clawing inside your sleek, sloping shoes, you most likely will have problems. A hint when trying on shoes: when you step down you shouldn't be able to feel the tops of your toes against the shoe. If you can already feel them rubbing in the store, they're certain to rub more when you wear them regularly.

Corns between your toes are often soft, because they're moist all the time from perspiration. If you soaked your feet in water, the hard corns on top of your toes would turn into soft corns. They can be best dealt with by inserting a wad of lamb's wool between the toes to spread them and keep the corn dry. Spreading the toes takes the pressure off the corn; sometimes they'll just go away. And keeping it dry reduces the possibility of infection. Because soft corns are moist, they're much more likely than dry corns to become infected. In that case, they can be a real problem. The temptation is to put something handy like foam between the toes. Foam will keep the toes apart, all right, but it won't absorb perspiration as lamb's wool can. Keeping the toes apart by itself won't help things. You must get rid of the moisture.

BLACK TOENAILS

Black toenails are the result of bleeding under the nail. The easiest way to get a black toenail is to drop something on your toe—and you don't need to be an athlete to do that. In sports they're most common in long-distance runners, although you see them in dancers and other athletes as well. They're usually the result of an overly long toenail banging into the front of your shoe over and over and over. Eventually the nail shears off, and the skin underneath begins to bleed.

What to do about it

If the bleeding comes on gradually, the toe usually doesn't hurt very much. But if the blood gets in there quickly, it can hurt like mad. The thing to do then is drill a hole in your toenail to let the blood out and reduce the pressure. Don't worry, it may sound awful, but actually it's a pretty simple procedure. You can sterilize a little ⅛- or 1/16-inch drill bit in alcohol and then work it through the nail by spinning it between your fingers. A particularly slick trick is to take a paper clip, bend one of the ends out, and heat it over the kitchen gas burner until it's red-hot. Then simply push it through the nail. It sounds as though it would hurt like crazy, but remember that there's a pool of blood under there, and as soon as the paper clip melts through the toenail and hits the blood, it cools down. It can be a wonderfully gratifying moment when the blood seeps out—instant pain relief.

When the toenail turns black, you're eventually going to lose it. But you want to keep it as long as you can. It gives your toe nice sterile protection. So long as there's no sign of infection—it's not red, there's no sign of pus—it makes sense to leave the nail in place. You might even tape it to keep it in place. After the nail falls off, another will grow in its place; depending on your age, it can take six to eight months. But one way to avoid having to go through the whole thing in the first place is to keep your toenails trimmed.

INGROWN TOENAILS

Trimming toenails is not the most exciting thing in the world to talk about, but it is really important for two reasons: it helps avoid black toenails, and if you keep your toenails trimmed properly you won't get ingrown toenails. An ingrown toenail is literally that: a toenail that curls at the edges and grows into the fleshy part of your toe. It may not sound like much, but it can be more devastating than an ankle sprain. A severe ingrown toenail can be extremely painful and easily becomes infected. Sometimes it never heals, and sometimes the nail has to be removed surgically—that means *real* pain. Fortunately, ingrown toenails are almost always preventable. Trimming the nail properly is the key.

What to do about it

Toenails should be trimmed straight across, so that the corners clear the fold of skin at the edges. For women in particular it's important to trim the nails properly, because feminine footwear tends to be constrictive. If you're on your feet a lot in tight shoes, the flesh of the toe can roll up over the nail, especially if you taper the edges rather than trim the nail straight across.

If the nail does become infected you might soak your foot in warm soapy water, using an antibacterial soap like Dial or Zest. That can help draw out the infection by softening the hard, horny skin. A doctor might put a wisp of cotton under the corners of the nail to push the skin away while the nail's growing—you can do the same thing. Once the corners get beyond the skin, you're all right. Don't let ingrown toenails get away from you. The longer you ignore them, the worse they are to deal with.

PLANTAR NEUROMA

The nerves to the toes run between the metatarsal bones of the foot. Sometimes the nerve between the third and fourth toes can become pinched between the bones that straddle it, a condition called plantar (or Morton's, after the man who first described it) neuroma.

The pain that results feels like an electric shock that starts at the ball of the foot and travels to the tips of the toes. If you squeeze your foot, driving the metatarsal bones together, or pinch the webbed area between the bones, it can be a shock as dramatic as hitting your funny bone. And if you ignore the problem, the nerve can become not only swollen but permanently scarred. The bigger it gets, the more easily it gets in the way, and the more it hurts. Sometimes the only resort is surgery.

Almost always plantar neuroma is caused by tight shoes. That's why it doesn't hurt when you go barefoot—your foot can spread out and take pressure off the nerve. In fact, that's the best way of diagnosing the problem: if the pain goes away when you take off your shoe, you can be pretty certain that it's plantar neuroma.

What to do about it

The best way to treat it, then, is to take off your shoe whenever you can. That's not always practical, however, so there's a neat trick that can help you when your feet are inside a pair of shoes (which, by this time, should be a new pair, roomier than the ones that caused the problem). You actually make your foot narrower by putting more stuff in the shoe—to wit, a little pad on the bottom of the foot, right behind the area that hurts. The pad creates a bit of an arch, which raises your foot and makes it narrower, further reducing pressure on the aching nerve. You can buy these metatarsal pads at drugstores and shoe-stores.

If you eliminate the pressure on the nerve, it will eventually get back to normal. But if you try these things and the pain persists, better see someone.

BLISTERS

A blister is a callus that hasn't been given enough time to form. That is, instead of a long process involving a small amount of friction that slowly builds up dead skin, a blister is caused by heavy friction that over a period of an hour or two causes the skin actually to separate, slide over itself, and form a pocket that fills with fluid.

What to do about it

By far the best way to deal with a blister is to catch it before it forms, when it's still only red and hasn't any fluid in it. Then (and this is one instance when it's a good idea to put something *directly over* the problem) cover it with Spenco Second Skin, a slippery pad widely available in drugstores. The Second Skin will absorb the friction, allowing the blister to heal. *Usually* it will, that is. The only problem is that more often than not you'll notice the emerging blister three miles into your seven-mile run, or in the middle of point class, and your Second Skin is back home in the bathroom.

So the blister forms. Now what? If it's less than about ½ inch, you should probably leave it alone. If it's larger than that, and it's really hurting, then puncturing it will speed the healing process. Sterilize your foot, and then a needle, with alcohol. At the edge of the blister, right where it meets the skin, make a tiny hole and let the fluid leak out. Then spread on an over-the-counter antibiotic ointment to help prevent infection. Cover the blister with moleskin (if you spread the ointment completely over the blister, it won't stick to the moleskin) and leave it there. The blister is sterile, and if you've done all this without contaminating it, you've got a clean, built-in sterile bandage, exactly the right shape and size.

In three or four days the dead skin will work itself loose, and by that time the new skin underneath will have had a chance to toughen up a bit. You may want to cover it with Second Skin until it's no longer tender. Repeat this recipe the next time. Unfortunately, blisters are simply a fact of life—athletic life, anyway. You can get to be an expert at this kind of treatment if you have enough practice, and it's likely you'll have enough practice.

SESAMOIDITIS

If your big toe hurts right at the base where the ball of the foot begins, especially when you push off the toe in running or jumping, you may have sesamoiditis. The term is a catchall description for any irritation of the sesamoid bones, which are tiny bones within the tendons that run to the big toe. Like the kneecap, the sesamoids function as a pulley, increasing the leverage of the tendons controlling the toe. Every time you push off against the toe the sesamoids are involved, and eventually they can become irritated, even fractured. Because the bones are actually within the tendons, sesamoiditis is really a kind of tendinitis—the tendons around the bones become inflamed as well.

Runners tend to get sesamoiditis. So do dancers (female show dancers are at particular risk, because doing anything in high heels throws more weight on these bones). And in the worst of cases the bones refuse to heal. It can come to surgery to remove fragments of the sesamoids, an especially difficult and nasty procedure. Avoid it if at all possible.

What to do about it

Treat sesamoiditis as you would any tendinitis or stress fracture: rest, ice, aspirin, with pain as your guide. If it continues to hurt, keep resting. If it feels better, gingerly go back to your activity, but not enough to make it hurt again. If you remain pain-free, gradually increase the activity until you're back at your accustomed level. Putting a small pad below the area can help reduce the pounding the sesamoids take. But if everything fails, see a doctor.

Orthotics

Orthotics are custom-made shoe inserts. There are a few problems, like plantar fasciitis, in which the use of orthotics can really make a difference. Sometimes orthotics can help with knee pain (see Chapter 5, "The Knee"). But there's no evidence that the use of orthotics is going to prevent any injuries or solve all long-term problems.

For example: you're a thirty-three-year-old runner or aerobic dancer. You've been at it for ten years, and you've never had any foot problems. Suddenly your foot starts to hurt. It's probably an overuse problem, a transient thing. If you treat it right, eventually it'll go away. You may need some kind of orthotic support to get you through it, but that doesn't mean you'll have to wear one forever. One of the biggest problems we see involves people who have been successful runners, or dancers, soccer players, or tennis players, and they come up with a little tendinitis, say. It's because they did something dumb, or got into a bad pair of shoes, or laced them too tight. More often than not the treatment is nothing very exotic or difficult, but instead of trying the simple remedy, *someone relegates them to the orthotic ranks for the rest of their lives.*

One interesting thing about orthotics is that you can never get only one. You may have pain in just *one* foot, but you're never going to get just *one* orthotic. Like shoes, they come in pairs. The upshot may be that you can develop an injury on the *good* side because the extra orthotic has changed your running gait, or your body's general alignment. While helping to treat a temporary problem, the orthotics actually may cause another over the long term.

It's amazing that people do so well on such bad natural equipment. During the Summer '84 Olympics there was a stir in the press about running technique. Thousand-frame-per-second photography had revealed all the horrible-looking things people do when they run. You come down on your heel first, then as you move through your stride the foot sort of wobbles in, rolls to the inside, then sort of wobbles back as you go up on your toes and onto the other foot. And this is in normal people, people who aren't having any problems. Nevertheless, many were appalled: "How can I look so awful and still function?" The result was a new interest in orthotics as a means of correcting all these built-in defects.

But if you've been running for ten years, it means that your foot's been wobbling for ten years as well; and if you haven't been plagued with problems, then that wobble is just right for you. It simply happens to be the way your body works. Yet some people would have you wear orthotics indefinitely to correct what they perceive to be faulty functioning, even if you, the functioner, have never been bothered. It just may not be the height of wisdom to fool around with "problems" that are not problems.

And there isn't any evidence to suggest that orthotics improve performance, despite claims to the contrary. Athletes, especially the thirty- to forty-year-old born-again variety, are suckers for anything that might lower times or increase stamina and strength, and if it's something as accessible as an orthotic, all the better. For some people a sporting activity assumes an importance out of proportion to the rest of their life—if an orthotic will make them better dancers or faster runners, anything goes. (The tennis racquet and golf club industries do very well selling new technologies in the name of performance. People must have the latest thing.)

Be careful. You run or jump or dance in a manner that's inherently best for you. Indiscriminate use of orthotics comes under the category of attempting to fix things that aren't broken. If you're not having problems, don't fool around with them.

Footwear—How to Choose Shoes

First of all, when you buy any kind of athletic shoe, be sure to take along the kind of socks you'll be wearing when you use the shoes. Don't try on running or aerobic shoes in your dress socks or pantyhose. And whatever your activity, be sure to wear absorbent socks. Everyone's feet sweat, and the more you can do to absorb the moisture, the less chance of infections, and the more comfortable you'll be.

Next, don't be in a hurry. There's only one way to select a pair of shoes that are right for you—do the thing to the shoe inside the shop that you're going to be doing to it outside the shop—and that takes time. The more thoroughly you get to know the shoe before you buy it, the less grief you'll experience later. If it's a running shoe you're after, try to run in it as much as you can without mowing people down. (Some shoestores provide treadmills for this purpose.) If it's an aerobic shoe, get up on your toes and bounce around. If it's a ski boot, at least walk around in it for a while (and some shops have mini-slopes or a device called Ski-Legs, so you can do more than that).

Leave one of your old shoes on one foot, put one of the new ones on the other foot, and walk around for a while—that gives you a valid basis for comparison. Then reverse the process. Then put both new shoes on and see how they feel. Remember, if you measure the length of a shoe, it should always be while you're standing up. It may be a good idea to shop at the end of the day when your feet are a bit swollen—if the shoes fit then, they'll always fit. Above all, test for comfort. Generally shoes will not stretch in length at all, although they may spread a bit in width. But for the most part, shoes are never going to feel much better than they did in the shop.

A few other things to remember:

1. If there's a problem with fit—the forefoot fits, but the heel doesn't, or vice versa—it's easier to put something in the heel (a heel cup, for instance) than it is to change the front part of the shoe. Heel cups, which come in various styles from soft leather to rigid plastic, can readily fill in the back part of the shoe, but there's not much to do about the front. If in doubt, *fit the shoe for your forefoot.*

2. When you step down on the heel of a shoe, particularly a court shoe, you shouldn't sink into it. Often shoe manufacturers will raise the heel of a shoe by softening part of the innersole in the heel area. When you try out the shoe, push up on your toes, then sink back into the heel, go up on your toes, sink back into the heel. Try this sequence a few times, and if you find yourself sinking down into the shoe a quarter of an inch or more, it's likely that when you're actually using the shoe it will rub into your Achilles tendon. Besides the irritation, the result can be bursitis and tendinitis.

The proper way to cushion a shoe is to put the resilient material *outside* the shoe, between the soft innersole and the hard outersole. That way, when you step down the whole shoe sinks rather than you sinking inside it. But the manufacturers know their customers. It's so appealing to stick your thumb in a nice soft heel and say, "Gee, that feels great." But it won't feel so great when you wear it. Until you flatten out the foam in the heel for good, you're going to be sliding up and down whenever you take a step. So look for shoes that cushion *below* the heel area rather than inside it.

3. Another problem with heels is that they are contoured to what the manufacturers consider a "normal" foot. Shoes cup forward in the heel. In profile, they resemble a shallow C. But all feet aren't so regular and symmetrical. Some people's heels are indeed nicely cuplike, but many others are more nearly straight from Achilles tendon to the bottom of the heel. These people, in tennis shoes in particular, will notice that the counter of the shoe cuts into their heel. The solution: crush the back of the shoe with your foot. Yikes! sixty dollars down the drain! But, no, it won't hurt the shoe, and it could make life lovely for your Achilles tendon.

4. Young people's outdoor athletic shoes: look for the ones that have cleats molded to the sole. These are much safer than the longer, conical, screw-on cleat. There are fewer knee and ankle injuries with the shorter and more numerous molded cleats. The long ones tend to get hung up in the ground. They dig in too far, and your foot won't release readily—the result is a higher frequency of injuries. Some high schools have even forbidden these older-style cleats.

A problem is that most of these shoes are flat—no raised heel.

There's nothing intrinsically wrong with a flat heel, of course, but these days most young people go to school in running shoes (which are well designed but don't last very long), or a variety of other styles, most of which have raised heels. In and of themselves, there's nothing wrong with raised heels, either. The problem arises when the students change to the flat heels during school sports, the most active part of their day, dropping their heels a good ⅜ inch. It's as though they're doing Achilles tendon stretching exercises every time they run. (Except for sprinters. The only shoe that really doesn't need a heel is a sprint shoe. When you sprint you're up on your toes the whole time.) Then they change back to the raised-heel shoes, shortening the tendon until the next day, when they again don their athletic shoes and give the tendon an abrupt workout. That kind of abuse often leads to Achilles tendinitis.

Manufacturers pay lip service to the problem by making the cleats under the heel longer, so when the shoe is sitting on the store shelf it looks as though the heel is raised. Don't be fooled. When you lace it on and start running in it, the cleats will simply sink into the ground, leaving you with a flat shoe. We suggest that people buy a ¼- or ⅜-inch heel pad to stick inside their athletic shoes. These can be made of cork, or you can use real felt, just so long as the pad doesn't flatten under pressure. Spenco has a new product that combines the benefits of both materials.

Athletic shoes don't have much of an arch either. There's a soft little foam-rubber cookie in the shoe, but it collapses easily. A fairly rigid over-the-counter arch support can make a real difference, especially in young people. Spenco and Dr. Scholl's make good ones. Kids can grow so quickly that they actually outgrow their muscles, which puts strain on the tendons attaching those muscles to bone. When the tendons are tight they're particularly susceptible to injury. If the arch is not supported, or the heel is allowed to drop, there's even more of a tendency to injury, particularly tendinitis. Arch and heel supports can go a long way toward keeping young people healthy.

5. Be sure to look at quality control in shoes. Shoes should be mirror images of each other, but sometimes they're not. There's no reason for shoes to be asymmetrical unless they're designed that way. Some shoes are made badly enough so that they actually affect your gait. They can force your ankles to turn in or pronate. You can usually trust name-brand companies that have had particular models on the market for a couple of years. Problems in those shoes have most likely been weeded out by now.

6. Ski boots: the days of breaking in ski boots are gone. Now, with boots made of rigid plastic foam, what you do is break your foot in, hoping that you'll get used to the boot. But if the boot doesn't feel comfortable in the store, it certainly isn't going to feel more comfort-

able later. So give ski boots particular attention. If you have other equipment to buy as well, look at boots first, then, when you find a pair that feels good, clomp around in them while you look at skis, parkas, and goggles. If they begin to hurt in the shop, they're not going to feel any better outside.

7. Aerobic dance shoes: by the end of 1984 there were over twenty-eight kinds of aerobic dance shoes on the market. At first glance the shoes may look different, but they're all pretty much the same—a bastardized running shoe, with less shock absorption at the heel, which is a good idea, and a nod in the direction of increased shock absorption in the forefoot. That would be a good idea if manufacturers didn't equate shock absorption with softness. If you step into a pair of shoes and they feel soft, you're probably not going to get much shock absorption out of them. If they're soft enough to feel soft, then you'll bottom out in them quickly, and when you're jumping up and down it's unlikely that there is going to be any significant amount of energy dissipation. It's similar to walking on synthetic turf. It can be spongy, and you kind of float. You may think, "Boy, this is neat," but when you run on it, it's a different story. It's like an old mattress—once you get to the bottom of it, it's as hard as asphalt underneath. Players who run on synthetic turf regularly will tell you that it causes aches and pains and promotes the recurrence of old injuries.

But any shoe absorbs banging better than your bare foot. Some of the original aerobic dance studies were done when a lot of dancers went barefoot. The studies directed a lot of the blame for injuries at those overworked bare feet. In our culture we're not prepared to do anything barefoot—not walking around the yard, much less anything so strenuous as aerobic dancing. When you're barefoot and you get on your toes, you take the weight of your entire body at the base of the big toe, the bunion joint, first, and then at the base of the little toe. If you put anything with a halfway-rigid sole on your foot, you're going to spread the force into a triangle that's perhaps five times as large. That seems to solve most injury problems. So if you're doing aerobics, you should wear shoes, and if you wear shoes, look for the firmest pair you can find that are still comfortable.

Test the shoe by doing some exercises in the store. Get up on your toes, bounce around some. Make certain the shoe is not too short, or the toe box too low. There's a certain amount of lunging in aerobics, and your big toenail can go into the end or top of the shoe pretty easily if the fit is not right. That can become mighty uncomfortable after a while, and can in time lead to a black toenail.

Point your toe to see if the counter in the back of the shoe cuts into your Achilles tendon. Sometimes manufacturers put padding in the counter to make the shoes look attractive, but that soft padding can rub against the tendon every time you point your foot. (Other dance shoes don't come above the ankle bone—the manufacturers have learned how to deal with the problem.) Some shoes have a split counter, so nothing rubs against the tendon. They're hard to get on, however. Make sure such a shoe is comfortable for you.

In a survey we did of the popular brands of aerobic dance shoe, there was no difference in the injury rates at all. None! The most popular shoe was the best-looking, but in every one of the other seven categories in which we compared them—including durability—it was below average or tied for last. And still people buy them. Unfortunately, it seems that the most important feature of aerobic dance shoes, so far as the customers are concerned, is looks.

Bottom line: the main thing you should look for in a shoe, no matter what athletic demands you're going to place on it, is comfort. All the business about traction, shock absorption, durability, etc., won't make a bit of difference to you if your feet hurt. So *buy a shoe for comfort.* Consider anything else frosting on the cake.

4 The Lower Leg

I was doing fine ..." Carlton Gillenwater is nervous. He can hardly sit still on the examining table. "... I was back in shape, down to a hundred and forty-nine pounds. I was jumping, making it through entire shows, and then it started again. It's just so tight. Go ahead and feel, there, next to the fracture." Garrick runs his fingers along the shin of Carlton's right leg. "That hurts. Look how black and blue it is. As soon as I build up strength it gets tight again. You know, in one month it will have been *two years* since I got it."

"You might have to change your line of work," Garrick says quietly, and he means it. Carlton, a ballet dancer, has suffered nine stress fractures in the past two years, five on one leg, four on the other. He can't seem to shake the injury.

"It's taken two years, and it just won't finish healing," he says. "I don't get pain, I get irritation. I feel it pulling, and I know what's coming if I don't stop and rest. So if I rest for three weeks, I can go back and dance another three months with no problem. And then after the three months I'll start getting irritation again. It's a never-ending cycle."

"What are you doing now?" Garrick asks.

"I'm not with anybody because I haven't been able to dance. I'm a volunteer counselor at a youth center, I teach some, I do all kinds of crazy stuff to keep myself occupied. Since it's a job-related injury, I'm still on Workers' Comp."

"So you're kind of treading water until you—"

"*Floundering* is a better word. I'm really floundering. I just want it to be over. I just want it done with. Even if I can't go back to dancing, I just want to know that my legs are in a permanent state. That either they'll always hurt or never hurt. Twelve years of dancing from the age of twelve will do that to you."

"Well ... " Garrick takes a long look at Carlton's leg.

"And in ballet, you know, we're all brought up with this work ethic that you just don't stop. So you start with one stress fracture, and then you get two, and three and four. I was on tour for six weeks, dancing four ballets a night, riding in buses and flying in planes all day, and it got worse and worse until I just *had* to stop."

"Why don't we measure the pressure in the muscle compartment?" Garrick says. "It's not a horrible thing. All we do is make you exercise with a little tiny needle in your leg. All right? We can do it in a couple of days." He looks at Carlton fidgeting on the examining table. "You be nice to yourself in the interim."

If the measurement indicates too much pressure in the muscles around the shin, Garrick can do an operation to open the fascia envelope surrounding the muscle. The surgery relieves the pressure, thereby relieving Carlton of his chronic pain. But, surgery or no, Garrick is not optimistic. Carlton has had the problem too long. The fact that it keeps coming back is not a good sign. His body may be trying to tell him something, and that something may be that life is much more pleasant offstage.

But although Carlton's problem is extreme compared to that of most people, it's really nothing more than a variant on a common theme. You know the scenario: you've broken through to the next plateau, and now you're running an extra two miles a day. Or you've advanced to the intermediate aerobics class and are in the studio five rather than three times a week. You feel great. This is the beginning of a new chapter in your life. You know that soon you'll feel and look better than you ever have before. If it just weren't for that nagging pain in your leg.

You first noticed the pain after you ran—a dull ache along the shin. Or it hurt while you were walking home from aerobics class, and that evening it hurt while you were watching the late news. It's nothing, you figure. You're simply tired—it'll go away by itself.

But it doesn't go away. And soon it starts to hurt at the end of your run, or the end of class. Still, you figure it's nothing. You'll simply work through it. What is it they say? No pain, no gain? It'll go away in a couple of days.

A couple of days go by. It doesn't go away—it gets worse. Now the leg hurts at the beginning of your run. Soon it hurts when you're warming up. And still you decide to ignore it.

But when it begins to hurt when you wake up in the morning, and gets worse *before* you even warm up, and continues to throb when you collapse into bed at night, you might start thinking that it's time to stop ignoring it. And you'd be right. You're probably suffering from an overuse injury, the most common problem that afflicts the leg between the knee and the ankle. It might be a stress fracture, shin splints, or a compartment syndrome. But whatever it might be, there's one thing that's certain: better not ignore it. If your leg hurts after your activity, and doesn't hurt any other time, and doesn't get worse, and the pain is gone by the next day, then most likely you can let it go. But if the pain starts creeping up on you, into the activity and beyond, you've got a problem.

Overuse injuries are almost always the result of change. Change in distance run, change in stride length, change in speed, change in terrain, change in floor surface, change to a new instructor, change in shoes. The change may be the result of illness. If you've had the flu and you go back to your old activity too quickly, you may suffer an overuse injury. Muscles deteriorate unbelievably fast. They'll fall apart twice as quickly as they build up, *at the least*. If you've had the flu for a week, it's as though you haven't run in two weeks (and most likely worse than that, because the illness itself results in a decrease in muscle tone and strength). Or the change may be the result of another injury. If you have an ankle sprain that isn't completely healed, you may start favoring the ankle and putting inappropriate stresses elsewhere. The result: two injuries instead of one.

In such cases your body is crying out for attention. And the more attention you can give it sooner rather than later, the better off you'll be. The key word is *overuse*. Once these injuries gain a foothold—or, rather, a leghold—they will do nothing but get worse. A word to the wise: nip overuse injuries in the bud.

STRESS FRACTURES

It seems an unlikely combination of words. *Fracture* suggests a break, conjuring up the image of a skier breaking a shinbone as the result of a fall or collision. *Stress* suggests something much less violent—tension, pressure, strain. How can tension cause something to break?

The answer is that in a stress fracture the bone doesn't really break in two, not quite. It *almost* does. Imagine an airplane wing. It looks rigid, indestructible. Indestructible? Usually—at least one hopes so. Rigid? Not so. It may be disconcerting to look out the window at thirty thousand feet and see an airplane wing flapping, but if it didn't flap it would break. The flapping is a way to dissipate the stress that the wing undergoes. Bones work the same way. They bend under pressure. A stress fracture occurs when the bone bends almost to the point of breaking. The result may be a hairline crack, too fine to show up on X-rays but not too fine to cause you pain.

The situation is made more interesting by what is known as Wolf's law: when you change an activity, your bone adjusts appropriately. For example, a continuing problem for astronauts is the fact that they lose bone strength at zero gravity—as though the bone says to itself, "There's no force on me, why should I be strong? I'll let the body use energy for other things."

Bone also adjusts when you make it undergo more force, but in a curious way. When you put heavier demands on bone by increasing your activity, it says to itself, "I'm too weak. Not only am I not dense enough, I'm not designed right." And rather than simply laying down new bone on old bone, it actually eats itself away, removing bone substance and calcium so it can then lay down new bone more effectively. All well and good, but while the old bone is disappearing like mad and the new bone has not yet had a chance to establish itself, you run a particularly high risk of stress fractures.

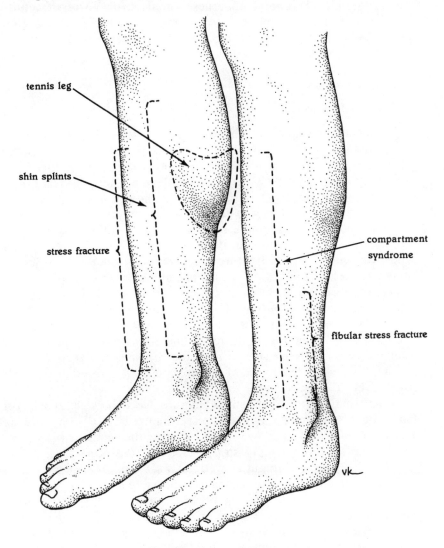

Lateral and Medial Views of the Lower Leg

The tip-off for stress fractures is that they're tender before they're painful, and the area of tenderness is well defined. At the beginning your leg might hurt when you pull your socks on or get into leotards, but it might not hurt during the actual activity. So if you are changing an activity in any way, it might not be a bad idea to run your hand down your shinbone from time to time to check for the possibility of a stress fracture. If you feel a discrete area of tenderness, a spot you could cover with a fifty-cent piece, you might start being concerned. All the more so if you move your finger up or down an inch and it doesn't hurt at all. That kind of pinpoint tenderness usually spells a stress fracture. And if, over time, the pain grows worse, takes longer to disappear after activity, and gradually creeps into the activity itself, you can be sure you have a problem.

What to do about it

The most important thing is not to let the stress fracture become serious in the first place. The sooner you recognize its onset, the better you will be able to treat it. That takes awareness, a little foresight, something all athletes develop (or should develop) anyway. The longer you let it go, the longer it will take to heal. The rule of thumb is that it will take you at least as long to get well as it took you to get injured. If you've ignored the stress fracture for two months, it'll take you at least two months to get back to your original level of activity. And, what's worse, an ignored stress fracture can eventually snap in two, just as though you broke it in a skiing accident—an unenviable fate. Normally a stress fracture crack affects only part of the bone, but if subjected to pressure over too long a time it can work all the way through. Then what you have to look forward to are all the joys of caring for a serious fracture—cast, immobilization, long rehabilitation—and none of the compensations of being able to describe the spectacular accident in which it happened. The moral of the story: it's not wise to ignore these things. They'll get you in the end.

So you've discovered your stress fracture. Now you want to back off and let the bone catch up. But you don't want to rest too much, because then you'll have to start all over again, wasting the conditioning you've already built. If you simply stop exercising, the bone says, "Gee, nothing's happening. I might as well get weak again." The trick is to find a level of activity that is as heavy as possible and at the same time pain-free. Then you're killing two birds with one stone; you're treating the stress fracture, because the way to promote healing is to maintain a pain-free level of activity, and you're continuing your conditioning, pushing the bone to become stronger, so that when you're able to get back to the level that caused the problem in the first place, the bone will be able to handle it.

It's not as hard as it may sound. First, *do whatever's necessary to become pain-free*. Usually it takes only a day or two of complete rest, perhaps including a short bout with crutches, to rid yourself of the pain. Then very gradually begin experimenting with what you can and cannot do. This is a test you don't want to fail. If you push yourself so severely that the leg hurts again, you'll have to start all over. So sneak up on your activity so carefully that you never push yourself over the brink. None of us is that smart, unfortunately, so occasionally you may push yourself to the point of discomfort just to find out where you are.

For example, if you're a runner, you may start by rapid walking. Three to four minutes the first day, then, if it doesn't hurt, six minutes the next day. When you can walk twenty minutes without pain, try running the first three minutes and walking the last seventeen. Then four and sixteen, six and fourteen, gradually changing the ratio of walking to running. Be sure to do the more stressful exercise—in this case, running—at the beginning, when you're not tired. Don't save the frosting for last; your body will not thank you.

Gradually get back to your activity, letting discomfort be your guide. If your leg doesn't hurt, then you're not doing too much too fast—if it does, you are. In that case, drop back to the previous pain-free level, stay there for a few days, then pick it up again. Once you're all the way back, be aware of the danger signs for stress fractures—tenderness before pain, fifty-cent-piece size area of tenderness—so that if they show up again you'll be able to shut them down at the beginning. Especially if you change the level or kind of your activity once again.

Remember that it takes time for the bone to destroy and then regenerate itself. The high-risk period is around the third week after you've begun any new training regimen—that's when the bone removal is at its maximum. So you can really hit it a lick for the first couple of weeks, then flatten out during the end of the second week and through the third. Don't increase your activity; even back off a little bit. Go with that pace for a week to a week and a half, then pick up again. That bit of caution might keep you from getting a stress fracture in the first place.

It used to be that the military had a terrible problem with stress fractures in recruits during basic training. And most of these injuries seemed to show up during the second or third week of basic, coinciding with a ten- to fifteen-mile forced march with field pack and weapon. The army began to call the injury a "march fracture." The military tried everything to solve the problem—different conditioning, different shoes—none of which worked. Finally one group decided to postpone the forced march to the ninth week and substitute the original ninth-week activity, target practice. Instead of slogging up and down hills in full gear during the high-risk period for stress fractures, these lucky recruits got to lie on their bellies and sight along rifle barrels. The result: stress fractures decreased by over 50 percent.

A little caution can go a long way, but if all these measures fail and your leg pain simply continues to get worse, better see someone.

COMPARTMENT SYNDROME

Sounds like a luggage problem—and the analogy is not as far-fetched as it might seem. The muscle groups in the body are enclosed in cases: tough, gristlelike envelopes called fasciae. Muscles swell with exercise, and the fascia, being slightly elastic, allows this swelling to happen. But the muscles just behind the shinbone are bounded on three sides by things with no flexibility: the shinbone (tibia) to the front; the fibula (the other, smaller bone in the lower leg) to the side; and a big, ligamentlike membrane to the back. When these muscles swell after aerobics class, a long run, a tough game of tennis or soccer or basketball, or, as in Carlton Gillenwater's case, too much time onstage, they quickly press against the fascia, which, hindered as it is by its inflexible neighbors, is unable to stretch in response. The result can be compartment syndrome: the muscle keeps on swelling, up to a third more than its usual size, but the fascia compartment can't keep pace. The muscle strains against the fascia like clothes in an overstuffed suitcase, and the compartment grows tighter and tighter. At this point, the blood vessels bringing blood to and from the muscle begin to press closed. As the veins shut down, the blood within the muscle becomes trapped, and when the arteries go they actually shut off the blood supply to the muscle, until it can take no more.

At that point a number of things can happen. The least of these, and the most common, is that the area to the outside of your shinbone starts to hurt. A compartment syndrome hurts over a larger area than a stress fracture, and, rather than hurting earlier as it grows worse, a compartment syndrome hurts at precisely the same point every time you exercise. It might be a third of the way through your barre, four miles into your run, twenty-two minutes after the beginning of aerobics class—your leg always hurts at the same time. It won't hurt if you run only three and a half miles or only do a twenty-minute class. It happens at the same time every time, because that's the point at which the muscles swell enough to begin shutting off the blood supply. When you stop the activity, giving your muscles a chance to relax, the pain usually goes away.

Often a tip-off that your pain is the result of compartment syndrome rather than anything else is the presence of what are called fascial hernias. These are little balloonlike bulges or defects under the skin in the lower outside shin area, just above the ankle. There are normally tiny holes in the fascia to allow blood vessels and nerves to get through. Sometimes the holes grow bigger, allowing muscle itself to poke through, and sometimes muscle and nerve actually becomes pinched against the edge of the fascia. These fascial hernias can cause tenderness and even numbness and tingling in the foot. At least half the people with overuse compartment syndrome have fascial hernias as well. You can test yourself by running your fingers down your shin after exercise. Dab some hand lotion or baby oil on your fingers—it makes them much more sensitive to feeling all the little nooks and crannies. If you feel little balloons or defects under your skin, and if your leg aches at the same point of exercise every time, you can be almost certain that compartment syndrome is the culprit.

What to do about it

See a doctor. You *can't* work through compartment syndrome. No one knows why overuse compartment syndrome may suddenly appear when an athlete has enjoyed years without injury. Sometimes it shows up in your mid-twenties. In women it appears more frequently just before menstruation, when there is a tendency to retain fluid and the muscles become a little bigger. You might get off your feet, elevate your leg, apply ice, and hope that the swelling goes down, but once established it's awfully hard to change the pattern.

There are very sophisticated ways of confirming compartment syndrome. With tiny needles doctors can measure the pressure inside the compartment and compare it to the other leg; that's what was done for Carlton Gillenwater. Sometimes the only resort is surgery. World champion distance runner Mary Decker Slaney was one of the first athletes to have an operation for overuse compartment syndrome. It's a relatively safe and effective procedure. The surgery was more common six or seven years ago than today. The ability to measure pressure in the compartment has made a big difference in prescribing treatment.

A caution: sometimes compartment syndrome can be the result of a blow to the leg—a swift kick in the shin during a soccer game, for example. In such cases the muscle and surrounding soft tissue can actually bleed into the fascia compartment, with devastating results. It doesn't happen often, but sometimes the swelling can be so dramatic that it will *shut off,* rather than simply curtail, the incoming supply of blood. The pressure from the excess swelling becomes so high, and the arteries and veins are so constricted, that blood cannot flow into or out of the compartment. Without nourishment, the muscle can die in a matter of hours. Almost always this acute, dangerous compartment syndrome is diagnosed late, because people think they're going to get better despite the pain, and take more and more pain medication. A rule of thumb: *injuries between the ankle and knee that result in pain and any kind of numbness and tingling, or pain that doesn't go away with rest, might be emergencies.* Get yourself to a doctor or emergency room as soon as possible.

CONTUSIONS

When we did a study of soccer players at the high-school level (perhaps surprisingly, there weren't many injuries), one of our conclusions was that more than the ball gets kicked. And those kicks to the shin were the major source of injury.

Contusion—a direct blow. You don't have to play soccer to experience one. Anybody who has ever hit a shin against a coffee table knows how much it can hurt and how long it takes to heal. That kind of contusion can be tender for six months, and the knob *never* seems to go down. A direct kick in the shin can hurt even worse. If it occurs right over the bone, usually it won't cause a fracture. But it can cause bleeding under the bone; that's why it hurts so much—the resulting swelling lifts all the nerve endings away from the bone, baring them to the environment. They can be excruciatingly tender and stay tender for what seems like an eternity.

A kick in the soft tissue adjacent to the bone can cause even more bleeding (and can lead to acute compartment syndrome, as suggested). Pain, swelling, and discoloration are the results here as well.

What to do about it

Compression and ice can help keep the swelling down; staying off the leg may keep pain to a minimum. But a contusion is one of those things you simply have to gut through. You know it will heal eventually. There's little to do except wait it out—except, that is, taking care to make sure that it doesn't happen again. A good preventive measure is to wear shin guards during activities, like soccer, in which contusions are a strong possibility. People grouse about wearing shin guards. They can't imagine that the padding on the back of a little piece of plastic can make any difference. But it can be the difference between taking the force of a kick over the area of eight square inches as opposed to one. Shin guards do a good job of protecting the leg, and they don't impede ankle motion. So you may not be able to successfully navigate around the sharp edge of a coffee table in the middle of the night, but in sports like soccer, at least, contusions can be prevented.

TENNIS LEG

It happens to the tennis player who gives a little bit extra to get to a ball that's just barely out of reach. It occurs in the hiker who strains to jump a stream that's wider than it appeared when he took off. Baseball, football, basketball, and soccer players, racquetball and handball players, participants in running sports that demand quick thrusts and sudden changes of direction, all are susceptible to tennis leg. Especially so if they're between the ages of thirty and forty-five. Tennis leg never shows up in children, and rarely in people past middle age.

It goes by a much more mundane name: calf strain—the ripping away of part of the calf muscle from the Achilles tendon. (It's similar to an Achilles tendon rupture, only higher up in the leg, and usually not so severe. And the onset is similar as well.) It feels as though you've been hit in the calf. A tennis player thinks she's been hit with a ball; a hiker reports turning around, thinking his wife has thrown a rock at him. There's little pain, usually, and sometimes you'll hear a noise—a popping sound. Frequently you can continue doing what you're doing for a while, because a good 75 percent of the muscle is still attached to the Achilles tendon. You know something's wrong, but everything still works.

Eventually the muscles will go into spasm, contracting violently, and you'll find that your foot begins to point downward. No matter what you do, you can't bring your foot back up to neutral—women often report that the only way they can get around is in high heels—and this awkward position will be accompanied by a lot of internal bleeding. Sometimes the entire calf will turn black and blue. Sometimes, because the blood flows down with gravity, you'll see discoloration in your ankle, or in your foot, or even in your toes. It can be alarming for people to look down days after being treated and see that their toes are black and blue. The blood simply travels downhill until it can find its way to the surface. And you can end up with a huge, puffy calf.

So you feel—and most likely hear—a pop, and soon your foot wants to point down. Your calf is puffing up rapidly, and the whole area from your knees to your toes may be turning black and blue. If you run your fingers along the inside lower part of your calf muscle, you'll usually feel an area that is exquisitely tender, and sometimes you can actually feel a defect. The tender area marks the point where the muscle fibers flow into tendon fibers. It is there that the rupture takes place.

The upper calf muscle, which is called the gastrocnemius, attaches at the top in the lower thigh, runs behind the knee about two thirds of the way down the lower leg, and connects to the Achilles tendon, which itself attaches to the heel bone. Thus the gastroc spans two joints, the knee and ankle. Muscles that rupture, like the gastroc, almost always span two joints. The hamstring muscle in the thigh, which spans the pelvic and knee joints, is another. You have double the probability of stretching a two-joint muscle.

Usually the body protects against too much stretching. For example, in walking, when the knee is straight, thereby stretching the upper end of the gastroc muscle, the ankle is relaxed. When the ankle is flexed, stretching the lower part of the muscle, the knee is bent. (Take a few strides and try it out. It's a slick, complementary movement.) It is when you get in positions that stretch both ends at the same time that you flirt with tennis leg.

So when you're a little tired, with your muscles beginning to tighten up, and you push off hard, straining for that serve that spins just out of reach, you may put enough pressure on both ends of the muscle to pull it apart.

What to do about it

Stretch right away. Keeping your knee straight, foot pointed ahead, and heel on the ground, slowly bend forward over your ankle and then bring your foot back to neutral. The motion stretches out the gastroc and also provides a measure of internal compression for the injured part, slowing down the rush of blood into the area, thus reducing swelling. (See the illustration on page 31. The exercise is the same as that for stretching the Achilles tendon.)

Another way of stretching the muscle is by sitting with your leg straightened out in front of you. Hook a towel around the front portion of your foot and pull it back toward you. It may be a bit harder to stretch that way—gravity doesn't help you out, as before—but if you just don't feel like pushing to your feet it might be the technique for you. As with the standing stretch, you'll be able to feel the pull against the gastroc from the ankle all the way to the knee. It may be uncomfortable, but slowly, firmly stretch as much as you can. The results will be worth it.

Next apply compression and ice. Start at the toes with an Ace wrap and work all the way up to the knee. If you wrap your leg only at the calf, you could wind up with swelling below. You want constant compression all the way so the blood won't pool. But immediate stretching lessens the likelihood of much swelling. It even makes compression and ice less crucial. All three together—stretching, compression, and ice—make an especially potent course of action.

Most likely you'll have to have the injury treated by a doctor sooner or later. People with untreated tennis leg can take months to get their foot back to neutral, much less return to action. Even if you're treated, it may be four to six weeks before you're back to playing reasonable tennis. It used to be that doctors put tennis leg in a cast, with the foot pointing downward, which meant that the leg healed in that position and it took up to five months to get the foot back up. Nowadays, especially if you stretch right away, you might be able to bypass all that and begin rehabilitating much more quickly. We continue people on a gentle stretching program and begin a restrengthening program as well, because the rest of the muscle that is still attached will waste away if you don't use it.

Eventually the muscle reattaches to the tendon, but not in the same place. It heals a bit shorter than it was. Why not sew the muscle and tendon back together? It doesn't work. The tendon takes stitches very well—it's gristly stuff—but sewing muscle is like sewing hamburger. It looks very nice, but as soon as the muscle contracts all the stitches come out. Tennis leg responds well to nonsurgical treatment. The trick is to do the rehab exercises diligently. And be patient.

FRACTURES

First the bad news: when you think of a broken leg, you think of skiing. With reason. There's an occasional broken leg in soccer, but lower leg fractures in sports other than skiing are relatively unusual. Now the good news: ski fractures look spectacular in X-rays, but they occur in a better spot than they used to. When plastic ski boots first came out, they were very stiff but not very high, and fractures involved the ankle joint. Those were devastating injuries, because they disrupted the construction of the joint itself. Not much could be done about them. Boots are still stiff today, but they're higher, so ski fractures are higher as well. Now isolated bones break, rather than joints. It's usually the shinbone, the tibia. That's a big bone, and it takes a long time to heal, but it *does* heal. These days ski fractures come out pretty well.

What to do about it

See a doctor. A fracture is one injury you simply can't treat yourself. But there is one thing you can do: be sure that your doctor—or someone who knows what he's doing—prescribes a good course of rehabilitation exercises. Too often people come out of a cast with a stiff ankle and a calf that looks like a chicken leg and no idea of what to do next. What you *won't* do next is get right back to skiing or anything else. That will become abundantly clear the minute you start to bear weight on your "new" leg. You'll wonder what that funny, useless thing is beneath your knee. (Sometimes fractures require that the joint above be immobilized, which means that you might find yourself in a cast up to your groin. In that case, we might as well be talking about thigh muscles. See Chapter 5, "The Knee," for advice on how to rehabilitate your thigh.) The reason your cast was changed at least once was not that it stretched, or simply because your swelling went down. It was changed because your muscles disappeared. Muscle wastes away at least twice as quickly as it builds up. If you've been immobilized for a month, it will take you two months *at the least* to get back to where you were before the injury. The most graphic way to become aware of the problem after you're out of the cast is to look over your shoulder into a mirror while you go up on your toes. Notice the nice bulge in your healthy calf, then look at the matchstick that's supposed to be your other calf. Until the two legs begin to look symmetrical, you've got work to do.

Sometimes people just don't get very good advice—either because they don't ask for it, or they don't listen, or it simply isn't good advice. Often people are so happy to be out of the cast and done with the doctor, they never want to talk to him again. Don't penalize yourself by assuming that when your leg comes out of the cast your recovery is complete. Your fracture might have been managed very well—set right, held in a cast for the right period of time—but, if you don't build back your strength intelligently the residuals of the fracture can be almost as troublesome as the fracture itself. The results can include some of the things we talk about in this book: Achilles tendinitis because you've got a stiff ankle, calf problems because your muscle has virtually disappeared, ankle sprains because you don't have enough muscle to protect it, knee problems from favoring the leg. A word to the wise: after you get out of the cast, rebuild the strength of your leg in a solid rehabilitation program.

SHIN SPLINTS

Depending on your point of view, shin splints are either a brilliant, all-encompassing category or an embarrassment to the medical profession. It is a diagnosis of exclusion. We know all these other fine things about causes of pain in the lower leg; everything we don't know falls under the umbrella of shin splints.

It is one of the two most common complaints in aerobic dancing (foot problems are the other). You see it in gymnasts who are working hard on vaulting technique or doing a lot of tumbling runs. Rope jumpers complain of it, as do basketball players, especially during preseason conditioning, and runners, usually untrained runners. And there seem to be two kinds of shin splints (if you can say that there are two kinds of something you don't understand): those that disappear in two to three weeks, and those, perhaps as many as 20 percent, that simply don't go away. These are the ones that are tough to treat.

The onset is familiar to most people. You change your training regimen in some way—you run greater distances, say, or over different terrain (a day of walking around San Francisco can do it)—and your leg begins to ache. It's usually the front of the leg, not right on the shinbone but where the muscle and bone meet. A tip-off that it's shin splints and not something else: run your fingers down your leg. If the soreness encompasses a large area—two dollar bills laid end to end, say, rather than a fifty-cent-piece-size spot, as in stress fractures—it's shin splints. At first it aches after the activity, then during, but if you stop for a few days it goes away. And after a few weeks of this on again, off again behavior, it simply goes away for good.

The most readily acceptable explanation for shin splints is that it involves muscle pulling away from bone. Muscle is attached to the tibia along its length, except for that front area that's directly under the skin. There really isn't any tendon along most of the bone's length—these muscles attach directly to bone. Probably the pain of shin splints is the result of tiny muscle fibers pulling loose, because they tighten up from fatigue, or the activity is too violent for them, or some such thing—no one knows for sure. In any case, it's the result of an activity for which you're not prepared.

What to do about it

In the great majority of instances shin splints are not a problem, because by the time you've sorted out the fact that something's wrong and you want to treat it, it's already gone. But sometimes it doesn't go away, and if our knowledge of the cause of shin splints is vague, treatment can be even more so. The medical literature on shin splints is almost like witchcraft. People describe similar symptoms and then describe a myriad of treatments, some of which are bizarre and all of which seem to work, at least some of the time.

Some people apply a concoction called tobacco poultice, a mixture made with moist tobacco. It works—for some people. Others rub in red-hot or analgesic balm and cover it with tape—that works for some people. Some simply tape the leg to constrain the muscles, reasoning that the tearing was caused by too much muscle movement. This works as well. If you put a band around certain people's legs just a couple of inches above the ankle bone, they're able to run without pain. And some years ago a sports trainer felt that improper use of the toes led to shin splints. He made a cigarette-sized roll of fabric and inserted it in runners' shoes just below the curl of the toes. Allowing the toes to curl over the roll changed the length of the muscle-tendon groups, he reasoned, and it worked—for some people. *All* these things work, *when* they work, which makes it difficult to sort out just what's working for whom. It probably means that the problems doctors call shin splints are really eight or ten different things, none of which we understand very well, but which we group together out of desperation.

The most common initial treatment for shin splints involves an effort to increase the flexibility and strength of your lower leg muscles, especially the dorsiflexors, those muscles that pull the foot back toward the leg. The simplest way to strengthen them is to nail the ends of a piece of inner tube or surgical tubing to a piece of board and stick your foot under the loop. Pull your foot up against the tubing. As you develop strength, decrease the slack in the tubing to provide more tension. Stretch your calf muscles before and after your activity, and apply ice as well.

Sometimes putting an arch support in your shoe can help. You can get hold of a Dr. Scholl's or Spenco semirigid arch at any large drugstore or running shoe store. Sometimes raising your heel a little bit will help. Heel inserts or pads are also widely available. These are all experimental things, but none of them is expensive, none of them is a big hassle, none of them is going to make you worse if it doesn't work. Stretching and strengthening is something you can do at home. Ice, arch and heel supports, even aspirin—you just start wading through these things from the least expensive, least time-consuming to the most, and hope you will get well. If nothing seems to work, see a doctor, and you can experiment together.

Commonly Asked Questions

Does running on the beach strengthen the legs?

It may be that there's some value in the added work running in the sand demands from your feet and legs. But in general, for most people, running in the sand won't do any more for you than running anywhere else. In fact, it may do you some harm. The main reason is that your foot sinks into the sand as you run, and your heel, which bears the brunt of your weight, drops lower than the rest of your foot. There's nothing wrong with that in and of itself, but it's just opposite to the condition we're used to. Most shoes raise the heel—running shoes certainly do—which in time tends to shorten the Achilles tendon and calf muscles. Suddenly lowering the heel stretches that entire linkage, and the upshot can be injury. (See Chapter 2, "The Ankle.")

The other reason that running in the sand can be hard on you is that usually you have to deal with a side slope. The sand slopes down to the water, sometimes fairly steeply, throwing off your center of balance as you run and shortening one side of your body as it stretches the other. Make sure you come back the way you came so as to balance the effect of the slope. And make sure you take a dunk in the water afterward. Otherwise, why bother to go down to the beach at all?

How can I slim down my calves and ankles?

Spot reducing isn't easy. Perhaps your best bet is a combination of lifting weights (see Chapter 11, "Exercising to Stay Fit") and diet. Aerobic exercise reorients your metabolism to burn excess fat more efficiently. A general rule of thumb is that the more fit you are, the better you look. Muscle is more attractive than fat, and, in contrast to fat, muscle can be toned.

5 The Knee

"All I know for certain is that I was getting on the board and somehow I fell off and hit a rock. I heard a crack, and my knee buckled."

"Were you conscious of your knee being out all the way?" Garrick asks. "Or was it partially bent?"

"No, it was completely locked. I'm positive about that."

"What happened next? Did it swell up?"

Bettina Miller doesn't particularly want to remember what happened next. A slim, intense brunette, Bettina was windsurfing in San Francisco Bay two weeks ago when it happened. Not that it hurt all that much. It's just that it was the last time her left knee worked normally. Two weeks ago her life changed—irrevocably. That's the part that's tough to accept.

"No, it didn't swell much," she answers. "I hung out in my wet suit in the water for a while, trying to figure out how bad it was. It was cold water. That probably kept it from swelling."

"Probably that and the pressure from the wet suit," Garrick says. "Could you bear weight on it?"

"Not then. And not for several days afterward. It just collapsed every time I tried to put weight on it."

"Collapsed because it hurt so bad? Or just collapsed?"

"It just collapsed. It didn't even get a chance to hurt."

"And what you've done since then is stay on crutches with your knee wrapped up. It feels better?"

"Much. It's more mobile. But it's still not completely working."

"Hmm. Let's see." Garrick begins to examine the knee. With one hand bracing the knee, he gently swings Bettina's lower leg from side to side. The movement is slight. The knee remains firm and tight. Then he moves her lower leg front to back. Here the result is different. He tries the other leg. Then back to the injured leg.

"See that?" he says. "When I try to take your lower leg and move it out from under your knee on the good side it doesn't move very far. Feel it come to a halt? It's like taking a piece of cloth and pulling it tight. Bang. It stops. Now, on the bad side, it moves much farther and then kind of mushes to a stop. It doesn't have that nice, abrupt pop. That means a problem with the ligament."

Garrick holds up a plastic model of a knee. It shows four of the seven ligaments of the knee, the major ones. Two run along the knee, one on each side, connecting the thighbone to the shinbone. Called the collateral ligaments, they keep the knee from moving sideways. The other two are within the knee, dead center, crossing each other as they rise from the middle of the tibia below to fasten to the middle of the femur above. It is these, the cruciate (or crossed) ligaments, that keep the shin centered beneath the thigh. The anterior cruciate ligament, the forward of the two, restrains the shin from moving forward; the posterior cruciate ligament, the one toward the back of the knee, keeps the shin from moving backward.

"Your anterior cruciate ligament isn't working too well," Garrick announces.

Bettina's face falls. "You mean it's torn?"

"Well, it's kind of a moot point as to what's wrong. We have a tendency to think of ligaments as pieces of paper—either intact or not intact—and that's not really the case. Ligaments have some elasticity. They can stretch a bit, but if they stretch over about 10 percent of their length, then they're like Saran Wrap—you stretch it too far and it stays that way. It won't go back. I think that's what's happened. Your ligament is longer than it was two weeks ago. Too long. And because it's too long, your knee is less stable than it was. In a way, it doesn't matter why. Instability is instability is instability."

Gulp! Instability. That horrible word, resounding with all sorts of undesirable connotations, whether it be emotional, spiritual, or physical. And when it comes to the knee, it's a word that you hear a lot. Over 25 percent of all sports injuries involve the knee (75 percent when it comes to surgery), and many of those involve some kind of instability.

But it's not that the knee is ill-designed, necessarily. It's just that it has to put up with all manner of stresses and strains. In fact, when you think of it, the knee is very well designed—ingeniously designed. Imagine: it's fantasy time. You're a mechanical engineer, and you've just been given a new commission: create a hinge. But not just any old hinge. This hinge must be flexible enough to bend a good 150 degrees front to back, another 3 or 4 degrees side to side, and it must be able to rotate 90 degrees as well—all at the same time if need be. It must be able to withstand anywhere from 100 to close to 2,000 pounds of pressure. It must be self-lubricating—no periodic grease jobs allowed. And it must be decidedly high tech: this hinge must be able to adapt internally to the changing demands made upon it. If it undergoes great stress on one side, it must be able to strengthen the other side, so as not to break.

And that's not all. The hinge must be durable, able to last sixty, seventy, eighty years. And it can't be too big. It may be the largest hinge in the machine of which it's a part, but if it extends more than three inches across in any direction, that's just too much. And, by the way, leave some extra room inside—the power train for the rest of the machine has to go right through the hinge.

All right, got it? If you can pull this one off, you've got a bright future in the firm. And don't worry about working overtime. On the seventh day you can rest.

So you begin. The first problem is this flexibility business. Since this hinge (might as well start calling it a joint) must bend and rotate at the same time, there's no possibility of a positive linkage like a door hinge. And you can't get too exotic in design, because the more flexible you make this joint the less stable it becomes—and it has to hold together for a long time. So you decide simply to have the two sides of the joint abut, one against the other, so that they can bend and twist and do all sorts of tricks. You mold them so the top part ends in two convex mounds, much like two scoops of ice cream side by side in a single cone. The bottom part you hollow out into two shallow cups. When you place one part against the other, the ends fit. Next, you protect the ends by coating them with some tough, white, rubbery stuff called cartilage, and between them you place rings of thicker cartilage called meniscus to further cushion the joint and provide shock absorption. So far so good. Now, how to hold the two ends together?

With stays and guy wires, that's how. Central Supply provides tough ropes called ligaments and tendons. You hook them up in the middle of the joint and along the outside (the collateral and cruciate ligaments) so that they're able to loosen and tighten their grip as needed, as though there were a mini-computer aboard controlling everything. Now your joint can bend, twist, push and shove, and withstand immense pressure. It will give but not break. And you enclose the whole business in a tough, flexible sac that not only protects the joint from the outside world but produces its own lubricant as well.

One problem remains: the business of the power train. Finally it comes to you: why not let the joint function as a pulley? From the power source above, run a cable across the joint to its tether on the other side. As the power source contracts, it reels in the cable along the joint, lifting the weight on the other side (which happens to be your lower leg)—a prototype giant crane. And to increase the leverage, thereby increasing lifting power and making the whole business more efficient, simply make the pulley larger. But, of course, this joint has no turning wheels. Its pulley is a sliding mechanism. To increase its efficiency you must increase the angle over which the cable slides. So a bold stroke: you place a small, lens-shaped piece of bone on top of the joint. The cable now must run *over* the piece of bone, which itself slides along the upper side of the joint. As the cable moves, the bone increases the angle between the power source and the weight to be lifted. The result: more strength.

Now you might well sit back and admire your work for a moment—you deserve to. And when you tinker with the final adjustments, make sure that you leave in some slack. If the tolerances are too tight, the fit is too precise, this joint of yours will degenerate too quickly—just as your car's transmission will grind itself to death if its gears are too tightly aligned. Even the best design must incorporate some slack.

The result? *Voilà*: the knee. The lens-shaped piece of bone is, of course, the kneecap. The sides of the hinge, above and below, are the femur—the large bone in your thigh—and the tibia—the shinbone. That ingenious drive train begins in your thigh with the quadriceps, the body's largest and most powerful muscle, and turns into tough tendon that extends all the way to the lower leg. This artful conglomeration of bone and muscle, soft tissue and gristle comprises the largest and most complicated joint in the body, and the most frequently injured in

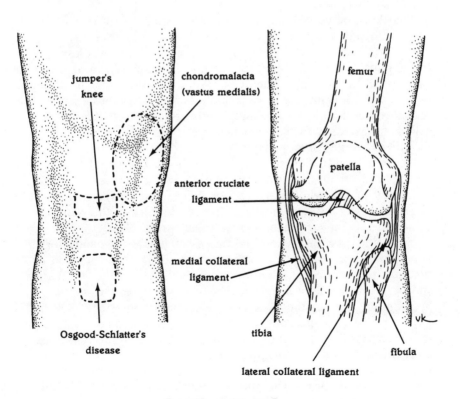

Front View of the Knee

sports. (Ankle sprains are the most common single injury, but the variety of knee problems outrank that of any other joint.) In runners knee problems are unquestionably the most common complaint. In aerobics they rank either first or a close second. The same goes for ballet. In football knee problems are number one. They keep doctors' offices and operating rooms hopping. One athlete might as well greet another by asking, "How's your knee?"

But, as you can see by now, the knee isn't ill-designed. It has changed less in our long evolution from scurrying rat to upright athlete than any other joint. It's just that we subject it to so much abuse. And because it's so large a joint, and so busy, there are a lot of things that can go wrong. There's lots of bone in the knee; seven distinct ligaments; more and thicker cartilage than anywhere else in the body; one huge tendon, as well as smaller ones; and a full complement of bursas to develop into bursitis at any time. But by far the greatest number of knee injuries has to do with what is called the extensor mechanism.

THE EXTENSOR MECHANISM

Your knee actually functions in two ways: as a joint that you stand on, that bends and twists, and lets you endure back seats, crowded movie houses, and lotus positions; and as a lever that allows you to move, jump out of your chair, run, kick a soccer ball or football, or the cat outside for the night. The drive train that powers this lever begins as the quadriceps muscle in your thigh, consolidates into a tendon that runs through the knee joint, and finally attaches to the shinbone. It's called the extensor mechanism because it allows you to extend your lower leg. The key to it all is the kneecap, which actually resides within the large tendon that crosses the knee. It is the kneecap that forces the tendon away from the joint, increasing the angle and thereby the efficiency of the whole linkage. As the tendon moves, the kneecap slides over the bone beneath it like a skier over the slopes (and sometimes it can seem every bit as injury-prone).

You could do without your kneecap if you had to. It sounds horrible, but if for some reason your kneecap had to be removed, you could function pretty much as before, even continue to play professional sports. With one major difference: because the tendon would then drop back onto the joint—the pulley become smaller, in effect—you would have to be 30 percent stronger just to do the things you did before. The muscle would have to compensate with brute strength for the loss of mechanical advantage. Imagine what another third as much strength would demand of the quadriceps, already the largest and most powerful muscle in the body. The kneecap, the smallest part of this linkage, is simply vital.

And vital to the kneecap is how efficiently it's able to slide over the end of the thighbone beneath it. As you bend your knee, your kneecap slides up and down the femur. It touches an entirely different part of the bone when you're sitting on the floor, say, than when you're standing up. (It never touches the shinbone—the tibia—which is about an inch away at least.) But this is no free and fancy flight, no relaxed glide along the slopes. The kneecap must tolerate tremendous pressure. Just walking down a flight of stairs will put three times your body weight across an area that's little larger than a fifty-cent piece. A full squat can subject the kneecap to pressures up to seven and a half times body weight. For an average-sized person, that's around one thousand pounds per square inch, an incredible amount of force. The cartilage that covers the end of the bone is thicker in the knee than anywhere else in the body—up to a quarter of an inch—just to cope with these forces. They can be so great that even when the joint is relaxed on the operating table, the slightest bend will produce pressure so strong that if your surgeon happened to stick his finger behind the kneecap he simply wouldn't be able to tolerate the pain.

So imagine skiing down the slopes with bone-crushing pressure on your shoulders. Bumps and moguls can be bad enough in the best of circumstances—now they would be disastrous. The most insignificant crack in the snow's surface would be as dangerous as a chasm. You'd navigate the smoothest course possible and be glad if you survived. The kneecap, too, navigates the best possible course—in this case, a groove in the femur, almost as though it were on a track. But, rather than being smooth, the cartilage covering the back of the kneecap is faceted like a gem. When you bend or unbend your knee and the kneecap travels up or down the femur, it absorbs the pressure generated by the movement on one and then another of its facets. As it moves, the angle between it and the femur changes, and more of its facets come into play. It's a highly synchronized and sophisticated progression, and usually it works very well.

Usually. When it doesn't, it can cause a whole range of problems. The most common of these is the kneecap's tendency to jump the track.

It doesn't have to jump off by much; the engineering of the extensor mechanism is so precise that the tiniest deviation from the blueprint can cause trouble. That's where the knee's ability to adapt to different circumstances becomes so important. Because the guy wires that hold the knee in place are not static (in contrast to those holding up a flagpole or a tent) and can change their tension constantly as your knee moves, the kneecap is able to stay on line. Your knee may bend and twist as you run, scrunch together as you dismount an apparatus, or extend as you stretch for a lob, but all the while the kneecap stays in its groove, sliding up and down as always, because some of the guy wires loosen up and others tighten as the need arises.

Most of these support wires are tendons attached on one end to the kneecap, on the other to various portions of the quadriceps muscle. They are able to tighten and loosen because the quadriceps constantly contracts and expands. But—and it's a big "but"—there's something in the design of our bodies that can work against the efficient functioning of this extensor mechanism. It's apparent when you stand with your knees together in front of a full-length mirror, even more apparent when you look at an anatomical drawing of the lower torso and legs: we are wider in the hips than we are through the knees. The thighbone on either side angles inward from the hips to the knees, and from there the tibia and fibula—the other, smaller bone in the lower leg—drop pretty much vertically to the ankle and feet. The effect is a kind of Y shape, certainly not the most direct route from beginning to end. If a crow were to fly from your hips to your ankles (a very small crow), it would fly in a straight line outside the Y. But the quadriceps muscle and tendons don't go as the crow flies. They run in line with the bones, with the result that they have to turn a corner at the knees before attaching to the lower leg. When the muscle contracts, however, the tendency is to try to establish a straight, crow's line—the shortest distance from point to point. The contraction tends to pull your kneecap to the outside, and that pull can, at the least, cause it momentarily to jump its track, at the worst actually to dislocate.

Your insurance policy against this happening is a tiny section of the quadriceps muscle called the vastus medialis. It's located just above and to the inside of the kneecap—you can feel it—and its job is to counteract this tendency of the kneecap to drift to the outside by tugging at it from the opposite direction and holding it in place. Unfortunately, the vastus medialis is the first muscle to get weak when you don't use your thigh properly, and the last muscle to get strong when you're coming back from an injury. Which means that the first thing that happens when you limp, or favor your knee, is that this stabilizer goes and your kneecap is left to its own devices—not the happiest circumstance for it.

It needn't be a knee problem that weakens the muscle—almost any injury can do it. An ankle sprain, for example, will cause you to lose strength in your thigh because you no longer walk normally. Achilles tendinitis, even ill-fitting shoes—anything that makes you limp can make you lose muscle in the thigh. And heading the disappearing-muscle act is invariably the vastus medialis. The result: a painful, swollen knee. So if we posted a sign that said

IF YOU STRENGTHEN YOUR VASTUS MEDIALIS YOU WILL NOT
HAVE TO READ ANY FURTHER

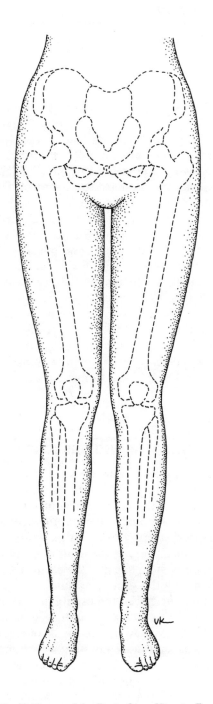

The Y Shape of the Body from Hips to Feet

probably three quarters of the people with knee problems could close this part of the book. Proper alignment of the extensor mechanism is that important. (If you're still here, stick around. In a few pages we'll suggest how to do the strengthening.)

So onward to extensor mechanism problems and other knee injuries resulting from overuse, misuse, and abuse. (The sudden injuries caused by such things as stepping into a hole or falling off your windsurf board are more dramatic, but it's hard to deal with those by yourself. We'll take a look at such acute injuries later in this chapter.) These overuse injuries can be hard to recognize. Often they sneak up on you, and sometimes they become submerged in subsequent and related problems. For example, a subtle kneecap problem can cause the knee to swell, which can change your gait, affect your hip alignment, and lead to what looks for all intents and purposes like a back injury, first and last. But it all started with a kneecap pulling to the outside. Until you deal with that, all the rest will not get better. Discovering the cause can be like eating an artichoke: you have to do a lot of stripping away before you reach the heart. To follow: suggestions to help you recognize and treat the heart of your knee problems. When it comes to these overuse injuries, there are many things that you can do on your own, simple things that surely aren't going to make anything worse and have a high likelihood of making things better.

Overuse Injuries

EXTENSOR MECHANISM INJURIES (CHONDROMALACIA)

They go by many names—runner's knee, quadriceps insufficiency, chondromalacia—and, like most overuse injuries, they are a result of change. For a runner, it can be new shoes that change your gait. It can be going from a pair that's badly worn at the heel to a new pair of the same brand. It can be starting to run hills—when you run uphill you shorten your stride, because you run with more of a bent knee; downhill you lengthen your stride, because the earth is falling away from you and your foot doesn't hit the ground as quickly. It can be from training on a track. About 60 percent of the usual quarter-mile track is curved, and when you run on an unbanked curve, you bank yourself.

For a dancer it simply may be the result of working toward a new role, one that involves a lot more jumping, say. For a gymnast it can be no more than changing floors (and it doesn't have to be a bad floor; there's some evidence that any kind of change, even from an awful floor—concrete, for example—to a good, sprung wooden floor can do it).

Hikers often develop knee problems while trudging downhill rather than up. The reason may be that it's harder on the muscles to constantly lengthen than to contract. For example, it's easier to get out of a chair slowly than it is to sit down in one slowly, and sitting down in a chair, so far as the quadriceps is concerned, is what you're doing when you go downhill. People who go camping in the mountains are often fine going up. They pitch their tent, fish, cook out, and have a grand old time. But when they come down they have fits. The Grand Canyon, into which you go down before coming up, is notorious for causing people who may have had only minor knee complaints to be in such difficulty by the time they reach the bottom that they must resort to a burro to make it up to the top. And in day-to-day living people will frequently complain that they can go up stairs but can't come down.

Ironically, fitness programs, whose purpose is to make your knee stronger, can cause the extensor mechanism the injuries they purport to prevent. So far as the quadriceps is concerned, lifting weights by extending your leg is just like going downstairs. Essentially what you're doing is hanging a weight on your foot and trying to straighten out your knee against it—not a terribly natural thing to do. People subject their knees to this kind of abuse because it's an effective way to isolate muscles, but if the vastus medialis isn't strong enough to hold your kneecap in place, and you hang seventy or eighty pounds on your foot, your kneecap just may try to find a new groove.

Skiers who lift to get in shape at the beginning of the season often experience just this problem. Their legs were hard as steel at the end of spring, so they start big, lifting at a level that the large part of the quadriceps may be able to handle but the vastus medialis, which falls out of condition more quickly than the rest of the thigh, cannot tolerate. The upshot: a sore and tender knee. It's important to build up slowly, with weights light enough for the vastus, then gradually increase.

Squats can be the most harmful of all. At the least, a squat subjects the back of your kneecap to about seven and a half times your body weight—around one thousand pounds per square inch—but imagine the forces on the knees of people who do their squats with 200 pounds of barbells on their shoulders. And when you ski you're really in a semisquat—or you should be—and if the vastus isn't strong enough, or if you start out in good shape but ski too long and the muscle runs out of gas (and the first part to run out of gas will invariably be the vastus because there isn't as much of it in the first place), it's a solid bet you'll find yourself in the first-aid station before long.

So these changes can be type-of-activity changes, level-of-activity changes, terrain changes, footwear changes, even changes as well meant as trying to get in shape.

The pain of this kind of injury is like all overuse type pain in that it creeps up on you. Frequently you first notice it *after* the activity. Then you start noticing it toward the end of the activity, then earlier in the activity, and pretty soon it's there all the time. Usually it hurts in the front of the knee, but in a diffuse way. It's not like a torn cartilage (which we'll get to later in this chapter), where you can put your finger against a spot on the knee and say, *"That's* where it hurts, right there." When you ask people where an extensor mechanism injury hurts, 75 percent of them will rub a finger up and down along the inside of the kneecap. For another 15 percent it will be on the outside of the knee, and the last 10 percent can't quite figure out where it is—just somewhere around the front of the knee. It's worse with activity, better with rest. And as it gets worse, you develop problems elsewhere. So if you would describe your pain this way, you may have something else going on as well, but you certainly have a problem with the vastus medialis and the kneecap. From now on we'll call the injury chondromalacia. *Chondro* means "cartilage," *malacia* "wear"—to wit, cartilage wear. The kind of problem we're talking about may not have anything to do with cartilage wear; nevertheless, the term is used to describe it. (More on that later.)

One of the next tip-offs to appear, and the last to disappear, is what is called the positive theater sign: you're unable to sit with your knees bent for a long period of time. People with this problem are the ones you're always tripping over in a crowded theater because they sit on the aisle and stretch their legs out. These are the people who have a hard time in the economy section of airplanes, or who can't take long rides in VWs. If you're one of these people, and you've been sitting for a long time, you may get up and discover that your knee just won't work. It might take four or five steps to get it to straighten out. The knee isn't locking, really, but doing something that's called gelling (as in "gelatin"—rubbery; hard to move).

Next you may start to get some swelling in the knee. That causes the knee to ache, usually in the back, where the capsule surrounding the knee is softest and the fluid accumulates most readily. When you bend your knee, the fluid squirts into the back, and it may feel as though there's an orange stuck back there. At the least it will feel tight, as though something's in the way. Something is indeed in the way: fluid. But people usually don't realize that that's the problem. They just know that they can no longer get into a squat. Not because the knee hurts so much, but because it feels tight, full, sort of boggy. As the fluid continues to accumulate, your knee will begin to look, as well as feel, different.

It takes quite a bit of fluid in the knee to call attention to itself— about an ounce to an ounce and a half will just begin to make a difference for most people. But if you really know how to look at your knees, you can tell. Stretch them in front of you on the floor, or on top of a coffee table, all the way out, without tightening up the muscles (if you tighten your muscles you push all the fluid to the back of the knee).

Then check to see if both knees look the same. There should be hollows on either side of your kneecap—look for them. If one knee is less delineated than the other, then it's time to stop ignoring it.

One thing leads to another: now the pain in your knee may be sharper. If there's a lot of fluid in your knee, your kneecap can't possibly be where it belongs. It may have been displaced a bit to begin with; now it's more out of place, pushed to the side by the fluid. It may start rattling around a bit, making clicking sounds, or popping—repetitive noises. And now you're using your knee differently. You're reluctant to straighten it—that's an extreme motion and it hurts—and you're just as reluctant to bend it all the way. In fact, you *can't* bend it all the way; it's stiff, as though filled with gelatin. So you start limping, keeping your leg somewhere between too straight and too bent. Which means that you must walk on your toes, because your partially bent leg isn't long enough otherwise.

When you walk on your toes, your calf starts to hurt, as your calf muscles are the ones that keep you up on your toes. The gastrocnemius muscle in the calf begins above the knee, and the strain on it may itself cause more knee pain. Or the hamstring muscles may begin to hurt where they connect in the back of the knee, because they're helping to keep the knee partially bent all the time. And your quadriceps aren't being used normally, so they get weaker, especially the vastus medialis, which was too weak in the first place. Then your knee may start giving way. It just won't hold you up. You'll be walking and suddenly feel as though you stepped into a hole, with nothing there for support. But before you fall you catch yourself—until the next time.

All these things feed on themselves. The more problems you have, the less normally you're going to use your knee. The less normally you use your knee, the weaker it gets. The weaker it gets, the more likely you are to have problems. And once this cycle gets started, it's *not* going to get better by itself, especially because it sneaks up on you. Without thinking much about it, you start altering your activity to fit your diminishing capabilities. You used to run five miles a day; after a month you're down to two, then one. You used to take aerobics class five times a week; now you go three times, and a month later it's all you can do to take any classes at all. A month after that you have trouble walking to the studio from the parking lot. You always take the elevator now, and you drive around the block four times just to find a parking place that's three blocks closer because it's going to be hell walking down the hill to the office.

And all this time you figured it would just go away. Didn't it go away last time, when you were ten years younger? Or, more likely, there was no last time. You just haven't had to deal with something like this before. The temple of your body has up to now remained inviolate, and you can't quite believe that it's happening to you. Except that it's happening, all right, and you'd better do something about it or it'll simply continue to happen, and get worse.

Gutting it through is *not* the answer. Neither is simply stepping up your activity rate. Some people figure, rightly, that if the knee is weak there's only one thing to do: make it stronger. So they lift weights even more than they used to, walk, run if they can, in spite of the pain. And the knee simply doesn't come around. It's not that these activities aren't making you stronger, it's that they're making both sides stronger at the same time. So the bad side remains weak by comparison. You've got to do something to get the bad side up to the level of the good one—otherwise, the discrepancy will remain, along with the pain. You've got to do something *extra* with the side that's bothering you. And that extra isn't nearly as hard as you might think.

What to do about it

You must break the vicious circle, get rid of the pain so you can again use the knee normally, get rid of the swelling, and build some muscle. The solution (and, indeed, the solution for other problems as well) is to make the quadriceps on the bad side, specifically the vastus medialis, stronger. If you can cycle, one-legged cycling will make it stronger, but frequently by this point you're no longer able to do weight exercises (and cycling is really a weight exercise). Usually about the only thing to do is tightening exercises.

It's simple: straighten out your leg in front of you. You can sit on the floor, or sit in a chair and rest your leg on a coffee table, or even sit on the edge of your chair and extend your leg, with your heel on the floor, so that the knee is perfectly straight. Just make sure it's relaxed. Then place your fingers about an inch above the top of your kneecap and an inch to an inch and a half toward the inside of your leg (toward the midline of your body) and tighten your thigh. If you're doing it right, you should feel the small muscle below your fingers get tight—*really* tight. If that's the case, you've found your vastus medialis, and you're in business. Tighten up and hold it for six to eight seconds, relax for a couple of seconds, tighten and hold for six to eight seconds, relax for a couple. Do three or four of these sets ten to fifteen times a day.

Sometimes it may be difficult to tighten the muscle. You may find that when you tighten your thigh much of the muscle is rock-hard but the portion beneath your fingers remains soft. In that case it's a matter of learning how to control the muscle in order to exercise it. One easy method is to roll up a towel and place it beneath your knee. Then push the back of the knee down into the towel. When you do that, you'll find that the vastus medialis beneath your fingers tightens automatically.

You can accomplish the same thing by putting your fist underneath your knee and pushing down. It really doesn't matter what you have to do to persuade the muscle to work—you may have to put the dog under your knee to get it right—a rock-hard contraction is the bottom line. Continue doing the exercise in this way until you find you can tighten the vastus without anything beneath your knee. Again, tighten for six to eight seconds, then relax, tighten again, and relax, three or four times in all. And do these sets ten to fifteen times a day. (If everything fails, you might want to try an electrical muscle stimulator to help you figure out how to do the exercise. The problem is that now you'll have medical bills—doctor, physical therapist, machine rental—but it's better than not getting the exercise at all.)

It may sound horrible, but what we're really talking about is no more than seven minutes of work—thirty seconds of exercise ten to fifteen times a day. You can easily fit that much effort into your schedule if you tie it to something you already do a lot. If you're in school, do the exercise set every time the bell rings. If you're in the office, do it every time the phone rings. (Do a set every time somebody puts you on hold, and in a week you'll probably have a quadriceps that'll lift buildings.) If you're at home watching the tube, do it at each station break. *Don't* try to do fifty of these at a time, in line with the theory that if four are good, fifty must be better. Not so. For one thing, it's boring—doing fifty of these is like watching paint dry—and for another, it's almost impossible to do more than a few really good-quality tightenings at one time. Don't worry, you'll be able to *see* the increase in muscle in two to three weeks. And the odds are better than four out of five that you'll get better. It takes the most discipline in the beginning. Later, when your knee starts letting you know that it's improving, doing the exercises is a pleasure.

Sometimes the kneecap is so badly out of alignment that it hurts even to do the tightening exercises. If that's your case, pushing the kneecap toward the center of your knee with your fingers can make the exercise more comfortable. Some people prefer to wrap the knee with an Ace bandage or wear a neoprene knee sleeve. Such sleeves are available at hospital supply shops and some sporting goods stores. Pro and Ortho-Tech are the names of a couple of good ones. They keep the knee warm and may help hold the kneecap in place. Icing after activity helps knock down inflammation, as will aspirin or other anti-inflammatory drugs. But all of these things are no more than adjuncts. They may make life a little easier for you, but you're not going to get rid of the problem—if you're going to get rid of it at all—until you make the bad leg stronger.

You might discover that you're among the 15 percent or so of people who just don't respond to this kind of treatment. It may be that the problem has gotten so bad that the back of your kneecap is chewed up (see the following section), or the capsule may have been scarred and has become too tight. If the exercise hurts (and as a general rule you shouldn't try to strengthen things that hurt), and displacing the kneecap with your fingers or a bandage doesn't help, then maybe you should see somebody. The exercise simply may not work for everyone.

But if you've experienced the symptoms we've described, and the swelling isn't too bad, and your knee isn't locking or doing any other horrible things, and doing the exercise doesn't hurt, then it won't harm you to back down on the pain-producing activity and try the program for at least two to three weeks before you think about going to a doctor. A doctor who deals with these kinds of things regularly is going to give you the same advice, anyway. He may give the knee a thorough exam, take X-rays, test your strength, but at the end of the visit he's going to tell you to make the muscle stronger—and it'll cost you $200.

If you do the exercises and develop lots of good muscle and it doesn't change things, then you're between a rock and a hard place. You may have to do something more spectacular. Like seeing someone. As a last resort, there is an operation that can help chondromalacia. It involves detaching the ligaments that hold the kneecap to the *outside* of the knee so that the vastus medialis can pull more effectively to the *inside*. But most likely you'll never have to go that far. First things first. Try the exercises. Odds are you'll have to do no more. And once back on the track, or the court, or in the studio, *keep* the muscle strong.

The vastus medialis—so much depends on so little.

CHONDROMALACIA: DEGENERATION OF THE CARTILAGE

As promised, here's a word about the "real" chondromalacia, the kind that is more closely associated with the meaning of the word itself—wear and tear of the cartilage. In the precise use of the term, chondromalacia suggests that the back of your kneecap is wearing out, that the normally smooth, faceted surface of articular cartilage has begun to roughen like sandpaper. Sometimes the surface of the back of the kneecap softens and literally falls away in strands, like a hanging garden of cartilage.

This degeneration of the back of the kneecap may be caused by the slow, subtle extensor mechanism problems most of us suffer to one degree to another, or it may be the result of a fall that drives your kneecap so hard into the thighbone that it cracks the cartilage. It might have happened ten years ago, and you've only begun to suffer the consequences now. It's a tough one to deal with—it may even require surgery—but in general strengthening the vastus medialis will help here as well.

What to do about it

This kind of chondromalacia is rare compared to the problems that the more general use of the term describes. But if you try the treatments suggested in the previous section and your pain just won't go away, you might be in the select group that has the real thing. See a doctor.

PATELLAR TENDINITIS (JUMPER'S KNEE)

One of the big differences between the effects of patellar tendinitis (that is, tendinitis of the patella—the kneecap), and chondromalacia is that tendinitis sufferers are much better able to locate the pain. Whereas people with chondromalacia may rub their fingers up, down, and around the knee to indicate where it hurts, when you have tendinitis you can put a fingertip right on the spot. It's so tiny and specific that you can put the tip of a ballpoint pen right on the spot and just about levitate yourself into the air with pain. And that spot is right at the bottom of the kneecap, where the tendon that goes on to connect to the shinbone begins—hence the name, patellar tendinitis.

It's also called jumper's knee, as it was first described in the takeoff leg of high jumpers. But it turns out that basketball players probably have more jumper's knee than anybody else. You also see it in dancers, runners (and it's very hard to deal with in runners, for some reason), volleyball players—anyone who runs and jumps regularly may suffer from it. And, like chondromalacia, it sneaks up on you, first hurting after your activity, then toward the end of the activity, then during, at the beginning, and finally all the time. It's not nearly as common as chondromalacia—nothing is—but it's more difficult to deal with. It's probably the second most frequent knee injury.

All that said, we must admit that no one understands patellar tendinitis very well at all. Judging by the discomfort it can produce, you might expect a great deal of inflammation, but when you get to the point of having to operate on these people, often you can't see anything wrong. Sometimes the tendon looks red and inflamed, but many times it doesn't. It's probably because we're not capable of looking at things at the microscopic level; these changes may be very subtle.

Not so subtle, however, is *acute* patellar tendinitis—that is, tendinitis caused by a specific incident rather than a problem that sneaks up on you. It can be the result of a misstep while running (a hurdler, for example, who confuses his steps between hurdles and tries to correct, or a sprinter who slips out of the blocks), a blow on the knee, even snapping out your leg while dancing—anything that puts an overload on the knee *quickly*. And you'll know it when it happens. You'll have sharp pain at the bottom of the kneecap, swelling, difficulty in moving the knee. In this case, part of the tendon actually tears away from the kneecap, but often much less than you'd think to cause so much discomfort. It may be that only a few of a couple thousand fibers in the tendon have broken away, but that is enough. (It may be, however, that you've actually pulled your kneecap *apart*. Sometimes, although not often, the tendon is actually stronger than the bone, and instead of giving way the tendon stays intact and the bone splits in two.)

Again, the tip-off that it is patellar tendinitis that is troubling you, not something else: the pain is sharp, specific, easy to locate—right at the bottom of the kneecap.

What to do about it

If it's acute tendinitis, the result of a particular incident, then two aspirin with meals, icing three times a day, a rest from your particular activity, and maintaining muscle strength during that period is a way to begin. But if it really hurts, and the knee is hard to move as well, you should probably see somebody about it.

Some people think that the overuse variety of patellar tendinitis, the kind that sneaks up on you, can result from an inappropriate balance between the strength of your quadriceps and hamstring muscles. That's not at all well documented, but there does seem to be some association with tightness of the quads. That goes along with the general philosophy concerning tendinitis: tight tendons are tendons that are likely to be irritated. The thing to do, then, is stretch out the tendon, and the way to do that is to stretch out the quadriceps muscle itself. You can lie on your stomach and have someone gently bend your leg to the point where either your knees hurt or your quadriceps feel tight. Hold the position for a few seconds, and then do it again. You can do the same exercise yourself by lying on your stomach, reaching behind you, grasping the foot of the opposite leg, and gently pulling your heel toward the small of your back. Or stand supporting yourself with a hand against the wall, and pull your foot toward your back as you did on the ground. The important thing is to stretch *without* pain. If it hurts, don't stretch so far. Gradually it will come.

Interestingly, about half the people with jumper's knee find that it hurts to extend the knee and tighten their thigh muscles—the kind of vastus medialis strengthening exercise described in the preceding section. But if you put your fingertip on the outside of the kneecap and push toward the inside of the leg just a tiny bit, sometimes an imperceptible amount, the pain disappears. That suggests that the vastus muscle—wouldn't you know it—is involved in this injury as well. It's probably an alignment problem. The tendon isn't pulling in quite the right direction because the muscle is weakened, allowing the kneecap to stray too far to the outside. So if you can get your vastus to take over for your finger (because it would be tough to walk around with your finger on your kneecap for the rest of your life), it can help alleviate the problem. Vastus medialis strengthening exercises are always a good bet.

So vastus muscle strengthening exercises and quadriceps stretching exercises most likely will help, as will doing all the other things that you do for tendinitis in general—warming up well before activity, icing afterward, perhaps wearing a neoprene sleeve over the knee (which can help push the kneecap to the inside—basketball players seem to like that), taking aspirin or a stronger over-the-counter anti-inflammatory drug like Advil, and, in case there's anything to the quadriceps-hamstrings strength ratio business, making sure that the hamstrings in both legs are equally flexible. Just lie on your back with your legs straight and lift one leg up, then the other. If there's a noticeable difference in flexibility, stretch the tight leg—but gently.

Both patellar tendinitis and chondromalacia, because they involve kneecap alignment problems, can sometimes be helped by orthotics. Anything that decreases the angle in the knee around which the quadriceps have to pull decreases the likelihood of the kneecap's slipping out of alignment. If your arch collapses, forcing you to pronate to the inside when you walk or stand, then your knee rotates to the inside. That makes the angle on the outside of the knee greater. Arch supports or orthotics can help straighten things up and decrease the angle. Seeing someone for an evaluation might be a good idea. But it costs you nothing to try exercises first.

Sometimes patellar tendinitis can result in surgery. It can be successful, but it's a last resort. At the Center for Sports Medicine, we would look at the possibility of orthotics before operating on anybody, *but not before telling people to start doing exercises.* You always treat things the simplest, least invasive way you can. If the easy things don't work, then you can try the more invasive, and expensive, things. But the vast majority of people are going to get well by doing the easy things. It's just a matter of recognizing the problem and knowing how best to go about dealing with it. That's what this book is for.

OSGOOD-SCHLATTER'S DISEASE

It's not really a disease, but rather a form of tendinitis at the *other* end of the patellar tendon, where it goes into the shinbone. You can easily locate the spot. Simply run your fingers up the shinbone toward your knee. When you come to a small lump a couple of inches below the kneecap, you've found the place. That would be enough said about the problem—how to deal with tendinitis should be pretty clear by now—were it not for one thing: Osgood-Schlatter's disease affects only people who are growing. That is to say, young people, usually between ten and sixteen years old. (And it used to affect males only, but that was because women just didn't do many sports. In recent years young women have come into their share of Osgood-Schlatter's disease. An unwelcome by-product of the women's movement.)

The reason for this being a young people's problem is interesting: when bones grow they don't just stretch like elastic; rather, they expand at certain spots near the upper and lower ends of bones, called growth centers. It is in these centers that new bone is made, pushing out to lengthen and thicken the existing bone and jack up kids to adult size. Once we've finished growing, the growth centers close down. (Although the bone, like the rest of the body, constantly regenerates itself, it doesn't become appreciably larger.) It just so happens that the patellar tendon connects to the shinbone at just this spot—a growth center. Which means that the tendon encounters *forming* bone, bone that is not yet as hard and resilient as it will become. It's in between bone and cartilage at this stage, not quite one or the other. In X-rays it resembles a cloud in the midst of the more solid bone at either end. Normally, if a tendon pulls away from the bone the tendon tears, not the bone. But when a tendon strains against a growth center, it can pull away pieces of the soft, forming bone instead.

And that's exactly what happens in Osgood-Schlatter's disease: the tendon pulls against the forming bone and actually tears away tiny pieces of it. But wait—the story isn't over. The forming bone, now connected to the tendon rather than the shinbone, isn't about to stop doing what it's doing. Its job is to turn into new bone, right? And so it does, right there at the end of the tendon. The result is a lumpy knee. You already had a lump at this point—now you've *really* got one.

What to do about it

Because the tendon is so near the skin, often it will get red and swollen, and very, very tender. Treat it with ice, aspirin, and rest to the point where you're not limping during normal activities. And, as before, you must strengthen your quadriceps, especially so because people who are growing very quickly often have tight muscles. The bones grow faster than the muscles can stretch; they just can't keep up. So the quadriceps muscles of people with Osgood-Schlatter's disease are often tight. Or more likely it's vice versa: tight quadriceps muscles can lead to Osgood-Schlatter's disease. It's important to start nice, long, gentle, sustained quad stretching exercises, as described earlier.

The only other treatment besides strengthening, stretching, and getting rid of the inflammation is to wear a horseshoe-shaped pad around the lump. You'll be amazed at how often you fall onto or kneel on the lump, or bump your knees into all sorts of things. As with any injury, you become very conscious of the tender part of the body. But don't expect the lump to go away. Most likely it's yours forever, no longer a sign of injury, but not necessarily the most attractive thing to have sticking up from your leg. Unfortunately, surgically decreasing the lumpiness is a tough, involved operation. You have to take the tendon off the bone, shave down the bone, then reattach the tendon. Most people are better off with a lump.

HAMSTRING TENDINITIS

Chondromalacia, jumper's knee, and Osgood-Schlatter's disease are the most frequent knee problems, but there are a number of less common kinds of tendinitis that can attack the back of the knee. One of those is tendinitis of the hamstring tendons. These are the tough wires in the back of the knee, one toward the outside of the leg, the two others toward the inside, in the direction of your other leg. If you place your hand at the back of your knee and bend your leg, you'll feel them. They're obvious to the touch as well as the eye. They connect the hamstring muscles, the large muscle group in the back of your thigh, to the lower leg. It's these muscles that pull your lower leg up toward the body, allowing you to bend your knee. If any one of the hamstring tendons becomes sore and inflamed, it's probably due to tendinitis.

Usually the tendinitis is from overuse. You can get it from running hills (running downhill, especially, stretches the hamstrings and can cause hamstring tendinitis if the muscles are tight), and limping with a bent knee to favor another injury can bring it on as well. It's the hamstring muscles that keep the knee bent—too much limping can overtax them, straining the tendons. Sometimes you can cause hamstring tendinitis by trying to solve other problems in your knee. If you bandage your knee too tightly, for example, the hamstring tendons will chafe against the wrap every time you take a step. Even wearing a knee sleeve can give you tendinitis.

Another possible cause is less obvious: changing to a lower-heeled shoe. It's easy to associate Achilles tendinitis with a low heel, because it makes sense that if you lower your heel, you stretch the Achilles tendon. It takes a bit more thought to realize that the hamstrings are part of the same chain. (That's the beautiful—or frustrating, depending on your point of view—thing about the body: everything is interrelated.) When you run and your heel hits the ground, your knee is partially bent. If your heel doesn't come down as quickly, as when you're running downhill, or if you lower the heel in your shoe, your knee must extend a bit farther for your foot to make contact with the ground. That can stretch the hamstrings. But if they don't stretch, something has to. That something is the hamstring tendon. The result can be tendinitis. So running in a tennis shoe, which has almost no heel at all, rather than in a running shoe, which has a raised heel, can often cause hamstring tendinitis, as can running on the beach barefoot. It's like running in a negative-heel shoe, because your heel sinks into the sand.

What to do about it

The first thing to do is deal with the inflammation. Try ice, aspirin, gentle stretching and strengthening of the hamstring muscles, as suggested earlier. But none of those treatments will have a lasting effect until you find out why you have tendinitis in the first place. What change—and overuse problems are invariably the result of some kind of change—have you made in your training, in your footwear, in the kind of activity itself? When you figure that out, avoid the activity for a while and continue to deal with the problem by strengthening and stretching. When you feel better, either ease back into your training or change back to the kind of activity (or footwear) that caused you no problems earlier. And one temporary thing you can do while getting back is to raise your heel a quarter of an inch or so with a cork heel pad. That'll help relax the tendon while you're sorting out all this stuff.

The important thing is to get on it quickly. The longer you walk with a limp or an abnormal gait, the harder it will be to get rid of the problem. But if your hamstring tendons don't get better, or if they're red and swollen and really tender to the touch, you might be better off seeing somebody. A doctor can prescribe stronger anti-inflammatory drugs and teach you physical therapy that might get you on your way a bit sooner.

TENDINITIS OF THE ILIOTIBIAL BAND

There's a long, thick, rigid tendon that runs from the upper part of your hips (the ilium) all the way down the outside of the thigh, through the knee, and connects to your shinbone (tibia). It's called the iliotibial band. You can feel it just above the hamstring tendon on the outside of the knee. It feels like a cable and, indeed, acts mostly as a stabilizer, almost as though it were a ligament. It's also involved in straightening the knee, for about the last 15 degrees of motion, and flexing it as well. It can be irritated by the difference in gait demanded by running downhill, or by other gait problems in runners.

What to do about it

Stretching and strengthening can help if you catch it early. Gently pull your injured leg to the outside and toward the back to strengthen. You can do this exercise standing or lying on your side, and it doesn't matter if you point or flex your foot. To stretch, stand up and cross your injured leg behind your other leg—it's called a cross-leg stretch. And, as with any other tendinitis, try ice, aspirin, and rest. But you may have to see somebody, as the exercise programs involved with iliotibial band tendinitis are very specific and require demonstration.

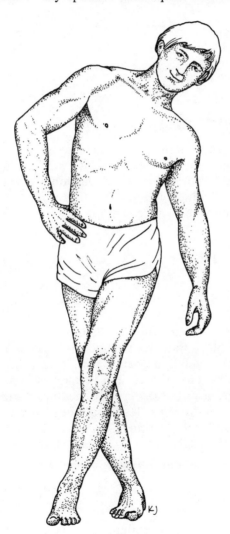

Iliotibial Band Stretching Exercise

Iliotibial Band Strengthening Exercise

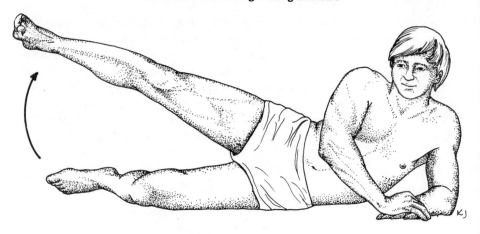

POPLITEAL TENDINITIS

There is a tiny muscle in the back of the knee called the popliteus. It helps flex your knee. Its tendon winds its way up and around and crosses the outside of your knee, the only tendon that's really inside the knee capsule itself. Popliteal tendinitis will give pain in the outside of the knee, most often when you're running downhill.

What to do about it

See someone. It's a tough problem to deal with, difficult to either stretch or strengthen the muscle, as it's so small and its role is so specific.

In fact, with outside-of-the-knee problems in general, if a little bit of stretching doesn't help, a footwear change doesn't help, and an activity change doesn't help, you'll probably have to see someone. These problems can demand a lot of precision in diagnosis and very specific rehabilitation programs. And there are a number of other things that can cause problems in this area. It's simply beyond the capabilities of most people to handle these things at home. Indeed, some of the problems are so difficult that it's beyond the capabilities of physicians to handle them.

BURSITIS

Bursas are envelopes of paper-thin, slippery tissue that act as the body's slipping and sliding mechanism, its friction reducer. Wherever two things in the body rub over each other—tendon over bone, tendon over ligament, tendon over tendon—you might find a bursa to grease the way. Because so many tendons run through the knee, there are more than a dozen different bursas around the area. These can become irritated and inflamed. Usually they don't involve enough swelling so that you'd notice it, but they can hurt.

The exception is what's called prepatellar (in front of the kneecap) bursitis. Here the bursa directly over the kneecap swells, most likely as the result of a fall or a blow. (It's also known as housemaid's knee, after those legions of women who through the years spent much of their time on their hands and knees.) It can grow so large that it looks as though someone has stuffed a lemon under your skin.

What to do about it

Once it's that size, you should definitely see someone. It may have to be aspirated and injected with cortisone to decrease the inflammation. Until that point you can try icing it three times a day for twenty minutes and taking two aspirin with meals. If a few days of this treatment produce no results, it's off to the clinic.

BAKER'S CYST

Unlike baker's yeast, it has nothing to do with bread. But it does rise. A Baker's cyst (named after the surgeon who first discovered it) is a large swelling in the back of your knee. In adults, it usually forms because you've got something else going on in the knee that is producing too much fluid. The knee capsule is much firmer in the front of the knee than in the back. When you tighten your quadriceps muscles, the capsule tightens around the kneecap and the fluid gets smooshed to the area of least resistance, the back. If enough fluid is pushed to the back of the knee enough times, the capsule can become permanently deformed, ballooning outward like a bulge in an inner tube. Sometimes people have one the size of an orange.

What to do about it

We used to remove them surgically, but they tended to come back because we didn't deal with the initial problem. So the idea is to get rid of whatever it is that's causing the fluid to form in the first place. If you let air out of a bulging inner tube, the bulge disappears. If you persuade the knee to quit forming fluid, the Baker's cyst disappears. Often the cause is a torn cartilage. That may require surgery. But the cause can be chondromalacia as well. Whatever it is, if you deal with the problem, you almost never have to take out the Baker's cyst. It simply goes away. Better see someone. It can be a frightening thing to discover that you've got an orange in the back of your knee.

Children sometimes develop something called primary Baker's cyst. The symptoms are the same, but in this case there's nothing wrong with the knee. The cyst forms for unknown reasons. Often these have to be removed surgically. See a doctor.

MENISCUS CYSTS

What we think happens is that you tear part of a meniscus (the cushioning cartilage in the knee joint) and it heals abnormally. In the process, cells that are capable of forming fluid somehow get trapped in the meniscus and form a cyst filled with jellylike fluid. As the cyst grows, frequently to marble size, it pushes toward the outside of the knee. You'd think that something that small wouldn't cause as much pain as it does, but things are pretty tight in the knee, and as the cyst grows it pushes against the ligaments and the knee capsule itself. That hurts. Often you can feel and see these cysts. As you bend and straighten your knee, the cysts appear to change in size, but they're only reacting to the amount of tension exerted against them.

What to do about it

If they hurt enough so that you simply can't live with them, sometimes these cysts can be aspirated and injected with cortisone to shut down their ability to make more fluid. But they can be difficult to drain, because the fluid is gummy, the consistency of cold maple syrup, and it clogs up the needle. Usually, however, as the cause of the cyst is a torn meniscus, surgically removing the tear gets rid of the cyst as well. Here's an instance in which the arthroscope can be very useful. (See Chapter 16, "So You're Going to Have an Operation.")

DEGENERATIVE DISEASE IN THE KNEE

It's not something that most people like to think about too much, but it's certainly true: little by little our bodies wear down. If we live long enough we're going to wear out our joints, and often the knee is the first to go. We're allotted our portion of cushioning meniscus, and although our body makes day-to-day repairs, it can't always keep up with the abuse we heap on our knees. As we get older, we wear down the meniscus. It begins to age, becomes less rubbery and more granular, and begins to get microscopic tears. These gradually become larger, are chewed up in the joint, and can start getting in the way. And if you've had any major problem that disrupted the mechanics of the joint—a torn meniscus removed, a ligament tear, long-term chondromalacia, so that the kneecap doesn't track properly—then this degeneration is accelerated.

Degenerative arthritis is one term to describe these degenerative changes. People blanch when they hear it, but it *is* arthritis. Not rheumatoid arthritis, which can deform the joint, but wear-and-tear arthritis. And it may sound worse than it actually is. For most people, the consequence is that their knees become less tolerant of the kinds of problems we've discussed in this chapter. If it would normally take a 50 percent change in your daily running mileage to bring on tendinitis, say, now you might get those same symptoms with just a 20 percent change. If running up and down hills never bothered you before, now your knee may ache after a workout. If five days a week of tennis, racquetball, or aerobics class used to be your norm, now you may notice that your knees are talking to you toward the end of the week (or the middle, or the beginning).

So the upshot is that you lose the luxury of being able to ignore things. Little problems are less likely to go away by themselves. You're less tolerant of change. And it can be very frustrating for an active person to realize that the little aches and pains that always simply disappeared by themselves are now things that have to be dealt with, that now it's necesssary to become *aware* of what's going on in your knees and plan your activities accordingly, instead of simply bludgeoning through as before.

These degenerative changes will show up in the guise of overuse problems. Your knee may ache after an activity and stiffen up. Usually as the day goes on you get a little stiffer, notice a little more loss of motion. But you can't put your finger on any particular spot that hurts, nor can you point to any particular cause. The damn knee just hurts. And if the pain goes away after a night's sleep, there it is again the next day, this time before you're done with your workout. Soon the knee aches while you're lacing your shoes. And so it goes.

What to do about it

The realistic way to deal with degenerative changes is to do all the things that you would do for overuse problems: ice, aspirin, rest, and maintain as much strength and flexibility as you can. There's some information to suggest that if you remain strong you can handle these changes better, because the joint is held together more firmly than if you were weak. And if you stay strong you retain a greater range of motion.

So degenerative changes usually mean that you'll have to alter your activity but not necessarily stop it. For example, if you're a runner and your knees are wearing out, you may have to start training without running. Alternate running with cycling. That cuts in half the amount of weight your knees have to bear, while continuing to maintain strength and cardiovascular conditioning. A few years down the pike you may have to do three quarters of your training on the bicycle and only one quarter running. After you run a 10-kilometer race you may have to cycle exclusively for the next two weeks to give your knees a breather.

Eventually the day might come when running simply isn't in the best interests of your knees, and you may have to figure out a way to maintain your conditioning and have some fun while running only occasionally—or not at all. It's easier to make that kind of change these days, for the fitness movement has helped diversify the kind of activities people do. Five years ago if you were involved in fitness you were almost certainly a runner. Now, with aerobics, cycling, cross-country skiing, racquetball, swimming, Universal gyms, and home exercise, people no longer rely on just one activity. That's good, because if something goes wrong you have other activities to fall back on. Your life doesn't have to fall apart because you can't run the way you used to. Now you can spread abuse around your body.

It's a matter of adapting. No one can reverse these changes. Knee joint surgical replacement techniques do exist, but so far they're more suitable for salvage operations than anything else. And it may be scant comfort, but rest assured that for all practical purposes you *won't* outlive your knees. They'll most likely carry you through most of the things you're interested in doing until that time when it no longer matters much.

REPLACING THE KNEE

You see people with artificial hips scampering—well, maybe not *scampering*—around on the tennis courts all the time. Why not artificial knees? The answer is that you *can* replace the knee joint, but the surgery isn't nearly as successful as hip replacement. For a simple reason: the hip is a very simple joint, a ball and socket, the easiest kind of joint to work with. But, as we've seen, the knee is a very complicated joint, a hinge that can rotate as well as bend, and that is held in place by a system of restraints rather than positive linkage. You have to depend on the body's natural guy wires—the ligaments and tendons—

to hold the artificial joint in place, and that's often a problem because they're not in such great shape after the joint has become so chewed up that it needs replacing.

The second problem with knee replacement surgery is that the knee is a huge joint, the largest in the body. It has four or five times as much surface area as the hip. So you're faced with inserting big pieces of metal or plastic in an area that's just under the skin, not covered and protected by muscles as in the hip joint. The body likes to get rid of foreign things that are near the surface, and because of the immense forces acting on the knee those things are more likely to loosen and break down—especially because you have to replace both sides of the joint at the same time, whether they need it or not. No one has yet come up with a single compound that will coexist with the cartilage and bone in your knee. If it's too hard, it wears away the cartilage on the other side of the joint; if it's too soft, the cartilage remains but the artificial bone wears out. So you have to insert two synthetics that are mated to each other—usually plastic on one side, metal on the other. And if the kneecap needs replacing as well, it must be done in conjunction with the new joint. Putting a new kneecap in your existing joint doesn't work for the same reason that prevents you from replacing only one side of the joint—the synthetic replacement material is simply not compatible with what it has to rub against.

The moral of the story: hold on to your knees. Treat them *right*.

OVERUSE CHECKLIST

About 60 percent of all overuse knee problems involve chondromalacia—a kneecap out of alignment. You'll know because it's hard to put a finger on the pain. It's there, all right, but it seems to spread around the knee. And if it persists, it can become submerged in other problems. Best get to it right away. Ice, rest, and aspirin can help, as can exercise: *strengthen the vastus medialis muscle.*

About 15 percent are other tendinitis problems: jumper's knee, hamstring tendinitis, popliteal tendinitis, iliotibial band tendinitis. They, too, can involve the extensor mechanism. Try ice, rest, aspirin, and exercise.

Another 15 percent are degenerative changes. They show up in the guise of common overuse problems. There is nothing to do but treat them as you would the overuse problems themselves. And stay strong. The healthier your muscles, the healthier your knee joint.

The remaining 10 percent are various little things: bursitis, cysts, etc. These are difficult to diagnose and difficult to treat. They require somebody pretty good at doctoring.

Acute Knee Injuries

Overuse injuries creep up on you. A minor discomfort turns into a nagging irritation, which turns into a chronic pain, and before you know it you're hurting all the time, really hurting, and you can't quite figure out when and how it happened. Not so with acute injuries. These you can date from a single incident. In fact, you can probably recall the hour, the minute, the second it happened, and *precisely* what you were doing at the time. Even if it happened years ago, the incident is burned into your mind forever.

Would that we could recall pleasant moments so vividly. For often all it takes to make you relive the incident is overhearing someone describe their own injury or reading through a book like this one that describes such moments in detail. Your knee can get *that* feeling all over again. Be strong. People have been known to get physically sick during lectures describing their particular problem. Once injured in the flesh, often reinjured in the mind.

All this to say that if you suffer an acute knee injury, you'll know it. You'll simply be able to *feel* that something serious has gone wrong, something that has never happened before and that you want *never* to happen again. Trust your own insight in such a situation, and go with your better judgment, not against it. In other words, don't deny to yourself that something serious has happened and try to ignore it. No one likes to go to the doctor, no one wants to have surgery (and acute knee injuries are the most frequent cause of surgery in all sports), no one wants to have to do all those awful things to rehabilitate the knee. The temptation is to go home, hit the sack, and hope that when you wake up it will all have been a bad dream, just as when your car acts up you put it in the garage for the night and hope that miraculously it will start the next morning.

Well, in the morning your car still may not start, but it will be no worse—your knee will be. And not only will it be worse, it will be *a lot* harder for somebody to figure out what's wrong with it. If you're examined soon after an injury, you're half again as likely to get an accurate diagnosis as when you wait. The reason is simple: when you injure your knee severely, the muscles in your thigh go into spasm—that is, contract violently and immobilize the knee, just as though you were wearing a splint. The longer the muscles are in spasm, the more tightly they hold the knee. The tighter the knee, the more it hurts. And the more it hurts, the more difficult it is for you to relax enough so that someone can move the knee to examine it. And soon the knee will start to swell. If you finally go to a doctor after a couple of days, and your knee looks like a softball, then there's little alternative than to resort to X-rays—a cost of $60 to $70 right there—or, because in probably 95 percent of acute injuries X-rays won't disclose the problem, to more invasive procedures like arthrography or arthroscopy (again, see Chapter 16).

One of the reasons why professional athletes receive such good care is that someone is always available to examine an injury within a minute—literally—after it occurs. At that point an athlete is still in shock, with no pain, so it's possible to do a superb examination. You can manipulate the knee in ways that an hour later would probably land you a punch in the nose. You can make an accurate diagnosis and start the athlete on a rehabilitation program, which should be done as soon as possible, almost immediately. So if you suffer one of these semi-dreadful things, it may not be necessary to call an ambulance, but to have somebody drive you to an emergency room right away. That kind of fast response will save you much unnecessary difficulty later.

ACUTE INJURY TIP-OFFS

If you're not sure what happened to you, and any of the following kinds of behavior describe your knee, you'd be wise to haul yourself off to a doctor and have it looked at.

1. *Noise*. It is not good to hear things in your knee. A lot of people may have a creaky knee, a knee that makes noise when they go up and down stairs, say, or bend into a squat. That's a different sort of thing. It's been around a long time; it's nothing new. The kind of noise that should snap you to attention is a noise that's the result of *doing something* to your knee—changing direction, slowing down, speeding up, landing after a jump, cutting hard. The gymnast who lands after a dismount and has her foot stick in the mat, the dancer who comes down off balance from a jump, the football player who cuts to avoid a tackle, the runner who decelerates too quickly, all might suddenly hear a sound in their knee they haven't heard before. A pop or a snap—a sharp, short sound—can signify a torn cartilage or ligament. A dislocated kneecap is marked by a long, drawn-out sound, like a chicken leg being disjointed. And certainly if you hurt your knee and *someone else* says, "What was that?" you'd better have it looked at. Knee sounds that other people hear bode no good.

The sound is important, for although your knee may hurt, you can't always otherwise tell that something serious has happened. For example, most people don't know when they've dislocated their kneecap, because as soon as they straighten their knee the kneecap slips right back into place. They look down and the knee looks all right. The tip-off is the noise. So sounds that you either sense, hear, or that other people hear should be viewed almost as absolutes. Get your knee to a doctor.

2. *A sense of instability.* If the knee doesn't feel the same as it did before the incident, before you heard the sound, then there's a good chance that you've torn a ligament. It may be an obvious difference—your knee now bends the wrong way; it used to be a hinge, now it's closer to a universal joint—or it may be subtle, no more than a feeling that something has changed. And it may not hurt enough to raise your suspicions otherwise. Be smart—see someone.

3. *Rapid swelling.* Certainly if the swelling occurs before your eyes—which will happen with a dislocated kneecap—you should see someone immediately. If your knee is obviously more swollen now than it was a half hour ago, better make a trip to the emergency room.

With some injuries, like a torn anterior cruciate ligament, perhaps the most common acute knee injury, the swelling occurs a bit more slowly. It may not be until morning that you realize that your knee is swollen. You'll notice it first in the back of the knee, where the capsule that surrounds the joint is softest. And even then you may not *see* the swelling so much as *feel* it. You'll notice that you can't bend your knee back as far as you used to. It feels tight, sluggish. Then the next thing you know, you can't stretch it out completely, either. The extremes of movement tighten the capsule, packing the fluid that causes the swelling tightly around the joint, preventing motion. And then you'll begin to see the swelling. Waste no more time—let someone see your knee.

4. *Locking.* It's important to understand just what locking is. It is *not* your knee becoming stiff after you've been sitting for a while. That's not really locking; it's something called gelling, probably caused by swelling that eventually is absorbed away when you move your knee. Locking is just what the term suggests: a sudden rigidity that occurs abruptly and then unoccurs just as abruptly. True locking implies unlocking. So if you think your knee is locking, ask yourself what you have to do to get it moving again.

If the answer is that walking around and getting the kinks out unlocks it, then it probably isn't of much concern. Simply walk around and get the kinks out. But if you're forced to twist it with your hands, or jiggle your foot, or have a friend pull on it, and if then you feel a snap like the one when you originally hurt your knee and suddenly it works again, you've got honest-to-God locking. And that means something is getting in the way.

That something may be a loose piece of cartilage, or cartilage and bone, that's caught in the joint. And that means that it won't go away by itself. It may be that you have an operating room in your future. Better see a doctor.

Once again, noise, a sense of instability, the rapid onset of swelling, and locking are the primary tip-offs for acute knee injuries. Two other things also might cause you concern:

5. *Compromises in the use of the knee.* If you hurt your knee and

afterward you're unwilling to bear weight on it, better let someone take a look at it. As with ankle injuries, people often will try to get back on the knee, sometimes successfully. That's how you find out if it's loose, or tight, or doesn't work at all. But if something happens to your knee and you're simply unwilling to put your foot down afterward—you just *know* that it's not a good idea—it could mean that something significant has happened.

Likewise, if you're unwilling to move the knee at all, you should have it looked at. With most knee injuries people will try to move the knee, and often it will move, at least in one direction. But if something tells you that you shouldn't move your knee at all, don't. *Do* go see someone.

6. *Bruising around the knee a couple of days later.* You can have a lot of bruising with an ankle sprain, and it may not mean much of anything. But if your knee develops a bruise larger than a silver dollar, say—and often these bruises will involve an area four to five inches in diameter—it means that there's bleeding underneath the surface, a tip-off that something is going on in the knee that shouldn't. Better have someone take a look.

Now, on to specific injuries.

TORN CARTILAGE

It is the most famous knee injury. In fact, you sometimes hear people with undiagnosed knee problems stating unequivocally, "I've torn a cartilage." And they well might be right, for if cartilage tears are not the most common acute knee injury—that dubious honor may go to torn anterior cruciate ligaments—they are plenty common enough. And they can result in all sorts of problems, pain and a locked knee most notably. Often they lead to surgery. But you don't necessarily have torn cartilages removed because of pain; you do so because the torn piece may damage the surface of the knee joint, which is another kind of cartilage, and which doesn't repair well at all.

Your knee contains two types of cartilage. The ends of the two large bones in the knee, the tibia and femur, are coated with one kind, the articular cartilage. If you're preparing a meal and you crack the joint between a chicken leg and thigh, you'll notice that the ends of the bone are covered by a glistening white cap. That's articular cartilage. The ends of our bones are white and glistening, too—at least they are when they're in good shape—as though they've been dipped in liquid latex. This articular cartilage cushions and protects the bone, but it's hardly indestructible. You can indent it with your fingernail and it stays that way. Try it with the chicken bone sometime. If your articular cartilage becomes indented, or cracked, or a piece is knocked out, it likewise stays that way. It's not like bone; it simply doesn't repair itself. You start out with all the articular cartilage you're ever going to have, so you might as well be nice to it.

And one way to be nice to your articular cartilage is to keep the other kind of cartilage in your knee—the fibrocartilage, or meniscus—whole. The menisci (plural; pronounced "men-isk-eye") are rings of dense, rubbery shims that perch on the end of the shinbone, the tibia, and act as shock absorbers between the two parts of the joint. But they don't just rest there. They're actually attached to the capsule that envelops the joint, so when your knee moves, they move. When you flex and extend your knee, the menisci move with the tibia. When you rotate the knee, they move with the upper leg bone, the femur. In that way they're always in the most advantageous position to absorb the forces in the knee. And the movement of the bones themselves is not simple. They sort of twist, glide, and slide at the same time. Nothing about the knee is simple. It's easily the most complicated joint in the body.

So it's very important that these menisci stay whole and function as they're supposed to. That doesn't always happen. If you twist your knee while bearing weight, you can tear them. If you tear them badly enough, the torn piece can float away within the joint and in the worst cases can lodge between the moving bone, like a wedge stuck between gears. Your knee is so sensitive that something the thickness of a credit card loose in the joint would hurt so badly that you couldn't bear to stand. A ¼-inch-thick piece of meniscus can be excruciating. It's these floating pieces that can cause the locking and pain cartilage tears are known for.

And even if a torn piece doesn't lodge in the joint, it can cause damage by ripping or chewing away the articular cartilage. A torn meniscus might never bother you directly, but later on, years after the injury, your knee may start to exhibit the kind of degenerative changes we discussed earlier, all because the torn piece has been grinding around in there all that time. So if you even suspect that you may have torn a cartilage, it's a good idea to have someone take a look.

The medial meniscus—the part on the inside of the leg, toward the midline of the body—tears with cutting-type maneuvers. The classical example is a football wide receiver who goes down the field, plants his foot, cuts, feels a snap in his knee, and can no longer straighten out his leg. Medial tears are more likely to cause the knee to lock and are more easily diagnosed.

The lateral meniscus, on the outside of the knee, tears when you're bearing weight on a bent knee. A wrestler on the mat with his knee bent underneath him, an aerobic dancer folding her legs behind her and leaning back over them to stretch, a person simply squatting and inadvertently twisting a knee—all of these actions are likely causes of torn lateral menisci. (Wrestlers, who spend an inordinate amount of time with their knees bent fending off attacks, are more likely to suffer lateral meniscus tears than people in other sports. Asians have a higher frequency of lateral tears than people elsewhere in the world, simply because they use chairs less and squat more.)

People in their teens and early twenties are more likely to have abrupt, spectacular meniscus tears than older people. As we age, our meniscus loses some of its fluid content and becomes granular, more brittle. So often tears in older people begin as degenerative things and gradually extend, like a crack in a windshield, until finally cartilage may break away within the joint. It's much harder to diagnose a meniscus tear in older people. The signs are often more subtle.

With ligament injuries and dislocations—as well as certain overuse problems, as we've seen—you may hurt, certainly, but the pain is spread over a large area. But with a torn meniscus, you can usually tell *exactly* where it hurts. You can put a fingertip right on the spot. So if any of the tip-offs discussed above sound familiar, and you can pin-point the pain, it's likely that a torn meniscus is the culprit.

And you need not have a swollen knee with a meniscus tear. Seventy percent of the meniscus has no blood supply. You can tear it and it won't bleed inside the knee. You may get some swelling later, because the inside of the joint becomes irritated and produces fluid to protect itself, but not necessarily. Your knee may even be locking and not swell appreciably.

What to do about it

Sometimes the meniscus will simply heal by itself, especially if it's in that 30 percent that receives blood. There are times when we look into a knee with the arthroscope and it's hard to tell just where the tear was—it's all kind of smooshed back together. But usually something needs to be done. If the tear is in the part of the meniscus that gets blood, it's possible to sew it back up. But nine times out of ten you have to remove the torn portion. You might ask, "Isn't it harmful to have the meniscus taken out? Don't I need that shock absorption?" The answer is yes, you do. And yes, it isn't particularly good to have it removed. But it's better than having a torn piece lodge in your knee. And it's better than letting the fragment chew up your articular cartilage. It's six of one and half a dozen of the other—almost. Yes, your knee will wear out more quickly without a whole healthy meniscus, but not so fast as it will wear out with a torn piece in there scraping away your remaining shock absorbers. And chances are pretty good that the rest of the body will come to a screeching halt before the knees do, anyway. It's simply not good to ignore these things. Bite the bullet.

TORN LIGAMENTS

Now we're in a different world. The hazards of a torn cartilage involve reduced shock absorption, increased wear and tear, and the possibility of locking—not to mention pain, of course. With ligaments we're dealing with the guy wires of the knee, the stays that hold it together. If one of these goes, the knee suddenly finds itself able to move in brand-new directions, none of which it was designed for. You experience that dubious freedom as looseness, instability, the "trick knee" that painfully bends in directions you never dreamed of, and always at the wrong time. It's no fun.

ANTERIOR CRUCIATE LIGAMENT TEAR

What was it Bettina Miller said? "It just collapsed. It didn't even get a chance to hurt." Hard to say it any better than that. It's the classical description of an anterior cruciate ligament tear. You hear a pop or a snap and fall down, but you're not quite sure why you're on the ground. It's not terribly painful, but you have a sense of instability, although you'd be hard pressed to say just where. The knee doesn't feel right, but you're not quite sure just why. Some people say that their knee shifts in position—which it actually does. Others more nearly feel the pop rather than hear it, and just know that something's wrong, although they can't tell you what. It's one of those serious injuries whose onset can be disarmingly ... well ... *friendly,* so much so that it may be the single most common acute knee injury. No one knows for sure, as it's just in the last five to ten years that tests have been developed to make possible a dependable, accurate diagnosis. It's likely that there are a lot of people walking—or running—around with anterior cruciate tears who were never treated for them, who never even knew they had them. And, interestingly, some of them don't have any problems, never have had, even though it's a big ligament, the size of your little finger. Some people can tolerate not having one without batting an eye. Eventually they'll come to the clinic for something else, and you'll examine the knee, discover it's as loose as can be, and ask them, "Do you have a lot of trouble with your knee?" They'll look at you as though you were from another planet, and then they remember: yes, twenty-three years ago, while playing high-school basketball, they missed half a season because they did something to their knee. But they can't quite remember what, and it makes no difference anyhow, because it hasn't bothered them since.

And that's lucky, because we don't understand as much as we should about the reasons why these ligaments become injured, perhaps because the injuries seem to occur in a variety of ways, many of them incongruously simple. There are films of NFL players tearing their anterior cruciate ligament in which an individual runs a wide, sweeping turn and suddenly grimaces and drops to the ground without being touched. You can see the stride where his ligament went out, you can isolate the instant it happened, but you can't see what was different about it. The ligament simply seems to give way of its own volition.

More often, though, you *can* discover reasons for the injury, and they are similar to those for cartilage tears: cutting from one direction to another, decelerating quickly (especially if you jam your foot ahead to stop yourself), coming down from a jump awkwardly. Basketball players frequently suffer anterior cruciate tears—they are knocked off balance in the air and come down wrong—as do volleyball players and dancers. Usually your knee is relatively straight when it happens, so it doesn't often show up in racquetball or tennis players, whose knees usually are—or should be—bent. Skiers sometimes tear this ligament, especially as the result of a twisting fall. But you rarely see it in runners, unless they step into a hole.

What to do about it

It's a difficult injury to deal with because there's such a wide range of reactions to it—from nothing, just a lot of looseness during an examination, to real disability, in which your knee goes out on you all the time and you really chew up the joint. The treatments are correspondingly various—and none are right or wrong. In fact, other than ice and compression on the spot and getting off the leg—all of which are only stopgap measures—we really don't know the best way to treat it, part of the reason being that there's no way of determining whether someone is going to be in that group of one third who don't even know there's something wrong or in the larger number who will have at least some disability. If you operate on everybody, you know that a third of the people are going to get great results because they never needed the operation in the first place. But who is in that third? It makes it hard to evaluate how effective the surgery is. How to deal with anterior cruciate tears is one of the most controversial issues in sports medicine.

One thing that most people will agree on is that sewing this particular ligament back together doesn't generally work. Because it's in the middle of the knee, inside the joint capsule, the ligament is constantly bathed in the joint's fluid, which is fine except that the fluid prevents a clot from forming around the stitches. For a ligament or anything else to heal it needs a clot around it. The clot forms a kind of seal, and the new blood vessels grow into it. Without the clot, healing is inhibited.

So if people do go ahead and operate on these tears, they repair them and augment them at the same time. They borrow a tendon from somewhere else around the knee and build a new ligament, then sew it directly into the bone. There are even some synthetic ligaments that are being used now—carbon fiber and Gore-tex, a nylonlike synthetic—but none of these has been in use long enough for anyone to know if it's going to hold up over the long run. There are over half a dozen ways of doing this surgery, all of which claim essentially the same results. And there are those who don't do surgery at all, just rehabilitate the knee, and they claim the same results.

It comes down to the approach—and wisdom—of your orthopedic surgeon. You have to find someone you can trust, but realize that whoever you see will be used to following a certain approach. It may be that a second opinion would be worth the effort, especially if the person is too quick to prescribe surgery as the *only* course. At the Center for Sports Medicine we assume that everybody is going to be in the group that doesn't have any long-lasting disabling problems. Or at least we try to give everybody the opportunity to find their way into that group. If you're quick to do surgery, you may do some people some good, but for other people, the people who don't need it, you've just performed an unnecessary operation. No one knows the answer for sure. If anyone says he does, be suspicious that he simply hasn't treated enough anterior cruciate tears to know better.

POSTERIOR CRUCIATE LIGAMENT TEARS

It's not really very often a sports injury. It's more likely in automobile accidents, say, in which you're thrown into the dashboard, which hits the front of your shin and drives it back under the femur. The majority of people can probably manage without having the ligament replaced.

Sometimes, instead of tearing, the ligament pulls loose a piece of bone. These injuries are usually operated on, because you get great results—bone-to-bone healing. It's a rare injury in athletics.

MEDIAL COLLATERAL LIGAMENT TEAR

Another biggie—next to the anterior cruciate ligament, probably the most frequently injured in sports. The medial collateral (middle supporting) ligament runs along the inside of the knee, connecting the thighbone, the femur, to the shinbone, the tibia. To injure it, you generally need an outside force. The common cause is a hit from the outside—a clip in football, say—that collapses the leg sideways, in toward the other leg, forcing open the inside of the knee and tearing away the medial ligament. It's almost impossible to injure your medial collateral ligament by yourself, unless you step into a hole—or are wearing skis. Medial collateral ligament tears are the most common ski injury. You catch one ski in the snow and continue skiing on the other, driving your legs apart and causing you to fall into the center. That wrenches open the inside part of your knee, just as though you had been hit from the outside.

As painful as they sound, these injuries are deceiving: you can completely tear the ligament and hardly know it. Often, the more severe the injury, the less pain involved. It hurts when you feel the ligament rip, but the pain rarely lasts more than a minute. Then you can get back up on your feet as though nothing had happened. Over half the people who injure themselves on the slopes ski down after the injury. And their subsequent complaints rarely involve pain: my knee bends the wrong way, it feels loose, I can't turn because my knee won't hold me. It's likely that the majority of football players who injure their medial collateral ligament go on to play another down or two. Only then will they figure out that something is wrong, that their knee no longer works as well as it did.

So with this injury the question to ask yourself is, how does the knee feel? Not, does it hurt? If it feels loose—even if there's no pain—you might have a significant problem.

What to do about it

We used to operate on all these injuries. We don't operate on many anymore. They heal well on their own. We use a hinged splint, and because the quadriceps muscles are capable of taking up almost any slack resulting from the torn ligament, we prescribe extensive rehabilitation exercises. If you rehabilitate faithfully, you'll be okay. There are many skiers—professionals, ski patrol, instructors—who have torn their medial collateral ligaments and lived to tell the tale. More than that, they're skiing as before, with little trouble. Of course, they have monstrous quadriceps (and they only need to work four months out of the year—that helps).

So if you've fallen while skiing, or been tackled from the outside, and your knee feels loose and unstable, ice the area as soon as possible, apply compression, and see a doctor. And count yourself lucky in your misfortune. This is one injury that heals well and may bother you very little.

LATERAL COLLATERAL LIGAMENT TEAR

Not much to say about this one. The lateral (side) collateral ligament is the smaller sibling of the medial collateral ligament. Its jurisdiction is the outside of the knee. It's not very often that this ligament is injured in sports. The reason: the kind of thing that would stretch the ligament enough to tear it would be a blow on the *inside* of the knee. That takes some doing, as your other leg is usually in the way. It's more likely that the other leg would absorb the force itself, putting the pressure on its own medial ligament.

DISLOCATION OF THE KNEECAP

Finally we return full circle to the extensor mechanism. Remember all that busines toward the beginning of the chapter about how important it is that your kneecap is seated properly? That it travel smoothly along its groove and not drift to the side? Now we're back in the same territory, but in its acute phase. A patellar dislocation is the culmination of all the subtle and not-so-subtle tendencies we discussed earlier, accomplished in one climactic stroke. The kneecap simply jumps its track once and for all.

First-time dislocations are the most dramatic. They can sound like chicken bones being separated—crruuunch! They usually occur with the knee partially bent and the foot turned out—and out, and out. It's a twisting injury that wrenches the kneecap out of its groove and to the side, stretching and tearing the securing ligaments and muscles along the way. As soon as you straighten your knee, the kneecap will flop back into place, but it won't stay there. With its medial support gone, the kneecap will tend to drift back to the outside as soon as you bend your knee.

The physical quirk that predisposes us to such injuries has to do with the fact that we're wider in the hips than we are at the knees. The quadriceps, the body's largest muscle, begins at the pelvis and runs all the way along the thigh and across the knee and finally ends at the upper part of the shinbone. The kneecap resides in the lower quadriceps tendon and acts as a pulley for this extensor mechanism linkage. When the muscle contracts, your knee straightens. You might think that this linkage transcribes a straight line. Not so. Because the body is wider at the pelvis than at the knee, this extensor mechanism actually pulls around a corner (see the illustration on page 93). The more you turn your knee in and foot out, the more of a corner it has to pull around. But it's not content with such a state of affairs. Like many other systems in nature, it would rather find the shortest distance between two points—enough of this turn-a-corner-at-the-knee business. So when it pulls, it exerts pressure to the outside, and nowhere greater than against the weakest part of the linkage, the pulley.

Your pulley, the kneecap, is held in place from side to side by small ligaments without specific names that are part of the capsule that surrounds the knee joint, and by the vastus medialis muscle, a tiny part of the quadriceps. They're reasonably efficient in their job, but not particularly strong. It doesn't take too much of a twist to tear them loose. And when they go, the kneecap jumps off track and sets up shop where the rest of the extensor mechanism has been pulling it all the while, on the outside of the knee.

Kneecap dislocations are more common in women than in men. When you think about it, the reason is obvious: women have wider hips than men, so the angle from the pelvis through the knee to the lower leg is greater. Women's kneecaps are under proportionally greater pressure to jump the track. And frequently women are not as strong as men (which may be a cultural thing, and may be changing, but is true nevertheless) and so don't have as much vastus medialis to hold the kneecap in place. Young women—teenagers, specifically—suffer more dislocations than their elders, for the simple reason that people are most active during the high-school years. Basketball, volleyball, tennis, cheerleading, dancing—all are good breeding grounds for kneecap dislocations. The injury has even been called "twist knee," after the dance that spawned a particularly high percentage of them. (With the twist you alternately try to dislocate one kneecap and then the other. At the height of its popularity some years ago, one wit suggested that the twist was invented by orthopedic surgeons.) Because of its exaggerated turnout, ballet would seem another prime cause of kneecap dislocations, but not so. If ballet dancers have been trained properly, they dance very precisely and under great control—lessening the chance of kneecap injury. And their turnout should come from the hips rather than the knees, so there really is no great increase in the extensor mechanism angle.

These injuries can swell amazingly quickly, especially the first time. Because so much soft tissue tears away, there's a huge amount of bleeding into the knee. It's one injury that allows you to look down and watch your knee grow before your eyes. People with first-time dislocations can swell so much in just an hour that you have to cut their clothes away to take a look at the joint. The knee just turns into a cantaloupe.

What to do about it

As always, ice and compression can only help matters. Then see a doctor as soon as you can. It's likely that you'll be able to avoid surgery. With most dislocations, immobilizing the knee in a splint and then going through a rehabilitation program will do the trick. It's a long and rigorous road back, because if you're going to keep your kneecap in place you've got to strengthen the little muscles that hold it in the center. These will have been torn during the injury. They'll heal, but most likely they were never very strong to begin with, or you would not have dislocated your kneecap in the first place.

The danger is that there's so much force involved during the injury that you can actually shear away a piece of the back of the kneecap or the inside of the joint, giving you a fracture to deal with as well as the dislocation. And a loose piece of bone can prevent the kneecap from returning on track. In this case, surgery is the answer, not only to remove the loose piece of bone, but to reattach the vastus medialis. And because dislocations have a tendency to recur, a surgeon might cut away some of the outside attachments to the kneecap, thereby reducing the pressure to the outside. It's called a lateral release, a reasonably common and successful operation.

A word to the wise: it may be that there's no practical way to prevent kneecap dislocations, but it certainly can't hurt to keep your thigh muscles in general, and vastus medialis in particular, strong and healthy. Since strength is one of the main ingredients in the smooth functioning of your extensor mechanism, and since a kneecap dislocation is no more than an extensor mechanism malfunction in the extreme, it stands to reason that a strong vastus medialis muscle might keep you out of all sorts of trouble. Of course, the body doesn't always stand to reason. But, just in case ... all together now, *contract* that muscle.

KNEE FRACTURES

The preceding example to the contrary, fractures in the knee are uncommon. Occasionally injuries that will cause ligament problems in adults will produce growth center fractures in children, but not very often. An area you don't have to worry about.

LOOSE BODIES IN THE KNEE

Sometimes injuries such as kneecap dislocations may knock off a piece of the joint surface—cartilage and bone, or just cartilage—inside the knee. It may be a flaked-off piece no larger than the end of a pin, but because the bulk of your cartilage receives its nutrition from the fluid in the joint rather than from blood supply, the loose body can actually grow while it's floating free in the joint. Through the years it can grow large enough to make trouble by lodging inside the joint to cause locking.

Sometimes we don't know where these loose bodies come from. Some of them may be the result of a portion of the joint surface somehow losing its blood supply, so that a part of the surface simply flakes away. The condition is called osteochondritis dissecans (see

Chapter 2, "The Ankle"). It's not that unusual, but we don't know why it happens. And these loose bodies won't show up until they're big enough to cause trouble. There's plenty of room in the knee for a loose body to float around, grow, and finally lodge someplace where it shouldn't.

If you have a loose body in your knee, you'll know it, even if it isn't bothering you. More often than not you'll be able to make the diagnosis every bit as accurately as any physician. Sometimes you'll even be able to find the culprit, push it around with your fingers. It's when the body is middle-sized that it causes problems. If it's tiny it can travel the back roads of your knee with impunity, slipping away from all sorts of sticky situations. If it's large, the size of the end of your thumb, say, it's just too bulky to do much of anything except find a corner somewhere and stay out of trouble. But if it's the size of a bean, it can wreak all sorts of havoc. It's small enough to travel the knee easily, small enough to hide, yet large enough to lodge somewhere and cause locking and pain.

What to do about it

For most people, such locking is an annoyance more than anything else. They develop a system to unlock their knee quickly and go about their business. These people find a way to peacefully coexist with the loose body in their knee—they just live with it. But for those who are involved in certain activities, loose bodies can be more than an annoyance. With hikers, for example, and rock climbers, it may be very important to find these particles and remove them. You don't want to be deep in wilderness country, twenty-five miles from any ambulance, and suddenly catch a loose body in the knee and be unable to free it. When a body lodges in the knee, all the muscles momentarily give way so that there's no danger of injuring the joint. That's why you invariably fall to the ground when it happens—everything immediately stops working. If you're lost on a remote trail, or inching your way up the face of a cliff, a lodged loose body can quickly become more than a mere annoyance. It can be life-threatening.

So it can be important to remove these loose bodies, but often that's easier said than done. The knee is so big that a foreign particle the size of the end of your finger can get lost when you go to remove it. You simply can't find it. And these bodies are very slippery, with sides worn smooth from tumbling through the knee, perfectly suited to slide through the joint, but less so for someone to grab hold of and remove them. The best way to deal with a loose body is for the physician and patient to attack it together: trap it between your fingers, then put local anesthetic in the knee and skewer it—impale it with a needle. Then you can either take it out using the arthroscope or simply make a cut directly over it and lift it free.

DISLOCATION OF THE ENTIRE KNEE

This is a really devastating injury, but it doesn't occur very often in athletics. Maybe a couple a year in football, once in a while in wrestling, but most of these injuries are the result of automobile accidents, parachute jumps, and the like. Because you can tear the blood vessels in the back of the knee that supply the whole leg, a knee dislocation can result in amputation. The blood vessels tear in an area where one vessel branches into three, so surgically repairing that junction is very difficult. You can actually lose the blood supply to your leg. All the ligaments in the knee tear as well, and there's extensive tendon and muscle damage.

What to do about it

Hope it doesn't happen. The knee is pretty stable—to do that kind of injury requires monumental force. If it does happen, see somebody.

Commonly Asked Questions About Knee Injuries

If I have an acute injury, will my knee ever again be as healthy as it was?

If you've had any of the acute injuries we've discussed, then no, your knee will never be the way it was—but you may never know it. If you tear a ligament, say, it may be that after you rehabilitate your knee you can go back to doing pretty much everything you did before, but if you worked at it hard enough, you'd find things that you could no longer do. Most of us aren't going to work at it that hard, and if we do it may be that those things aren't so important after all. So most people will find themselves functioning pretty much as before.

That's not always true, of course, and it's hard to predict exactly who will be able to get back to what activity. If you tear an anterior cruciate ligament, for example, getting back to basketball or volleyball will be tough, maybe impossible. But you'll be able to run, play tennis, ski, even play football (there are pro football players doing just fine without their anterior cruciate ligament). What happens is that other mechanisms in the knee rise to the occasion and take over the function of the missing part. It's as though your knee has a number of built-in redundancies. Training helps, however. With an anterior cruciate tear, you train the hamstring muscle to act as a surrogate and keep the shinbone in line. More often than not, it will.

Torn cartilages present a different picture, because rather than causing instability they reduce shock absorption. And there's nothing in the knee to act as shock absorber surrogates. The entire joint has to absorb the extra pounding. The result is that there's a significant increase in wear and tear in the knees of people who have had a meniscus removed. Still, the difference may not be of any real consequence. By the time your knee gets bad enough so that you notice it, your activity level may have dropped to the point where it no longer matters. In fact, you may stop functioning before your knee does. Considering the amount of abuse we heap on it, the knee is quite a forgiving joint.

But you must become vigilant and aware of what's going on in your knee. If it starts acting up, do something about it. You just don't ignore things in your knee if you've had any significant injuries. If you do, you run the risk of more knee problems and problems elsewhere as well. If your knee begins to hurt when you run, say, especially going up and down hills, and you ignore it and persist in running up and down hills, your body simply won't stand for it. Without your realizing it, your running gait will change to accommodate the pain, and the next thing you know your ankle will hurt, or your hip ache, or your back stiffen up, and then your knee will begin to act even more weird.

If you've had any serious knee problems in the past, stay on top of the situation so you won't have any more problems, in the knee or elsewhere, in the future.

If I have a cartilage removed, what will replace it?

Nothing will replace it. There's no such thing as an artificial meniscus. You've just got to learn to live without it. It takes a while to get used to it, longer if you've lost your lateral (outside) meniscus rather than the medial meniscus, but sooner or later you'll be able to go about your business as before without pain. The knee compensates.

If I don't have surgery for a torn ligament, will my knee heal?

It depends on the ligament. The cruciate ligaments won't heal by themselves, but the collateral ligaments (the ones on the outside of the knee) will. When you repair them surgically, all you do is put the torn ends together (stitches provide little strength), but the torn ends are never that far apart in the first place. They'll heal by themselves, and they may heal as tightly as they would have had you sewn them back together. Even if they don't, though, having to go through surgery may be harder on you than a little bit of looseness. No operation is completely benign. Any surgery involves trauma and risk. It should be well thought out, done as a last resort, when it's clear that leaving things as they are is more hazardous than the operation itself. Your knee may not be as tight as before, but it isn't necessary for it to be as tight as before. You may be able to function very nicely with a looser knee. In fact, most of us do, all the time.

Everyone has some instability of the knee; a lot of people have almost breathtaking instability. The system is not so precise that it doesn't have some slack in it. Like the clutch in your car, things work best when there's some play. If there's too much, we have muscles to tighten things up. So if a ligament injury loosens up your knee even more than usual, you can depend on your muscles to rise to the occasion. Most of the time, with a little (maybe a lot of) training, they do.

If rehabilitation is a lot of work, can I just have surgery instead?
That's not the choice. The choice is, are you going to have surgery and go through rehabilitation, or are you just going to rehabilitate your knee? Surgery may or may not be necessary. Rehabilitation always is.

If I have arthroscopy, do I need a general anesthetic, or can I just have a local?
If you just have what's called diagnostic arthroscopy, a quick look around the knee to see what's wrong with it, you may be able to get away with local anesthesia. But usually no, for this reason: during arthroscopy the surgeon must fill your knee with fluid, a clear saline solution, because otherwise the knee tends to collapse in on itself and there's no room in there to look around. If the solution dooesn't remain clear, it's hard to see. It's like trying to look into a cloudy aquarium, only worse. Just one or two drops of blood in the fluid cloud it enough so that the surgeon can't see. To prevent that, 30 to 60 percent of all arthroscopies are performed with tourniquets on the upper leg to control the blood flow to the knee. Tourniquets hurt, more than a little. And you can't give local anesthesia for the knee *and* the tourniquet. We used to do arthroscopy with local anesthesia, but we got tired of chasing people around the operating table while they tried to crawl away from tourniquet pain. A general anesthetic makes for a much more relaxed—and therefore successful—surgery. (Again, for more on arthroscopy see Chapter 16, "So You're Going to Have an Operation.")

Is fluid in the knee serious? Should I have it removed?
That the knee can become inflamed and swollen is common knowledge—not so the fact that there's *always* fluid in the knee, at least a little bit. The knee constantly lubricates itself. And, more than that, it feeds itself. The cartilage in the knee doesn't have a blood supply of its own, but it has to get its nutrition from somewhere. It gets it from the

knee capsule, that sac that surrounds the entire joint. Normally the wall of the capsule is no thicker than cigarette paper, and its underside is very slippery, covered with a fluid-producing lining called the synovial membrane. The membrane secretes fluid all the time, bathing the cartilage and the rest of the joint in a fluid that's full of nutrients, much like blood with the red cells removed.

If the capsule is irritated in any way, it reacts by producing more fluid. And any injury to the rest of the knee tends to irritate the capsule, which surrounds the joint in a kind of protective embrace. Producing fluid is the only way it can react—how else can it tell you it's being picked on? So it makes fluid, and more fluid, and if you've been overusing the knee, running too many hills, taking too many dance classes, pretty soon you're going to have to cut back and be nice to it, because it simply isn't going to bend anymore. The excess fluid functions as a splint. It's as though your knee is trying to tell you to lay off for a while, and if you ignore it, it'll *make* you lay off by forming enough fluid so that it simply doesn't work.

The fluid in the knee is dynamic, in an equilibrium of coming and going. The synovial membrane has the capability of absorbing the fluid as well as producing it—the fluid that's in your knee tonight most likely will not be the same fluid that's in there tomorrow night—so usually there's no reason to take out the fluid *until the knee is ready* to have it taken out. The important thing is to find out why it's there and do something about it. Otherwise, it'll simply continue to form.

If the fluid is drained prematurely, or worse yet, you have cortisone injected into the joint (cortisone is great for reducing swelling—it will shut off the fluid—but it will also stop the healing process in the joint), you may never discover why the fluid was there in the first place. Once the effect of the cortisone wears off, the fluid will come back as before, and you'll be right where you started. And perhaps worse off, because now you may have caused damage in the joint itself. Be very cautious with cortisone, especially with children. Other kinds of anti-inflammatory medications, such as an over-the-counter drug like Advil, may be better, because they don't have the side effect of shutting down the healing process. Such remedies may get you through a game or a performance, but sooner or later you'll have to find out why the fluid formed and do something about it.

6 The Thigh and Hip

W ell?" Garrick says, raising an eyebrow.
"Oh, God." Leslie Friedman crosses her arms over her chest, hugging herself. "He gives me that eye, and I cannot tell a lie. The hip started to pop a lot again. No, *popping* is too gentle a word. Every time I flex it, it sounds like a car going into a wall."

Leslie is a modern dancer. About a year ago her left hip started to bother her. Soon thereafter she went on tour. And so it went: every time she had time off to rest the hip, she would go back to dancing with a vengeance and undo any gains she might have made. Finally she just couldn't stand it any longer. She first came to the Center for Sports Medicine a few months ago.

"I'm thirty-eight years old," she says, "old for a dancer. That's why I took so long before coming in to have it looked at. I thought, 'You're getting old, your joint's wearing out, time to shoot you soon,' and I just didn't want anyone to tell me that."

Garrick squints at her.

Leslie laughs. "That's the 'stay in line' look. I know, I know, I have to take care of myself."

"I think you have a tendency to feast-or-famine it," Garrick says.

Leslie sighs. "Yes."

"When you do things, you tend to overdo them. I'm not saying this is wrong or anything—you know how you're built. You know what your schedule is. But when you feel good enough to do *anything,* you do *everything.*"

"Yes."

"And when you don't feel good enough to get away with doing everything, you go in the other direction."

Leslie nods, hugging herself.

"And, you know, when people have long-term things like you've got, and are used to them, they seem to have some kind of a built-in mechanism that always keeps them at the same level of discomfort. This may not be the case with you, but if your hip hurts, and then you have a good day when it doesn't hurt, then tomorrow you go out and—"

"Trash it," Leslie says.

"You kind of keep unconsciously testing yourself."

"That's me."

"And admittedly," Garrick says, "you've spent years burning the candle at both ends. You may be running out of wax."

"*Moi?*" Laughter. "*Moi?*"

Leslie's problem is a knotty one. When she first came in, X-rays showed a stress fracture high on the thighbone, the femur. Garrick was sure he would have to operate and strengthen the bone. But a bone scan indicated that either the X-ray was inaccurate or the fracture had healed on its own—an unlikely prospect, given the fact that stress fractures demand rest, and the pace of Leslie's life is anything but restful. The mystery remains, but the bone is strong, and Garrick now thinks that the problem has to do with the muscles in the area and was around long before it began to bother her a year ago. Most likely it started with little things that Leslie neglected until they became big things.

"At this point it's just hard to tell," he says later. "It's been going on for so long. It's just that her thermostat is set too high. You can keep her off that pace for a while, but when she feels good ... well, it's been the way she's lived. She's gotten along for years ignoring these little signals, but now she's getting a little older, and it's a tough pace to keep up. But she's so good at what she does that her hip has worked out every compensatory mechanism known to man. It's really difficult to sort out."

It's a familiar story when it comes to overuse muscle problems, and nowhere more than in the hip and thigh. The two areas are intimately related. Little goes on in the thigh that isn't affected by the hip, and vice versa. In fact, one of the joys, and difficulties, of dealing with the body is the fact that everything—*everything*—is interrelated. And that's never so clear as when you're injured. If you have a stiff neck, you'll know it when you shrug your shoulders and move your arms. If you strain a muscle in your chest, it can hurt to turn your head, laugh, sneeze, or even breathe. And if you irritate a muscle in your thigh, you'll probably feel it in your hips, or maybe even in your toes.

All that makes life very interesting. It's not always enough simply to know where it hurts. Because although you may hurt in one spot now, the problem may have begun elsewhere, and unless you find out where that place is and do something about it, little is going to change. For example, let's say that, like Leslie, you're a dancer and your hamstrings, the muscles in the back of your thigh, are weak. The hamstrings supply the brunt of the power necessary to bend your knee and straighten your hip—needless to say, important functions for a dancer. If your hamstrings are weak and you continue to bend your knee and hip, other muscles must step in to help, most likely the gluteal muscles in the buttocks.

But the gluteals are not designed to be hamstrings. They have their own tasks, primarily extending the hip and leg backward—in arabesque position, for example—and helping you to rotate your hip and leg; good turnout depends a lot on strong gluteal muscles. Yet now, besides keeping up with their own duties, they're forced to lend a hand to their cousin in the thigh. The combination can be too much. Like anyone who is overworked, the gluteals can become irritated. Irritation usually means pain. And pain, if it lasts long enough and grows severe enough, can mean that a dancer stops dancing and learns some new steps—those leading to the doctor's office.

So you go to the doctor and tell him your hip hurts. What follows separates the wheat from the chaff in doctoring, or at the least (and most charitable) the experienced from the inexperienced. Your doctor may conclude, in effect, that your hip hurts (you know that already, you just don't know what to *do* about it), tell you to stop dancing for a while, perhaps prescribe anti-inflammatory drugs, and maybe even give you a shot of cortisone to bring down the inflammation in your hip immediately.

Well, for a dancer to stop dancing is the kiss of death. There may be other activities in which you can get away with a layoff and then come back strong as ever, but dancing is not one of these. To be able to dance, a dancer must dance—one of those sweet, Zen-like conundrums. But let's give this treatment the benefit of the doubt and say that you do get off your hip for a while, the irritation goes away, and finally you're back at the barre. Rusty and stiff though you may be, it feels terrific to be able to move again without pain. You're forever grateful to your wise physician. And then a funny thing happens: it may take a week, it may take a month, but sure enough, little by little, the pain returns, the irritation grows, and more quickly than you thought possible you're right back where you began.

Why? Because no one bothered to find out *why* the problem occurred in the first place. And *why* involves the fact that everything is interrelated. It's not enough to treat the hip; you have to find out what *caused* the hip to flare up. You have to work back through the chain to that first incident, that first difficulty, that first inadequacy that started the whole business—in this case, weak hamstring muscles. Knowing that, it well may be that the best treatment is *not* to get off your feet, but rather to strengthen the hamstrings, continuing to dance, albeit at a reduced level, while you do special exercises to bring the muscle strength up to the level where it needs to be. (More on that later in this chapter.)

Which brings us back to where we started: the thigh and hip (as well as the rest of the functions of the body) are intimately related. A problem that surfaces in one place can be the result of a problem that began elsewhere. To successfully deal with these things, it pays to become aware of what's going on inside your body, aware of activity changes, aware of the initial, bothersome little things that can eventually grow into debilitating big things. And when choosing a sports medicine doctor, you want someone who will suggest treatment based on an appreciation of the interrelatedness of things. In other words, someone who will give the effort necessary to deal with problems in what may not be the quickest or easiest way. (For more on that, see Chapter 18, "How to Choose a Sports Medicine Doctor.")

The Thigh and Hip

The hip is the most stable joint in the body. It's well protected, as it lies deep inside the body, surrounded by muscle on all sides. It holds together very well, and it allows you a lot of motion—front to back,

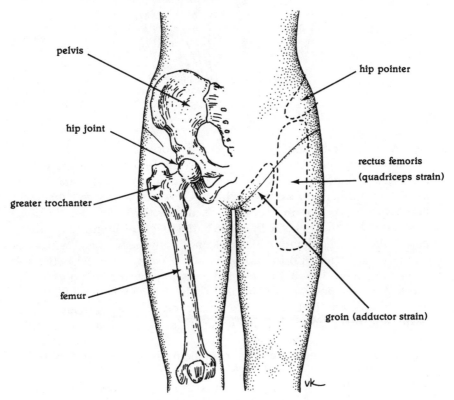

pelvis

hip pointer

hip joint

rectus femoris
(quadriceps strain)

greater trochanter

femur

groin (adductor strain)

Front View of the Thigh and Hip

Back View of the Thigh and Hip

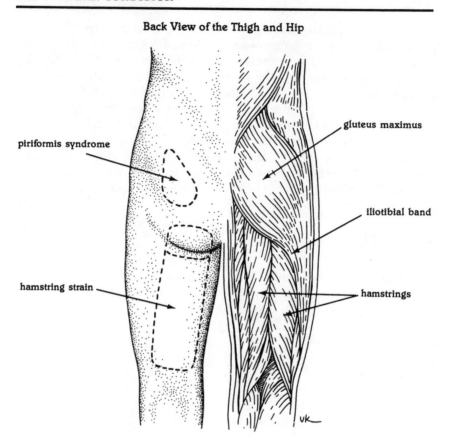

piriformis syndrome

gluteus maximus

iliotibial band

hamstring strain

hamstrings

side to side, and rotation. The joint is formed by the end of the thighbone, the femur, which inserts into the lower part of the pelvis, that thick ring of bone that anchors all manner of muscles and bones, providing a transition from your body's torso to your legs. Imagine a butterfly resting flat in a collector's display box—the pelvis looks something like that. The body of the butterfly corresponds to the lower part of the spinal column, which descends between the two "wings" of the pelvis to taper into the tail bone, or coccyx. Like the butterfly's wings, the pelvis is wider on top and narrower toward the bottom. You can feel the top portion of your pelvis—it's where you hang your skirt or pants—but not the bottom, which is deeply embedded in muscle and flesh. And that's good. It helps to keep the hip joint safe from most injuries.

The stability of the hip comes from the design of the joint itself. It's truly a ball and socket, with a deep socket in the pelvis and a lovely round ball at the end of the femur. In contrast to the knee and shoulder, other large joints with a wide range of motion, the hip doesn't depend on muscles and ligaments to hold it together. It's designed to hold together. There are few substantial ligaments in the hip, and the muscles that surround it serve to move it rather than keep it from falling apart. So there are few joint problems in the hip. Injuries tend to show up in the muscles and tendons themselves.

The ringlike structure of the pelvis, all that bone, makes it ideal as a muscle attachment, and, appropriately enough, the muscles of the spine and abdomen, above, begin at the pelvis, as do the hip muscles, and the hamstrings and part of the quadriceps, below. Except for the gluteal muscles in the buttocks, which are large, and which allow you to rotate and abduct your legs, or pull them outward, these muscles in the hip tend to be smaller than those in the thigh, shorter and fatter, more suited for precision work like rotation and stabilization. But they're no less important than the bigger muscles. Many problems around the hip arise from these short muscles being forced to do things other than what they're supposed to be doing.

The thigh is not much more than a big bone surrounded by big muscles. The bone, the femur, is the largest in the body, and at least half of the thigh, the entire front portion, is dominated by the quadriceps, the body's largest muscle. Almost the whole back of the thigh is taken up by the hamstrings, and the upper inside is defined by the groin muscles, or adductors. These big muscles are responsible for big movements, for propulsion-type things like walking, running, going up and down stairs and hills. All knee bending comes from the thigh muscles, and all knee straightening. You depend on the thigh muscles to adduct, or pull your legs together, and the thigh muscles stabilize your hip as well. They're very strong and absolutely necessary for the most basic needs of most sports, not to mention simply getting around from day to day. There aren't many subtle things about the thigh.

Interestingly, however, the largest and most powerful muscle in the thigh, the quadriceps, is so sensitive that no other muscle in the body atrophies more quickly when it's not used, as after an injury, or misused. As we discussed in Chapter 5, "The Knee," lack of quadriceps strength can be at the heart of a myriad of problems, and it's as easy to have weak quadriceps as strong ones. Something to watch out for.

Acute Injuries
MUSCLE TEARS AND STRAINS

These affect the thigh, primarily, and are some of the best-known injuries in sports. Who has not heard of, or experienced, a hamstring strain or pull (the most common), or torn a quadriceps muscle? These injuries are endemic to running sports. And except for contusions—the result of direct blows—they are pretty much the *only* serious problems to affect the area. (People don't break their femurs very often, and it takes a lot to dislocate a hip. These are such awesome injuries that nobody's going to run home and look them up in a book. Instead, you'll be writhing on the ground awaiting an ambulance. Suffice it to say that there's no question about fractures and dislocations in the hip-thigh area—they don't happen often, but you'll know it when they do. Get thee to an emergency room.)

A muscle tear might occur in a sprinter who's trying to accelerate harder than usual or a football player who needs a couple of extra-long strides to get under a pass that's overthrown. Whether it's because the muscle itself tightens up and so can't tolerate the increased demands made upon it, or because the opposite muscle tightens, forcing the first muscle to work harder to accomplish the same task, you suddenly feel something pop. Other times it may feel as though someone has thrown a rock at your thigh. Either way, the next thing you know, you're on the ground. There's no doubt that something bad has happened.

*Over*stretching can cause tears. This can occur if you miss your footing, say, presenting your body with a situation it doesn't anticipate. The body does anticipate movement. Everyone has had the experience of going down a flight of stairs and encountering one more (or fewer) stair than you expected. It takes a real effort to overcome the body's inertia and not land flat on your face. Why? Not because one more stair is inherently so dangerous, but because you just didn't expect it. The same thing happens in sports. A runner coming out of the blocks anticipates a certain kind of surface, a certain degree of traction. But if he slips, all bets are off. A slip of no more than an inch can fake out the muscles. They're going to go ahead and contract powerfully, because they expect the resistance of the surface to slow them down—and if that resistance isn't there, the muscles can't react in time. The contraction continues, becomes monumental, and something's got to give. That something is not the track. The result, a muscle tear.

Not being warmed up can be another cause of tears. Track meets early in the spring are a problem because it can be cold and thereby difficult to stay warmed up. When a muscle gets cold, it gets tight. And just stretching it out isn't going to help—you have to keep it warm, working and flowing well.

A relatively new source of thigh tears is, of all things, stretching for exercise. Stretching has become something of a cult, as though being well stretched in and of itself is good for you. It may be, but probably stretching is more useful in combination with something else—before and after another activity, to prepare the muscles for action and relax them afterward. And, as with any cult, many people don't do the activity properly. They throw themselves into stretching, start doing bouncing toe touches and quick torso twists rather than long, slow stretches. Sometimes the result is a torn muscle.

Sports medicine doctors usually separate these injuries into three categories. Grade Three is the worst kind, in which the muscle actually pulls apart. It feels like a hole in there (reminiscent of ruptures of the calf muscles—see Chapter 4, "The Lower Leg").

Grade Two strains are not so bad. You may feel a pulling sensation, you know something's wrong, but it really isn't dreadful, and, rather than cause you to collapse, these strains will allow you to slow down and then get off your feet.

Grade One strains involve the least pain, the least discomfort. It's as though your thigh just tightens up over a few strides. You know something's happened, but it doesn't seem like much. Rather than stop their activity, people often go ahead and try to keep doing what they're doing.

What to do about it

For the worst of these, if you feel something pop and you're immediately unable to move, you should see someone. And that someone should know how to deal with athletes. If you go to someone who isn't used to dealing with athletic injuries, the likelihood is that you're not going to be treated right. You might be rested too long, put on crutches, put in a splint. These injuries must be treated aggressively—rest is *not* the answer here—or it'll take you forever to recover. The milder ones you may want to try to deal with yourself. Here's a way to go about it:

All muscle tears and strains, no matter how severe, probably involve at least some tearing of the muscle fibers. (A tear is no more than an extreme strain, or pull. In a tear the fibers completely separate, leaving behind a gap. In a strain the tearing is more subtle—some fibers hold together, others separate, but the fabric of the muscle remains whole.) And since muscles are generously supplied with blood, the tearing means that many blood vessels tear as well. As a result, the severed vessels bleed into the muscles. With big tears there can be big bleeding. The vessels can drop a pint of blood into the muscles just like that. And that bruising may not show up until a few days later, and usually not at the site of the injury. The blood migrates where gravity takes it, and you won't see it until it gets close enough to the surface to show up. A hamstring tear today may mean a discolored calf next week.

So *you* may not see it, but the *muscles* know all that blood is there. The problem is that they don't know what to do with it. They're used to blood that's contained in vessels. Now it's as though something foreign has been injected into the body, and the muscle is capable of only one reaction to any foreign invasion: go into spasm. It's a protective reaction, just as a turtle retreats into its shell or a snake winds tightly into a coil. Scrunch! The muscle tightens down violently, as though you have a cramp.

That's fine, but once the muscle goes into spasm, it tends to stay in spasm (as anyone with a cramp knows all too well). And the longer it stays in spasm—days, weeks, months—the longer it'll take to straighten out. Meanwhile, as the muscle is starting to heal, the likelihood is that it will heal in spasm as well. That means you end up with a shortened muscle.

So one thing you can do immediately is try to limit the amount of bleeding into the muscle. Ice and compression are good for that, but in contrast to the ankle, say, where compression is very effective after sprains, it's hard to apply ice or compression to the thigh. There's too much fat and muscle in the way, making it difficult to apply enough pressure to do any good. If you've suffered a hamstring tear, sitting on a bag of ice is a pretty good way to achieve icing and compression at the same time, but otherwise it's pretty tough to do. (How do you sit on a torn quadriceps?) If the tear is in a place you can reach, pressing your hand against the spot that hurts for ten or fifteen minutes can help. But there's another thing you can do to treat a tear, which may be even more effective, and is certainly less obvious: stretch it.

Everybody knows that ultimately you're going to have to stretch out your torn hamstring. The thing that people usually don't know is that all the time the muscle spends shortened in spasm is lost time. Even though it remains tight, it really doesn't do anything. So it gets weak. It gets smaller. It gets flabbier. And when you finally do get around to stretching it out, it won't stay that way—it just isn't strong enough to stay stretched out. You stretch it, you go ahead and get back to your activity, the weakened muscle gets tired much too easily, and it goes right back into spasm. That old adage about recurring hamstring injuries— "Once a hamstring tear, always a hamstring tear"—is often true, simply because people don't realize that the muscle has withered away into nothing during the time it wasn't used. So a tight muscle is not only an uncomfortable muscle, one that will tolerate only limited motion, it's a muscle that's getting weak right before your eyes.

The best way to deal with these injuries is to *never let them get weak in the first place.* As soon as you can, begin gentle stretching— immediately, if possible; certainly within twenty-four hours or so— even though it may be a little uncomfortable to do so. Pain is the guide. Keep the stretching just on the edge of being really painful. The more stretched out you can make the muscle sooner, the better off you'll be later.

And the better off you'll be sooner, too. Muscles are contained in tough, gristly tubes called fasciae. Even though a muscle may tear, it's likely that the fascia will not. When you stretch, you stretch the fascia as well as the muscle, making the tube longer and narrower, tightening it around the injured muscle and reducing bleeding. You *internally* compress the muscle, curtailing bleeding, which is good, while stretching the muscle, which is good. A neat trick.

So it's important to do something soon. If you suffer only a mild strain, get up the next morning to find that the muscle is tight and hurts when you move it, and decide that you're not going to use it until it's really well, then what should be a minor injury can become as devastating as a really severe tear. With muscle injuries in athletes at least, *the magnitude of the injury is a much less important determiner of disability than the way you treat it.* A small tear that you coddle, babying it while it heals on its own, can be a lot more disabling than a substantial tear that's dealt with effectively. As a general rule, *muscle injuries won't heal as quickly if you just leave them alone. You have to work to get well.*

That work can be easier than you might think. One notable by-product of being injured is that you soon come to realize the many ways in which that injury connects with everything else that's going on in your body. You never dreamed that moving *that* would make it hurt *here.* Well, if you do something that makes the injured area hurt, you must be doing something right. More likely than not, that something involves stretching the injured part. Simply keep it up. You don't have to know any anatomy, don't even have to know just what it was you injured. If getting out of a chair or out of bed or into a shower or a car hurts, you'll know what you need to do to stretch the muscle. Don't shy away from the activity. Find the motion that gives the most discomfort and gently repeat it, stopping just short of real pain. That way your rehabilitation can become part of your daily activity, rather than something you do specially. You just naturally keep the muscle stretched and active, in contrast to avoiding activities that hurt. If it doesn't hurt, you'll know that you're not exercising the muscle at all. You'll pay for it later.

Restrengthening the muscle involves the opposite motion. If you stretch out your injured hamstring, say, by extending your leg when you step into the shower, you can strengthen it by bending the leg. If it's a torn quadriceps, and bending your leg to get into your car stretches the muscle (it will hurt), then extending your leg out straight after you close the door (if you're not in a VW, that is) will strengthen it. It involves listening to your body, being aware of what it's trying to tell you. Don't worry, it'll tell you the truth. You may not know what muscles you're working with, but you're doing the right thing—you're on your way to getting well.

If you prefer a more formal rehab program, here's one:

To stretch the hamstrings, do what's called a hurdler's stretch. While standing, straighten your leg out in front of you and rest it on a chair, say, or a coffee table, or the hood of your car. Keeping your hips square—that is, at right angles to your extended leg; you *don't* want your leg out to the side—slowly lower your chest onto your thigh far enough so that the back of your thigh starts to hurt. Hold that position for fifteen to twenty seconds, then lean forward a little more, again until it starts to hurt, and hold the stretch for about the same amount of time. You may find, soon after the injury especially, that you can't bend over the leg much at all without pain. That's okay—simply do as much as you can. In time the muscles will stretch and your flexibility will increase. Stretch in the morning, during the day, and before you go to bed—if you stretch at night, you won't be so stiff in the morning. As the muscle stretches and heals, bend farther and stretch more often.

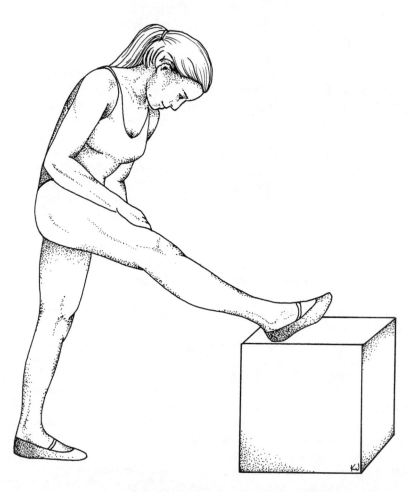

Hurdler's Stretch—Hamstrings Stretching Exercise

To strengthen the muscle, go the other way and bend the leg against resistance. That resistance can be your other leg, a chair, the floor, your child or dog, or an inner tube. Take the strengthening to the point of fatigue; when you feel the muscle start to burn, then back off. Three series of ten contractions, just as with stretching, is a reasonable schedule. In fact, combine the two when it's comfortable to do so. Stretch, strengthen, then, because the muscle tends to tighten after being contracted, stretch again.

Do all this through a *comfortable* arc of motion. It's *not* necessary to go from a straight knee to your heels pressing up against your buttocks. If you're able to accomplish half the range of motion, or even 10 percent of it, that's fine—what does the muscle know? It may be that your leg will hurt enough at first so that you can't bend it at all, and you may have to do the exercises isometrically, simply tightening the muscle. It'll still do some good.

For quadriceps tears, simply turn around all these procedures. The quadriceps and hamstrings complement each other. When you bend your knee, the hamstrings contract and the quads stretch; when you straighten your knee, the quads contract and the hamstrings stretch. They're always working in opposite directions. So to stretch the quads, do the exercise that tightens the hamstrings—that is, bend your leg. Here's a good way: while standing, bend the injured leg and grab the foot with your hand (make sure it's the hand of the opposite arm—grab your right foot with your left hand, left foot with right hand). Then pull back on the leg. As with the hamstrings, you may be able to bend only a little bit at first, but be not discouraged—it will come. To strengthen the quadriceps, extend the leg against resistance, at first only as much as you can handle without hurting, then increase the resistance and the number of repetitions as the muscle heals.

The important thing is to do something. You don't want to let the muscle just lie there and do nothing. If it lies there, it's going to get weak and stay tight. And the weaker it gets, the longer it will stay weak and tight. Don't let that happen. Again, *you have to work to get over muscle injuries.*

Perhaps the best exercise technique of all is contract-relax stretching. To exercise the hamstrings, lie on your back and have a friend extend your leg up toward your head until the injured area begins to hurt. Then push your leg back against your friend's resistance, using the muscle, contracting it a little, but not too much. Hold the contraction for fifteen seconds, then relax. Then ask your friend to extend your leg farther toward your head. Surprise! You've picked up another 15 degrees of flexibility. Stop when you again feel discomfort and again push back against the pressure. Stretch again, and stop.

With this exercise you momentarily fatigue the muscle so that it kind of gives up the ghost for a few seconds, then pick up the slack and

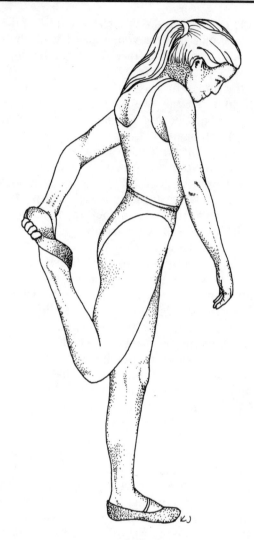

Quadriceps Stretching Exercise

stretch it again. It may be the most effective stretching exercise you can do—it feels good, too—but its disadvantage is that it usually requires two people. However, with some ingenuity you can do contract-relax exercises by yourself. You have to get into a position where you stretch yourself against resistance—a table leg or a doorjamb. Push against the table leg, then relax, move forward to take up the slack, and push again. Contract-relax exercises are the way a physical therapist would stretch you, charging $50 a shot for the pleasure. Might as well go to a therapist once, learn how to do it on your own, and take care of yourself thereafter.

So you've worked on your injury, it's started to come around, and you're back to the activity that put you down in the first place. A couple of things might happen: one is that the muscle might hurt at the beginning of the activity, but as you exercise it loosens up and things get easier. That sort of thing is likely with ankle sprains, where you milk some of the swelling away as you move and gradually your range of motion increases, but not so common with muscle injuries. More likely is the second possibility: you'll be partway through your work-out, a couple miles into your run, say, and your hamstring will start to tighten up. If you try to run through it, it just gets tighter and tighter, to the point where you have to stop running or risk hurting yourself again. A way to deal with that kind of problem is to stop running (or stop playing tennis, or step away from the barre, or drop out of aerobics class), go off to the side, and do three or four good, long, slow stretches right on the spot. Then start running again. In nine out of ten instances the leg will be comfortable once more. It may stay comfortable only for another few minutes, however, in which case you simply stop and stretch again, then continue running.

If you keep up this regimen day after day, the intervals between the stretching will become longer and longer. If during the first couple of days you have to stop and stretch every quarter of a mile, the next week you may have to stretch only every half mile, and the third week every mile and a half, to the point where you may have to stop only once during your run, or not at all. It can be a bother to have to put up with all that stopping and stretching, at least at first, but it can be a very effective way of getting back to your activity.

But only if you can do the activity comfortably. You may be able to go back for only a minute or two at first—that's better than nothing, and most likely it will be longer than that soon enough. But if the tightness comes on and you can't stop it by stretching, *don't continue*. The muscles will just get tighter and tighter, may cause you to change your gait, or your stroke or technique, and you'll eventually either reinjure the muscle or injure something else. Instead, drop back from the activity, do the home stretching and strengthening regimen that got you back this far, and gradually try again. Ease back into the activity, slowly, and with patience. A word to the wise: *don't* try to bull through muscle injuries. They'll get you in the end.

A couple of words of caution:

1. When you rehabilitate a muscle injury, you have to *stretch the injured side specially*. You can't do two-handed toe touches to deal with a hamstring problem because, although you may be stretching the injured side, you're not doing much for the good side, and it may be tightening and weakening as the bad side improves. Always stretch each side separately and appropriately. Otherwise, the more flexible side is always limited by the lack of flexibility of the injured side.

2. If you're treating your injury on your own and it doesn't respond, but just continues to get worse, *see someone*. That kind of situation can be ominous, nothing to trifle with. But, happily, such is not usually the case. So long as you're smart about things and listen to what your body is telling you, rather than grit your teeth, bite through your lip, and abuse your body because you've decided that, by God, no injury is going to make you lose even one inch of flexibility or one minute of down time, you'll be okay. Better than that, you'll be on the road back sooner than you might have anticipated. And you'll learn a lot about yourself, besides.

CHEERLEADER'S HIP

It's an injury that occurs in young people, often for the same reasons as muscle tears. Overstretching or overcontracting, sudden, unexpected demands on the muscles, cold muscles being forced to work too hard—all these things, which would most likely do no more than injure a muscle in an adult, can do something quite different in a growing person. They can actually pull the muscle away from its tether, popping off a piece of bone in the process. Bouncing into the splits can do it—thus the name cheerleader's hip. It can actually pop the hamstrings or the adductors (the muscles in the upper inner thigh) away from the pelvis. If the quadriceps contract violently, the portion of the muscle that connects to the pelvis, the rectus femoris, can pull a piece of bone away.

Why will the same incident pop off a piece of bone in a young person but tear a muscle in an adult? The answer is that in young people bone is still forming. It's geared to grow and heal. Accordingly, it's covered with a dense, blood-rich tissue called periosteum. Adults' bones are covered with periosteum as well, but whereas in a grown person it is usually paper-thin, in a child it can be as much as 1/16 inch thick. In kids, the muscles and tendons, where tears occur in an adult, are actually stronger than their interface with the bone, so if anything is going to pull loose in a child, it will be bone. And that's just what happens in cheerleader's hip.

So all of a sudden a chunk of periosteum and bone that might be as big as your thumb finds itself no longer connected to the pelvis but floating somewhere in the muscle-tendon area. "What am I doing here?" it asks itself. "I should be doing something." What it does is the only thing it knows how to do: it makes more bone.

So into the doctor's office comes a teenager with a half-baseball-sized lump of bone in the buttocks, say, from a hamstring tear. The unhappy kid is very uncomfortable, has become a one-cheek sitter, and hurts whenever she moves. And besides the discomfort caused by the lump of bone itself, a bursa that formed over the bone to provide a cushion has become irritated and is swollen to the point where the poor teenager feels as though there were two baseballs in there. All this from a little piece of misplaced bone.

What to do about it

See a doctor. But make sure that it's a doctor who's used to dealing with athletes, and young ones at that. In an X-ray these bone growths can look just like malignant bone tumors, and it's not uncommon to hear of people being operated on and biopsied because the physician feared the worst. As a doctor, if you don't know that this sort of thing can happen to kids in athletics, especially teenagers who are in the middle of growth spurts, and you don't ask a lot of questions to find out exactly what happened in the beginning, the X-rays can scare you to death. Here is where experience can make a big difference.

Sometimes surgery is the answer. The wayward piece of bone can be screwed or stitched back to the pelvis. Sometimes the bone will build up and then taper back down by itself, and by taking it easy, not picking on the area, you can wait it out. But the important thing is to *know* what the problem is; then you can act accordingly. See someone.

CONTUSIONS

Contusions, or bruises, are almost as common in the thigh as in the lower leg. They're the result of direct blows, the kind of charley horse you get from being hit, and are the bane of contact sports such as wrestling, football, even basketball and baseball. They almost always occur in the quadriceps, that fine, big, meaty target for well-aimed football helmets and knees alike.

A contusion usually affects people in one of two ways: either it's so devastating, hurts so badly, that you can't do anything but lie there and suffer; or, more often, you take the blow, continue what you're doing for a while, and then pause for half a minute or so, during which time the muscle goes into spasm and ceases working very well. Then it's obvious that it's a bad sort of injury. In a few hours the pain will be accompanied by swelling and soon after the familiar black and blue splotches.

What to do about it

The pain, swelling, and discoloration are the result of ruptured blood vessels below the skin bleeding into the muscle, and the blood can accumulate into massive amounts very quickly. With contusions in the lower leg, ice and compression together can slow down the bleeding and reduce swelling. In the meatier thigh, it's harder to apply either effectively—there's too much fat and muscle around the injury. If you could sit on a bag of ice, that might work, as it would supply cold and compression at the same time. But it's hard to sit on an ice pack with your quadriceps. So don't neglect ice, but don't expect miracles from it. The best way to apply compression is to put your hand over the point of the blow and lean on it for ten to fifteen minutes.

More effective still is stretching the muscle. If you're bashed in the quads, you can stretch the muscle by bending your knee. Stretching the muscle stretches the fascia surrounding it as well, tightening it and turning it into a kind of internal tourniquet. You apply compression from within, inhibit bleeding, *and* get a head start on stretching the muscle, keeping it from remaining shortened and in spasm.

Then take it easy. In contrast to muscle tears and strains, with contusions you *do not* want to push to the point of pain. Keep the muscle stretched and start moving in ways that are comfortable. And you might well see someone. These can be painful injuries, and you don't want to overdo things and make the problem worse.

MYOSITIS OSSIFICANS

With a name like that it's got to be bad, right? Well, it ain't particularly good, but it is interesting. This is the contusion equivalent of cheerleader's hip. If you're hit while the quadriceps muscle is contracting (and it usually is during contusions), the blow not only crushes the muscle and ruptures blood vessels, but because the muscle is under tension by being contracted it can pull away from the bone. Except for one portion (the rectus femoris, which connects to the pelvis), the quadriceps begins in the thigh. It connects to a good two thirds of the front part of the femur. And that's muscle-to-bone connection. There are no tendons here to act as intermediaries. More to the point, it's muscle-to-periosteum, that dense bone covering that's supposed to heal fractures and otherwise keep things shipshape.

So when the muscle pulls away from the bone, it takes some periosteum with it. Meanwhile, the ruptured blood vessels are pouring blood into the area, bathing the periosteum, which has set up shop in the muscle, an inch away from its former home in the femur. In the face of such adversity it knows how to do just one thing: make bone. And with so much nutritious blood around, it does so at an unbelievable pace. You can actually see new bone on an X-ray within a couple of weeks of the injury—that's almost unheard of. It can grow as large as a flashlight, and often it has very sharp edges. And all that bone is forming precisely where it shouldn't, inside the muscle. Needless to say, it does not promote good muscle function. It promotes pain.

What to do about it

See someone. The problem is that there's no way of knowing at the beginning whether your contusion will develop into myositis ossificans—which literally means "bone forming in muscle"—or not. Again, here's where it's particularly important to see someone who's had experience with such things, because the way you treat the contusion from the beginning will most likely have a bearing on if, or how badly, bone forms in the muscle. And if the bone is already there, a doctor who's not used to dealing with athletes might easily draw the wrong conclusion from X-rays that show a rapidly forming mass that looks suspiciously like a malignant tumor.

Usually these injuries are *not* treated well; in fact, they're abused. Someone—a high-school football coach, say—decides that it's nothing more than a bruise, and tells the athlete to work through it, get into the whirlpool, go into a massage program. And often the injury can lead to another, simply as a result of mistreating the myositis—by vigorous massage, say, or too much activity. Like simple contusions, this injury should be rested. Pain is *not* gain when it comes to myositis ossificans. Once the bone forms, you have to wait until it has run its course and formed all the bone it is going to form. Usually, especially if you're nice to it, it will reverse itself and reabsorb nearly all the bone, a process that can take from three to twelve months. And the muscle will eventually reattach to the femur. You simply have to wait it out.

If it doesn't reabsorb, then surgery might be the only answer. In any case, don't muddle through this one on your own. Have someone see it.

HIP POINTER

Blows to well-protected bones like the femur are painful enough; a blow to the virtually naked bony ridge of the pelvis can be devastating, one of the most painful athletic injuries possible. If you run your fingers along your hip just below the belt or skirt line you'll run into this ridge. There's little between it and your fingers but skin. When this exposed bone is given a whack by a football helmet, or baseball bat, or sharp fall, the pain can be unbelievable, frequently requiring injectable drugs to help people tolerate it. In fact, if we could get detailed enough X-rays, we'd probably see that the bone is actually fractured, even crushed.

And it's not just impact pain that causes the problem. The abdominal muscles attach to this ridge, and the blow causes bleeding into these muscles, just as in myositis ossificans (without, in this case, the added complication of displaced bone). In reaction to the bleeding, the abdominal muscles go into spasm, and when the abdominal muscles go into spasm, they *really* go into spasm. The entire front of your body becomes absolutely rigid. You don't want to breathe, laugh, cough, God forbid sneeze. To the inexperienced eye it may look like a ruptured appendix or colon, because these problems are accompanied by a rigid abdomen as well. And because the pain is so great, people don't want you to touch them to find out any different. It's one of the most dramatic illustrations of the interconnectedness of things in the body, a reminder that most people would be happy to do without.

What to do about it

See someone. You'll hurt so badly that it won't cross your mind to do anything else. And be patient. It's important not to go back to your activity too soon. Too many people have gone back too quickly and, to compensate for continued pain, have consciously or unconsciously altered their gait, or their stroke, or their throwing style. The upshot can be another injury to another part of the body, one that may be more serious than the hip pointer in the long run.

OTHER ACUTE PROBLEMS IN THE HIP

There aren't many others. And those are so obvious that, as with hip pointers, it would be surprising if you had to be persuaded to see someone. Fractures fall into that category, as do other, less-well-defined problems with the hip joint itself. As a general rule, if you have a serious hip joint injury you'll experience substantial loss of motion, and you won't be able to bear weight on the joint. It will hurt, a lot, deep in the hip. These things should be seen.

Overuse Injuries

Back to the world of Leslie Friedman. Overuse injuries are the problems that creep up on you, that begin with the slightest of irritations and build to the point where they can be more painful, and more difficult to deal with, than the kind of dramatic injuries we've been discussing. They're usually the result of overusing a particular muscle, or tendon (or bone, even), and they often first breathe life because of some change in your activity. A change in distance run, number of classes taken, sets played, rehearsals attended, terrain traversed—even a new instructor, or a new racquet, or pair of shoes—can bring on an overuse injury. Most people ignore them until they're so painful, or debilitating, that they simply can't ignore them any longer. By then, something minor may have turned into a real problem. Especially so as these injuries tend to migrate—the old body-interrelationships business again—and what began in the quads, say, might lodge in the hip. You may be able to treat the latest symptoms, but it's harder to track it all back to the source. And if you don't get back to where it began, it'll just keep recurring.

Funny we should mention the quadriceps. Well, not so funny, because, as you might have suspected by now, weak quadriceps are the single most common source of overuse problems from the waist on down. We've discussed how weak quads can affect the knee (see Chapter 5, "The Knee"); they can cause problems in the hip as well, and most overuse problems in athletes are in the hip rather than the thigh. Probably the only people who have lots of overuse injuries in the thigh are track and field athletes, and they are often residual problems from old thigh tears and strains. Overuse injuries usually lodge at one end or the other of the muscle, where it attaches to tendons—in this case, the hip area, where so many muscles begin. (Muscles that begin at the femur lack tendons. The muscle simply connects directly to the bone.)

To treat overuse injuries effectively, you have to be aware of these changes, aware of the subtle beginnings. That's where a doctor who takes the time to talk with you, to ask questions and listen to answers, can be of real service in helping you monitor your activities. But it may not be necessary to go to a doctor for many of these things. If you don't, you must become your own monitor. For the only lasting way to deal with overuse injuries is to find out why they occurred, to track them back to their source and snuff them out there, so *they* won't come back after *you* go back.

GLUTEAL PROBLEMS—PIRIFORMIS SYNDROME

We return to that solid wad of muscle in the buttocks, so important in athletics, and so prominent in dancers, skaters, and gymnasts. It's primarily made up of three specific muscles, the gluteus maximus, gluteus medius, and gluteus minimus. That is, the "greatest," "middle," and "smallest" rump muscles—glutes, for short. The glutes are responsible for rotating your hip and leg outward (ballet dancers, take note) and for extending the hip and leg backward. When a dancer does an arabesque, it's the glutes that pull the leg back, up, and out. When a skater glides over the ice, it's the glutes that both rotate and extend the legs. When you run or walk uphill, the glutes provide the power to push your body ahead of your trailing leg. When you do a dolphin kick in the pool, it is the glutes that pull your legs up against the water.

There are smaller muscles in the buttocks as well, muscles that lie underneath the glutes and assist them in rotating and extending the hip. One of these is the piriformis muscle, which is only a couple of inches long. These small muscles can be irritated along with the glutes for a variety of reasons. We've already discussed how weak hamstrings can lead to overused gluteal muscles. The same can happen with weak quads. If the quads aren't. strong enough to do so on their own, the glutes can actually be called upon to help tighten your knee—not their preferred task. And overuse of the muscles' natural functions can lead to irritation as well.

You'll know it when it happens—painful and aching buttocks are no fun—but you may *not* know it, as well. This interesting tale involves the piriformis muscle. In about 20 percent of the population, the sciatic (pronounced "sigh-at-ic") nerve—that large nerve that supplies sensation to much of the body from the hips downward—descends from the lower spine and runs right through the piriformis muscle on its way down the legs to the feet. In the other 80 percent of us, the nerve runs over the muscle. Either way, if the piriformis goes into spasm, which is what muscles do when they're irritated, it can squash or pinch the sciatic nerve.

That can mean pain that runs down the back of the thigh and calf all the way to the foot. The condition is called sciatica, and it can be accompanied by numbness and tingling as well. Meanwhile, the piriformis and the other muscles in the buttocks are in spasm, which means that you have pain in the hip that is particularly sharp when you try to rotate or extend your leg. Not only do you hurt in ballet class, but it's getting pretty tough even to get out of the car or out of a chair. And then the muscle tightens further, which throws your leg into a semipermanent external rotation. You start favoring the hip, altering your gait, moving and bending in strange, awkward ways, all of which starts to affect your back.

Finally you sort it all out and go to the doctor, who says, "Where does it hurt?"

"Well," you answer, "my back is killing me, and I have this pain in my buttocks that goes all the way down my leg to my foot."

"Aha!" the doctor replies. "Disk disease."

For such are the classic symptoms: back pain caused by a degenerating or abnormal disk that pinches the sciatic nerve to produce pain all the way down to the foot. And heaven help you if X-rays expose a bulging disk that you may have had for fifteen years and that never bothered you all that time. It's off to the operating room. It happens all too often, and it can be scary.

But it may not be disk disease. It may not be a back problem. It may be the little ol' piriformis muscle. And what may be necessary is not surgery at all, but the kind of treatment that works so well for muscle and tendon injuries: stretching and strengthening.

How can you know? There are a couple of ways to test yourself. Lie on your stomach with your knees together and bent, so that the soles of your feet point heavenward. Then just let your legs fall apart, out to the sides. The motion causes your hips to rotate *inward,* stretching the *external* rotators, the gluteal and piriformis muscles. If the muscles hurt, it's a pretty good chance you've located the problem. (We'll see the exercise again, slightly modified, as a way of measuring turnout in Chapter 12, "Ballet.")

Another test is to sit in a chair or on the floor, place the heel of one leg against the outside of the knee of the other leg, and pull the knee of the first leg (which should be on the side where it hurts) toward the middle of your chest. You should feel a good stretch in the buttocks in any case, but if it really bites, you may be looking at irritated glutes and/or piriformis muscle. (An interesting thing about this test is that if you really and truly do have a disk problem, this stretch probably *won't* bother you. And doubly interesting is the following: the common test for disk-disease-caused sciatica is the positive straight-leg raising test. That involves lying on your back and lifting your leg straight up and back, which, if you do have a disk problem, should cause sciatic pain. But if you pull up your leg with the knee bent, there should be no pain—if the problem is caused by a disk. However, if the piriformis or glutes are at fault, then the sciatic pain will occur in *either* case, leg straight or bent. So if you get the same pain with knees extended or bent, you might look to the muscles and think about canceling your appointment with the back surgeon.)

Gluteal and Piriformis Stretching Exercise

What to do about it

Stretch and strengthen the muscles. It's easy to do. One strengthening technique is to lie on your stomach and raise your leg behind you. You may find that you're able to raise the leg only a few inches off the ground, or not at all. It doesn't matter. Do the best you can, even if that means only tightening the buttocks at first. If you stay with it, you'll start to notice results.

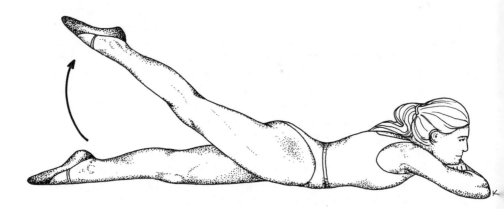

Gluteal Strengthening Exercise

Another way to strengthen is by simply reversing the stretching motion discussed earlier. If you're sitting in a chair, the heel of your bad leg resting outside the knee of the other, and you pull the knee of the bad leg toward the middle of your chest to stretch the gluteal muscles, strengthen them by pushing your leg back against your hand. The more resistance you offer with your hand, the harder it will be to push against it, and the greater the strengthening.

You can do contract-relax exercises this way. Pull your knee toward the middle of your chest as far as is comfortable, then push back against your hand. Hold the push—which contracts the muscle—for about fifteen seconds, then relax. Pull the knee toward you a bit more, then push back with your leg. Hold it for fifteen seconds. Relax. You may have to start with a relatively straight knee and hip, then gradually work the knee back toward the chest. The more the knee and hip are bent, the greater the glutes are extended, and the greater the stretch. It's pretty slick—you can stretch and strengthen the muscles all by yourself with the same test you used to determine the cause of the problem in the first place.

But remember, once you're relatively pain-free and back to your favorite activity, the only way to stay that way is to deal with whatever it was that caused the problem. And with gluteal injuries, that something may have begun in the thigh—weak quads or hamstrings—or might involve the way you go about your activity. Getting rid of the symptoms, no matter how much relief it may bring you, won't guarantee that you will not face the same problem again. The only way to escape that merry-go-round is to find out why you hurt yourself and change the way you go about things.

A caution: it's certainly worthwhile to see if sciatic pain is the result of a piriformis or gluteal injury. But if you try the things we've suggested and the pain persists, or if you have a great deal of numbness or tingling, and you feel weakness along your leg, strange sensations you've not experienced before, then don't assume that you've done the exercises wrong and you should give them another try. See someone.

Sciatica is nothing to play around with. Nor is numbness, tingling, or weakness, no matter where it might show up. If you have any of these sensations, *see someone*.

CHRONIC GROIN INJURIES

The adductors, those fanlike muscles in the groin and upper thigh, are responsible for pulling your legs together. There are few sports that demand such movement (equestrian sports come to mind—it's the adductors that allow riders to tighten their legs against the horse), but people experience adductor problems because the muscles have another job as well: they work to stabilize the hip. Ballet dancers use their adductors a lot as pulling-up muscles, very subtle rotators. And the adductors change their function depending on how much you flex or extend your hip. They're good-sized muscles, and they're used, and abused, more than you might imagine.

Some adductor injuries can be awful to deal with. Although stretching and strengthening probably will help most adductor problems, the rest seem never to get better. Some people hurt for *years* without relief. They may improve, but whenever they get to a certain level in their activity, back comes the pain again. These cases are a mystery to everyone involved.

What to do about it

Stretching and strengthening the muscles is the best bet. You can stretch the adductors in a number of ways. If you're standing, simply pull your leg out from your body—the farther the pull, the longer the stretch. To strengthen, bring the leg back to the midline and then beyond, crossing your legs in front of you. An inner tube looped around a table leg can provide resistance, as can someone holding on to your leg. You can pull against the presence of any relatively inert impediment.

You can also exercise the adductors by sitting on the floor with your knees bent and the soles of your feet together. Hold your feet with one hand and with the other gently push against the bad leg—the inside of the leg, not the knee. The longer the push, the greater the stretch. To strengthen, pull the leg back against the resistance of your hand. You can do contract-relax exercises in this way as well.

If the muscles don't respond, see someone. You may be in that 50 percent or so of athletes whose injury is simply a bear to deal with. If so, you and your doctor can struggle through the dark together.

TENSOR FASCIA LATA INJURY

There's a little fist-shaped muscle in the hip, right under the bony ridge of the pelvis, where your pants pockets begin. It's called the tensor fascia lata. It hooks on to the iliotibial band, the long tendon that runs all the way down the outside of the thigh, across the knee, to the lower leg. Small though it may be, this muscle helps extend your knee, going to work during the last 15 degrees of movement and then holding on to help keep your knee extended. (If you tighten your knee and hold it in front of you, you can feel how tight the muscle and tendon become. Simply run your fingers from the muscle just below the point of your hip down the outside of your leg to the knee.)

When you bend your knee, the tensor fascia lata, versatile little character that it is, helps flex it as well. But if your quads or hamstrings are weak, the tensor fascia lata is forced to bear too much of the load. Weak thigh muscles can lead to irritation of the tensor fascia lata, as well as to iliotibial band tendinitis.

What to do about it

Strengthen the thigh muscles, the quads especially (by now you know all too well how to do that), and stretch and strengthen the tensor fascia lata. Side leg raises will strengthen the muscle; crossing your leg *behind* the other—the cross-leg stretch—will stretch it. (See page 107 for an illustration of this stretch.)

STRESS FRACTURE OF THE FEMUR

The femur is the largest bone in the body, and it's monstrously strong. It's almost two kinds of bone, really: the shaft, which gets its strength from being an almost rigid cylinder, and the neck. The neck is very sophisticated in structure. Because of its curve and the stress it has to put up with, it's built like a bridge, with bone laid down in complicated arches. It's a spongier kind of bone than in the shaft, but still very strong for what it's designed to do.

But as mighty as this bone is, stress fractures can be its undoing. Stress fractures are almost invisible cracks that invade the bone (for an extended discussion of stress fractures, see Chapter 4, "The Lower Leg") and in the worst of scenarios can spread all the way through it, actually severing one part from another. The stress fracture can become a real fracture, and it's not unusual for it simply to knock off the head of the femur. That can be devastating. In young people especially, the severed portion can lose its blood supply and simply die. You can be looking at a hip replacement at age twenty-two.

The problem is made more difficult by the fact that stress fractures are tough to spot because they really don't have any particular symptoms. The strongest diagnostic criterion is that there *isn't* any diagnostic criterion. You have pain somewhere in the thigh, usually the upper part. It's worse when you exercise, better when you don't—well, that sounds like a lot of things. You try all the treatments you know about, and nothing works. Finally you go to a doctor who, after hearing your frustrating story, takes an X-ray—still nothing. Finally, if you're lucky, the light dawns, and your doctor gives you a bone scan. And there it is, a tiny crack that you can't believe could cause so much trouble.

It can. We see femoral stress fractures in runners and aerobic dance teachers primarily (not students—the number of classes makes a difference). They show up with some frequency in the army, which is so cautious about them that you'll find yourself in bed before you know it and after that on crutches. They seem to be caused by overuse—running, jumping, perhaps changing surfaces and terrains—and training errors, trying to do too much too soon. They can show up anywhere in the femur, from the neck all the way down the shaft, and we really don't know why it's one place and not another. (You can also get stress fractures of the pelvis where the muscles begin. These, too, are often missed.) They all take a long time to heal, sometimes as long as six to nine months, and if the fracture is in a particularly hazardous spot, it may require surgery to pin the bone together.

What to do about it

See someone. The stakes are simply too high not to. And it's vitally important to do what you're told to do—in most cases, not much of anything. That's what makes things hard. Active people don't like to do nothing. It's hard enough to get active people to slow down, much less stop doing their favorite activity, but that's just what you have to do with a femoral stress fracture. You simply have to make the area free of pain so the bone can start to heal, and that may involve crutches and a wheelchair around the house. No fun. Some people have actually had to go into formal psychiatric care to deal with the necessity of doing nothing. The rule of thumb here is that if it's not hurting, you're not doing anything wrong.

Then, when the pain is gone, you try to get back to as much activity as you can without hurting the area again. The tricky thing about stress fractures is that the bone originally broke because it wasn't strong enough for the demands you put upon it. So it's not enough simply to let it heal, you've got to exercise it to the point where it will gain enough strength not to break when you impose those demands again but not to the point where you reinjure it while trying to rehabilitate it. Risky business.

So the tip-off is activity-related pain in the thigh that you can't put a finger on and that doesn't respond to any treatments. If that describes what's happening to you, see a doctor.

SNAPPING HIP

And now, welcome to the haunted house of sports medicine, a world in which things happen for no apparent reason and quit happening just as mysteriously. How many dancers (and others, too, but mostly dancers) have to get up in the morning and pop their hip before they can go ahead and dance the rest of the day? It's a common thing. It's lucky that most snapping hips don't hurt because we don't know why they pop, and God knows we don't know why they feel better afterward.

One theory says that tendons snap across the front of the pelvis, or each other, as they change position during activity. If they snap enough, they can become irritated. And that can mean swelling and pain—the symptoms of tendinitis.

What to do about it

If it doesn't hurt, ignore it. And count your blessings. If it does hurt, see someone. The task then will be to find out which tendon or muscle is involved, and then do the familiar things: stretching, strengthening, even ice and aspirin. But we may be in the realm of cracking knees, ankles; and toes here. You learn to live with it, shaking your head in wonder, and go about your business.

SNAPPING HIP—OUTSIDE VARIETY

There's another kind of snapping hip that's on the outside of the joint, by the greater trochanter, which is a protruding knob at the upper end of the femur, just below where it goes into the hip joint. We know about this one—it involves the tensor fascia lata muscle and the iliotibial band. The muscle helps to flex and extend your hip, and as it works the iliotibial band can actually snap over the greater trochanter, which sticks out from the bone, just asking for it. Especially in lean people who don't have much fat to lubricate that sort of thing (there's a bursa in there to help out, too—sometimes it doesn't), the tendon can become irritated.

It can also occur in people who lie on their hip and move their leg, as in aerobics and calisthenics. The pressure can push the bone against the tendon and irritate it that way. These people feel the irritation right next to the skin.

What to do about it

This one is something you can deal with, because it usually involves tendinitis, or a muscle that's too tight or too weak. Stretching, strengthening, icing, aspirin.

MERALGIA PARESTHETICA

Another little thing that can cause big problems. One of the nerves that supplies sensation to the front of the upper thigh comes out of the spine and crosses over the bony ridge of the pelvis. It's called the lateral cutaneous nerve, and it doesn't take very much to bother it. Just enough pressure barely to pinch it against the bone will cause pain down the upper front of the thigh. We used to see it when women wore girdles, because the girdle was tightest over the pelvic bone. Now it shows up once in a while in dancers and other performers who wear costumes that are very binding across the hips. Occasionally we'll see it in a man wearing a dance belt or in people with really skintight jeans, even in people whose running shorts have too much elastic. It doesn't take much.

The pain is always hard to pin down. It isn't muscle pain, it doesn't respond to treatment, and it comes and goes depending on what you have on. Once the nerve is irritated and inflamed, though, it'll stick around for a while.

What to do about it

The treatment is pretty simple: get rid of the pressure. A change of clothing and anti-inflammatory drugs will usually calm it down. But it can take some doing to arrive at that point. It might be best to see someone, just to be sure what the problem is. It can masquerade as other things, but it doesn't respond as other things do. One test involves tapping across the bony ridge of your pelvis. When you come upon the irritated nerve, you'll feel the pain down your thigh, often like an electric shock.

Fortunately, the problem is rare.

Frequently Asked Questions About Thigh and Hip Problems

My hip feels like it's dislocating. What can I do about it?

It's probably the iliotibial band tendon snapping over the greater trochanter. The tendon can be so tight, and it's so big and prominent, that when it snaps it can feel as though your hip is actually shifting in position. It isn't, but the muscle and tendon are, and the abrupt change can be striking and disconcerting.

Treatment involves stretching and strengthening the muscle. Best to see someone about it.

I've been bothered by a recurrent hamstring (or quadriceps) strain for years. Why does it keep coming back?

Almost without exception, the answer is that the muscle has never gotten strong enough. It may be flexible, but it's not strong. So it keeps getting injured.

People think they can exercise themselves back into shape after these injuries by doing the same things they always did. If they run, they run again. If they play tennis, it's back to the courts. Or back to the studio, or the gym, or the health club. That's all well and good, but once one of these muscles gets weak, it no longer starts at the same level as your other muscles. As you exercise, all the muscles get stronger, but you never erase the discrepancy between the injured muscle and the others. So even though your injured hamstring may be stronger than it was when you began, compared to the rest of your body it's still weak.

You must do *specific exercises* for the *specific muscle* that was injured. That doesn't mean more exercise, necessarily; it just means different exercises. And that's why it's so vitally important to discover just what it was that went wrong in the first place. If you don't know which muscle was injured—precisely which muscle—you won't know which muscle to exercise.

7 The Back and Neck

Y ou landed on the beam?" Garrick says. "You're not supposed to do that."

"Not on my back, anyhow," replies Karen Bevis. Karen is a fourteen-year-old gymnast. In two and a half years, she's been to the Center for six separate injuries. Garrick refers to her as a "permanent resident." Her mother nods sadly. This back problem is just the latest.

"What did you do?" Garrick asks.

"A backflip."

"Well, better your back than your face, I guess. No numbness or tingling or anything like that?"

It's an important question. Almost everyone, in or out of sports, has had back or neck problems. Most are things like stiff necks or sore backs rather than anything really serious, which is lucky, because serious problems involving the neck and back can be ominous. The reason, of course, is the backbone, which is, among other things, a conduit that houses the spinal cord, that stalk of nerves that connects all parts of the body with the brain. When you get involved with nerves—with sensation, electrical impulse, the brain's ability to control the body—you're entering a fragile world, the disruption of which can have frightening consequences. From paralysis to partial loss of bodily functions, the hazards of spinal injury are real. But they represent a small minority of all back problems. This chapter will not deal with these relatively few serious back problems, because they're obvious, often the result of contact sport injuries or other equally violent accidents, and they *absolutely* require professional care. No home treatments here.

Some, though, sneak up on you. But not without warning signs:

1. *Your pain is not just in your back or neck but radiates down your leg, or down your arm, or into your groin.*

2. *You have numbness or tingling, or disturbing sensations in your legs or arms.*

3. *You notice any sudden weakness in your arms or legs—you can't get up on your toes, for example, or your foot slaps when you walk.*

4. *Any straining—coughing, sneezing, moving your bowels—makes your back or neck pain sharply worse.*

If *any* of these conditions describes your experience, then stop reading and *see a doctor.* And you should see one pretty quickly. Any of these symptoms might be a tip-off to injuries involving the nervous system. Don't mess around with them, hoping they might go away. *See someone.*

Karen Bevis has none of these warning signs. Her back bothers her mainly when she does long, slow back arches—back walkovers, for example.

"It doesn't hurt with normal daily activities?" Garrick asks. "Just with gymnastics?"

"Yes."

"Gee." Garrick puts on his best innocent face. "There's an easy solution to that problem."

The remark elicits a laugh all around. The point is that the "easy solution"—stopping gymnastics—is not easy in the least. Although Karen's injury would mean little in the "real world" outside gymnastics—many of us would be very happy to go through life with no more pressing problem than pain when we do a back walkover (many of us would be happy even to be able to do a back walkover)—Karen's real world is defined by the walls of the gym. Any gymnast worth her salt, especially a beam specialist like Karen, must be able to do back walkovers. So Garrick searches for a way to keep her inside the gym.

"I can't find anything that would suggest you've broken something, or you have a disk, or anything horrible is going on. I think you've bruised the muscle, and what happens when you do something like that is that you get some bleeding in the muscle. The muscle doesn't know what to do with blood that isn't inside blood vessels, so it goes into spasm. It's tight—you can feel it. When you get into certain positions, the muscle bites you. I think the best thing to do would be to get you on some really vigorous—not fast but vigorous—stretching exercises."

He calls in a therapist to help Karen find positions that stretch out her lower back muscles. He suggests that she start an abdominal strengthening program as well. And, he tells her mother, a round-the-clock regimen of aspirin wouldn't hurt anything.

"When's your next competition?"

"In another month," says Karen.

"Well, I think you can safely go back. You can do ninety percent of the stuff now without hurting, can't you?"

"Right."

"So do those things and hold back on the others for a while. It's not the end of the world. It's just that you hurt yourself in a bad place. If you bruise a muscle in another spot you can work around it, but you've got to use your back in everything you do."

True enough. Gymnast, runner, dancer, walker, athlete or not, you just can't escape the back. It's the body's lodgepole, its center of support. You might compare the backbone to the center pole of a circus tent. Much as the pole holds up the tent, radiating guy wires in all directions, the backbone must support the entire upper body. It provides attachment for guy wires—the muscles in the back and elsewhere—and internal stays—like the pelvis, the rib cage, and the shoulder bones.

Still, it must do more than that. In contrast to a circus tent pole, the backbone must bend. Forward, backward, side to side, twisting double on itself, and all variations in between, the backbone must be flexible as well as strong, a reason for the fact that it's not simply one rigid bone but a series of twenty-five blocks called vertebrae, connected by hinges called facet joints, cushioned by spacers called disks, and held upright against any strong wind, internal or external, by its structure of muscles and bones. At this point all comparisons fall away. The backbone is unique.

And that's not all. As we've discussed, the backbone must perform yet another vital task: channel and protect the spinal cord in its journey from the brain to the pelvis, and provide outlets for the nerves that branch off along the way. So the backbone is a conduit as well.

A lot to ask. It's a wonder there aren't even more back and neck injuries. Yet, for all its success in providing a myriad of services simultaneously, almost anything you read about the backbone suggests that it's not well designed. That is, it's not designed for an upright posture. In this view, the backbone works best when supported at both ends, as with most animals, and as with us humans back a few years when we too scurried around on all fours. Although we readily made the jump to getting around on two legs, our backbone did not.

It's a debatable contention, made all the more difficult to prove one way or the other by the fact that it's hard to ask other animals if their backs are bothering them (although we do know that there are certain dogs that have frequent disk problems). But whether or not we should be wearing two pairs of running shoes instead of one, it is true that many back problems have to do with the way the backbone is designed.

To explain: in contrast to the center pole of a circus tent, the backbone is not perfectly straight. It curves front to back—it's designed that way. To begin at the top, your neck, which is supported by what's called the cervical spine, curves forward. The part of the

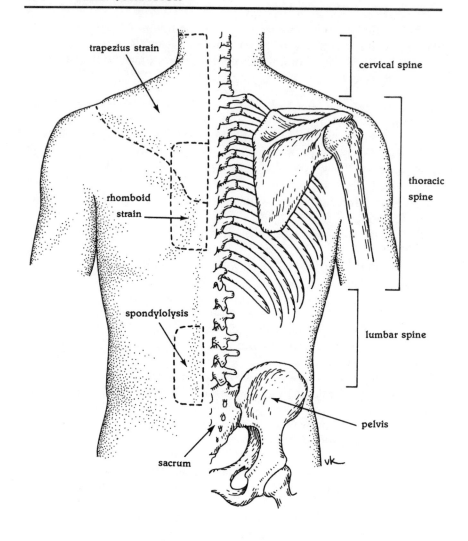

trapezius strain

cervical spine

thoracic spine

rhomboid strain

spondylolysis

lumbar spine

pelvis

sacrum

Back View of the Back and Neck

backbone to which the ribs are attached, the thoracic spine, meanders backward, and then the lower backbone, the lumbar spine, moves forward again a bit. The effect is a gentle S curve.

The vertebrae are cut at just enough of an angle to sustain this curve, likewise the cushioning disks between. The guy wires—the muscles— are just taut enough on every side. And although the backbone is very flexible, at rest it returns to this gentle curve.

That is, it should. Problems arise when for one reason or another the backbone is forced into positions that stretch and strain the muscles and bones that hold it in place, so that it remains out of line, and therefore out of sorts. The reasons include disease and injury and are often unavoidable. Some suggested treatments follow a bit later on. But often you *can* avoid mistreating the backbone. The keys are twofold and very simple: keep your back straight and strengthen your stomach muscles.

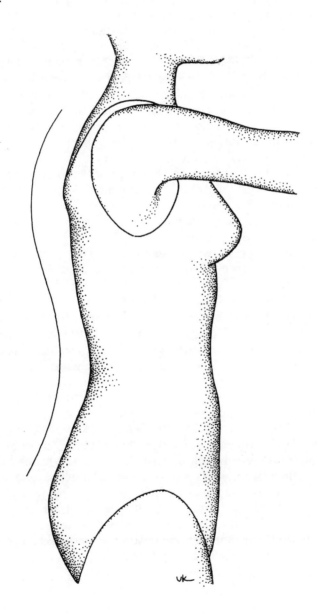

S Curve of the Backbone

The Importance of a Straight Back

Many people dread back injuries, but they're very common and usually not terribly serious. Of the twenty-five vertebrae in the backbone, the ones in the lower back, the lumbar spine, cause the most trouble, three or four times as much as those in the rest of the back. In fact, in athletes these five vertebrae, particularly the lowest three, cause more problems than all the other vertebrae put together. It's hard to know just why that's so, but it's probably because these largest vertebrae in the backbone are not connected to stabilizers, like the ribs, that help secure them in place. There's a lot of movement in the lumbar spine, just as there is in the cervical spine, the part of the backbone in the neck. But in contrast to that upper part of the spine, which only has to support your head, the lower back has to worry about almost half of the weight of your body. And it's subject to terrific stresses as well. The twistings and turnings of the torso above and the legs below can deposit hundreds of pounds per square inch of force on the lumbar spine. So it's potentially a troublesome area, and that potential is made greater when people inadvertently accentuate the lumbar spine's already existing curve.

Everyone has seen a swaybacked horse. The animal is a staple source of jokes. It hurts even to look at such an animal's sagging back; Lord knows what it must feel like to the horse. People, too, have swaybacks, which are nothing more than overarched backs. Some of us come about our swaybacks naturally—we're born with them—but more often we give ourselves temporary swaybacks without realizing it. It's usually a function of fatigue or lack of strength. Next time you go to a fitness center, watch people work out on the weight machines. Invariably, whether it's back exercises, leg presses, or arm conditioners, as people get tired or stack too many plates on the machine, they begin to arch their backs (many people simply arch their backs from the beginning—they've never been taught otherwise). Take a peek into the free weight room. The experienced lifters know better, but novices, especially those who are trying to take on more weight than they can handle, arch their backs with each lift. And it doesn't have to happen at the gym. Whenever your back is involved in lifting (and when you think of it, there are few times when it is not), be it rearranging the furniture, carrying out the garbage, picking up the dog, or just supporting the weight of your body, if you're tired or not strong enough, you arch your back. It's a way of trying to get more of the big muscles in your torso to help out.

Not good. So long as the vertebrae in your backbone are stacked as they should be, they absorb force effectively all along the chain; they compress one onto the next as they are designed to do. But when you overarch your back, distorting the backbone's normal curve, in effect you stack the blocks off center. They sheer off course when they compress and tend to want to slide *off* rather than *against* one another. (It's awfully hard for them to do that, of course, as they're locked together at the back by the facet joints. But it's not good for the joints to undergo such stress. These connectors are pretty small compared to the forces against them.) In this position, you lose the advantage of bony stability, and suddenly you have to stabilize your back purely with muscles. The muscles will tolerate that kind of overwork only so long. Then you start having all sorts of problems. At the least you can develop temporary back pain, at the worst a real injury.

And it's not just in lifting activities where the tendency to arch the back shows up. In gymnastics, especially in women, the arched-back, bottom-out pose is *de rigueur* when finishing a routine. In ballet, dancers without enough turnout tend to tilt back their pelvis (and sometimes bend their knees, too) trying for more; when they straighten up, their back arches and bottom sticks out. And the need for good turnout isn't limited to ballet. Gymnasts, figure skaters, even discus throwers depend on turnout. Overarched backs are common here also.

An arched back doesn't just show up in turnout problems. Dancers whose hip flexor muscles—like the sartorius and rectus femoris, those muscles in the front of the pelvis—are overly tight tend to overarch their backs. Many dancers are in this boat. Their hamstrings are plenty flexible—they can pull their foot up to their ear—but they don't have as much flexibility in the other direction. The demands of arabesque and attitude simply don't stretch out the hip flexors as much as they might. The result can be a tendency to tilt the pelvis forward, which in turn accentuates the arch in the back.

Aerobic dancers, too, overarch their backs. Often it's because the students tend to do what the teacher does, not what she says (a tendency in any activity that is taught by demonstration, not just in sports. How many parents through how many generations have in frustration told their children, "Do what I say, not what I do"?). The teacher introduces an exercise, a donkey kick, say, that should be done with a perfectly flat back, perhaps even with elbows on the floor. While demonstrating, she looks up to see how the students are doing, thereby arching her back. The result? A studio full of students donkey kicking away with arched backs.

Ballet teachers try to circumvent the problem by teaching students to pull up through the pelvis and stomach and tighten their buttocks. Physical therapists tell you to tuck your tail beneath you. Either technique works, and either points toward the same end: keeping the lower back as straight as possible. The straighter the lower back, the more abuse it will take, which is a real boon, because most of the activities athletic people do abuse the lower back.

PELVIC TILT

It's important to know what it *feels* like to have a straight back. Many of us don't know; we're used to the other. One way is by learning to do a pelvic tilt. Lie down on your back and bend your knees toward you. That's all, just bend your knees. The mere act of bending them tilts your pelvis beneath you and correspondingly flattens your back into the floor. If you want to tilt your pelvis even more, all you have to do is curl up into a ball. (A very good way to stretch your lower back, by the way. Now you've reversed the curve of your backbone, which is just the ticket to stretch out your overly contracted muscles.)

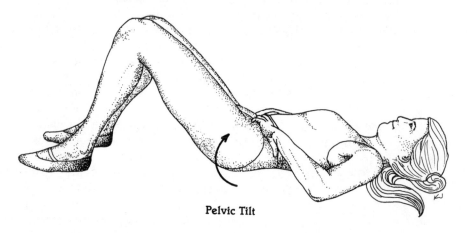

Pelvic Tilt

But it's hard to go through life on your back with your knees bent. It's that feeling of flattening the lower back that you want to remember, so that you can reproduce it anytime. Have a friend slide a hand underneath the small of your back, and then push your back into the hand, knees bent or no. That's the feeling. You can do this exercise standing against a wall, too. You don't even need your friend's hand— simply flatten your lower back into the wall. Just the act of doing it is good exercise, and eventually you'll be able to tilt your pelvis and straighten out your back anytime.

You can make it a conscious thing: when standing, think about tilting your pelvis beneath you; when sitting, neither slump nor over-arch—simply keep your back straight. If you're sitting in a straight-backed chair, press the small of your back against the support. When lifting, bend from the legs, not the lower back (another way of saying keep your back straight). And when you're working out on weight machines, be sure to flatten your lower back into the backrests of the equipment. Always aim to feel the pressure of the back support against your lower back. If you can't, you're arching too much.

And there's another thing you can do to prevent overarching. It's not obvious, like straightening your back, and it may even be surprising. Yet perhaps it's the most important thing of all: strengthen your stomach muscles.

The Importance of Strong Abdominal Muscles

Back to the circus tent. The center pole not only supports the guy wires radiating from it, but it's supported by them as well. If the guy wires to one side pull too tightly, the pole leans in that direction, even bows out in the center. A similar fate can befall your backbone. If any one of the groups of muscles that attach to the backbone is significantly stronger than the others, it can exert undue influence on the backbone, actually pulling it out of shape.

The two main muscle groups that influence the backbone this way are the strong ropes of muscles that run along the spine, the paraspinous muscles ("near to the spine"—you can easily feel them on either side of your backbone; when well developed, they surmount the spine like banks of a canal), and your stomach muscles. Although these abdominal muscles attach at the pelvis and ribs and so don't pull directly on the backbone, they still act as guy wires (the old business of interrelationships again—as the song says, "the rib bone's connected to the backbone, the backbone's connected to the hipbone ..."). For life to be pleasant for your backbone, the paraspinous and abdominal muscles must complement one another. Unfortunately, while the paraspinous muscles tend to be strong in everyone, kept toned and conditioned by the everyday demands of living, the same can't be said of the stomach muscles. As the beer drinkers and candy eaters among us know all too well, the stomach muscles can easily become soft and weak. And when that happens, it's no contest—the back muscles take over. When unopposed back muscles contract, they tend to shorten the distance between the skull and pelvis, just as a drawn bowstring shortens the distance between the two ends of a bow. The result: an accentuation of the spine's curve. You need strong stomach muscles to keep things in balance.

So when you're talking about prevention or treatment of back injuries, you have to be flexible and strong, but not only in the back. You have to strengthen the muscles in front, too. A good abdominal strengthening program will probably prevent, and treat, more back problems than any other course of action. Here's a way to go about it:

Curl-ups

No, not sit-ups. Curl-ups. There's a difference. It's not that there's anything wrong with sit-ups—along with push-ups and chin-ups, they're probably the most universally done strengthening exercise—it's just that if strengthening the stomach muscles is your aim, there's nothing more effective than curl-ups. And nothing safer. They have a built-in warning system. When you reach the point where you're too tired to continue exercising safely, you'll find that you can't do the curl-ups correctly. In that case, simply stop. At first you may stop sooner rather than later.

Here's how curl-ups work: lie on the floor with your hands resting together over the lower part of your chest. (Don't put your arms behind your head, because the tendency then is to pull your head up with your arms, rather than doing what you're supposed to be doing.) With your arms resting on your body they're closer to your center of gravity, making the exercise easier. Then tilt your pelvis, pressing the small of your back into the floor, and *slowly* curl your head and shoulders up, to the point where your shoulder blades have cleared the floor and then just a little beyond. Hold it for a moment, then *slowly* curl back down. Try it again. If you're doing it right, you should feel it in your stomach and no place else.

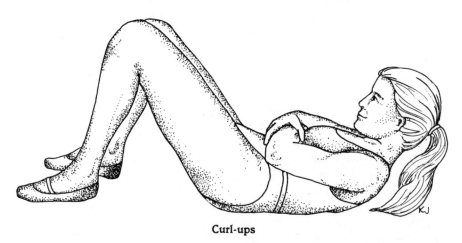

Curl-ups

If you hook your feet you won't feel it in your stomach as much because then you've created a fulcrum that allows you to use your hip flexor muscles as well. That dilutes the exercise so far as your stomach muscles are concerned. And if you don't hook your feet, then you can't cheat by letting other muscles help pull you up. Curl-ups keep you honest.

V-ups? When you V-up you use your stomach muscles, but you also use your hip flexors. Any time you involve your hips in an exercise, you shortchange your abdominal muscles. There's nothing wrong with V-ups, certainly. It simply depends on what you're exercising for. If it's to strengthen stomach muscles, to provide more stability for your back, then curl-ups are the ticket. It may be that you'll want to do curl-ups besides your usual sit-ups or V-ups.

Count to six as you curl up, hold for a count of six, then curl down to a count of six—all very slowly, always making sure that your back is flat. That's the important thing: your back must be flat, pressed into the floor. It's the tip-off as to whether you're doing the curl-ups correctly, and to whether you're too tired to do them any longer. As soon as your back begins to arch, and it will when fatigue sets in, stop the exercise. In contrast to sit-ups, during which people do all sorts of things just to keep going—arching their back, throwing themselves into the exercises, speeding up to be able to finish—curl-ups shouldn't be done if you can't do them correctly. And that means slowly as well. If you do them slowly, you can't cheat. The whole point is to strengthen the stomach muscles so as to provide better support for your back. Anything other than a pure curl-up brings in other muscles to help out, in which case the exercise won't do as much for your back.

So slow, flat-back, pure curl-ups will do your back a lot of good. Five sets three times a day is a good number to shoot for, but don't be discouraged if you can't do that many at first, or even later. Curl-ups are tough. One is worth at least fifteen regular sit-ups. If you can do even five at a time you're doing very well. A few years ago we tried out curl-ups on a junior national gymnastics team (a number of whom went on to the summer '84 Olympics). These are some of the best-conditioned athletes in all sports, people who can do two hundred conventional sit-ups just like that. *Not one of them could do five curl-ups.* It wasn't that they didn't have muscles—one look at them dispelled that notion; their muscle definition strained belief—it was just that these muscles weren't functioning as back stabilizers. They were doing other things. When they were called into play in curl-ups, which condition the stomach muscles to work for your back, they weren't equal to the job. So, as virtually all gymnasts have some back pain, curl-ups work for them, as well. A number of gymnastic clubs now use them as part of their conditioning routine.

You can even use curl-ups on a spot basis. If your back aches from bending too long over the desk, or the drafting table, or the stove, or the sawhorse, a few curl-ups on the spot can clear things up. Again, the cardinal rules are: 1. Be sure your back is flattened into the floor. 2. Do the curl-ups slowly. 3. It doesn't matter how many you can do so long as you do them correctly (if you can do two hundred of these, you're doing them wrong). 4. When your back starts to arch from fatigue, stop.

Back Injuries
BACK STRAINS

It's one of the most common experiences in all sports. You're a little tired. You're in the midst of just one more set, which is one more than you usually play, and you lunge to get your racquet on a ball at the shoetops. It's your best shot of the day, worth the extra half hour on the court and your mounting fatigue. But as you stretch to make contact, you feel something odd happen in your back.

Nothing much. It feels weird, but it certainly isn't going to stop you from playing. You finish out the game, then walk off the court for a drink of water before changing sides. And there as you're standing by the side of the court, cooling down a little, resting for a moment, it happens: your back tightens up, and suddenly it doesn't work very well at all.

You finish out the set anyway, gutting it through, then go home with a throbbing back and go to bed. In the morning the sun rises, but you don't. You discover that what used to be a human being is now a pretzel. You not only can't get out of that position, you can't even get out of bed. All this for one extra set and a hell of a passing shot.

It doesn't have to be tennis, of course. Running, swimming, team sports, dance, weight training—anytime your back becomes weary, or when you do something to it that it isn't accustomed to, the result can be a back muscle strain. It can happen to a football player doing pass blocking drills or a gymnast practicing one routine over and over. (Gymnastics puts your back into horrible positions, but its saving grace is that for women it involves four different activities, for men six. The variety of demands probably saves the day so far as even more frequent, and awful, back problems are concerned.) Dancers attempting a new or especially strenuous role are subject to back strains, particularly men whose shoulders and arms aren't strong enough for the demands of partnering. Often they have a tendency to muscle their partners up with their back, much like trying to lift too much weight in a gym.

Wrestlers strain their back by doing arches in an attempt to strengthen it. A tough aerobics class can do it, as can something as mundane as working too long on your tennis serve. At the top of your preparation, with your racquet all the way cocked, your back is hyperextended, a position it doesn't exactly savor. And when you think of all the ways of mistreating your back around the house—digging in the garden, moving furniture, mopping floors—it's easy to see how it doesn't take much in any athletic activity to push it over the edge.

What we think happens with a muscle strain is that you tear at least a few muscle fibers, which then bleed into the muscle. As muscles aren't used to encountering blood except in vessels, where it should be, the blood acts as an irritant, and the muscle scrunches up and goes into spasm. And these are big muscles, dense, long cords with a diameter of a good inch and a half or more. When they go into spasm, they *really* go into spasm. There is no muscle injury that is more debilitating.

They're going to stay that way, too, because they're trying to protect themselves. They don't want you to get in positions that might cause further injury, so they do their best to keep you from moving much at all. Very successfully, too. The muscle clamps down so hard it feels like a rock. You can often find the spot that really hurts, the trigger point where most of the damage has been done.

The strain doesn't have to be in your back, per se. It can show up in your neck as well. You might wake in the morning and, because you overstretched a muscle by sleeping in an awkward position, find that your ear is pressed to your shoulder and you can't do a thing about it. Or it can be the result of doing something the day before to your trapezius, the big shoulder-neck muscle, or another muscle in the area. With stiff necks the cause can be mysterious as often as not, but not so the result. The number of people walking around with hunched shoulders and heads tilted to one side attests to the frequency of this kind of strain.

What to do about it

The only way to deal with these things is to stretch out the afflicted muscle. You want to break up the muscle spasm as soon as possible, primarily for two reasons. One, of course, is pain and disability. So long as the muscles are in spasm, you're going to hurt, and you won't be able to do the things you like to do because your back will be tight as a knot. The other is that the longer the muscle remains in spasm, the harder it is to get it out of spasm, and the weaker it becomes. Which means that you'll be a long time working to restrengthen the muscles, and they'll be especially prone to reinjury in the meanwhile.

If there is anything good about a back strain, however, it may be that because it's so disabling, you're likely to get around to doing something about it more quickly than with strains elsewhere in the body. It's one thing limping around with a hamstring strain. It's another not being able to get around at all. So it's more likely that you won't allow the back muscles enough time for much weakness to develop, and re-strengthening the injured muscle might not be as daunting a task as it can be in other places. It's simply hard to ignore things that happen to your back.

So what to do: as elsewhere in the body where there's pain and perhaps swelling involved, aspirin can help, as can other anti-inflammatory drugs. Icing? Almost always the answer would be an unqualified yes. But the back is one area where there may be some legitimate disagreement about ice as opposed to heat. Usually you'd never want to apply heat to an injury that involves swelling, as heat tends to increase the blood supply, which increases swelling. Conversely, ice shuts down the blood vessels, helping to keep swelling to a minimum. If your injury occurred dramatically, suddenly, the pain appearing immediately, then icing is probably better, because you most likely tore quite a bit of muscle. In that case, you want to keep the bleeding down as much as possible, and since you can't really compress the back muscles, icing is the next best thing to do.

But if your back strain is similar to the one we described earlier, one that doesn't seem all that much at the time but only later clamps down and bends you out of shape, then it may be that getting into a nice, warm Jacuzzi or hot tub is just what you need, so long as you *do something* in that nice warm water other than play with your rubber ducky. Muscle strains demand an active effort if you're going to get over them. *Stretch* the muscle in the warm water. Take advantage of the wet warmth for something other than just comfort.

So ice if that feels best; use heat if that's the ticket. Go with what works, always remembering that you have to break up the spasm before the injury will get any better.

It's easy to stretch the back muscles. If your injured back bends you in one direction, then stretch in the other. For example, if your ear is glued to your right shoulder, then trying to put it on your left shoulder is the way to stretch that muscle. If you're stooped to the left side from back spasms, then bend over to the right. The way to do it is with long and slow stretches. These are the longest, slowest stretches for any muscles in the body. It may take you three or four minutes to get a decent stretch at first; be patient and stay with it. Once the spasm is broken, it will be easier the next time.

If the pain is in your lower back, there are a number of ways to stretch, all depending on how flexible you are and how much you hurt. One way is to curl up in a ball. Simply lie down, grab the back of your thighs, and very slowly curl up. Another is slowly to pull one leg at a time toward your chest. In both these exercises, bending your head and shoulders to meet your legs increases the stretch. If you hurt too much to be able to do these stretches, just lying on your back and bending your knees automatically tilts your pelvis, providing a gentle stretch. And an even more gentle method than that is simply to lie on your back with a firm pillow underneath your feet. Just raising your feet the thickness of a pillow helps to tilt your pelvis, providing some relief. Any of these simple movements will allow the spastic muscles a bit of relaxation.

Another way to stretch for people who are in such lower back pain that it hurts even to make contact with the floor, or a bed, is to lower

Back-Stretching Exercises

yourself slowly into a toe touch (or as close to a toe touch as you can manage). This kind of stretching can feel very good, because it takes no effort on your part. Gravity and the weight of your head and arms and upper torso gently pull you down. The problem is, however, that it can be hard to get out of that position. Gravity has stretched you out, but now you have to use your inflamed muscles to work against it to pull yourself back up. Don't. Simply bend at the knees, then straighten up. It won't hurt at all. Toe touches have been criticized as an exercise for people with back pain not because of bending down but because of the difficulty of having to get back up. Bending the knees makes all the difference.

Sometimes just pressing on the injured muscle for thirty or forty seconds will give it some reflex relaxation. And then you can stretch it. It's like a bit of mini-massage, self-acupressure. And you'll know where to press. A strained muscle will have a hot spot, a place that's hard as a rock, the bull's-eye of the whole area.

Sometimes just doing pelvic tilts or abdominal strengthening exercises can help back injuries, even the worst ones. Curl-ups might bring relief. Anything, so long as you're able to break up the muscle spasm, and the sooner the better. And then as soon as you're able, again go about your business. If your back or neck starts to tighten up, just flop down and do the stretches. (It can take some courage to roll into a ball on the office floor, but after all, what's more important, your image or your back?) At first you may have to stretch every ten minutes for the first two hours, then every twenty minutes, then thirty, and so on. In time, stretching before you go to bed, stretching when you get up in the morning, and stretching before and after any athletic acitivities will probably do the trick. And once you've learned what kind of exercises work for you, you have become in effect your own physician and exercise therapist. You can use the same approach the next time, and most likely prevent the frequency of next times. Again, if you get to doing back muscle stretches early, you're likely to save yourself untold grief and wasted time.

Strains account for probably three quarters of the back problems that we see, maybe more. Unaccustomed activity, unaccustomed positions, staying in one position too long, reaching for something too quickly, not being prepared for any particular movement—the causes of back strain are many, and the results are all too similar. Get on them quickly. But, again, although the muscles may be very uncomfortable, they *should not radiate pain or numbness or tingling, produce any weakness in the extremities, or become worse when you cough or sneeze or otherwise strain.* Those symptoms can indicate a serious problem. In that case, see someone right away.

STIFF NECK

It may be the most common problem of all, as prevalent in non-athletes as athletes. You need do nothing more than sleep in an awkward position to have a stiff neck (although you may legitimize it by having an athletic dream), or it can come from something very active, like practicing your serve for an hour after playing a couple of sets. All that looking up and over your shoulder can cause the muscles in your neck all sorts of fatigue, with the result that you wake up the next morning with your ear plastered to your serving shoulder.

What to do about it

The best remedy for a stiff neck is to stretch out the muscles so that they can't stay in spasm. Your neck goes in six directions: forward, chin on chest; backward, looking at the ceiling; to either side, ear to shoulder; and twisting, looking over your shoulders. So those are the directions to stretch, opposite from the way your neck is tilted. If you wake up looking over your right shoulder, stretch by turning to the left. If your ear is tilted toward your left shoulder, tilt to the right. All these motions should be long and slow.

You can contract-relax stretch your neck as well. Stretch, then push the other way against your own arm, then stretch some more. And isometric neck exercises are easy. Football players do them against each other; you can do them by yourself. Push your head and neck against the resistance of your arm.

CONTUSIONS

Contusions, or bruises, are the result of direct blows. The impact can cause blood vessels below the surface to rupture and bleed into the muscle—that's why the area becomes discolored and swollen. If the blow is strong enough, the muscles themselves can tear. And, as we've seen so often in this book, when muscles tear and are confronted with blood that isn't contained in vessels, they know how to do only one thing: contract violently and go into spasm. And when the muscles in the back go into spasm, you'll know it.

Back contusions usually involve football players who are struck by a helmet or knee. Sometimes they're the result of larger collisions—from inadvertently running into your tennis partner to serious contact sport things—and again football players are conspicuously among those who suffer this kind of injury. And contusions can be the result of bizarre accidents, such as Karen Bevis landing on the balance beam on her back.

At the worst these collisions can break things that are much better left unbroken. These can include the little bumps of the backbone that you can feel just under the skin, the spinous processes. They're little nubbins of bone, maybe an inch to an inch and a half long, that are used as muscle attachments. They're a long way from the spinal cord, so breaking one is not such a big deal. Breaking your back, per se, is awfully hard to do.

Not so breaking your neck, however. You can break your neck pretty easily if it's in the wrong position when you receive the blow. Diving into shallow water is probably the most common cause. Broken necks also show up in equestrian sports—being flipped off a horse and landing on your head—and just occasionally in wrestling. Trampolines produce more than their share of broken necks, from very skilled people using them for training—pole vaulters, high jumpers, gymnasts—to kids playing on them. (That's why you don't see many trampolines anymore.)

In football, if you take enough force your neck can break even though it isn't in an awkward position. All you have to do is hit somebody hard enough with your head and the vertebrae in the neck can literally explode. The results can be devastating because this relatively small section of the backbone doesn't protect the spinal cord as effectively as it does elsewhere. When these vertebrae break, the danger is that the spinal cord can tear or sever as well. At the worst such a tear can cause paralysis of the arms and legs—quadriplegia. Probably three quarters of the football injuries that have led to quadriplegia were not the result of the player having his head in an awkward position, but simply the fact that he hit somebody with his head.

Recently, it has become illegal to tackle with your head at the highschool and college level—just plain illegal in high school, illegal if done intentionally in college. You're supposed to be penalized for a head tackle, but as a rule the penalties are rarely called. Still, it's better than it used to be. There's been a decrease in the rate of quadriplegics in football, and it could probably be even lower if the rules were more stringently enforced. If nothing else, football coaches are pragmatists. The first time they had a couple of players thrown out of a game for hitting with their heads would be the last time. The technique would never be used again, intentionally or accidentally. But, as it is, we've made a start.

Interestingly enough, the reason there was an upsurge in quadriplegics for a time was that football players weren't suffering serious head injuries any longer. Helmets were improved to provide such good protection that head injuries became almost a thing of the past. Now you could use your helmet as a weapon because it no longer hurt your head when you made it a battering ram. Unfortunately, there's still a weak link between your helmeted head and padded shoulders: it's called the neck. And making your neck stronger has little to do with it all. The liability is not in the muscles but in the bones.

What to do about it

Treat contusions the same way you treat muscle strains. As with muscle strains, it's important to break up the muscle spasms as soon as possible and try to keep the bleeding, and therefore swelling, to a minimum. If you can apply ice to the injured area, fine. More effective still is stretching the muscle. Whichever way it hurts, that's the direction to stretch. Make the stretches long and slow. They not only break up the spasms, they help control swelling by compressing the muscles from within. (See the previous section for more detailed suggestions.) But if it's a severe contusion, with a lot of pain and swelling, it might be best to see someone.

If there's ever any possibility that someone might have suffered a neck injury—a person falls, say, and lands on his head or neck, and is unconscious or unable to move his arms or legs—assume the worst, a broken neck. It's very important that you not do anything except try to make the person comfortable, *keep him from moving,* and get help. Don't try to diagnose the problem, don't try to treat it, don't try to straighten his back or neck, don't remove his helmet or uniform—just get help. If it's raining, cover him up. If it's sunny and hot, supply some shade. Above all, *get help.*

DISK PROBLEMS

Everyone has heard of ruptured disks and slipped disks, but few people know what they mean or what disks really are. These days the word *disk* suggests nothing so much as a Frisbee, or perhaps a high-tech laser recording. The popular image of a spinal disk may be one of a hard, round, flat piece of bone or cartilage somehow wedged into the backbone, performing some obscure function, and ready at any moment to "rupture" or "slip" or otherwise bring about devastation and disaster.

Well, the shape is right—disks are disklike—but the consistency is wrong. Rather than being little round blocks, disks are more nearly like undersized jelly-filled Danishes (ones that have been left standing too long and have gotten a bit stale on the outside). The outside is tough, fibrous tissue; the inside is a watery, gelatinous material. As you bend your back, the disks act as cushions, spacing the vertebrae in the backbone and allowing them to twist and bend without bumping and scraping against each other. The jelly in the disk acts something like a kitchen sponge between plates—at rest the sponge holds the plates apart, but if you press them together it displaces to one side or another according to the pressure you exert.

As we grow older, this jelly loses some of its fluid, becoming stiffer and less effective as a shock absorber. And under the constant pressure exerted by the movement of the backbone it can begin to push against its fibrous outer surface. If there's a defect in the tissue, the surface will bulge out like a worn inner tube. Sometimes it can even fragment, a piece of disk breaking free. Thus, a ruptured, or slipped disk.

By itself the bulging or fragmenting isn't much of a problem, so long as it doesn't impinge against anything important. However, the backbone shelters something *very* important: the spinal cord. If the disk bulges toward the front of the body, you're safe. There's nothing there for it to interfere with. But if it presses back, or back and to the side, it will soon encounter the spinal cord (that is, if the disk is at the level of the first lumbar vertebra or higher—the spinal cord descends only that far) or press against nerve roots branching off from the cord. The spinal cord sends off two nerve roots at the level of each vertebra. Where it ends at the first lumbar vertebra, the cord then trails nerve roots, like the tail of a kite, into the four remaining lumbar vertebrae and then into the sacrum and coccyx, which form the "butterfly body" in the pelvis. Those roots continue to escape the backbone two by two and descend into the rest of the body, supplying all our sensations thence downward.

The nerve roots exit the body cage of the spinal column through little holes in the bone called foramina (pronounced "for-ay-mina"), which are hardly bigger than the nerves. If the disk protrudes in that direction, two things can happen: it can crimp the spinal cord or it can bulge into the foramina, squashing the nerve root against the bone. Either obstruction brings about a similar result, radiating pain and loss of nerve function. And when you move, stretching the nerve over the bulge in the disk, it hurts all the more. That's why one test for disk problems is straight-leg raising. If you raise your leg up and down and that causes pain from your foot to your back, it's likely that you're pulling the nerve back and forth over a protruding disk. Other tests look at strength and reflexes—heel and knee jerk, for example. If the nerve's ability to conduct impulses is in any way impaired, you'll lose your ability to function as usual. And if the problem is at a certain level in your lower back, the loss can even include bladder and bowel function. All this from an undersized jelly-filled Danish losing its shape and mucking up your electrical system.

What to do about it

See someone. Disk problems are not something you should ignore or try to manage yourself. The stakes are too high.

Treatments vary. Sometimes long periods of rest do the job, with the help of a corset or back brace to stabilize you in the meanwhile. Sometimes anti-inflammatory drugs can reduce the swelling of the disk enough to get rid of the pressure. A relatively new approach involves injecting the disk with a substance called chymopapain, which is derived from the papaya fruit. That may inhibit the swelling as well. Sometimes a disk problem comes to surgery, and even then the treatment can vary. The procedure is called a laminectomy, and it involves removing the part of the disk that's ruptured. Sometimes people remove the entire disk, sometimes fuse vertebrae together, but not as often as they used to. There's still a lot of controversy over the best way to manage disk problems.

But that controversy doesn't extend to your best course of action. If you're experiencing numbness, tingling, pain radiating into your extremities; if you have any weakness in your limbs, and bowel or bladder dysfunction; if your back hurts more when you squeeze, cough, or strain, then there's only one thing to do: *see someone* right away.

STRESS FRACTURES—SPONDYLOLYSIS

Stress fractures, those hairline breaks that are the result of overusing or misusing the bone rather than any one dramatic incident, show up in the backbone, too. Here they're called *spondylolysis* (pronounced "spon-de-lo-*lie*-sis)—literally, "vertebra loosening."

Spondylolysis occurs in the little knuckle-sized facet joints at the back of the spine, and most often in the low lumbar vertebrae, just before the backbone descends into the pelvis. The tip-off is usually pain when you arch your back. (Indeed, spondylolysis may be caused by overarching—more on that in a minute.) Dancers may feel pain in their up leg when they do an arabesque, or pain in their lower back on the up leg side. With this problem, any activity that demands arching the back may produce pain.

No one knows for certain just what causes spondylolysis, but there's an interesting piece of information to back up the suspicion that it's a result of overarching. High-level teenage girl gymnasts, who overarch as a matter of course—nowhere more obviously than when posing after dismounting an apparatus—suffer from spondylolysis *four times* as frequently as female nongymnasts their age. It may be that football linemen, who tend to overarch when they come out of the down position to block, suffer it more frequently than other people, and ballet dancers most certainly do. At least 10 percent of the San Francisco Ballet company has spondylolysis. And it well may be more common in figure skaters, too.

So perhaps it's not only overarching that causes spondylolysis. In ballet and figure skating you don't arch that much, as having your back swayed and tail sticking out in these activities is not considered aesthetically desirable. It may be jumping that does it, or simply the constant pounding the lower back undergoes in these kinds of demanding activities. There's obviously something more to it than we yet understand.

Some people think that tight hamstrings or tight hip flexor muscles may be the culprit. And it's true that usually, among not-so-serious athletes, anyway, tight hamstrings will show up in association with spondylolysis. But it's hard to know which is the chicken and which is the egg. It may be that tight muscles are the result, rather than the cause, of the problem.

And it may be that the older you are, the less likely it is that you'll have to do anything more about spondylolysis than read this section. Most of the bone-scan evidence of the problem is in young people, teens and upward. When it shows up in adults it most likely has been there for some time and is surfacing because of some recent change in activity. But again, we're just not sure.

What to do about it

It depends how much it hurts. If your back doesn't bother you a lot, then there's no reason to do much of anything except be careful with it. And you certainly should spend some time working on straightening your backbone—pelvic tilts, curl-ups—because the more you arch your back, the worse the problem will be.

If it does hurt, see someone. The important thing here is to have the problem diagnosed correctly. For even though it may not be absolutely killing you now, like any stress fracture it will get you later if you don't treat it effectively. And that treatment involves staying away from activities that hurt. Again, the barometer is pain.

The good news is that in a third of the cases the bone will heal as a result of nothing more than keeping the area pain-free for a length of time. The bad news is that the time required can be as long as six months. For most of us, that might be an inconvenience; for a young person seriously involved in an activity, a six-month layoff can mean a twelve-month departure from meaningful competition or performing. And that can mean a devastating gap in a budding career, if not the end of it.

So spondylolysis is one of those problems that may be no problem for some of us, an inconvenience for most of us, and a serious blow for the rest of us. As a general rule, once you stop the activity that provoked the problem, it disappears (even though a bone scan may say differently). The difficulty is getting along without your favorite activity. And it may not carry any horrible long-term implications. Although people with spondylolysis likely will have more frequent back complaints through the years than people without, the likelihood of their undergoing surgery or experiencing other major disruptions is very small.

And again, it is one of those problems that respond well to using the backbone as it was designed to be used. Straighten your backbone and strengthen your abdominal muscles.

SPONDYLOLISTHESIS

One thing that can happen to people with stress fractures (but rarely athletes) is that the crack can become so pronounced as to sever the facet joint and, if you have breaks on both sides of the spine, cause one vertebra actually to slip forward on another. The word *spondylolisthesis* (pronounced "spon-de-lo-*liss*-thesis") means "vertebra shift," and that's exactly what happens. In the worst cases, the vertebra can slide forward as much as an inch and a half. That's a long, long way when you're talking about a space as confined as that of the backbone.

Fortunately, this shifting tends to occur in the lower vertebrae, below the level of the spinal cord, so there's little danger of a wayward vertebra pinching or chopping the cord in two. At these lower levels there are only nerve roots, and they float inside the spinal column, with more than enough room. So you rarely see any disastrous problems with spondylolisthesis, and rarely does the slip ever come all at once. It tends rather to slip up on you over a long period of time.

What to do about it

Again, the tip-off is lower back pain, and again it's *how much* that counts. With spondylolisthesis, it probably will hurt enough to motivate you to see someone. In the milder cases, the treatment can be rest, perhaps some kind of body brace. If it's really bad, it may require surgical fusion so it can't slip any farther.

SCOLIOSIS

Gulp! It's one of those words that strike fear in the heart.

"What are they testing us for?" asks one schoolgirl to another.

"Scoliosis," comes the reply.

"I'm glad I don't have *that*," says a third girl. "It's horrible. It means you have to wear a brace for the rest of your life, and you can't run or dance or do *anything*."

"That's right," a couple of others join in, "it ruins your life."

Well, what would these girls say if they knew that the odds are pretty good that one of them already has some degree of scoliosis, that she hasn't been bothered by it yet and most likely never will be, and, were it not for the test she is about to undergo, would never even know she had it? It's that common and in most cases that insignificant.

The word *scoliosis* literally means "a curve," and it denotes just that in the backbone, but a curve in a distinct direction—laterally, or side to side. Whereas the backbone is designed to curve front to back, it isn't supposed to curve side to side—that is, not stay that way. And with scoliosis you never get just one lateral curve. Your body will not tolerate your spine's bending in just one direction. It will figure out a way to keep your skull centered over your pelvis and that usually means that your spine will make another curve in the opposite direction from the first one, either above or below it, or both. So although your head stays perfectly aligned over your hips, all sorts of interesting things may be going on in between.

Scoliosis curves are not just side to side, however. Usually they also have some rotation, and it's the rotation that testers look for in school-kids. They have the kids bend over, and they sight along their backs. If one side of the back is higher than the other, then it's likely the kid has scoliosis. And they'll find it in quite a few of them. It's a disease of teenage girls. More than one girl in ten has some degree of it. Why, no one knows. In fact the most common kind is called *idiopathic* scoliosis, which means that we don't know what causes it.

In the worst cases the curve can be severe to the point of deformity. It can get so bad that it can actually collapse a lung and part of the chest. And those cases may, indeed, have to be treated with braces and even surgery. But most of the time the curvature is so mild as to be almost unnoticeable and certainly not disabling. There are people dancing professionally who have significant scoliosis. Professional skaters have it, as do top-level gymnasts. Frequently women will notice it when they try on slacks, say, and one hip is more prominent than the other. Or when one breast is higher than the other. Women forty years old may notice it for the first time, but it's never bothered them before and probably never will.

You can get temporary scoliosis from muscle spasms in your back. When one of the big ropes of muscles on either side of your spine goes into spasm, it will pull the spine to one side just like a bow. So one of the offshoots of the kinds of back injuries we've been discussing can be scoliosis.

What to do about it

In the case of temporary, muscle injury-caused scoliosis, do those things we've suggested to treat the muscle injury. Or, if it's severe enough, see someone.

In the case of idiopathic scoliosis, you probably won't even know you have it unless someone calls your attention to it, perhaps during a physical exam. In that case you're already with a doctor, and it's a good bet that there's nothing much to do about it, anyway. For more pro-nounced cases, see someone for sure. There are new treatments that may preclude the necessity of bracing or surgery. One of these is applying an electrical charge at night to the muscles on the other side of the curve. The charge stimulates the muscles, causing them to contract and pull the spine back to normal. The technique shows promise if applied early enough.

And, contrary to what may be the popular perception of scoliosis, it's good for people with the problem to stay active. The story of one teenage girl is a case in point, albeit an ironic one. An equestrian, she didn't let the fact that she had to wear a brace get in the way of practicing or competing. Until the time when the judges forced her to remove it during a competition. Why? Because they felt it gave her an unfair advantage: it enabled her to sit her horse with a straighter back than the other contestants.

OSTEOPOROSIS

It's in the news these days, a loss of bone strength affecting primarily postmenopausal women. In these women it shows up as a tendency to become stooped and round-shouldered, and it can lead to recurrent backaches. It's the result of hormonal changes and can, in extreme cases, actually lead to a collapsed spine because of increasingly soft bone. What isn't as well known is that some of the same problems are beginning to show up in young high-level female athletes, whether menstruating or nonmenstruating, almost like a kind of youthful menopause. The tip-off here is recurrent stress fractures.

What to do about it

See someone. Often women who suffer from osteoporosis are calcium-deficient. If you're a serious female athlete, it may be a good idea to supplement your diet with a multivitamin and additional calcium and iron. (A little extra iron won't hurt—most people use Teflon-coated pots and pans, so we don't get iron from cooking utensils anymore.) A cheap and readily available source of extra calcium is—are you ready?—Tums antacid tablets. Two Tums a day provide the right dosage of calcium in easily absorbable form. (Might settle your stomach, too.)

SCHEUERMAN'S DISEASE

How many parents are constantly nagging at how many teenagers— usually male—to stand up straight? Uncountable legions. Well, some of those gooselike necks and rounded shoulders actually may be, as he insists, beyond the beleaguered kid's control. They could be a result of Scheuerman's disease. It's an odd malady affecting the growth centers in the vertebrae. It is in these areas that new bone is formed, which then pushes out to lengthen and thicken the existing bone. In this case, however, the growth centers fragment and produce wedge-shaped vertebrae rather than squarish building blocks. As the wedge shape increases over time, the backbone curves forward, the shoulders round, the neck sticks out, and parents start complaining.

What to do about it

See someone. It can be diagnosed by X-ray, and there are little things that can be done. Sometimes a brace can help things. But it's a rare problem. There are infinitely more parents telling kids to straighten up than there are kids with Scheuerman's disease. No matter how appealing it may be to parents to have the medical profession on their side, most of the teenagers who slump don't have back problems, don't need a brace, and probably don't need to see a doctor.

Back Injuries in General

You can deal with a vast majority of back problems yourself, *if you catch them early.* Again, it comes back to the old business of *being aware* of what's going on in your body and, rather than ignoring it, *doing something about it.* Your approach should be two-pronged:

1. Figure out what's caused the problem. It may be easy to do. Your neck might be stiff, say, because you've been practicing serves more than usual, and the constant looking up and over your shoulder has overworked the muscles. Or it may be a tough task, worthy of a medical detective (and here's an area in which seeing somebody can produce real benefits), all because of the body's delightful predilection, much discussed in these pages, of being everywhere connected to everything else.

Your lower back is killing you, say. So much so that the muscles on one side have gone into spasm, and you're walking around like a human question mark. Why? You haven't done anything to your back. In fact, you're always respectful of your back; you wouldn't do anything to upset it. Ah, but two months ago, while running barefoot on the beach, you stepped on a rock that bruised your heel so badly that you've hardly been able to walk normally since. In fact, you've been limping, tiptoeing around on that leg while walking normally on the other. Could that have something to do with your back problem?

Yes, indeed it could. In order to protect your bruise, you went up on your toe, which caused one side of your pelvis to tilt up, as though you were walking with one foot up on a curb. That threw your backbone off kilter, overworking the muscles on one side. But your body won't tolerate an off-kilter backbone for too long; it likes to keep your head centered over your hips, and the only way to do that is to pull the upper part of the backbone around to compensate for the lower part's being askew. So the back muscles clamp down, twisting your back in a way it's not meant to be twisted, and you not only hurt in the lower back, you hurt just about everywhere, and can't stand up straight besides. All that from a stone bruise a good four feet from the spot that hurts now. And no matter what you do to your back to alleviate the pain, until you straighten your gait the problem simply won't go away. You have to find out the cause of things.

2. Stretch and strengthen the muscles involved. The way to stretch is to move in the direction that hurts—that is, the opposite direction to that in which you're being pulled. If you're twisted to the left, turn to the right. If your chin is down on your chest, look up to the sky. If you're bent over at the waist, lean back. It may be that curling into a ball helps alleviate your low back pain, or maybe bending down to touch your toes will help. And all these stretches should be long and slow. If you can manage only a few inches at first, be not daunted. Keep at it, and your flexibility will increase as your pain decreases.

And try curl-ups right away. Few people have strong-enough stomach muscles, so the curl-ups can do nothing but help you. Remember to do them right. The key is to keep your back flat. Have a friend periodically slide a hand under the small of your back as you're learning. If there's room for a hand, your back is arched and you're not doing the exercise correctly.

Then, when you're no longer hurting too much, ease back into your activity. Go slowly at first, then gradually build up steam. Continuing to stretch and strengthen the back and stomach muscles will go a long way toward preventing the same problem from happening again. But if it should recur, or something similar happens, then attack it as you did this time. The sooner you get to back problems, the better.

And once more, for good measure: *if your back pain radiates into your arms or legs; if you feel any numbness or tingling in your arms or legs; if you notice any sudden weakness in your arms or legs; if coughing, sneezing, or other straining makes your back pain worse—see someone.*

Commonly Asked Questions About Back Injuries

What about home exercise equipment? Is it safe to use?

Yes, if used correctly. But it's a big "if." After spending that much money on equipment, the tendency is to go home and see what you can do. After all, an investment like this should produce tangible results, and quickly, right? So you hit it hard, too hard, piling too much weight on top of too much weight, checking the scales and making the measurements as you go. And if they're not what you're looking for, you hit it even harder. All with no supervision, no one to remind you that in all likelihood, as you pile the weights high, you're committing the cardinal sin in lifting: arching your back.

Supervision is a problem at fitness facilities as well. In the best of circumstances it's not easy for a few staff people to keep track of the crush of bodies in the weight room, and often those staff people, dependent as they are on commissions for attracting new members, are busy giving tours, answering questions, and making juice drinks rather than advising members on their lifting technique. But at least at fitness facilities there *are* people around—at home there's no one. And often at home there's no mirror to help you keep track of yourself. As a result, the risk of back problems is greater at home.

A rule of thumb: *if you can't lift without arching your back, drop back to a weight you can handle with your back flat*. Press the small of your back into the backrest, and make sure it's there for the duration of the exercise. Remind yourself to *feel* your back against the support. Go on to a heavier weight only when you can handle it with a flat back.

It's not how fast you proceed from level to level that counts, but whether you're doing the exercise correctly. And perhaps one advantage of home equipment is that there's no outside pressure motivating you to progress too quickly. If you're secure at home, with no brute next to you lifting fifty pounds more than you did, or spared from the embarrassment of someone half your size doubling the weight on the machine you just vacated, then maybe you can relax and go at your own pace. Whew! What a relief. Just remember to keep your back straight.

When I stretch my back by flexing forward or rolling into a ball, it hurts. Is there another approach that might work better for me?

We've found that perhaps as many as 15 percent of the people we see get more relief from extension exercises than flexion exercises. Another name for extension exercises might be press-up exercises, or controlled arching. If you lie on the floor, flat on your stomach, and slowly arch your back by pressing up with your arms, you're doing extension exercises. Although these exercises actually contract the back muscles rather than stretch them (they do stretch the abdominal muscles, although not very well), they open up the front of the disk space between vertebrae in your backbone, allowing the gelatinous center of the disk to shift into a different configuration from that which it's used to. At least, such is the logic behind the exercises.

Whatever the reasons, the approach does work for some people. If you're one of those people, you should learn the techniques from a physical therapist rather than experimenting at home. The key here is *controlled* arching. With all the problems that might be caused by overarching your back, you don't want to run the risk of overarching on purpose.

If I have a weak back, how do I make my back stronger?

By making your stomach muscles stronger. For the most part back muscles are pretty strong. They may be too tight, and stretching them might be in order, but because we constantly use them for everything from lifting to bending and twisting to just holding us upright, our back muscles rarely need much extra strengthening. It's the stomach muscles that often aren't doing their job to stabilize your back. Try curl-ups. Abdominal stretching is like drinking water—it's good for everybody.

What activities are dangerous for my back?

Whenever you can't quite handle an activity, you wind up using your back wrong. It's very interesting—if something's too heavy to lift, you misuse your back lifting it. If your shoulders aren't flexible enough to twist around and hit a serve, your back bends to compensate. If your hip muscles cramp and tilt your pelvis, your back suffers the displacement. If you wrench your knee and limp around too long, your back eventually will go into spasm. If you're not strong enough, you use your back, and if you're not flexible enough, you use your back—never correctly. The poor old back takes it in the seat of the pants whenever something's wrong elsewhere.

So the most dangerous activity for the back is *doing any activity incorrectly.* Get the rest of your body in shape, and your back will stay in shape.

When are my back problems bad enough to go to the doctor?

Three tip-offs:

1. When it hurts so bad that you can't sleep. If you don't get a good night's sleep, you'll never get better. You need a window of comfort in the midst of your misery to make any improvement. Often a doctor can provide that.

2. When you've tried these home remedies for a few days and things aren't getting better, or they're getting worse. That's a tip-off that either your approach is not the right one or the problem is too difficult to handle on your own.

3. When you experience any of these warning signs: (a) The pain is not just in your back or neck, but radiates into other parts of your body. (b) You have numbness or tingling in your arms or legs. (c) You notice sudden weakness in your arms or legs. (d) Coughing, sneezing, or other straining makes the pain worse. See someone.

8 The Shoulder

wo years ago Harriett Burnette was racing her friends down the mountain on the last run of the day. It was beginning to snow, the surface was icy, and Harriett was tired. The trail was narrow, bounded by the mountain to the left and a steep drop to the right. Harriett was bringing up the rear.

Suddenly she caught an edge on a patch of ice and instantly knew that she had two options: if she recovered to the right, she risked plunging off the trail and down the mountain. If she recovered to the left, she would stay on the mountain but would crash full force into the side of the hill. She chose left and took the impact on the point of her left shoulder.

The first-aid people at the ski lodge decided that the shoulder was not dislocated and advised her to go either to an emergency room or home to her own doctor. Harriett decided to go home. By the time she got there, her shoulder had stiffened to the point where she couldn't move it at all. So she went to an immediate-care facility. The people there X-rayed the shoulder, decided nothing was broken, put Harriett's arm in a sling, and told her to go home. It would be fine in a couple of weeks, they said. If not, go see an orthopedic surgeon.

So Harriett waited a couple of weeks. Nothing changed. The shoulder still hurt, still was stiff, still kept her from straightening her back, moving her arm, doing much of anything at all. Eventually she made an appointment to see an orthopedic surgeon.

The doctor thought that maybe she had a hairline fracture that so far had been missed. He took X-rays. Nothing. Finally he suggested a couple of exercises to loosen the joint and sent Harriett on her way. The exercises didn't work. When Harriett returned to him, he started talking about cortisone shots.

Meanwhile, Harriett had started to ski again—if being unable to straighten your back, swing your arm through a full range of motion, and move without pain allows for much skiing. And now her elbow had started to hurt as well. While on the slopes, a medic at the ski facility advised her not to let anyone give her cortisone or anything like it unless it was a last resort. He suggested that she see a sports medicine doctor.

So, six months after the original injury, Harriett came to the Center for Sports Medicine. Garrick's conclusion was that she had separated her shoulder slightly in the initial ski accident and that the elbow problem was the result of a pinched nerve in her shoulder, a consequence of the abnormal, scrunched way Harriett had been holding herself since the fall. (The injury is called thoracic outlet syndrome; it's discussed later in this chapter.) And her problem was compounded by the fact that in the months since the injury her shoulder muscles had wasted away from lack of use. Garrick suggested that she begin a stretching and strengthening program to rehabilitate the joint. Daily sessions were set up with a physical therapist at the Center, and Harriett began to improve rapidly.

Finis. Happy ending. Soon Harriett is back to normal, skiing better than ever before and even stronger because of the exercise therapy. But not quite.

"I was doing great," she says. "I was coming in for therapy every morning. My goal was to get back in shape by the end of the ski season. I was working so hard, and we could see marked improvement. And that night I fell, and it started all over again."

A reporter for a San Francisco newspaper, Harriett had just finished an interview on a dark January afternoon. On the way out of the building to her car, she slipped on an unlit stairway. The impact of the fall traveled up her outstretched arm and crashed into her left shoulder. And so, a year after her initial injury, six months since she had begun to rehabilitate the joint, Harriett found herself right back where she had started.

Now Harriett stands in the examining room and demonstrates her hard-earned mobility, the result of *another* full year of rehabilitation therapy.

"Well, you know, your shoulder motion is much cleaner," Garrick says.

"I know." Harriett grins. "I'm standing up straighter, not cheating. I'm going skiing this weekend." She laughs. "I already went last weekend. I did fine. And I didn't fall."

But today she has developed a hard knot in her upper trapezius muscle, probably from an overzealous use of weights in an exercise and posture class she's taking. The rigid muscle prevents her from turning her head to the side or even straightening her shoulder.

"The reason it's so sore is that a portion of the muscle is in spasm," Garrick explains. "If we could figure out a way to selectively stretch that area, that would help. That's the first thing. The second thing is that weights are not a bad idea, but two pounds may have been too much. So try going through that whole series of exercises with no weights to start—just the weight of your arm can be plenty. Then work up to one-pound weights and see how it goes. Let's go over to the therapy room to get rid of the knot in your traps."

And so it goes. You give a little, you take a little—life is a series of compromises. Nowhere is the maxim more evident than in the shoulder. While not exactly typical—two years of struggling to regain strength and mobility is not necessarily the norm—Harriett's experience is a testament to the delicate, complicated, interrelated nature of the shoulder. No joint can do so much, but no joint so constantly flirts with disaster.

To wit: the shoulder is the most flexible joint in the body. We can rotate our arm in a full circle. We can throw a baseball or football, serve a tennis ball, swim the freestyle. We can do a 360 on the sidehorse, lift a ballet partner, scoop a basketball from the floor and dunk it far overhead (a few of us can, anyway). What's more (and absolutely vital to athletics), we can navigate this huge range of motion with power. The shoulder is able to back up its extraordinary mobility with a lot of muscle.

People who hurt their shoulder and find their arm in a sling—or, worse yet, who don't restrain the joint and try to go ahead and do all the things they usually do—quickly discover how limited and frustrating life can be without a properly functioning shoulder. And not just in athletics. Think of combing your hair, tying your shoelaces, driving your car, brushing your teeth, turning the pages of this book—all the inconsequential daily movements we take for granted—without the freedom and strength provided by the shoulder. Unfortunately, there are many people in this boat. For the trade-off the shoulder must make for all its flexibility is in the realm of stability. The shoulder is at once the most mobile and least stable of all the joints in the body. Not only that, what stability it does have is maintained only by constant vigilance on the body's part.

To explain: the knee is not the most stable joint in the world. As we've seen, it too must make a compromise between flexibility and stability. But what stability it does have is reasonably constant, provided by its elaborate network of ligaments, all seven of them. The joint capsule, too, provides some firmness, as do the muscles and tendons—sometimes they even step in and take over for the ligaments. But the knee is held together primarily by the ligaments, guy wires that are there first and always to provide support.

The hip, on the other hand (or on the other joint, perhaps we should say) is very stable. If you had no ligaments, muscles, tendons, joint capsule, or anything else surrounding the hip joint, it would still hold together very nicely, thank you. With its ball in its deep cup of a socket, the hip is *mechanically* set up to stay in one piece until the cows come home. It's a simple, direct, efficient design (which is why hip replacements are more effective than those of other joints).

Now to the shoulder. In its defense we must repeat that neither the hip, nor the knee, nor any other joint can come close to the flexibility the shoulder offers. But not only doesn't the shoulder offer the mechanical stability of a deep ball and socket, not only doesn't it offer the guy wire stability of an elaborate network of ligaments, but it offers no stability at all except for that provided by the constant interrelated (that word, again) tension of the muscles and tendons crisscrossing the area. If something drastic should happen to these muscles and tendons, if some evil sorcerer should come and cut them in two, your shoulder would simply fall apart. And were your shoulder muscles to completely relax, as they do under anesthesia or in deep sleep, and somebody gave your arm a sharp pull, the joint would come apart just as easily.

Those are unlikely incidents, of course, evoked here to make a point. But as it is, in real life, the shoulder *does* fall apart—that is, dislocate—more frequently than any other major joint. The injury is common in contact sports. Even more frequent are less dramatic injuries to the muscles and tendons, which must constantly work, even when you're not moving your shoulder, just to keep things together. Strains, tendinitis, inflammations of one kind and another—these sneaky kinds of problems often attack the shoulder. And when they do, they can be particularly debilitating because a healthy shoulder is so important in everyday activities, not to mention athletic ones. If your knee is in a splint, you may not be able to go off on your run, but you can get around well enough to function day-to-day anyhow. But if your shoulder is out of commission, there goes not only the tennis game, the swim, and the run too (all that jarring readily transmits its way up to the shoulder), but day-to-day tasks as simple and necessary as opening a door or lifting a cup to your mouth or buttoning your shirt.

Yet the shoulder joint, like the hip, *is* a ball-and-socket assembly. Why then doesn't it hold together as well as the hip? The answer is that there are balls and sockets and balls and sockets. An analogy for the hip joint might be a tennis ball stuffed into a teacup so firmly that it can turn but not pull free. The shoulder's ball and socket, on the other hand, is more nearly like a racquetball resting against a tiny saucer. The ball is the end of the upper arm bone, the humerus. The saucer is part of your shoulder blade, or scapula. And the ball rests against, rather than on, the saucer, because the saucer is no more than a vertical depression in the shoulder blade. Besides that, the saucer is much too small and shallow to provide the ball any support; but at the same time its very size and shallowness allow the ball to swivel and turn almost limitlessly. The design problem is how to secure the ball to the saucer—it's vertical, after all, so gravity hinders rather than helps— and still allow such range of motion.

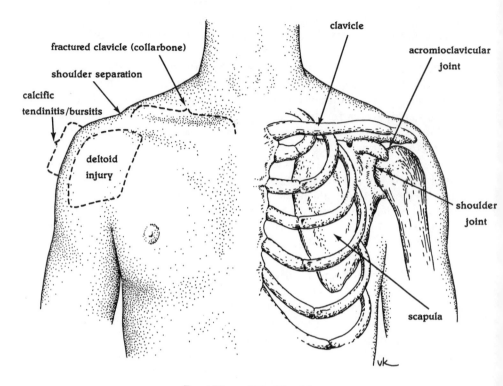

Front View of the Shoulder

The body's solution is to run muscles and tendons across the joint, as though securing a group of wires to the ball and the edge of the saucer. When the wires are suitably tight, the ball remains in the center of the saucer, where it should be. But if any one of the wires should come loose or break or, conversely, tighten too much, the ball tends to move away from the center of the saucer; and there's so little of it that the ball may even tip off the edge.

So a constant interrelated tension among the muscles and tendons acting as guy wires for the shoulder joint is absolutely essential. Otherwise, the ball will not remain in the center of the socket. It doesn't need to, really, when your arm is hanging to the side. But once you raise your arm and move it through all the loops the shoulder is capable of, the joint simply will not function effectively if the ball and saucer are not aligned as they should be. The mis-centered ball explores new ground, runs into things it should stay clear of. The result: pain.

One of those things it may run into is another part of the shoulder, the acromion. A combination of two words meaning "tip of the shoulder," the acromion is just that, a bony shelf that juts up from the shoulder blade to provide a kind of protective roof over the shoulder joint (and connects to the collarbone, or clavicle, at a small joint called the acromioclavicular, or AC joint). It was the AC joint that Harriett injured. (See "Shoulder separation" later in this chapter.)

And now comes an even more curious tale. First, to backtrack: "The hipbone's connected to the thighbone, the thighbone's connected to the kneebone"—all the other joints are secured to the body by bony attachments. The hip joint is part of the pelvis, which is itself part of the backbone really. The knee connects to the femur above and the tibia below. The ankle connects the lower leg bones to the bones in the foot. And so it goes, all solid, substantial connections. But in the shoulder, bless it, the only bony attachment to the rest of the body is through a bone, the collarbone, that's not much bigger around than your index finger and connects to the shoulder through a little joint—the AC joint—about the size of your fingernail. The entire remaining shoulder assembly—the shoulder blade with its bony ridge (which includes the acromion) and the ball-and-saucer shoulder joint itself, and thus your whole arm—is attached to the rest of your body by muscles only. As you move your arm and shoulder, the whole shebang—shoulder joint, shoulder blade, collarbone and all—moves up and down, back and forth along your chest wall.

That makes for super-flexibility, but it must be apparent by now that it can also make for problems. If you're not in very good shape, or if some of the individual muscles involved aren't in very good shape, or if the *relationship* among those muscles is out of kilter, then the shoulder can't twist and turn and move and slide as it must if you're going to do all the things you like to do. These can be subtle discrepancies, minor things that by themselves in another context might not even be noticeable, but that when functioning in concert with the rest of the shoulder's complex interrelationships can throw things decidedly out of tune. And that's not to mention acute incidents, sudden dramatic injuries that can produce the kind of well-known problems associated with the shoulder—for example, broken collarbones and shoulder dislocations.

So there's no other place in the body where rehabilitation is more important than in the shoulder. You can brace your knee and tape your ankle or fingers and still function—people do it all the time. Professional athletes often brace and tape themselves for extra support even if they're not injured. But you can't brace your shoulder, not if you want to be able to move it. With the shoulder you're really stuck with the consequences of injury. As debilitating as injuries in the rest of the body can be, in the shoulder they can *really* change your life. It pays to try to head off these things before they happen by being good to this particular joint.

Overuse Shoulder Problems—Tip-offs to Trouble

A very nice thing about the shoulder is that usually it gives you ample time to head off problems before they head you off. It'll give you little hints that something is up, and if you act on those hints—slow down, start rehabilitating *before* the problem gets out of control—you can often subvert the process before it fairly gets started.

There are two good tip-offs as to the general health of your shoulder. One involves the deltoid, that thick triangle of muscle that slopes over the shoulder into your upper arm. It's responsible for raising your arm away from your body. If you do just that and feel the now-contracted deltoid sitting atop your shoulder, which is, or should be, firm to the touch, you'll notice that the muscle separates into three leaves. The forward one, that little bump right in the front of your shoulder, is called the anterior deltoid and is probably the key to what's going on inside the whole shoulder assembly. The trick is to compare it to its sister in your other shoulder. A good way to do that is to face a mirror and hold your arms up in front of you. If the deltoid on one side is smaller than the one on the other side, or if it twitches when you use it and the other side doesn't, or if it has a ropier, more linear feel to it, then it's a good bet that something is going on in your shoulder that's not up to snuff. The size of the muscle is the most important indicator. It's just that you can't see most of the other muscles in your shoulder to be able to check them, and this leaf of the deltoid is particularly sensitive to changes and problems. So if your anterior deltoid fits any of these descriptions, it might be a good idea to start doing some of the exercises we'll discuss in a moment.

The other prime indicator of shoulder problems is how you use your shoulder. If, while raising your arms to the side, you hunch your shoulder toward your ear, or tuck it forward toward your chest, or degrees of both at the same time, then there's almost certainly some problem you're trying to compensate for. The mechanism works this way:

Usually the first thing that goes when you start having shoulder problems is the ability to bring your arm up from the side comfortably. The shoulder joint itself is involved in this motion only for the first 85 degrees or so—that's all the flexibility you have there. For the remaining 100 degrees or more that your arm can normally navigate, you're dependent on movement from the rest of your shoulder assembly. And move it does. Your shoulder blade slides up a good three or four inches as you continue to raise your arm. You can watch this process unfold in the mirror. Put your hand on top of your shoulder as you raise your arm and feel those relationships. They don't change. Every time you raise your arm, your shoulder girdle, as it's called, will start to move as your arm comes straight out from your body. You can see your shoulder blade, and the rest of the assembly, slide up as you continue to raise your arm.

That is, your shoulder blade *should* start to slide when your arm is at right angles to your body. But if something is amiss around the joint itself, something that restricts movement in the ball and saucer, your shoulder girdle will be obliged to start its motion earlier. The result of that premature motion is actually less shoulder mobility. Because the shoulder girdle has begun to move too early, by the time you raise your arm to the point at which your shoulder blade should start sliding, it may already be halfway to your ear. And by the time your arm lifts to the point that would normally cause the shoulder girdle to be halfway to your ear, it may be wedged up against the top of your neck. And that means no more movement. Your arm may only be three quarters of the way to its destination, but that's it. It will go no farther.

You can get away with partial shoulder mobility in some activities, but not those in which line is important, such as dance, gymnastics, or figure skating. There it's important to keep the shoulders relaxed and down. Any hunching at all is immediately apparent. Not only does it look bad, destroying your form, it reduces arm movement and can throw your head out of line as well.

So early movement of the shoulder girdle is a tip-off that there may be an injury around the joint area. And soon the injury may become so ingrained that you start carrying your shoulder hunched up all the time. You won't need to raise your arm to discover the problem. A quick peek in the mirror will suffice, especially if you see one shoulder where it should be and the other all the way up to your neck.

Another warning sign can be the habit of rolling your bad shoulder to the front, kind of tucking it into your chest. The muscles in the front of your shoulder are stronger than those in the back. When you think about it, that's obvious—look at the difference in size between the chest muscles and those that surround the shoulder blade in the back. Weight lifters walk around with their shoulders rolled forward and in because their chest muscles, strong to begin with, have become even stronger through training and pull the shoulder forward. You may not be a weight lifter, but if there's an imbalance between your chest and back muscles—and there often is—the chest muscles can become overly tight and pull your shoulder forward.

Again, a quick look in the mirror can tell you a lot. The key is to compare one side with the other. A bad shoulder not only has a tendency to hunch up, it rolls in, too. And, of course, it goes without saying that sooner or later these tip-offs will be accompanied by pain. If you're like most people, and don't make it a practice to conduct regular exploratory examinations of yourself, then it's likely that you won't look for tip-offs until pain and stiffness finally motivate you to do something. By then the tip-offs are largely superfluous. You've got a shoulder problem, all right.

What to do about it

The first thing is to get rid of the pain. Don't make the mistake that many of us make all the time, that of deciding that whatever it is that's bothering you will surely go away by itself. And then the next day, when it's still there, you decide that just one more day will clear it up, and so on and so on. Until a couple of weeks or a month later it's no longer just a minor ache, it's a major injury. Get on shoulder problems promptly. If you're hurting for a couple of days straight, come to grips with it. Knock off the serve or whatever it is that's bothering you until your shoulder is again comfortable. Just doing that, and the exercises we're about to suggest, may be all you need.

If you let things go on too long, the plot thickens. Then knocking off for a while may bring you some comfort, but when you go back to your activity it'll take less to bring back the symptoms than it did to develop them in the first place. Because by now your shoulder won't be in as good shape as it was in the first place. The muscles will have weakened and lost the ability to work together efficiently during the weeks you compensated for the pain so as to be able to continue playing.

And now it may not be so easy to get rid of the pain, either. You may find that what was once isolated to a particular activity—like serving a tennis ball—now shows up almost all the time. Everything you do hurts. To try to escape the pain you use your shoulder abnormally all day, not just when you're playing tennis. That's no good, not only for comfort's sake, but for your ability to get rid of the problem. It's hard enough to rehabilitate other places in your body when you're hurting—it's almost impossible with the shoulder. It's just that if everything you do is going to hurt, including rehabilitation exercises, you'll continue to use your shoulder abnormally even when you do the exercises. And that'll nullify any gains you get from rehabilitation. So it's important to deal with shoulder problems right away.

Again, the first step is to stop doing the things that hurt. Sometimes, especially if the problem is well along, that means doing absolutely nothing that involves your shoulder. That can be pretty hard to manage, unless you put your arm in a sling. As cumbersome as that might be, it can be worth it. It's not that a sling will absolutely immobilize your shoulder—almost nothing will do that but a body cast—but it'll force you to think about what you're doing. Instead of automatically shooting out your arm to open a door, or shake hands, or reach for the check, you'll have to think twice and use the other arm. Aspirin or other anti-inflammatory drugs can help during this period as well. Just don't cheat on yourself. Let the shoulder rest.

The next order of business is to rebalance and restrengthen the shoulder muscles. It can be hard to pinpoint, but the likelihood is that the crucial interrelated tension among the muscles in your shoulder has been thrown out of kilter. When these muscles don't work well, your shoulder doesn't work well. Without the consistent tension of these guy wires, the ball in your shoulder joint may no longer be centered in the saucer. When you move your arm, the ball rolls around and bumps into things it shouldn't. (Interestingly, if you use a weight or rehabilitation machine, something that forces your shoulder to stay in a perfect arc of motion, you may have no pain at all. It's just when you leave it to the muscles themselves to balance things and they're not working right that you have troubles.)

It used to be that people did surgery to correct this problem, actually going into the shoulder and taking off part of the acromion, the bony shelf above the joint, to provide more room. Now it turns out that in most instances you really don't need to do that. It's possible to reseat the joint through exercise therapy rather than surgery—a great boon to everyone.

So you've rested the shoulder and finally gotten to the point where you're free from pain. Now it's time to retune everything so you'll be able to stay that way.

Here is a series of four exercises. They're to be done without weights or resistance, simply by utilizing the weight of your arm. By the time you do all of them, you will have run through the entire range of motion of the shoulder, and if you do them as often as we recommend, you'll not only begin to restrengthen and balance the muscles, but develop endurance as well. They're awfully good, and most likely will do the trick. All they demand from you is perseverance.

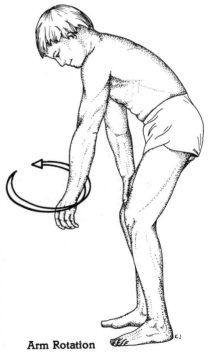

1. Bend over at the waist and just let the arm on your injured side hang in front of you. Then start swinging it in a clockwise motion. Not too hard or too fast—it's not like stirring a vat of molasses. Use just enough muscle to kick your arm into motion and keep it swinging lazily.

Arm Rotation

At first you may be able to bend over only a little way. That's okay. Continue to circle clockwise, then counterclockwise, bending over farther and farther as you go, until your torso is at a right angle, parallel to the ground. The key here is, *don't do anything that hurts.* If it hurts to bend too far, don't bend too far. If it hurts to circumscribe a circle, don't. You may have to make an ellipse, or an egg shape, or some other figure that feels all right. Then gradually work toward a complete circle, both clockwise and counterclockwise.

2. Stand up straight. Pretend that you're on one end of a double-handled saw and start sawing. Back and forth, in and out, way out and way back. As with all these exercises, the more repetitions you do, the more your range of motion will increase. You're stretching at the same time as you're strengthening. (And the exercise also puts your elbow through a complete range of motion.)

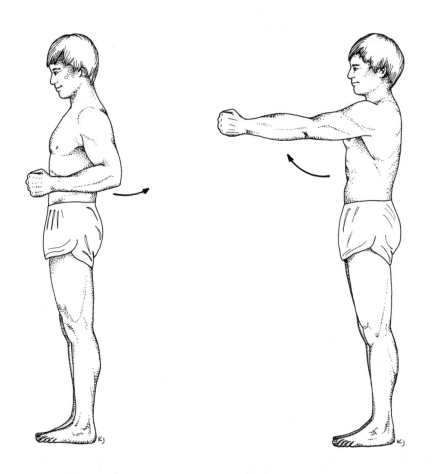

Sawing Exercises

3. Let your arm fall straight down to your side. Then raise your arm up at a right angle to your body and let it back down, up and down, as though you're slowly flapping an injured wing. These are called abduction swings.

Raise your arm to a comfortable level only. Even if you can bring your arm up only a foot or two from your side to start with, keep at it. As you continue, you'll become more flexible. And if it hurts too much to swing your arm up at all, start out by bending your elbow to form a chicken wing. Then flap it up as far as is comfortable. After you develop flexibility that way, gradually straighten out.

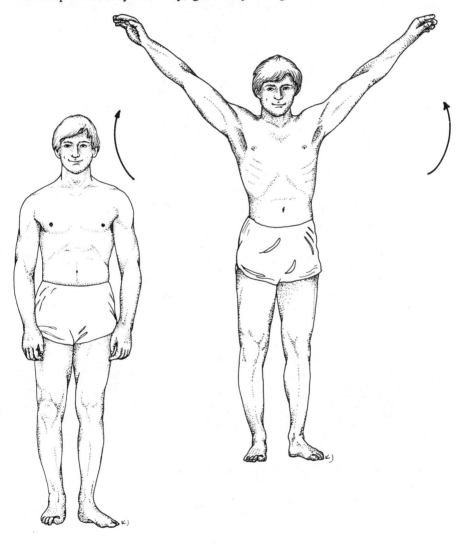

Abduction Swings

4. Last, but not least, shrug your shoulders. That's all, just shrug your shoulders. After doing so much sawing and circling and flapping, you may feel like shrugging your shoulders anyway. If you want to get fancy about it, you may want to roll your shoulders up and forward, then down, or up and back, then down, again making clockwise and counterclockwise circles.

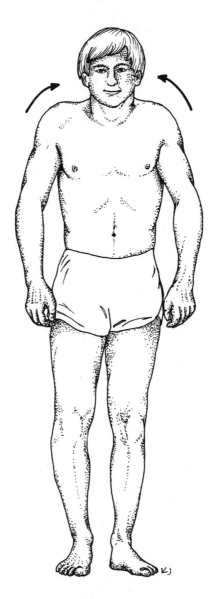

Shoulder Shrugs

Nothing to it, right? If you're having a fair amount of shoulder trouble, start out by doing the exercises ten times each, twice a day—in the morning and evening, say. And increase as you grow stronger and more flexible. What you're shooting toward is fifty of each exercise, three times a day. That's 750 reps. When you start doing that many, these deceivingly easy exercises turn into quite a workout. Don't worry if you work up to about thirty-five, say, and figure you must have lost count because nothing so easy could be so difficult. Only pretty good athletes, and young ones at that, can do that many reps readily. Use that number as a goal, a motivator, although getting rid of your shoulder problem should be motivation enough.

A week to ten days of these exercises is probably enough. You may find that you can go back to your activity, always taking it easy, of course, working into it a little at a time. But if you go back and find that your shoulder still bothers you, it's time for special exercise therapy to deal with just the specific muscles involved. And for this you should see a doctor or physical therapist. You have to do these more specialized exercises against resistance, in very specific positions, in order to isolate one muscle or another. They're best taught in person. You'll find, though, that at the very least these general exercises will tone and strengthen your shoulder. They'll make you use everything and use it right.

(To give credit where credit is due, the exercises were developed by Robert Kerlan, a Los Angeles orthopedic surgeon who for years has probably taken care of more baseball players than anybody else has. He uses the exercises as part of a rehabilitation program for pitchers. But they're so good, they'll work for anybody. And you can use them as a general toning procedure, a preventive thing that you can do anytime. Of course, they can be boring, and people don't like to do boring things, especially such simple boring things. They'd rather spend $500 for a glamorous, complicated machine that they can do boring things on. But no machine is going to do you any better than these simple exercises. Save your money and start circling and sawing and flapping and shrugging.)

RHOMBOID STRAINS

Now to more specific injuries. There are a couple of strains that recur with some frequency and are easy to diagnose. One of those is a rhomboid strain. The rhomboids are muscles in the center of your back that attach the edge of your shoulder blade to your spine. They help to pull the shoulder blade upward and toward the spine. (See the illustration on page 164 to pinpoint the location of a rhomboid strain.) People sometimes complain of back pain, when the culprit is really the rhomboid. The muscle will go into spasm, producing little knots. You can feel them—hard, painful spots in the center of your back, right where a woman's bra hooks. And because your shoulder blade no longer can move much, you'll have a tough time doing such things as raising your arm.

What to do about it

As always with muscle strains, the strategy is to rest the muscle, stretch it out, and then restrengthen it. Since these muscles pull your shoulder blades together, the best way to stretch them is by forcing the shoulder blades apart. Simply hug yourself. Reach around to your back with both arms, grasp hold of the shoulder blades, and stretch. It's a good way to relieve the pain. Another way is to grab the arm on the side of your body that hurts and pull it across your body with your other arm. Pull it high, middle, or low, depending on where you feel the stretch the most.

A good way to strengthen the rhomboids is by reversing the stretching motion (as everywhere in the body, the motions of stretching and strengthening are the reverse of each other). While leaning forward at the waist, pull your shoulder blades together. You can start by folding your arms like chicken wings and flapping backward. Then, as your strength and range of motion improve, straighten out your arms, thereby increasing their weight, and pull your shoulder blades together. Doing the exercises bent over at the waist enlists gravity as an aid, making your arms heavier, and thus further strengthening the muscle.

TRAPEZIUS STRAINS

The other recurrent strain is that of the trapezius muscle. The trapezius is a huge flat triangular muscle that reaches almost from the base of your skull, out to your shoulder, and then down to the middle of your back at the belt line. The top part of it forms the web that descends from the side of your neck to your shoulder. It moves your neck from side to side and helps move the shoulder blade as well. (Again, see page 164.)

It's this double duty that accounts for many trapezius strains. For example, let's say your shoulder bothers you. Your body's natural inclination is to try to protect it. How? By tucking it forward, out of harm's way. What muscle do you use to do that? The trapezius. But because the top part of the muscle is attached to your neck, the motion affects the neck, too. And as the trapezius struggles to keep your shoulder tucked in, little by little you may find that your neck doesn't work so well. In time it may hurt more than the shoulder did in the first place. All this because another muscle (or tendon or joint) acted up and the trapezius tried to make things better. So much for being a good neighbor.

What to do about it

Again, rest, stretch, strengthen. When you've stopped doing whatever it is that hurts long enough so that you're comfortable again, start gentle stretching. A good way to stretch the upper trapezius is to bend your neck away and a little bit forward from the side that hurts. Long, slow stretches will unknot the muscle.

Then strengthen. Shoulder shrugs will strengthen the upper part of the trapezius, because it's that part of the muscle that shrugs you. The lower trapezius is more difficult to deal with, but it's not as frequently injured. If the shrugs don't seem to help, then it might be a good idea to see someone. In fact, it's good to have a pretty solid idea of what's happening with injuries such as these, and as often as not the person to see for that is a physical therapist. A therapist knows how to do very discrete muscle testing and will be able to show you sharp, discrete muscle strengthening techniques.

BURSITIS

Yes, it shows up in the shoulder, too, as there's a large bursa between the acromion and the joint, but rarely does it appear in athletes. For years almost everything that hurt on the outside of the shoulder was called bursitis, but most likely these things were other things—tendinitis, say, or muscle strains.

What to do about it

If your shoulder hurts on the outside, rest it until the pain is gone, then try the circling-shrugging exercises we've discussed. More likely than not the pain will stay away. If not, see someone. If bursitis is truly the problem, a shot of cortisone may help a lot.

CALCIFIC TENDINITIS

Sometimes an interesting thing happens with shoulder tendinitis: besides the tendons becoming inflamed and irritated, something goes wrong and the body deposits calcium in the injured area, so much calcium that you can see it in X-rays. It looks just like bone, and that's disturbing to see in a spot where there shouldn't be any. (When you operate you find it's usually much like toothpaste in consistency and color.) The body's reaction to these calcium deposits is much the same—disturbed. It wants to get that foreign stuff out of there, and so the area becomes even more inflamed, which causes it to lay down more calcium, which causes more inflammation, and so it goes. It can turn into a bad situation, with reduced movement in your shoulder and much pain. In fact, "much pain" may be an understatement. It can be one of the most painful injuries possible, in the same league with passing a kidney stone. Often even drugs won't help.

What to do about it

Like true bursitis, calcific tendinitis is frequently treated with cortisone injections, successfully, too, as the cortisone stops the inflammation, which in turn stops the calcium deposits. Sometimes the body will then absorb the calcium, sometimes not. If not, or if the inflammation just won't quit, surgery can be the answer.

But sometimes people with large amounts of calcium deposits don't even know they're there. You may X-ray their shoulder for other reasons, and lo and behold the calcium shows up. The real problem is not the calcium itself but the tendinitis that causes it to be deposited. Calcific tendinitis is really nothing more than a visible evidence of chronic tendinitis. Nobody quite knows why the calcium forms, but we do know why people get tendinitis: overuse and abuse of the joint. So although a shot of cortisone may get rid of the immediate problem, it won't prevent the calcium from forming again. The only thing that'll do that is getting rid of the tendinitis, and the only thing that'll do *that* is the kind of rehab program we've been talking about. Try the exercises. If the problem persists, see someone. Just be careful not to confuse temporary relief with a long-term solution.

THORACIC OUTLET SYNDROME

Warning: as with anyplace else in the body, *if you have numbness, tingling, or weakness in your shoulder or down your arm, you should always see somebody.* Those are the symptoms of problems involving nerves, which in one way or another lead back to the spinal column, and you never want to risk serious injury in that area.

In this case, despite the name of the injury, the problem begins in the cervical spine, the seven vertebrae in the neck. All the nerves to your arm come from the top part of this portion of the backbone, exiting the base of your neck (thus thoracic "outlet" syndrome) to form big trunks of nerves deep in the armpit. From there the nerves run down your arm and do all the things that nerves are supposed to do. Along the way from the spine to the arm the nerves go over and around a lot of muscles. As with piriformis syndrome in the hip and thigh, if any of these muscles is injured or in spasm, or if you just hold your shoulder in an abnormal position, you can stretch and pinch the nerves. The result: pain, but not necessarily pain in the shoulder.

Nerves are interesting critters. If you hit your funny bone, you don't just feel it there, but also in your fingers, although you haven't done a thing to them. The same is true with your shoulder. If you irritate a nerve in your shoulder, you may feel pain in your elbow. Sometimes what people think is tennis elbow is really a result of thoracic outlet syndrome. It's what caused the pain in Harriett Burnette's elbow. If you stretch your neck in a certain way and your thumb starts tingling, it may not be your thumb that's causing the problem. If every time you reach over the back seat your fingers hurt, it may not be the fault of your fingers.

What to do about it

See someone. Although the culprit may be a stretched nerve in your shoulder, it could be anything, even a disk problem. You want to be sure just what the injury is. If indeed it is thoracic outlet syndrome, then stretching and strengthening the muscles involved may be the ticket. Again, it's important to find out just what the problem is.

CONTUSIONS

Contusions—direct blows—usually occur in contact sports. Football, wrestling, lacrosse, and soccer can produce a contused shoulder, as can such accidents as skiing into a barrier or running into a stage set or another dancer. It can be a painful injury, but in and of itself it's rarely serious. The reason is that contusions almost always affect the deltoid, the big muscle that caps your shoulder, and the only one that you can see reasonably well. It's the muscle that bulges impressively in body builders, that fills out the shoulders in tight T-shirts. But its very visibility is also the cross the deltoid must bear. The other muscles and tendons in the shoulder either lie sheltered beneath the deltoid or cluster in front and in back of the shoulder blade. So when a blow is on the way, it's the deltoid's lot in life to receive it.

The deltoid is the unsophisticated hulk of the shoulder. The muscles below it, called the rotator cuff muscles, are the fine tuners. The deltoid is responsible for doing most of the gross work, but the rotator cuff muscles hold the joint in the right position, balancing things so that the work can be done. It's more critical if these smaller muscles are injured by the blow, but happily for them, and you, they're almost always not. Thanks to the deltoid.

Since the deltoid spans only one joint, it rarely tears from the force of the blow. (Remember that muscles that span one joint are less likely to tear than muscles that span two joints, such as the biceps. More on that soon.) But, like muscles anywhere, it will go into spasm, which means that soon you won't be able to use your shoulder properly. Thus starts another of the body's seemingly endless number of vicious circles, and the reason why contusions, although usually not serious in themselves, can lay the groundwork for lots of other problems.

Your shoulder hurts, and you can't raise your arm. So you start enlisting other muscles to do what the battered deltoid is no longer able to do. You start moving your shoulder blade too early, say, and learn all sorts of other ways of cheating to keep your shoulder functioning. That may be okay temporarily, but once the shoulder learns how to cheat, it won't stop even when the original injury heals. One of the real problems with tennis and baseball players, and football quarterbacks, too, is that once the injury heals they continue to throw or serve as though their shoulder were still hurt. It may have been the only way they could function during the injury, but now it's an inefficient way. More than that, it can be a harmful way, because misusing the muscles can lead to other problems.

In effect your body has said to these muscles, "Stop doing what you usually do; I have a new job for you. The muscle that usually does this job isn't working very well. I want you to take over." The muscles must agree—after all, what choice do they have?—but your shoulder is designed in such a way that muscles do their original tasks best. Once new muscles step into situations they're not designed for, they get injured more easily. Or, because your shoulder now hurts, the muscles surrounding it, like the trapezius, find themselves asked to hold your shoulder in ways they're not used to—all hunched up, say, to reduce the pain—and they might start hurting. Often people go to the doctor complaining of neck or back pain when the real culprit is the shoulder. These can be tough problems to handle, because you have to work backward to the source. And it can be hard to set up rehab programs to cover such a multitude of sins.

So the real danger of a contusion is the far-flung problems it can set into play. That's why it's usually not a good idea to ignore the injury.

What to do about it

It's important to get on contusions right away and stretch out the injured muscle. The circle-shrug exercise regimen is a good way of stretching and strengthening any of the muscles in the shoulder. For more specific rehab exercises you'll have to see a physician or physical therapist. But it may be difficult to find someone who will offer you the time and expertise you need. Many doctors can provide cortisone shots, anti-inflammatory medications, and even surgery for shoulder injuries, but few as readily give good rehab advice. Unless you see someone who is used to taking care of good athletes, information on what to do with your shoulder for the long term can be hard to come by. And that's too bad, for, as we've seen, the shoulder is one area in which the healthy interrelationship of muscles is crucial. But so far as the importance of muscle functioning and rehabilitation is concerned, knowledge about the shoulder is probably about a decade behind that of the knee. The upshot can be shoulder problems that don't go away for a long, long time.

So it's very important to keep the shoulder healthy and to rehabilitate it as quickly and efficiently as possible after an injury like a contusion. We've offered some suggestions as to how; it's a good idea to see someone who regularly takes care of athletes to find out more.

BROKEN COLLARBONE

Probably the most common accident involving the shoulder is falling on your outstretched arm. And the most common result of that is a broken collarbone. The collarbone is the single most frequently fractured bone in young people. And that's not just in athletics, but as a result of play—falling out of a tree or the upper bunk, racing down the sidewalk, tripping, and reaching to break the fall.

The collarbone, or clavicle, is the only bony link between your shoulder and the rest of you. If you cut all the muscles away from your shoulder, the only thing left connecting it to your body would be the collarbone. As a result, any stress on the arm and shoulder is transmitted to the rest of your body through—guess what—the collarbone. So if you're skating, say, and you stumble and reach out to break your fall, the force of the impact, fueled by the weight of your entire body, goes right up your arm and through your shoulder to the collarbone, and finally to the spot where the collarbone attaches to the rest of the body, your breastbone, or sternum. Except that often the force doesn't reach all the way to the sternum. The collarbone, the weak link in the chain, so slender as to be hardly thicker than your finger, breaks first.

You'll know it when it happens. It hurts like crazy when you touch the end of the fracture, which is almost always in the middle third of the bone, and the whole area becomes tender. Soon it'll swell, and you'll have trouble moving your shoulder at all.

What to do about it

Applying ice may help reduce swelling, but there's little else to do except see someone. The bone must be set right for it to heal right. People usually set the break the same way it was done years ago, in a figure-eight dressing that pulls your shoulders back and puts some traction on the fracture. Almost all broken collarbones heal, and they all heal with a bump.

Collarbone fractures are something like rib fractures in that way— they rarely need any kind of surgical intervention, they almost all heal, and they heal with a bump. If your collarbone line is important to you, you might as well get used to the fact that a fracture will produce a lump, although it probably will get smaller over time. But there's little to be done about it. Surgery probably won't decrease the size of the lump, and it will give you a scar over the spot. And it's a bad place to operate, especially in women, as the weight of the breast stretches the skin, causing the scar to spread.

SHOULDER SEPARATION

The joint that connects the collarbone to the shoulder is called the acromioclavicular joint— "acromio" for acromion, the bony ridge of the shoulder blade, "clavicular" for clavicle. You can feel it. With your fingers, just follow your collarbone toward the shoulder—the little bump just before the end is the joint. It's tiny, only about the size of your fingernail, but well tethered by ligaments. Still, it's so small that falling onto the tip of your shoulder can sometimes push the joint apart, separating the collarbone from the shoulder. By a ratio of ten to one, it's a male sports injury. Wrestling, football, lacrosse, hockey— anytime a person's shoulder is driven into the ground or suffers a disabling blow, as from a hockey or lacrosse stick, the result can be a shoulder separation. In Harriett Burnette's case, the separation—a mild one—was caused by slamming her shoulder into the side of a mountain. Then she did the same thing again a year later by falling on her outstretched arm. As with a broken collarbone, the force travels up the arm to the joint.

Usually a shoulder separation is either bad or not so bad, with little in between. You may tear out the whole AC joint, completely separate the collarbone from the shoulder, or just partially tear the ligaments. In the case of a complete separation, the collarbone, no longer tethered to the shoulder, can stick up as much as an inch. If the tear is minor, the lump will be less severe. In either case, it hurts, especially when you try to lift your arm above your head. And if you press on the AC joint itself, look out.

What to do about it

In the case of complete separations, the strategy is obvious: see someone right away. But the minor varieties can be deceiving. Although the injury is painful at first, it soon gets better and can be easy to forget. But it turns out that a good quarter of the people with minor separations still suffer discomfort as long as five years later, especially when doing things that carry the arm across the body, like throwing a ball or setting up for a backhand. The motion pushes together the sides of the joint, which has degenerated over the years, causing the bones to rub against each other and hurt. And what's really a minor disability can lead to other problems, because, as elsewhere, your body tries to compensate for the pain by enlisting muscles and tendons to do jobs they're not supposed to do. They can then become irritated and inflamed, which leads to more discomfort, which leads to ... And so it goes.

So it may be worthwhile to see someone if you even suspect the possibility of a separation, no matter how slight. The doctor may simply put your arm in a sling until it's comfortable, then lead you through a rehab program and wait and see what happens. Or the treatment can be surgery, a reasonably simple operation in which the surgeon retethers the joint, sometimes with Dacron tape, sometimes with a screw or pins, and actually removes the tip of the collarbone to preclude the possibility of the joint's degenerating and rubbing together. You can go back to almost any activity without the end of your collarbone, and your shoulder looks better without the lump that would be there if the bone remained. It's just one of those injuries concerning which there are a lot of ideas, but little agreement, as to the best treatment.

DISLOCATIONS

Back to the old ball and saucer, the shoulder joint itself. And back to the theme of this chapter: you give a little, you take a little. What the shoulder takes is almost unlimited flexibility; what it gives is stability. And there's no better evidence for this lack of stability than the fact that of all the major joints in the body, not one of them dislocates as frequently as the shoulder.

The causes are many and varied. Having your arm wrenched out of the socket in wrestling; arm tackling in football; catching a ski pole in the ground and skiing on, leaving the pole, and your arm, behind; leading a horse that suddenly rears back, popping your shoulder. We recently saw a fellow who dislocated his shoulder when all of him except his arm fell through the hatch of a sailboat. But the most common cause is falling on your outstretched arm—the old transmitted-force business again. If you fall just right (or just wrong), you can squirt the ball of the shoulder joint away from the saucer. It doesn't take much.

Again, the reason we can go on like this ad infinitum is that the shoulder joint is held together not by a securely fitting ball and socket, not by stiff, reliable ligaments, but by the constant interrelated tension of the muscles and tendons around the joint. We just don't realize how protective of our shoulder we are, all the time. Just relax completely for an instant, and the shoulder will dislocate a bit (that is, sublex) all by itself, simply from the weight of the hanging arm. After shoulder injuries, when the muscles are really weak, people often walk around with their shoulder hunched up to their ear, because they can sense that if they relaxed, their shoulder would slide out. And it would, maybe as far as half an inch. Combine that natural instability with some outside force and it's easy to see why shoulder dislocations are so common.

You'll know immediately that something has happened to your shoulder that you never want to happen again. The shoulder muscles go into spasm, and any motion of your arm hurts. You have a tendency to hold it close to your body for protection. And the most telling sign is that you lose the ability to rotate your arm. Other injuries may cause you to hold your arm close, but nothing but a dislocation or fracture will take away your ability to rotate it. The area may appear swollen and become tender. Nothing feels right, neither straightening up nor crouching down. There's a strong sense that something is badly out of alignment.

What to do about it

See someone. The first thing that person will do is relocate, or reduce, the joint. Any other treatment comes later.

Most likely you'll never need to know how to reduce a dislocation by yourself, as most people are within reasonable reach of a doctor's office or emergency room. But what if you're on a camping trip, miles from any doctor? In that case reducing the injury can be vitally important. There are a number of ways to do it. Here's one that's both effective and safe: clasp your fingers in front of you (*if* you can get the hand on the dislocated side in front of you—it can take some doing), put your knee between your hands, and just relax. Let the weight of your leg stretch your arm away from your body. It may seem that that's the wrong direction, but you have to remember that when your shoulder dislocated the muscles went into spasm. Now they actually hold the joint apart. You've got to stretch out those muscles. When you do, in most instances the joint will simply pop back together.

Old hands at dislocations learn such tricks. And there are old hands, because for years one dislocation meant that there was between a 75 percent and a 90 percent chance that there would be others. People were so convinced that one dislocation was the prelude to many that they went ahead and operated on athletes as young as teenagers, hoping that surgical reconstruction would keep the joint in place. Recently, though, a physician named John Aronen took a group of Naval Academy midshipmen with shoulder dislocations and put them through a very precise, vigorous rehab program. He immobilized them for about three weeks in a sling and bandages and then started them on a couple months of combined strengthening and stretching. Then he sent the men back to their normal activities, which included demanding physical conditioning and sports. After three years, when according to previous records most of the recurrences should have occurred, only 25 percent of these men had suffered new dislocations.

So there's hope. If you rehabilitate dislocations well the first time, it may be that you'll be little more susceptible to more of them than anyone else. But once a dislocation does recur, all bets are off. Then the likelihood of recurrences gets really high again.

The moral of the story is that it's important to find somebody who knows about these things and will set up and supervise a really good rehab program—this is one case in which you don't want to do it yourself. Dislocations don't have to recur, and they don't have to be treated surgically. If you see someone who says that they do, he may be right. But he may be wrong. It can't hurt to get a second opinion.

SHOULDER SUBLUXATION

It's no more than a minor dislocation. Pop, it's out, pop, it's back in, all by itself. Your shoulder hurts for a moment, then feels pretty much as before. Then within hours the pain returns, and soon it's hard to move the shoulder. The causes are similar to those of dislocations.

What to do about it

See someone who knows how to rehabilitate such injuries. Like dislocations, subluxations can be difficult to deal with, with high recurrence rates (but probably a much lower recurrence rate if you rehabilitate well). The treatment is exactly the same as that for dislocations, even though the joint doesn't slide out as far: immobilize it, then rehabilitate.

Because the injury doesn't seem as bad, there's a temptation to ease off the rehab program. Don't. It can meant the difference between suffering and escaping an endless round of recurrent subluxations.

(Subluxations are actually more difficult to deal with surgically than dislocations. It's a lot easier to keep something from sliding out an inch and a half than it is to keep it from moving a quarter of an inch.) If you can get on top of the injury at the beginning, there's a much better chance that you'll never have to get on top of it again.

ROTATOR CUFF TEARS

The rotator cuff is much in the sports news these days. Baseball pitchers who a few years ago would have been described as having sore shoulders now suffer from injuries of the rotator cuff—whatever that is. Well, what it is is a cuff of four tendons that, like a hood, cover the shoulder joint. They're connected to muscles, none of which you can see, that attach at one end to the shoulder blade and at the other to a little ridge around the upper arm bone, the humerus, just below the ball portion.

These are muscles that rotate your arm—thus, rotator cuff—and keep your joint stable. They keep the ball centered in the saucer when you move your arm, stabilizing the fulcrum that allows the other muscles to do what they're supposed to do.

With any kind of violent movement you can tear the rotator cuff, but most of these injuries are attritional things. Anytime your arm is in an upright position, the tendons may rub against the shoulder blade, causing minute tearing and inflammation. The more your arm is overhead—pitchers, quarterbacks, and tennis players come to mind, but perhaps none so much as swimmers (see Chapter 15, "Swimming," for more on their special problems)—the more tearing. But you don't need to be a swimmer to have rotator cuff problems. Everyday activities will do just fine. A startling statistic is that over half of everyone over fifty years of age has rotator cuff tears. In people over seventy the rate is up to over 70 percent. It seems to be one of those unhappy realities of life that most of us can look forward to, if indeed we haven't experienced it already.

The tip-off is pain on the top of the shoulder, especially when you raise your arm above shoulder level. In the worst cases you lose the ability even to bring your arm up from your side. But most people handle rotator cuff tears without too much difficulty. Just another one of the things to adjust to as we age.

What to do about it

The circle-shrug exercises we discussed earlier can do you a lot of good here. But if the injury is really severe, you should see someone.

Sometimes rotator cuff tears are treated surgically. A professional athlete may find it the only recourse, but recreational athletes should be wary of surgery. The likelihood of a big-league pitcher coming back after rotator cuff surgery is not high at all. And that's somebody who has a lot of time to devote to rehab and is dealing with people who really know their stuff. It may be that for most of us, unless it's a large tear and a lot of disability, a strong and specific strengthening and stretching program will do the most good.

RUPTURED BICEPS

It's about the only muscle in the shoulder that frequently ruptures, and it usually occurs in older people. Often it's not connected with an athletic activity at all. You'll be lifting or moving something—the refrigerator, the piano—and all of a sudden you feel a pop. It's not particularly painful or disabling, but when you look down at your arm your biceps bulges like Popeye's after he eats a can of spinach.

What happens is that part of the biceps simply snaps off the shoulder and rolls down into your arm like one of those party favors that coil back when you stop blowing into them. The biceps connects to the shoulder in two parts: the short head, in which the muscle itself ascends high into the shoulder and attaches to the front of the shoulder blade by a short tendon, and the long head, in which the muscle ends below the shoulder and relies on a long, snaky tendon to go up the rest of the way through the joint. It's that long tendon that ruptures and causes the sudden bulge; the rest of the muscle stays in place.

What to do about it

There isn't much you can do about it. No one can put the tendon back where it was. If someone does operate, the idea is to tether the tendon into the humerus and let it go at that. But often the same thing happens naturally—the ruptured tendon simply scars into the bone by itself.

Then it's just a matter of letting the dust settle and gradually getting back to your activity. The body uses the half of the biceps that's still attached and recruits the other muscles that bend your elbow to do more than their share of the work. The result may not be as efficient as it was before, but we don't use our biceps for that much anyway. If you can tolerate a lumpy muscle, in time you may forget that you injured it. You can go back to tennis, swimming, a reasonable level of weight lifting, almost any activity with a ruptured biceps. But you'll always look like Popeye.

PECTORAL TEAR

The big muscle on the front of the chest that forms the fold over the armpit is called the pectoralis major (to differentiate it from the pectoralis minor, which lies above it). This is the muscle that allows you to draw your arm across your chest. It can tear, usually in weight lifters, sometimes in gymnasts, causing real pain and disability. Just as a torn biceps snaps back to form a sharp bulge, so does a torn pec. If your pain is accompanied by a big knot on one side of your chest, there's a good chance you've torn a pec.

What to do about it

See someone. It's not a common injury, but it can be serious enough to require surgery.

Commonly Asked Questions

If I dislocate my shoulder, do I need an operation?

Probably not. It all depends on what you do afterward. Ten years ago, especially if your shoulder dislocated again and again, the answer would have been, yes, if you're active, you really do need an operation. But now, with the increasing success of really good rehab programs, you probably won't need surgery. Just make sure that whoever treats the dislocation sets you up with a physical therapist who can give you thorough, specific rehabilitation instructions. And make sure that you follow them faithfully, especially with a first dislocation. Once it recurs, the more likely it is to continue to recur. And the more often it recurs, the more likely it is that you will indeed find yourself on the operating table sometime.

Do I have a torn rotator cuff?

With all the publicity about rotator cuffs, it's getting to be a frequent question. And the answer is, yes, if you're male and aged fifty or above, you probably do. If you're younger than that and do a lot of activities that involve raising your arm above your head—like tennis, swimming, and throwing sports—yes, you probably do, too. The rotator cuff seems to be one of those structures that wear out.

The important question is, however, does it matter? And the answer to that one is, most likely not. Most people go through life with a torn rotator cuff very well, thank you. The fact that evidence of tearing may show up during a shoulder examination is not necessarily reason to do anything about your rotator cuff—not if it doesn't bother you. Odds are that through the years you've noticed some changes in how your shoulder operates, and you've adapted to them in such a way that you're still doing what you like to do pretty darn well, if not in the same high style you were capable of in your twenties. Discovering that you have a torn rotator cuff doesn't change anything one bit.

That is, it shouldn't. Some doctors like to treat X-rays rather than symptoms: if it shows up in an exam, better do something about it—no matter that you may never even have known there was a problem. It exists; let's fix it, or try to, anyway. Be careful of encountering such an attitude. The bottom line is, or should be, this: if your shoulder isn't hurting and you don't have to compromise your strength or range of motion, then you shouldn't have anything done to your rotator cuff. Strengthening and stretching exercises, the circle-shrug set we discussed earlier in the chapter? Yes, anytime. Surgery? No. Not unless absolutely necessary.

Will I ever be able to use my frozen shoulder?

A frozen shoulder—that is, a shoulder that simply won't move—rarely shows up in athletes. We see the problem in people who injured their shoulder in one way or another and then simply stopped using it. If you keep your shoulder in one position too long, it'll resist moving into any other position. It may be because the soft tissue capsule enclosing the joint develops adhesions, kind of wrinkles down and adheres to itself, preventing movement.

The antidote is to start moving your shoulder. The answer to the question is, yes, you will be able to use your frozen shoulder, but it can take a long time—months or even years—to regain the flexibility you once had. Some doctors put you under general anesthesia and manipulate the shoulder, breaking the adhesions that way. You can do the same thing yourself just by exercising the joint, although it can be a slower process and it'll hurt, especially at first.

The best thing, of course, is to *never stop using your shoulder in the first place*. If you injure your shoulder, see someone or rehabilitate it yourself, but don't stop using it. That's the gateway to real problems.

Will my shoulder ever get better?

Yes, most likely it will. It'll just take a while. The shoulder involves the most intimately interassociated group of muscles and muscular functions in the entire body. No wonder it can take time to get over things. In the shoulder little glitches can make big problems and because one thing leads to another here more than anywhere else, you often have to deal with secondary problems at the same time that you're trying to come to grips with what started the whole awful thing.

And it's so hard to rest the shoulder, to give it a chance to regain its equilibrium. If your knee is in a splint, you limp around for a while, but you still limp *around*. If your shoulder and arm are in a sling, there go more of your daily functions than you ever imagined.

Perseverance helps, that and patience. But having a shoulder problem does have one advantage: you can do the majority of rehab exercises on your own. No need to run over to the therapy center or the fitness club for weight and rehab equipment. With the shoulder, weight and resistance aren't as important as the mere act of motion.

So look on the bright side. Circles and sawing, anyone?

Why isn't my shoulder getting better?

It's the flip side of the previous question, and herein lies an interesting tale: one of the biggest problems we see with shoulder injuries is that *people tend to manipulate their activities so that they stay at the same level of discomfort.*

Sounds crazy, no? But it's true. People whom we've put on a rehab program will come back month after month and say, "My shoulder feels the same. It hurts just as much." All this lack of improvement can be depressing until you learn to ask an important question: "Is my activity level the same month after month as well?" And there the answer will probably be "No, I'm doing more than I did before."

Without thinking, people will start playing more or harder tennis, or they'll work back up to three thousand yards in the pool, or they'll start opening doors again, or pick up the typewriter in the office and move it around—things they never would have done a couple of weeks ago. If it's a knee injury, they might increase their laps on the track, or start parking five blocks away from the office instead of in the parking garage in the basement. A dancer may start using the injured leg as her weight-bearing leg at the barre, whereas before she used it only as her free leg—again, all this without thinking about it.

So it may be that, no, you're really not getting any better. If so, it's time to have things reevaluated. But it may be that, yes, you're getting lots better. So much better that you've been able to increase your level of activity without even noticing it. It's just that people find a pain level that they can live with and then in one way or another work to stay right there.

Oh, well. No one ever guaranteed that life would make sense. Right?

9 The Elbow

I can't do anything around the house anymore. I dropped a coffee cup yesterday. I can't even begin to pick up a spoon, it hurts so bad." Arlene Jacobson's tennis elbow first surfaced six months ago. At first she felt some soreness after a match, but nothing alarming, and it disappeared as quietly as it had come. The next weekend, though, her elbow began to hurt before the match was over, and that time it took a couple of days to go away. And so it went, little by little creeping up on her, until finally Arlene did what now she considers a very stupid thing.

"I took a week-long workshop," she says. "Three hours every day." She looks sheepish. "It was spring, and some of my tennis friends had signed up. I thought it was just what I needed."

It wasn't. By the end of the week Arlene could hardly open a door. It was murder to get into and out of the car. Even making the children's lunch was a trial.

"My husband suggested I do some exercises," she says. "He told me to squeeze a tennis ball, but it didn't do any good."

"Not surprising," Garrick says. "Squeezing a ball exercises the muscles on the wrong side of the elbow."

"And I tried something one of the girls at the club told me about, an elbow strap. That helped a little, but still hurt." So she decided to see a doctor, who immediately gave her a shot of cortisone. "I thought it was a miracle. The shot was horrible, but the pain went away completely. In a week I was back on the court and playing as though nothing had ever happened."

Two weeks later she was hurting as much as ever. Maybe more. "I had another shot," she says, "and started playing again. This time it didn't last as long as the first one. Now I'm miserable."

"It won't get better," Garrick says, "until you get rid of the pain *and* rehabilitate it." He gently touches Arlene's elbow. "What you've done is pulled a few fibers of tendon away from the outside part of your elbow. Now, by itself that's not a heavy duty problem, but when the elbow hurts, you don't want to use it."

Arlene nods.

"So it gets weak. The cortisone removes the pain, but because the elbow's weak, when you use it again, it hurts all the more. And if every time you get rid of the pain you go out and play tennis and hurt yourself again, you may *never* get better. You've just got to rehabilitate the joint. I've had people go as long as two and a half years fighting this thing."

Just one of the joys of dealing with elbow problems, which may not be especially numerous but are certainly persistent. Part of the reason is the way the joint is constructed. It's lucky that whoever designed the elbow doesn't moonlight hanging doors, because although the elbow is a great hinge, it's a crooked one. You can see for yourself. Bend your elbow as far as you can, so that you're touching your shoulder with your fingertips. Now slowly straighten your arm, palm up. Surprise! Your arm doesn't extend absolutely straight. It veers out to the side from the elbow, especially so in women. That crook away from the straight and narrow is called the carrying angle, and herein lies the seed of one of the elbow's two dominant ailments. In large part because of this carrying angle, when you serve a tennis ball or throw a baseball the inside of your elbow tends to open up and the outside collapses in on itself. Were the elbow a more balanced hinge, it would more efficiently distribute the forces stirred up by these activities. But it's not, and it doesn't; thus, little league elbow, which, combined with tennis elbow, is one of the most common injuries of the entire upper body.

But that's just one of the elbow's peculiarities. It's a very interesting joint, unlike any we've yet discussed. It's really two joints: a joint that lets you flex and straighten your arm and a joint that allows you to rotate your wrist and hand—at the same time, if need be. You've already flexed and extended your elbow to demonstrate the carrying angle. To watch the elbow rotate, simply place your hand and arm, palm up, on a table in front of you. Your thumbnail should be touching the table. Then, without lifting your arm, turn your hand over so that the other side of your thumb now lies flat on the table. That's called pronation. Now rotate back again—supination. Pretty impressive. That's a full 180 degrees of rotation at the wrist. It's that capability, combined with the elbow's bending skills, that allows us to button our collar, deliver a karate chop, or play the piano, all with the same equipment. That combination of skills also allows us to drive home a hard, flat serve or scoop up a ball underhanded, chin ourselves on a horizontal bar, or bench press free weights—all, obviously, with power. Crooked hinge or no, the elbow is a pretty versatile, efficient instrument.

This joint that's really two joints connects the humerus, the upper arm bone, to two bones in the lower arm—the ulna and radius. That there are two bones in the lower arm is important. It's what makes possible the elbow's ability to bend *and* rotate. The ulna, the longer of the two, allows the elbow to bend. You can feel it run all the way from your elbow to your wrist along the inside back of your forearm. The ulna cradles the end of the humerus in a comfy hollow with a shoe-hornlike extension that allows the two bones easily to work with each other as a hinge, albeit a crooked one. If you place your cupped hand (which represents the ulna) over your fist (the humerus) and then increase and decrease the angle between your arms, you'll get the idea.

The shorter bone, the radius, sometimes runs parallel to the ulna, sometimes across it like an X, depending on what your wrist and forearm are doing. Again, rest your arm on a table in front of you, palm up. In this position your forearm is flat, with the two bones lying docilely side by side. If you rotate your wrist, however, interesting things begin to happen. Your forearm develops a transverse swelling, a small mountain range running from the outside of the elbow to the inside of the wrist. This muscular ridge indicates what the radius is doing underneath it—pivoting against the humerus and rotating around the ulna, which itself doesn't move much at all relative to its partner.

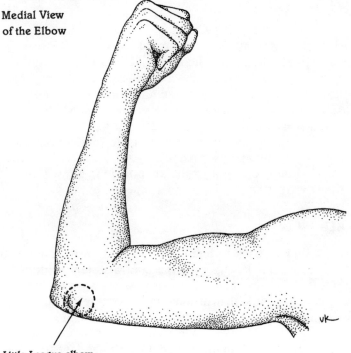

Medial View
of the Elbow

Little League elbow

Lateral View of the Elbow

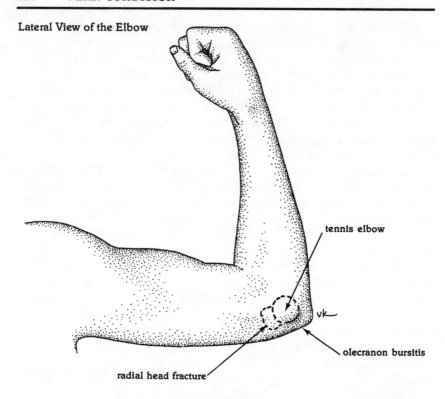

The radius's ability to rotate is a function of its shape. Whereas the ulna actually cradles the humerus, the radius abuts it. The end of the radius is shaped something like an ice-cream cone, the top of which has been hollowed out by pressing the scooper into it. It's an ideal shape for traveling along the convex end of the humerus, which it does to a lesser or greater extent, up to 140 degrees of rotation, every time you twist your wrist. So there's a lot going on inside your elbow all the time: bones not only swing against each other as in a hinge, but rotate along an arc, constantly changing relative position, all within the confines of a pretty tight space. Two joints indeed.

TENNIS ELBOW

All of which brings us back to tennis elbow, perhaps the dominant elbow injury. But, Arlene Jacobson to the contrary, tennis elbow is more common off the court than on. In fact, it shows up more frequently in trades or industry than it does in athletic settings. People who work with impact wrenches, who use hammers or staple guns, are all prey to tennis elbow. Framers, automobile mechanics, assembly line workers suffer from it. Ditto those who do nothing more strenuous than put up jam for the winter. Clinics are swamped by epidemics of tennis elbow during the fall canning season. So here's the $64,000 question: auto mechanics, homemakers putting up preserves, tennis players—what do all these people have in common that leads to tennis elbow?

The answer is that all of them tend to do things that demand sharp, quick twists of the wrist. A mechanic tugging a wrench against a stubborn spark plug, a canner twisting closed the top of the jar, a tennis player hitting (or mis-hitting) a backhand—all of them put demands on the wrist that it sometimes can't handle.

Which leads to the next question: what does all this wrist stuff have to do with the elbow? It comes down to the interrelationships business again. The muscles that bend back your wrist and straighten your fingers all begin at the elbow. And not just any old place in the elbow. In one spot, no bigger than a dime. It is, of course, the bump on the outside of your elbow, the very spot that hurts so much when you have tennis elbow. It's called the lateral humeral epicondyle (literally, "the outside top of the knuckle of the humerus"), a term that pretty well describes the precarious nature of this connecting point. It's where almost 40 percent of the muscles of your forearm begin—all that from an area not much bigger than your fingernail. Not the greatest mechanical arrangement in the world. No wonder it hurts.

The scenario goes something like this: all of us tennis players are taught to hit a backhand with our body, using our arm as a kind of rigid lever. We're taught to step into the ball, our elbow and wrist frozen, and swing through it using our legs and shoulder to provide power. The impact of the ball against the racquet then travels up the length of the arm and dissipates into our entire body. Fine. Makes sense. So what do we do instead? We forget our body and strongarm the ball to death, leading with our elbow—our first mistake. Then, to compensate, we use our wrist to whip the racquet through the ball—mistake number two. The muscles in the forearm, which are perfectly able to hold the wrist rigid, simply can't produce the power necessary to drive the racquet into the ball and handle the impact as well. And because the elbow is not rigid, as it should be, but rather loose and flexible, the bulk of the impact doesn't travel up the rest of the arm and into the body but goes up the muscles and tendons of the forearm and slams into the elbow with considerable force. Where specifically? Right into the lateral epicondyle, which, understandably, is simply not capable of absorbing so much. The result: tennis elbow.

It's probably unnecessary to describe how it feels, as so many people have experienced it. The tip-off is pain, of course, centered at the epicondyle but resulting from almost everything you do with the wrist and elbow. From opening doors to shaking hands (tennis elbow is a politician's nightmare) to picking up the kid, or the cat, or the evening paper—not to mention hitting a backhand—the pain is there. For perhaps one or two out of a hundred people, it arrives with a single backhand. In one stroke, these people may tear part of the tendon that connects the muscles to the bone, actually popping off a few fibers. They're the people who may receive a cortisone shot and suddenly feel good as new. What happens is that the cortisone quickly decreases the inflammation, which in turn gets rid of the pain, which, in an injury like this, is the real problem rather than the damage itself. It's likely that you've torn only a few of hundreds of fibers, but the danger is that because of the pain you'll be unable to use the joint, and so the muscles can quickly weaken. With the pain gone, you're able to go out and use your elbow and keep the muscles strong.

So much for the one or two percent of us. Most of us have to cope with the sneaky kind of tennis elbow, the overuse variety, which comes on gradually from almost imperceptible beginnings and, once ensconced, is much more difficult to get rid of. At first your elbow hurts a little after your match but is better the next day. The weekend player then forgets all about it until the next weekend, when it starts to hurt before the match is over and still hurts a day or two later. And so it goes, until finally it hurts so much, all the time, that you can't play tennis at all and you stop doing even the most simple everyday things. Would that there were a single treatment as effective as a cortisone injection for the problem. There isn't. But, paradoxically, it may be easy to get rid of. The crux of the matter is getting to it quickly.

What to do about it

The earlier you catch tennis elbow the better. When you first notice the pain is the time to do something about it. The first thing may be to figure out if it's actually tennis elbow that's bothering you rather than something else. One test is to put the backs of your wrists together and see if one bends more readily than the other. A stiff wrist might indicate tennis elbow. Another is to stretch the muscle involved by straightening your bad arm in front of you with your wrist down and pulling your hand under the arm and toward you. If your elbow hurts, you might have tennis elbow. And if none of these tests pan out, there's one other. Again extend your arm out in front of you with your palm down. Place your other hand over the top of your hanging hand and then push up against this restraining hand. If your elbow hurts when you do that, you've got tennis elbow for sure.

Now's the time to ice your elbow and stretch the muscles. Do so again before and after your next match. A good way to stretch is by repeating the exercise you used to test for the problem—that is, hold your arm out in front of you, elbow straight, wrist down, and with your other hand pull the hand on the bad side under as far as possible. That

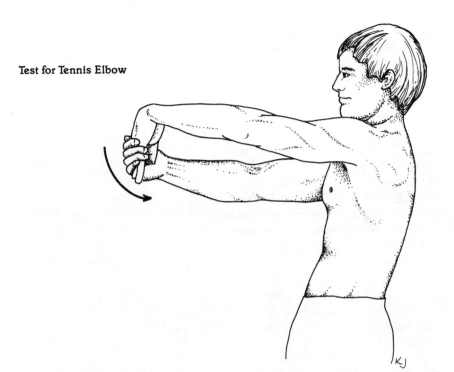

may hurt; if you do this stretch with your elbow bent, it's easier on you. So you may want to go through a progression by starting with the elbow bent and gradually straightening it out as you go. The muscle is stretched the most with your elbow straight.

Icing and stretching ought to head off the problem, but if the pain comes back again, and yet again, it's time to try another tack: see a doctor immediately. No, not a medical doctor. A tennis doctor. In other words, *get to the tennis pro and take some lessons*. Professional tennis players almost never suffer from tennis elbow because their fundamentals are sound. The best treatment for tennis elbow, better by a long shot than any kind of medical treatment—ice, stretching, cortisone shots, anti-inflammatory drugs, surgery, anything—is a series of lessons to improve your backhand. That, combined with ice and stretching, and done early enough so that the muscles haven't had time to weaken and tighten, will cure virtually any bout of tennis elbow. It's almost foolproof.

But let's say that, like most of us, you haven't done anything about your tennis elbow, and now the pain has increased to the point where you can't ignore it any longer. Perhaps you've tried various treatments prescribed by your friends in the locker room. (Lots of people do get well through these treatments; they're certainly not to be scoffed at. It's just that often they may work for the individual involved but not necessarily for anyone else. Tennis elbow is like shin splints in that way—there are almost as many suggested treatments as there are cases.) Let's say that none of them worked for you. Now what?

You must make the elbow comfortable enough so that you can rehabilitate it. That usually means stop doing those things that hurt, tennis first and foremost. If you hurt, you're not going to use the muscles properly, even in rehab exercises, and if you don't use the muscles properly, they won't get any better but will simply continue to hurt—it's an old refrain with overuse injuries like this. Sometimes we put people in a sling, not because there's anything magic about a sling but because it makes them think about how they're mistreating their elbow before they go ahead and do it. If you don't even try to open doors or pick up heavy objects because the sling reminds you of your mortality, you're ahead of the game.

Once the elbow stops hurting, you can start stretching and strengthening the muscles that attach to it. We've already talked about how to stretch the muscles. The best way to strengthen them is by doing reverse wrist curls. Rest your arm on a table with your wrist and hand hanging free over the edge. Then curl your wrist back as far as possible. If you run your fingers along the top of your forearm, you can feel the muscles contracting from the wrist all the way to the elbow. Repeat the curl ten times, say, three sets of each. If your elbow remains pain-free, then gradually add resistance in the form of a dumbbell or a piece of surgical tubing. Increase the weight of the dumbbell or the resistance of the tubing as you grow stronger.

Forearm Strengthening Exercise for Tennis Elbow

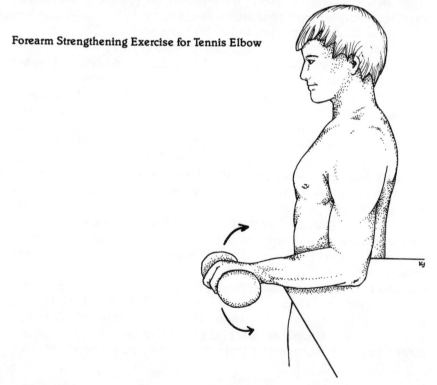

One of the old methods was to take a shortened broom handle, nail to it a piece of rope or string with a weight tied on the end, and roll up the string around the handle by rotating it with your hands and wrists. That'll work too, although the reverse wrist curls with weights or tubing work even better. Any of these exercises can be a good preventive measure as well. No need to wait until your elbow hurts before getting around to strengthening the muscles in your lower arm. Contrary to popular belief, squeezing a tennis ball will *not* do anything for tennis elbow. That exercise works on the muscles that flex your wrist, rather than the extensors. Not only are these muscles not involved in tennis elbow, they're usually relatively strong already. As most of us don't have forearms like Rod Laver, however, doing anything in the name of strengthening is admirable. Just don't expect squeezing a tennis ball to do much for your tennis elbow.

Now to the nether world of tennis elbow remedies, those things that may or may not do anything for anyone, depending on your mood, hair color, and the phases of the moon. Many locker-room cures fall into this category.

Some people swear by a certain brand or composition of racquet, or equally fervently avoid others. Aluminum racquets, graphite racquets, wood racquets, composite racquets, mid-size, large, regular, tightly or loosely strung—nobody has ever been able to sort out which does what to whom. In fact, so many kinds of racquets have been accused of causing tennis elbow that probably no one kind is the culprit. It's more likely that it's a change from one racquet to another that helps cause the problem, much as a change in running shoes, floor surface, or bicycle pedal alignment can help bring about tendinitis.

So if you're going to change racquets, it's a good idea to do so as an experienced runner changes shoes—gradually. Use your new racquet for just fifteen minutes the first day, say, then go back to your old one. The next time use it for twenty-five minutes, the next time forty minutes, and so on, until you can finally put the old one aside for good. The same strategy applies for a new grip size. There's some data to suggest that using a slightly oversized grip decreases the amount of torque transferred to your arm, thereby decreasing the amount of force your elbow must tolerate. But make any change in grip size gradually as well. Let your elbow and the rest of your arm ease into these things.

Of all the tennis elbow appliances, the bands and braces and magic amulets, the most effective is the band. Nothing more than a strap, sometimes called a counterforce brace, that wraps tightly around the muscle just below the elbow, it seems to help people. It may simply smoosh the muscle enough that you use it a bit differently, or change the direction of the pull on the muscle—no one knows exactly why it works. But so long as it does work, who cares? Ours is not to reason why . . .

Just don't make the mistake of using these aids as cures. If they control your pain so that you can play, great. But *treat* your tennis elbow in the meanwhile. If you don't, you may find that what controlled the pain for a while no longer works, and your elbow hurts more than ever. Stretching and strengthening, perhaps taking anti-inflammatories like aspirin or Advil, icing after you play—all these treatments will help. And again, don't neglect the most important remedy of all: take a tennis lesson. Improve that backhand. (Interestingly, you almost never see tennis elbow in people with a two-handed backhand, because a two-handed backhand is really more of an opposite-handed forehand than anything else. It may be that when all the younger players who now use two-handed backhands reach their forties, prime tennis elbow age, we'll see much less of it. Whatever else Borg, Connors, and Evert-Lloyd have done, by popularizing the two-handed backhand they've made great strides in getting rid of tennis elbow.)

If you deal effectively with tennis elbow early on, you should never have to see a doctor—except the tennis doctor, that is.

LITTLE LEAGUE ELBOW (MEDIAL TENNIS ELBOW)

If lateral epicondylitis is the tennis elbow of recreational tennis players, medial humeral epicondylitis, pain on the *inside* of the elbow, is the tennis elbow of really good players. Pros and top amateurs rarely get the outside-variety tennis elbow, because their fundamentals are sound. Rather, they tend to get wear-and-tear tendinitis on the inside of the elbow—but not from a backhand. They get it from a forehand or a serve, that big, sweeping, overhead stroke that happens to be very similar to the motion of a baseball pitcher. So it's no surprise that medial tennis elbow is better known by its other name, little league elbow.

And here we return to the carrying angle, the elbow's tendency to resemble a crooked door hinge. It causes the forearm to splay out to the side when you straighten your arm—remember? When you follow through after making a pitch or hitting a tennis serve or forehand, that tendency to veer to the side is amplified. In the elbow this outward force causes the inside portion of the joint to open up. It literally tries to pull itself apart from the inside out, especially when you throw or hit from the side rather than over the top. But the ligaments and muscles holding the joint together won't allow such a catastrophe; they hold on tight. Elbow opening up, muscles and ligaments holding on—something's got to give. As usual, that something is the weak link in the chain, the tendons (and occasionally the ligaments, too). Over time, with pitch after pitch and serve after serve, they weaken, stretch, give a little. The result is tendinitis of the tendons attached to the medial epicondyle. You experience it as pain on the inside of your elbow.

So it's the inside equivalent of the more common lateral tennis elbow, with one important difference: whereas tennis elbow is muscular in origin—that is, it comes from too much being asked of the muscles that attach to the elbow—little league elbow begins in the joint. The joint itself tries to pull apart, with the muscles doing their darndest to hold things together.

With young people the problem becomes compounded, as the tendon actually connects to a growth center in the bone. Classic little league elbow is really a kind of Osgood-Schlatter's disease of the elbow. (See Chapter 5, "The Knee," for a discussion of Osgood-Schlatter's disease.) As the elbow opens up and the tendon strains at the bone, the area becomes not only irritated but enlarged as well. About a third of all little league pitchers probably have an enlargement of the inside of the elbow, but it's not any more of a problem than the tendinitis itself. There are no long-term consequences. It's more nearly something that shows itself in X-rays but might go unnoticed otherwise.

The old saw that throwing curve balls at too young an age is the cause of little league elbow in sandlot players may be true, but it's more likely that elbow problems are the result of the sheer quantity of throwing rather than what you throw. Little league elbow is not so much the result of specific muscle overuse as it is of general overuse of the entire arm. And it simply takes longer to learn how to throw a curve ball than it does to throw a fast ball. If it takes you one hundred pitches a day to learn a fast ball, it may take four hundred to learn a curve. It's that extra hour and a half after dinner spent snapping off curve balls with Dad or older brother that causes little league elbow, not the kind of pitch you throw.

The tennis equivalent is the grocery cart full of balls or the ball machine. Hitting too many tennis balls causes elbow problems. With one can of balls, it's hard to get into trouble, because you spend half your match chasing and picking up balls. But if the pro stands across the net with a cartful of balls, or the machine is spitting them at you rapid-fire, you'll hit more forehands and backhands in a half hour than you do in a couple of weekends of three sets a day, especially if you play doubles. And most people encounter the grocery cart and ball machine at a particularly unfortunate time, the beginning of the season, when they're trying to get back in shape. Wham! From months off watching it rain or snow to hundreds of balls coming at you. Your poor elbow can't win.

The tendon involved in little league elbow attaches right next to your funny bone—really the ulnar nerve—which runs in a groove behind the elbow and down into the forearm and the outside of your hand. If the tendinitis is really bad, the inflammation can move over into the nerve groove and irritate the nerve itself. Then it's as though you're hitting your funny bone all the time, and your little finger and ring finger may become numb and tingly. If the tendinitis becomes chronic, the tendon gives way to scar and degenerative tissue, a condition that can require surgery to clean out the area and reattach the tendon.

Sometimes little league elbow (and tennis elbow as well) can lead to numbness and tingling all up and down the arm, and sometimes to pain that doesn't come from the elbow at all but from the shoulder. It's the old interrelationships business again. If your elbow hurts, you use your arm differently; and if you use your arm differently, you may start using your shoulder differently. As we discussed in Chapter 8, "The Shoulder," using your shoulder in unaccustomed ways can lead to thoracic outlet syndrome, a stretching and pinching of the nerves passing over the muscles in your shoulder on their way down to your arm. Those irritated nerves then send messages of grief to the ends of the circuit (nerves aren't choosy—if there's irritation in one place, you may feel it in another). So sometimes what's needed at first is not elbow treatment but shoulder rehab. These cases can become complicated fast.

What to do about it

Elbow surgery is reasonably effective, but it *is* surgery. With almost any kind of major joint surgery, people never quite come back to their previous level of ability. In the elbow, the primary by-product is reduced range of motion.

But, happily, most bouts of little league elbow don't require surgery. As with tennis elbow, resting your elbow is the first thing to do. Icing it after use can help, as can taking anti-inflammatory drugs such as aspirin or Advil. Stretching and strengthening the muscles involved is good. You can do the same exercises as with tennis elbow, but with opposite results. The exercise that stretches the muscles involved in tennis elbow—dropping your wrist and pulling your hand underneath your arm—will *strengthen* the muscles involved in little league elbow (see the illustration on page 226). Cocking your wrist up and pulling your hand back will *stretch* the muscles involved in little league elbow.

So a little league pitcher who complains of elbow pain should stay away from throwing for a while and only gradually get back to playing when the pain subsides, all the while icing, stretching, and strengthening as suggested. But if the elbow continues to hurt, he should definitely see someone and probably have X-rays. The rule of thumb, especially when it comes to kids, is *never ignore joint pain.* If you do,

Forearm Stretching Exercise for Little League Elbow

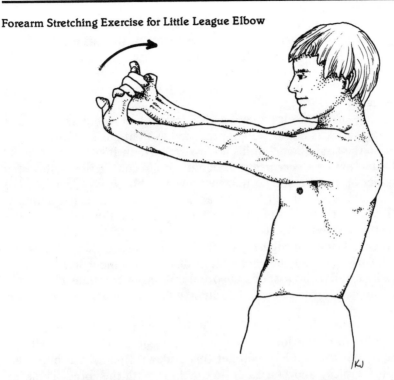

by the time a kid is sixteen he might have a chronically injured elbow, one that might bother him for the rest of his life.

But when all is said and done, because little league elbow is a function of overuse rather than poor technique or lack of strength, it may be one of those things that simply comes with the territory. If you hurt but want to continue playing tennis, say, you certainly should try the treatments we've suggested, and see a doctor if things don't clear up, but you should also realize that it may be a problem you simply have to live with. It comes down to weighing what's important to you—playing with some pain or playing less, or even not at all. It's the kind of dilemma that soon becomes very familiar to people involved in sports. And the only person who can decide which road to take is you.

JOINT MICE (SEVERE LITTLE LEAGUE ELBOW)

Joint mice are the little white loose things that scurry around in your elbow (in the knee, knee mice, in the shoulder, shoulder mice, and so on)—in other words, bone chips. They're caused by repeatedly snapping your elbow into full extension, as when pitching a baseball or serving in tennis. They can be the result of a bad case of little league elbow. Again, because of the elbow's carrying angle, which causes the inside of the joint to fly apart, the outside of the elbow tends to collapse in on itself, grinding the bones together. It's this mashing, the action of the head of the radius on the humerus, that can cause little pieces of bone to chip off into the elbow. And the more tired you get, the less able the muscles are to absorb the shock and fend off this smashing and crashing.

The role the muscles play in decelerating movements and thus absorbing shock is not as well appreciated as their ability to get things started in the first place, but it's no less important. It's a very sophisticated function, an *eccentric,* or lengthening contraction—almost a contradiction in terms. The muscle must be able to work against the direction of the movement, to contract at the same time as it lengthens, and all very rapidly. For example, when a pitcher follows through, the muscle that cocked the arm, the biceps, must now cushion the arm as it straightens. It must mitigate the effect of the muscle that extends the arm, the triceps, and the momentum of the movement itself. Otherwise, like a car without shock absorbers, nothing dampens the movement, and your arm can snap straight with an impact that can chip bones.

Joint mice can lead to pain and swelling, and the loose pieces can actually lodge in the joint, making it impossible to use your elbow. Suddenly, out of the blue, you get this godawful pain, like being hit with an ice pick, and you can't do anything with the joint. Then, as quickly as it came, the pain will disappear as the loose body gets out of the way. The problem can be especially serious when combined with osteochondritis dissecans, the strange tendency of bones to die in spots and simply flake away. (See Chapter 2, "The Ankle," for more on osteochondritis dissecans.) Pieces of loose bone as large as a marble have shown up in the elbow—almost half the volume of a joint that small. Children are more prone to this problem than adults, but, fortunately, it's very uncommon.

What to do about it

See someone. Sometimes the mice have to be removed surgically. The arthroscope is especially handy for this kind of operation. And another thing we sometimes do for people is overstrengthen their biceps. We put them on what otherwise might be an ill-conceived rehab program that actually makes them a little bit muscle-bound, so that the muscle will decelerate and cushion more strongly than usual and thus keep bone from bashing into bone.

Once more, with feeling: both tennis elbow and little league elbow become more frequent as we age. Women more than men are afflicted with tennis elbow—men more than women with little league elbow. One third to one half of all tennis players over forty years of age have some symptoms of one or the other. The likelihood of encountering either is related to how often you play now, how often you've played in the past and for how long (you've probably developed some degenerative changes in the tendons if you've played a lot), and the level of your technique. With tennis elbow, technique and strength are very important. The more of both, the less likelihood of getting tennis elbow. Little league elbow strikes without much regard to either. It's wonderfully democratic that way. It's pure overuse.

BURSITIS

Ever wonder why the skin at your elbow moves around so easily? One reason is that there's lots of it. It has to cover your elbow when it's bent as well as straight, and to do that it has to have lots of slack. The other reason the skin slides over the elbow so readily is that there's a bursa in there, a slippery fluid-producing sac that, as we've seen, tends to show up whenever something in the body needs to slide over something else. It's called the olecranon bursa, because it covers the olecranon process, that shoehornlike extension of the ulna into which the humerus fits. The bursa functions like a little pallet of ball bearings, reducing the friction between the bone and skin. We'd be much like a tin man without lubricating oil if we didn't have bursas.

The trade-off is that bursas easily can be irritated, and in the elbow especially, with its bony, exposed prominence, the olecranon bursa is often bumped. From bumping, the bursa produces more and more fluid, which causes it to swell, sometimes to the size of an egg. More than anything else, a swollen bursa is annoying, and it has a tendency to stay irritated because we so often rest our elbows against things, as, for example, when we read, write, work, and, often, eat (Emily Post, eat your heart out).

In the elbow bursitis is sometimes compounded by the fact that because the skin in the area is not only plentiful but thin (take a couple of fingersful and pinch it together—even in double thickness it's not very thick), the hair follicles are very close to the level of the bursa. If a follicle gets irritated from all the swelling, it can become infected and in turn infect the bursa. Elbow bursas are the most frequently irritated bursas in the body. And an infected bursa, already swollen and distended, adds pain to annoyance. They're no fun.

Sometimes, after a swollen bursa finally goes down, people will complain of what feels like tiny bone chips in their elbow. What happens is that the bursa isn't elastic, so when the fluid disappears you're stuck with a sac that's too big. The loose bodies in the elbow are really the wrinkles of the overlarge sac. In time they dry and harden, and then they feel even more like bone.

What to do about it

Ice can help reduce a swollen bursa. So can aspirin and other anti-inflammatory drugs. Be careful not to bump your elbow—a tough task.

If the irritation doesn't go away, you may have to see someone. Sometimes the only recourse is draining the bursa; sometimes people inject them with cortisone. The last resort is surgery to remove the thing. It's just such an annoyance to have this big, spongy egg at the end of your elbow all the time.

RADIAL HEAD FRACTURE

A fall on your outstretched arm and hand can break the head of the radius, that ice-cream-scoop-shaped bone that rotates against the humerus. The injury is the result of the force of the impact traveling up the arm to the joint, where it attacks the point of least resistance—the end of the radius. You'll know it from the pain on the outside of the elbow, and soon the joint will stiffen and swell. It may be the most common acute elbow injury that recreational athletes suffer.

What to do about it

See someone. Usually it's not a serious injury. You may not even have to immobilize your elbow, but rather protect it until it heals, which it tends to do very quickly.

EPIPHYSIAL FRACTURE

Since there are a number of growth centers (epiphyses) near the elbow, young people sometimes fracture these areas.

What to do about it

This is a painful, obvious injury, nothing that you'd ever dream of waiting out. See someone right away. It has some potential problems with injury to the vessels or nerves that cross the elbow and go to your hand. So it's a medical urgency, if not an emergency. Leave the elbow in whatever position it's in and call a doctor, or 911, or have someone get you to an emergency room. Again, *don't ignore sudden painful injuries to the elbow, or any other joint.*

DISLOCATIONS

Elbow dislocations show up in contact sports like football and wrestling, and, in particular, in gymnastics. Because of the elbow's carrying angle, a fall on your outstretched arm can push the joint apart. Female gymnasts are especially subject to dislocations, as their carrying angle is greater than that of males and so many of them have hyperextended elbows as well. Women's elbows are often not particularly stable and therefore more likely to dislocate. A dislocation is terribly painful, as it involves stretching or tearing of the ligaments around the joint and causes the muscles to go into spasm in an attempt to hold things together.

What to do about it

See someone. Often the treatment involves putting your elbow in a cast at an angle of 90 degrees for three weeks or so. For female gymnasts, though, that treatment might not work. The reason why offers yet more evidence of how sensitive the elbow is to injury.

With any injury, and especially after surgery, the elbow loses some of its ability to bend and straighten. For most of us the loss of the extremes of elbow motion would not present a major problem. We could continue running, playing tennis, swimming, biking, dancing pretty much as before. Not so the gymnast, however. Arm flexibility is crucial in this sport, especially because of gymnasts' need for the stability provided by a locked elbow. Carrying angle and all, if you can lock your elbow out straight, you can use it as a support member (in tumbling, say, or on the bars), much as a locked knee provides support—all without the necessity of muscle power. A locked knee or elbow is much like the spinal column in that it provides the stability of one bone perched on top of another.

If you can't extend your arm straight, however, you're forced to support yourself with the muscles that extend the elbow, primarily the triceps. Well, the triceps is not the world's strongest muscle, and female gymnasts in particular lack the upper body strength to rely on muscles alone. Males are better able to do it, but all gymnasts simply need skeletal stability.

So with female gymnasts, even though it's a bit more risky and requires a lot of attention, we cast dislocated elbows at less of an angle than we might otherwise. The hope is that when the injury heals the elbow will be able to extend farther than if it were bent at a greater angle in the cast. In any case, flexion comes back more readily than extension. Your biceps is stronger than your triceps. It'll crank your elbow bent even though the joint may be stiff. So when in doubt, we try to provide people with extra extension.

10 The Wrist and Hand

Alan Yamaguchi is short and sturdy, with impressive shoulders and arms. He looks as though he should be a gymnast, which indeed he is. The problem is that he hasn't been able to be much of a gymnast lately. His right wrist is red and swollen.

"Now I don't want to hurt you," Garrick says. "You tell me when you start to feel just the beginning of pain." He holds Alan's arm out and gently pushes the hand up and back, flexing Alan's wrist.

"There!" Alan says.

Garrick looks at Alan's wrist. It's flexed no more than 35 or 40 degrees from neutral, less than half of the 90 degrees a normal wrist will bend.

"Your problem is called impingement," Garrick says. "There's something getting in the way of your wrist flexing as much as you want it to."

"Tell me about it," Alan says. "I can't do the horse, I can't vault, I can't tumble. The only time it doesn't hurt is when I'm on the high bar or the rings. What is it, bone?"

"No," Garrick says. "It's not like impingement in the ankle, where you can see obvious bony spurs. Usually there's nothing obvious about wrist impingement. It's mainly soft tissue." He lifts Alan's good wrist. "See how the skin at the wrist wrinkles when you flex it? Well, the soft tissue under the skin wrinkles the same way. But if the tissue gets swollen for one reason or another, there simply isn't enough room in the wrist for it to wrinkle. The result is that your wrist won't bend all the way. It feels fine until you start to bend it, but at a certain point it starts to hurt."

Alan groans. "But I can still do push-ups," he announces.

"Show me," Garrick says.

Alan drops down to the floor and, balancing on his fingertips, without flexing his wrists, does five quick push-ups.

Garrick laughs. "It used to puzzle me how you guys could have impingement and still claim you did push-ups, until I asked somebody to demonstrate one day. You just don't bend your wrist, that's all. That's not fair. Not everyone can do that. It's not quite human."

The problem with impingement is that it feeds on itself. The wrist may swell in the beginning for a variety of reasons, but once swollen it continues to swell the more it's used. With enough use, some of that swelling may remain, permanently reducing flexibility in the wrist.

This may be no problem at all if you're not a gymnast. The loss of a few or even quite a few degrees of flexibility in your wrist won't bother your running at all, or your swimming, or even your tennis playing. It's another one of those injuries that's sports-specific, something that might not mean much to most people.

But that's not to say that most people are off the hook when it comes to wrist injuries. They're common. Even sports in which the wrist is not involved have a surprisingly high number of wrist injuries. It's hard to escape them. For example, roller skating and skateboarding are notorious for causing wrist injuries. Why? Because skaters and skateboarders fall, and the most common reaction on the way down is to thrust out a hand to break the fall. Well, you may break your fall that way, but you may break something else as well—your wrist. We've finally gotten to the bottom of the transmitted-force business that we've been talking about from the shoulder on down. Here the force is not transmitted—it's direct, and the wrist is the unhappy recipient. But the damage doesn't necessarily stop there. There's no guarantee that you might not injure something else higher up as well. Or lower down—that is, your hand.

A fall is just one of the ways in which you can hurt your hand. There are lots of others. Jamming your fingers is the most common; blows to and by the hand are not far behind. Dislocations, fractures, tendinitis, sprains—it's an impressive assortment. In fact, there are more acute injuries in the hand than anyplace else in the body. And that's just counting the injuries that are countable, those that show up at emergency rooms or doctors' offices. The bulk of hand injuries never see the inside of a doctor's office. People treat them by themselves, usually pretty successfully, but not always. The number of permanently twisted, crooked, bent, and gnarled fingers around testifies to that.

The hand and wrist may be small in comparison to other parts of the body, and their injuries not as dramatic as some we've discussed, but they can be as disabling as any of the others, especially for an athlete. A jammed finger can put a quarterback or pitcher or basketball player out of commission as surely as a dislocated shoulder or torn-up knee. A sprained thumb can as effectively prevent a dancer from partnering, a boxer from entering the ring, or a tennis player from stepping onto the court, as can a sprained ankle. And if any of you athletes out there are musicians or secretaries or surgeons or artists, forget it. Hand and wrist injuries can be the kiss of death.

The Wrist and the Hand

They're the body's last outpost, in a way the culmination of everything else that has allowed you to run, jump, bend, and stretch. The twist of a wrist and touch of a finger can make or break the entire body's athletic effort. Certainly that's true for a wide receiver stretching for a touchdown pass, a golfer lining up a crucial putt, or a basketball player putting up a last-second shot. From pool players to tennis players, handball players to bowlers, gymnasts to baseball players, how well your hand and wrist work is the key. A lot to ask of twenty-seven little bones, eight in the wrist and nineteen in the hand, even ones so artfully arranged.

The two forearm bones, the ulna and radius, are lashed together by ligaments at the wrist in a kind of shallow cradle. Sitting atop that cradle is a faintly oblong wedge of eight small bones, arranged in two rows of four, called the carpus. It's this junction of the forearm and wrist bones that is the joint proper; it allows the wrist its super flexibility. The wrist can bend up and back almost 180 degrees—the unimpinged wrist, that is; don't remind Alan Yamaguchi of the fact—and along with the forearm can rotate fully as much as that. As in the elbow, the radius rotates around the ulna to turn the wrist, but whereas in the elbow the radius slides along the humerus, which remains

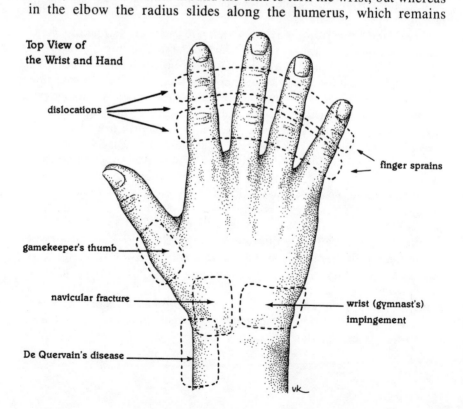

Top View of
the Wrist and Hand

dislocations

finger sprains

gamekeeper's thumb

navicular fracture

wrist (gymnast's)
impingement

De Quervain's disease

relatively stationary, here it takes the wrist along with it. When the radius rotates, the wrist rotates, while the staid old ulna stays pretty much where it is.

The wedge of small bones in the wrist is itself capable of some rotation, but its primary job is to provide a stable base for the hand and its fingers. Five columns of bones make up the hand, four bones for each finger and three for the thumb. The top three bones in each column (two in the thumb) are called the phalanges (from the Greek for "battle lines," which seems appropriate when you consider what the hands are often used for). The lower echelon of bones, the metacarpal ("beyond the wrist") bones, is masked by the fleshy part of the hand from wrist to knuckles, but you can easily feel the bones by running your fingers over the back of your hand, and if you wiggle your fingers you can see the dancing tendons that connect the bones to muscles in the forearm. There are muscles in the hand itself, but most of your hand's power comes from these muscles in the forearm, which operate as if by remote control, their agents long tendrils of tendons. One group of tendons runs up the back of your hand to extend your fingers and thumb; another group moves through your palm to enable you to bend your fingers. A web of ligaments holds the bones in alignment. The great majority of hand and wrist injuries in one way or another subvert this usually happy working family of bones, tendons, and ligaments.

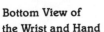

**Bottom View of
the Wrist and Hand**

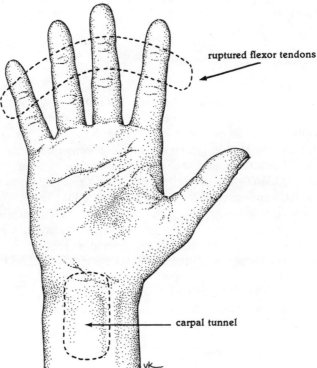

ruptured flexor tendons

carpal tunnel

NAVICULAR FRACTURE

It's the most common of the bad things that can happen to the wrist from a fall on an outstretched hand. And it's probably the worst. The navicular, or scaphoid (both words meaning "boat-shaped"), is a bone that lies at the base of the thumb, just beneath the hollow in your wrist that's accentuated when you extend your thumb. The bone is tiny, about the size of the last joint of your little finger, and it's the lowest bone in the wedge of eight that comprise the wrist. It directly abuts the radius. The positioning is important, because when you fall on your wrist the force may travel through the other bones in the carpus, as they have some give to them, but when it reaches the navicular all bets are off. The navicular has no place to go except right into the end of the radius. And in a test of strength between the navicular and the radius, the radius will win every time. The upshot is that often, caught in the middle, the little navicular will break from the impact.

That's not good. The navicular has a bad reputation for not healing back together. And because it's such a small bone, almost all of it is surface and in contact with other bones. That means that any kind of irregularity in the bone can cause even more trouble than it might otherwise. One of the first things that happens when you fracture your navicular—besides pain, that is—is that you permanently lose the ability to bend the wrist fully. There's no getting around it, navicular fractures are nasty. They're particularly common in wrestling and football.

What to do about it

See someone. Any fall on your outstretched hand that bends the wrist back and hurts for more than a day or so, not necessarily with a lot of swelling, even, should be seen by someone who knows what he's doing. And it probably should be X-rayed. This is one instance in which you should overreact and see someone more quickly than you might otherwise and take more X-rays than you might otherwise. If the X-rays don't show anything, and your wrist still hurts three weeks later, go back and get it X-rayed again. The adage in orthopedics and sports medicine is that anything that looks like a wrist sprain, particularly if it hurts on the thumb side of the wrist, is not a sprain until you've absolutely proved that it isn't a navicular fracture. Some people feel so strongly about the injury that if your wrist is sore on the thumb side but X-rays are negative, they'll put you in a cast and bring you back in three weeks to be X-rayed again, just to be sure.

Still, even after doing all that, it's a tough injury to pinpoint. It's hard to X-ray the navicular. Frequently people miss the injury, sometimes because they X-ray the wrong bone, sometimes because they X-ray the right bone but the fracture line simply doesn't show up (which underscores the advisability of getting another X-ray later on if the pain continues, as the fracture may be more visible once it has started to heal a bit). Once you are sure of the injury, there are two primary ways of treating it. One is to put your wrist in a cast and simply wait for it to heal. Some athletes, football linemen, for example, can get away with playing and wearing a cast at the same time. The drawback to this approach is that it can take nine to twelve *months* to heal. The navicular is a slow-healing bone, lacking a good blood supply to provide nutrients. The other treatment is surgery. Probably more than any other fracture in the body, a navicular fracture that won't heal back together requires surgery.

So the moral of the story is, if you fall on your outstretched hand and it hurts beyond a day or so afterward, especially on the thumb side, see someone. Overreact on the side of caution. As difficult as the injury is for a professional to treat, it's much more difficult, and dangerous, to ignore it and try to live with it.

OTHER WRISTBONE INJURIES

There are many different kinds, but they don't occur very often and are the result of very specific situations—nothing so general as falling on your outstretched hand. They, too, can be tough to live with, as the smallest displacement in the eight tiny wristbones can cause fits. Any wrist injuries that don't soon calm down should be seen by someone, maybe even a hand surgeon.

TENDINITIS

A variety of tendinitis can afflict the wrist, sometimes from nothing more offensive than taping your wrist too tightly. The most common wrist tendinitis is called De Quervain's disease, after the nineteenth-century Swiss surgeon who first identified it (and, incidentally, introduced iodized table salt). It affects the tendons that connect your thumb to the muscles in your forearm. These tendons allow you to extend your thumb, so that you can hitchhike or yell "Out at third!" You can easily see and feel them. There are three of them, two of which run closely together, and they straddle the hollow below your thumb that covers the navicular bone.

These tendons can become swollen and painful to the point where it seems as though they're infected. The cause can be any repetitive activity—tennis, weight lifting, gardening, rowing (feathering can bring it about, as you use your thumbs to help rotate the oars)—and the problem can become so bad that surgery is necessary. The sheaths that the tendons run in can become so scarred and restricted from the irritation that every time you move your thumb they squeak. That's one tip-off. The classic experiment, called Finkelstein's test, is to wrap the fingers of your hand around your thumb and squeeze toward your little finger. If you have De Quervain's disease, it'll hurt even to touch the thumb, much less squeeze it.

Another form of tendinitis affects the tendons on the bottom side of the wrist, those that allow you to flex your fingers. As with tendinitis anywhere in the body, it's the result of overuse or abuse. Again, tennis, lifting weights, rowing, or any other repetitive activity can bring it about. Tendinitis on this side of the hand, however, carries with it a special wrinkle. The tendons to the fingers, all eight of them (two for each finger), and one of the tendons to the thumb go through the carpal tunnel, which is literally a tunnel in the wrist and palm that protects the tendons on their long journey from your forearm to your fingers. But the tendons don't have the tunnel all to themselves. The median nerve that supplies sensation to part of your palm runs through there as well. Now the plot thickens. If the tendons become irritated, swell, and fill up the tunnel, they can squash the nerve, the only soft thing in there. It starts out about the same size as the tendons; if they get irritated, it gets scrunched.

So carpal tunnel tendinitis can not only cause soreness and swelling, it can bring about numbness and tingling from the thumb side of your palm all the way back to your forearm. And your hand might feel more swollen than it really is, just because you no longer have normal sensation in the area. It's most common in people with rheumatoid arthritis in their hands, and in women, usually older women, just before menstruation (because of the tendency to swell easily as a result of retaining water), but you see it in athletes as well. You can test yourself for it by tapping the area to see if you can reproduce the pain, by holding your hands with wrists cocked in prayer position, or just by letting them hang limp. If your wrist hurts in any of these positions, you most likely have carpal tunnel tendinitis.

What to do about it

The most important thing is to catch it early. Almost any tendinitis will do well if treated early enough.

Icing after activity will help. Contrast baths—warm water for four minutes, ice water for one, four or five repetitions two or three times a day—can be very effective. Just make sure you move your hand in the warm water. Anti-inflammatory drugs like aspirin or Advil can help. Wearing a splint will rest the tendons and so promote healing. Then, after the pain disappears and you're comfortable, gentle stretching is a good idea. To know which way to stretch, simply move your wrist and hand in the direction that hurts.

If you don't get to the injury early, you'll have to wait until the swelling goes down before doing any stretching. Ice and contrast baths can hurry the process along. If the muscles go into spasm, you'll want to immobilize the joint in a splint or removable cast to protect it. A good idea in any case is to splint your wrist at night—taping a little pillow around your wrist will do the trick—because your wrist can get into strange positions when you're sleeping and stay that way for a long time.

Again, you want to get rid of the soreness and swelling right away. Ice after activity, contrast baths, anti-inflammatories, maybe a splint. Then, once you're comfortable, on to gentle stretching. But if all fails, see someone.

IMPINGEMENT

For Alan Yamaguchi, impingement was a real problem, but most of us, athletes or otherwise, wouldn't even know it if we had it. It's one of those specialized sports medicine injuries that affect athletes who use their arms and wrists to bear weight, and none so much as gymnasts. Like a dancer who must be able to bend at least 90 degrees at the ankle in order to plié, a gymnast must be able to bend at least 90 degrees at the wrist to do a myriad of things. If you can't bend your hand back over your arm at a right angle, then all those tricks like handstands, cartwheels, back walkovers, and many more of the gymnastic repertoire of flips and twists become awfully difficult, if not impossible. If you can't dorsiflex your wrist—that is, bend it back—at 90 degrees, then you've got to do all sorts of spooky things with your elbow and shoulder to try to compensate for your stiffness. Otherwise, you can't get your body over your wrist.

It's not that bone builds up, as in the ankle, impinging on your dorsiflexed wrist, but that the soft tissue in the area becomes scarred and chronically swollen from the constant pressure exerted upon the wrist. And, interestingly enough, a gymnast with problems elsewhere, in the elbow or shoulder, may call upon the wrist to bend even more than 90 degrees to compensate for those other troubles. That added pressure on the wrist can lead to just what the gymnast can least afford: impingement. (Impingement also shows up in dancers and skaters who are partnering. It's definitely a weight-bearing injury, but it may not be your own weight that you're bearing.)

What to do about it

Like tendinitis, impingement responds to a regimen of rest, ice, contrast baths, anti-inflammatories, and, later, gentle stretching. Another thing we try to do is make the muscles on the bottom side of the wrist, the ones that pull the wrist down, so strong that they act as a brake and protect the wrist from unnecessary pressure. The logic goes like this: if you're not very strong and you do a cartwheel or any of the other tricks that load your body weight onto your wrist, then the wrist tends to sag until the soft tissue becomes so tight that it won't let you go any farther, or until the bones actually run into each other. That's not good. It's a kind of passive restraint that can lead to just the kind of irritation that causes impingement. If, on the other hand, you're really strong, then the muscles will prevent you from sagging over quite that far. That's active restraint, and it can help reduce the pressure on the soft tissue of the wrist by holding back a little.

You can further provide an external bolster by wrapping tape around your wrist, and there are mechanical aids, such as a splint, that can help protect the joint. But don't expect that, as in ankle impingement, an operation might solve the problem. Impingement in the wrist just doesn't respond well to surgery. Sometimes the only way to deal with the problem is to wear the splint for everything except actual competition, and simply grin and bear it during that time. Some people manage very well that way. It's one of those things that you may have to live with as best you can.

GANGLION

It's fairly common in racquet sports, or handball, but it's no big deal. A ganglion is a little fluid-filled cyst that grows on the back of the wrist. It's about the size of a marble and is especially prominent when you bend your hand down. People now feel that it's the result of a ligament injury that somehow went awry while healing. It's no cause for great concern, but it can become tender and bothersome, probably because it's pushing things out of the way as it grows. And it can cause tendinitis in the back of the wrist, because now the tendons have to navigate around this obstruction, and, as we've seen over and over in this book, any unaccustomed demand can disrupt tendons.

What to do about it

The traditional treatment involves the family Bible. Not prayer, that is, but smashing the Bible onto your wrist and breaking the ganglion (you do, however, want to be reasonably skilled when smashing it—you want to break the ganglion, not your wrist). The fluid is absorbed away after a few days, and if you're lucky, that's that.

These days, nontraditionalists tend to have ganglions aspirated or surgically removed. And sometimes ganglions just go away by themselves. The thing to ask yourself is if the ganglion is bothering you. If not, it'll cause no harm; you might just as easily ignore it.

JAMMED FINGER

It's the common finger injury. You jab your finger into a wall, catch a ball wrong, fall on the finger, inadvertently run into someone—the causes are many. The results are the same: a painful, swollen, stiff finger. It's probably a sprain, a stretching or partial tearing of the ligaments and capsule surrounding the joint. The difficulty is that these are tiny joints, so a little swelling can go a long way to completely disable the finger. And it seems to stay that way forever. Jammed fingers stay swollen for months, even if they're not very serious. And there really isn't much you can do about it.

What to do about it

What people *do* do about it, unfortunately, is try to get it back to normal as soon as possible. A swollen joint won't bend as far as a normal one, but people develop the habit of *making* it bend by worrying at it with the other hand. That irritates it more and makes it swell even more. People will come into the doctor's office complaining of a finger that hasn't gone down in four months, all the while pushing and pulling at it with their other hand as they talk. No wonder it hasn't gone down.

The thing to do with jammed fingers is leave them alone. That and contrast baths and anti-inflammatories are about all you can do. The next thing is to realize that even if you didn't jam it badly, it may stay swollen for a long time and you may lose a little bit of bend in it. But if you just can't bear to sit around doing nothing, then use the finger muscles themselves to exercise the joint, rather than your other hand. Hold the rest of the finger still and just move the tip, or whatever joint is injured. In that way, you won't bend the joint more than is safe—the muscles won't flex more than is comfortable—and you'll be strengthening the finger at the same time.

But, above all, patience is a virtue. Nine times out of ten the finger will come all the way back and the swelling will go all the way down, but you have to be nice to it in the meanwhile. And meanwhile can last an awfully long time.

DISLOCATIONS

Very common injuries. The causes are the same as those of jammed fingers: hitting a wall (dislocations are the bane of handball players) or someone else, falling on your finger, catching a ball wrong. And the results are similar as well: pain, swelling, stiffness in the joint. In fact, many jammed fingers are just shy of being dislocations, in which the joint capsule and ligaments tear enough so that the joint actually comes apart. You'll know it when you have a dislocation rather than simply a jammed finger. It hurts more, and it just doesn't feel right. Something feels and looks out of place, askew. And that something is, of course, the joint, usually the middle joint in the finger.

What to do about it

Since only about one in ten dislocations ever sees the inside of a doctor's office, people must be doing a good job of treating them by themselves. Most of them are popped back into place by the injuree or a friend, and most don't lead to any long-term problems. (Hand surgeons might not like hearing that. Some do lead to permanent instability, but the fact remains that there are just so many dislocations out there that heal and are forgotten that it's hard to recommend any more than reasonable caution concerning them.)

Icing is important, because these are little joints, and a little swelling can cause a lot of disability. Contrast baths, too, are an effective way of getting rid of swelling. And probably the best thing you can do is splint the joint, either by getting hold of a splint made for that purpose (never splint your finger on a tongue depressor, for example; the finger should not be straight) or by simply taping the injured finger to an adjacent finger. Like toes, fingers offer built-in splints, because the joints of one finger are seldom at the same level as those of the finger next door. The fingers lie comfortably against one another, joint against bone. Tape above and below the dislocated joint, and remember to allow the finger to bend a little. You should splint it in the position into which it falls naturally. Keep the finger splinted for two to three weeks. A word to the wise: don't remove the splint at night. It may be a great temptation to do so, as it can be tiresome to carry a splinted finger around all the time, but people often flex and extend their fingers while sleeping. If you leave your finger unsplinted, you may be awakened out of a dead sleep by a painful and throbbing dislocated finger tightly clenched into a fist. Keep the splint on until you can comfortably bend the finger. Then stretch the finger gently and gradually get back to your activity.

If there's any question about the joint, if it doesn't seem to improve and the pain just won't go away, then see someone for sure. It may be more than a dislocation—a fracture, say—and your fingers are too valuable to take any chances with them. See someone.

BASEBALL FINGER

Another common injury, also called mallet finger. Instead of catching a ball in your hand, you catch it against your finger. The impact drives the end of your finger toward the palm and pulls away the tendon that attaches near the fingernail. It may feel much like a jammed finger or even a dislocation, the other most common finger injuries, but you can recognize it by the fact that you can't straighten out your finger. You may be able to bend it—the tendon on the other side is still attached—but you can't straighten it. It's important to check for that right after it happens, because soon the finger will straighten up a bit just from the pressure of swelling.

What to do about it

If you can't straighten out your finger, better see someone. At the least your finger may have to be splinted for six weeks before the tendon completely reattaches, which it usually will do. At the worst the impact may have pulled off a piece of bone with the tendon, in which case surgery may be necessary.

For most of us it's not a horribly disabling injury; it's just annoying not to be able to straighten your finger. But for an athlete who depends on his hands, a baseball or handball player, say, it can be much worse than that. It can be a career-threatening problem. See someone.

FLEXOR TENDON RUPTURE

It's the football equivalent of baseball finger. As the sports are virtually opposite from each other in conception and pace, so this injury involves the opposite tendon, the one that flexes the finger rather than straightens it. In football it's usually the result of a player's grabbing the jersey of another, then getting his finger stuck in it while the other player moves away. The force can pop loose the tendon beneath the finger. In this case you'll be able to straighten the finger but not bend it.

What to do about it

See someone. It may be that baseball finger will heal by itself—not so this injury. The tendon usually must be reattached, and the only procedure that can accomplish that is surgery. Again, the test is to see if you can curl your fingers into your palm. If one finger sticks out, you've torn loose the tendon.

FRACTURES

Usually fractures in the hand or fingers are pretty obvious. They grate, they hurt, they swell. They're often caused by hitting something—or someone. An easy way to tell if you've fractured a finger, or even a bone lower down in the metacarpal area, is to straighten your fingers and just tap the tip of the one that hurts. If you feel a pain lower down in the finger, or into the hand, you've probably fractured it.

What to do about it

See someone. The danger of fractures in the hand is that the severed bones can rotate against each other, changing the alignment of the injured finger. If, for example, you bend your fingers toward your palm and one splays out in a different direction, it's the result of rotation, and you're in for a problem. A rotated finger can keep you from having a powerful grip, which can be a handicap in more than simply athletics.

Sometimes a splint will treat the fracture; sometimes surgery is necessary. Again, see someone.

GAMEKEEPER'S THUMB

It's the commonest injury of the thumb, and it may be the most frequent injury in skiing (it's hard to be sure, since, as with most hand injuries, people usually don't tell their doctor about it). It's a sprain of the ligaments at the base of the thumb, right where the web between the thumb and index finger begins. It's often called gamekeeper's thumb, which is what we'll call it rather than a "sprain of the ulnar collateral ligament of the metacarpal phalangeal joint" (huge sound of readers sighing with relief). The term comes from the custom of gamekeepers in jolly olde England of wringing the necks of birds and other small game animals between their thumb and index finger. If you wring enough pheasant necks you'll stretch out the ligament, and you end up with a joint that opens *way* up.

The problem is that when you lose the ligaments at the base of the thumb, you lose the ability to pinch tip to side. The joint is supported solely by ligaments in this direction—no muscles back it up. So although these are small ligaments, it can be a thoroughly disabling injury. Imagine trying to grip a bat, a tennis racquet, or a ski pole without being able to exert any pressure with your thumb. Which brings us back to why it's the most common ski injury, and why ski poles aren't made with straps any longer. People commonly acquire gamekeeper's thumb by falling with the pole in their hand. The impact slams the pole into the thumb, forcing it away from the rest of the hand and stretching or tearing the ligaments at the base. Now, with no straps to tether it to the hand, skiers are free to jettison their poles before falling.

What to do about it

If it's really tender, better see someone. The more torn rather than stretched the ligaments are, the more likely the necessity of surgery to reconstruct them. (If it *really* hurts, it could be a fracture rather than simply a sprain. In that case you should see someone for sure.) Otherwise, treat gamekeeper's thumb as you would any sprain: rest, ice, compression, contrast baths, anti-inflammatories. Then stretch gently and gradually begin to use the joint again.

MISCELLANEOUS INJURIES

Cuts in your hand can be a problem, especially anywhere in the palm. The tendons in the palm are right under the surface. A cut need only be three or four *millimeters* deep to reach a tendon. And, as with feet, the blood supply to the hand isn't so great. Infections can be another problem. Even blisters bear watching. Just don't ignore any kind of lacerations in the hand. Keep them clean and covered, and watch for infection.

There's a bunch of little muscles in the hand, but not much goes wrong with them. You can, though, get a lot of bleeding in the hand from something striking it, or from the hand itself doing the striking. The base of the thumb is an especially good place for internal bleeding. The bleeding, and the swelling that comes from it, can be very disabling temporarily but is not of a whole lot of consequence otherwise. Ice and compression will do the most good.

Bleeding under a fingernail can be the result of a blow (dropping something heavy on it is a great way to puff up the end of your finger). Sometimes the resulting pressure can hurt a lot. Just as in the foot, an easy way to get rid of the pressure is to puncture the nail with a hot paper clip or a sterilized tiny drill bit.

No matter what the injury, if it comes on dramatically, with a lot of pain and disability, it's a good idea to see somebody. If you've lost any function in your hands—you can't curl your fingers down, can't make a fist, can't straighten out your fingers—or if you get lots of swelling, or squeaking or cracking in the hand, then ice it for a day, and if the problem disappears, fine. But if it doesn't, *see somebody*. Your hands are simply too important to risk.

11 Exercising to Stay Fit—Aerobics and Weight Training

C arla French is an aerobic dance instructor, and she looks it. In her middle twenties, slim and solid, with sharp muscle definition, wearing tights and a French-cut leotard, Carla limps into the examining room. She's in tears.

"What's the problem?" asks Garrick.

Carla's story floods out. She had studied ballet since she was ten years old, then quit in her mid-teens when it was apparent that becoming a professional was not in the cards. Then, about two years ago, she discovered aerobics. She had been taking classes for a year and a half and loved it. She couldn't believe it had taken her so long to get back to the studio. Aerobics was nothing like ballet, of course, but in a way she liked it more. It gave her such a sense of freedom and exhilaration, and she loved what it was doing for her body.

Then she was asked by the manager of the studio if she wanted to become an instructor. Did she! Within a month she had quit her job as a receptionist in a dental office and was teaching full time. Her classes were popular, and it wasn't long before she was teaching three classes a day on Monday, Wednesday, and Friday and two classes a day on Tuesday, Thursday, and Saturday, beginning and intermediate.

That was three months ago. About three weeks after taking on such a heavy load, her right leg started to hurt. At first it just hurt after class, and only after the more advanced classes at that. Then it started to hurt after every class. She would rest it on Sunday, it would feel okay on Monday, but by the middle of the week it was hurting again. After almost two months of that—getting better and getting worse, getting better and getting worse—the leg started hurting all the time. She didn't stop teaching, but now she was able to do only a few of the exercises. For the rest she just stood there and told her classes what to do.

"Finally the manager told me that I couldn't teach another class until I saw somebody about it," Carla says. "She said that not only was she worried about me, but it was bad for business for people to see me limping around all the time."

"Can you put a finger exactly on the spot where it hurts?" Garrick says.

"Here," says Carla. She gingerly places her index finger on the outside of her right leg, about two inches above the ankle knob. "Right here."

Already Garrick has a pretty good idea what the problem is: a stress fracture of the fibula. He examines Carla more fully, then says, "If this is some weird variant of shin splints, you might be able to suck up the pain, and we can try to treat you and keep you teaching. But if it's a stress fracture, you're not going to get well until you back off from your activities, get pain-free for a while, then ease back into things. As teaching aerobics is your job, we'd better know for sure."

Stress fractures don't usually show up on X-rays, so the best way to know for sure is by the use of an isotope scan, a common diagnostic procedure that involves injecting a radioactive isotope solution that in effect searches out weakness in the bone. If the test is positive, and Carla does indeed have a stress fracture, what she has to look forward to is rest and lots of it. Of course, rest is a relative thing. To someone teaching fifteen aerobics classes a week, as Carla does, rest may mean dropping back to ten or five. The important thing is that she has to stop doing whatever it is that's making her hurt. For a stress fracture to heal, it must be absolutely pain-free.

"You don't mean it." Carla again breaks into tears. "What about my job?"

Garrick pats her on the shoulder. "I suspect you'll still have your job," he says. "More important, you'll still have your leg."

Aerobics

In one way Carla's experience is unusual: aerobic dance is remarkably injury-free. Compared to almost any comparably intense athletic activity you can think of, the rate of injury in aerobic dance is low. Even so, if you take on too much too soon, as Carla did, the result can be injury. It's a theme that runs through this entire book.

What is not unusual about Carla, in fact is typical of aerobic dancers in general, is her enthusiasm for her activity. Aerobics may be the most popular form of exercise in the United States. Estimates are that aerobic dance alone involves as many as 23 million people. The figures are particularly impressive with respect to women. There are more women doing aerobic dance than any other organized exercise activity, more even than in all the high-school athletic programs in the country put together.

And for good reason. Aerobic exercise can do all sorts of good things for your body. It helps lower blood pressure and cholesterol levels. It tunes up the cardiovascular system. Over time it actually changes your metabolism so that you tend to use accumulated fat for energy. When you go out for your run, say, the 300 calories you burn off come more readily from your spare tire than from your breakfast. (More on that later.) Aerobic exercise will help you do other athletic activities better (even if those activities consist of nothing more than walking up the three flights of stairs to your office without feeling as though you're going to collapse). And for many people it promotes a more healthy sense of self—you simply feel better.

Hefty benefits from such a simple activity, for aerobic exercise really is simple. All that's required to achieve a training effect is to keep your heart rate between 65 and 80 percent of maximum for as little as twenty minutes three days a week. It doesn't matter what you do. Running, rapid walking, cycling, swimming, dancing, rowing—these are the most common aerobic activities, but anything will do. Some people climb stairs (although you need a lot of stairs to keep it up for twenty minutes), some people skip rope, some people shoot baskets. So long as you *sustain* your heart rate at 65 to 80 percent of maximum for twenty minutes, you're in business.

Anything less than that certainly won't hurt. There's no magic in twenty minutes. It's just a guide. Twenty minutes three days a week will give you consistent benefits from your training. That's not to say that nineteen minutes won't give you some benefits as well, or that ten minutes isn't better than nothing. It's just not as good as twenty or more.

How can you figure out what heart rate to sustain? A good question. Here's an easy way to approach the whole business. A rough method to determine your maximal heart rate is to subtract your age from 220. Thus, a forty-year-old person's maximal heart rate is about 180 beats per minute. Now figure 65 to 80 percent of that—let's say 125 beats per minute (about 70 percent of maximum). If you're forty years old and you can keep your heart pounding along at 125 beats per minute for twenty minutes, you're giving yourself a healthy dose of aerobic exercise. If you're sixty years old, a good rate would be about 110 beats per minute. If you're twenty, 140 beats per minute will do—and so it goes. An easy way to measure your heart rate is by feeling the pulse in your neck, just below the jaw line. Count the beats for ten seconds, then multiply by six. Nothing to it. Twenty beats during that ten-second interval indicates about 120 per minute—right on the money for a forty-year-old.

If all this higher math puts you off, a quick and dirty way of doing the same thing is to approach any activity with the attitude that you should break into a sweat but always be able to carry on minimal conversations (except while swimming, of course, at once the most antisocial and nonsweaty of sports). If you're biking with friends and they can't understand what you're saying because you're simply too short of breath, you've probably gone beyond aerobics. If you can't ask your aerobic dance neighbor a question or can't respond to what she says because you're out of breath, you've probably gone beyond aerobics. If you finish your run in a pool of sweat, unable to move or talk, you've gone beyond aerobics. It's such a *civilized* activity, so reasonable and do-able—thus its appeal.

All this is not to say that finishing your run sweaty and out of breath is bad for you (not necessarily, that is, but it may be, depending on how you go about it; it can lead to injuries), but it probably isn't aerobic exercise. The term comes from the Greek words *air* and *life,* and that's the key: aerobic exercise involves breathing, the utilization of oxygen. Sounds obvious. We're always breathing, right? But when we're out of breath, our intake of oxygen can't match our output of energy. The demands of the exercise outstrip our ability to fuel it by breathing. Then the body must rely on its stored energy sources. Thus, the term *anaerobic* —without air life.

Activities such as sprinting, whether on a track, a bike, or in a pool, are anaerobic. A runner may not even breathe once during a sixty-yard dash. A swimmer may take one breath going out and a couple more coming back during a fifty-yard sprint. All that time the body uses its stored-up carbohydrates to keep going. This kind of exercise hurts more than aerobic exercise. Your muscles burn because you're depleting the available fuel and all that's left are waste products like lactic acid. "Go for the burn" means exercise to the point at which you hurt. Any serious athlete deals with that kind of hurt daily.

Done to excess, any aerobic exercise can become anaerobic, and there's nothing wrong with that. It all depends on your reason for exercising. Anaerobic exercise is the name of the game for building strength in specific muscles. When you abuse a muscle to the point where it burns, you begin to build strength in that muscle. Body builders bring their muscles to this point all the time. It's what pumping iron is all about. But if your intent is general fitness—and now we're talking about most people—aerobic exercise is an efficient and reasonable way to go about it. The results are not so quick and dramatic as those of anaerobic exercise, but they're attained at less cost of time and effort. And if you stick with it long enough, the benefits become measurable and lasting.

They show up in subtle ways. Some people exercise as a means of living longer, but there's no real evidence to suggest that you're likely to live one month longer if you do aerobics than if you don't. It's the quality of your life while you're still around that increases. The odds are that you'll simply feel better. You'll find that you're able to ski longer or survive an extra set of tennis. You'll be able to take a hike in the mountains without getting winded as easily as before, or walk up the hill to the office without huffing and puffing. Your weight might not change too much—aerobic exercise is not an efficient way to lose weight (combining exercise with diet control can produce results, however)—but slowly that weight becomes distributed differently. Muscle begins to replace fat. Muscle is heavier than fat, so you may not lose much weight, but it also looks better than fat. Muscle is more dense, takes up less space, so the exchange of a few pounds of fat for a few pounds of muscle can improve your appearance. And although none of these benefits shows up immediately, you don't have to wait too long either. Pulse rate and blood pressure changes often occur in a couple of months. Weight loss takes longer. The change in metabolism that allows your body to more readily burn off accumulated fat becomes measurable in three to six months. All this for twenty minutes three days a week.

But exercise, any kind of exercise, is not for everybody. Some people simply hate to exercise. Being browbeaten into it by a physician, a spouse, or a book can actually decrease the quality of one's life rather than improve it. If you'd rather curl up with a good book in front of the pool than swim twenty minutes of laps three times a week, that's okay. It depends on what you want from life. And the same reasoning applies to exercise. It's important to remember that any kind of exercise *may* be good for you. It all depends on your reason for doing it.

How to Pick Your Own Style of Aerobic Training

You need to know what you want from your exercise and how much you enjoy doing it. The activities usually associated with aerobic conditioning are those that are constant through a period of time—running, rapid walking, swimming, cycling, rowing, dancing—in contrast to tennis, say, which involves spurts of rapid activity combined with spurts of preparing for and recovering from action while watching the ball zoom by. But it's crazy to decide that swimming laps is going to be the exercise for you if you hate the water, or if you're trying to get in shape for skiing. By the same token, there's no sense running a few miles a day if you don't like to run, or if you're preparing for tennis season. And there's certainly no reason to do either activity if you don't like to be alone. Besides, lower-body workouts don't do that much for upper-body sports and vice versa, especially if you don't enjoy what you're doing.

So, if you have goals in mind for this conditioning, match the exercise with the goal. If it's skiing you're after, then running will help, cycling maybe even more so. If it's tennis, then an upper-body conditioner like swimming or rowing might be the way to go (some running won't hurt, certainly). If it's general conditioning, then pick an activity you like to do and one that's convenient for you to do. If you live in San Francisco and you can't manage running hills, it may not be worth it for you to have to drive twenty minutes to flat terrain, run for twenty minutes, and then drive another twenty minutes home. On the other hand, there's not one person in San Francisco who lives more than fifteen minutes from a fitness facility. In that case, aerobic dance might be the ticket for you, especially if you like the companionship and the idea of having an instructor, and don't mind paying for the privilege. Running, of course, is free.

Previous medical problems can determine what activity you choose. If you have knee problems, then running up and down hills may not be a lot of fun, nor will pumping a bike for a few miles. Low-back problems may not be the ticket for the jarring involved in running or the stretching demanded by the rowing machine. Hundreds of shoulder revolutions in the swimming pool might not be the best thing for chronic shoulder problems. You may have to test out activities, experiment a bit until you find what's right for you.

On the other hand, just because you've had a bad experience with one or another of these activities doesn't mean that they're out of the question forever. You simply may have to modify your approach. For example ...

RUNNING

Often people complain about running on a track—it's boring, it hurts, it gives them shin splints. Well, it can be boring, that's for sure. In fact, if aerobic conditioning is your aim, it may not be such a good idea to run on a track at all. Besides the fact that running through town or through a park can be much more interesting, some tracks simply are not designed for training. They're built for competition—synthetic tracks fall into this category—and although they may feel soft, they're actually too hard and unyielding for the constant pounding produced by frequent runs. The result of training on these tracks can be nagging injuries. If you must run on a track, be sure it's cinder or dirt, not synthetic.

Sometimes people complain of not being able to find a grassy area to run on. Well, today's shoes are designed to run on asphalt. The idea of the cushioned sole is to make asphalt as easy on the body as grass. You can even run on concrete in these shoes, but asphalt is much better.

It's softer, and the subtle irregularities of the surface allow your shoe to sink, providing even more cushioning. So, if possible, run in the road rather than on the sidewalk. Alternate directions, however. Always running against traffic is all well and good, but some roads are heavily crowned, with the result that you're always running on a hillside, with the right side of your body at a higher level than the left. After twenty minutes, the discrepancy can take a toil.

Many coastal dwellers prefer to run on the beach. As glorious as it can be to jump into the waves at the end of your workout, beach running has a couple of problems. One is that the soft sand converts your shoes (or bare feet) into negative-heeled footwear, because your heels sink into the sand as you run. There's nothing intrinsically wrong with a negative heel—some shoe companies have made their mark by claiming that it's a desirable commodity—but when you're used to having your heel raised above the rest of your foot, as is the case with almost all of the shoes people wear, suddenly dropping your heel below the level of the rest can put a lot of strain on your Achilles tendon and calf and hamstring muscles. If they're not pretty flexible, look out. Tendinitis and muscle strains can result.

The other problem at the beach is similar to that of running on the road: you're always navigating a hillside. The best thing to do is pick a beach that slopes as gradually as possible, and stick to the moist, hard sand. Low tide is often a particularly good time to run. And if you start out going in one direction, be sure to take the time to come all the way back in the other. Equalize the effect of the slope.

CYCLING

Lots of people have had bad experiences with cycling, especially people with knee problems. True, the nature of pumping a bike—up and down, back and forth, against resistance—can be hard on the knees, but more people suffer from cycling than need to, most likely because they haven't set up the bike well.

Before you take off for the first time, you should adjust your own bike. The shop where you bought your bike may not have set you up well. Often they adjust things for greatest efficiency, as though all their customers, like themselves, did hundred-mile excursions on their days off. That approach may not translate into the greatest safety and comfort for someone with a knee problem. And it can be a good idea to set up on an exercise bike to start with. It's easy to control, easy to adjust, and you don't have to carry a wrench and socket set around in your back pocket for the duration of your ride.

Begin by finding the ideal seat height for you. The higher the seat, the straighter your knee when the pedal is most distant from you. The lower the seat, the more bent your knee. You know when your knee hurts—find the position that bothers you least. (In general, your knee should be about fifteen degrees shy of full extension when the pedal is farthest away.) Then check your foot placement. That's a consideration that can be crucial in being able to cycle comfortably.

To wit: although bike pedals and toe clips point straight ahead, most feet don't. Most people's feet turn out, at least a little. Some people are pigeon-toed: their feet turn in. It's the rare foot that points absolutely straight ahead, as though milled that way in some factory. Yet bike designers don't seem to acknowledge the discrepancy. The pedals lie square to the sprocket, toe clips secured to the front, inviting the foot to slip in and stay there, parallel to each other and the bike. Yet forcing feet to be aligned that way would be like making runners fit into parallel shoe-wide troughs. That would be ludicrous, but cyclists do the equivalent all the time.

Don't let yourself fall into that trap. You can tell which way your feet fall by sitting on a table with your knees bent and legs hanging. Notice which way your feet point.. That's the way they should point on the pedals. Although they may not look it, toe clips allow you to vary the angle of your feet by about 5 to 8 degrees in either direction and still stay secured. That's enough for most people. Hardcore cyclists spend lots of time and money making sure that their cleats are attached at precisely the right angle for comfort on the pedals. Less serious bikers can do much the same thing by actually gouging out a ridge in their cycling shoes so that their feet fit onto the pedals the same way all the time. Don't do it, though, until you're sure you've found the right angle.

Once you're situated properly, with feet comfortably placed and height adjusted, you may find that most of your cycling problems fade away. If some still persist, it may be wise to try another sport. There are lots of ways to get your aerobic conditioning.

ROWING

Watch out for similar things in rowing. Are your feet situated properly? They don't have to point straight ahead in a rowing machine, either. The boot supports oarsmen use often are angled for specific foot demands. And you should be able to adjust the slide distance in the machine to accommodate your particular frame. It may be that bending forward is rough, or perhaps it's pulling all the way back that hurts. Do whatever's comfortable for you. Again, for general aerobic conditioning it's not so much what you do as whether your heart rate is high enough or long enough. Even a relatively short rowing stroke can offer you a good aerobic workout if you go at it hard enough.

Advice—Approach It Gingerly

For people who exercise, especially beginners, the woods are full of advice. Most of it is well meant, some of it is actually well taken, but much is not terribly well founded. The advisory columns in the national fitness magazines can fall into this category. They are often written by people who are in the upper echelons of their sport and are trying to wring that last tenth of one percent of efficiency from their activity. For such a person—a runner, say—subtle or not-so-subtle alterations in foot position and arm swing may pay real dividends. But for the rest of us mortals, those who are happy to run our few miles, get our heart rate up, and enjoy the scenery along the way, any conscious attempt to alter our form may lead to disaster.

If you look like a duck when you run, it's probably because your hips and knees are built in such a way that your most efficient form is ducklike. If your legs bow and feet point in when you run, so be it— that's the way you're built. For someone to suggest that your feet should point straight ahead, or your hips remain straight, or your neck and head stay motionless can be ludicrous and dangerous. Sports medicine physicians make a good part of their living seeing people who tried to change their running gait.

There is a time for refining technique, of course, but for the recreational athlete it shouldn't come at the expense of what feels comfortable. A word to the wise: when beginning any activity, or sustaining one for recreational purposes, *do what comes naturally*. And for heaven's sake don't change because somebody advises you to. The idea for most people is to enjoy what they do, remain comfortable and free of injury, and realize the benefits of exercise at the same time. Remember, it doesn't matter how you get your pulse rate up or how you look doing it—the benefits will come.

An Approach to Working Out

All right. The moment has come. After numerous fits and starts and solemn promises that you're going to start any time now, the day is here. You've locked the office, run the errands, paid the bills, washed the car, picked up the kids, and fed the cat—no more excuses, time to get going. You're wearing your new running shoes, matching shorts, latest tank top. It's a beautiful day, not a cloud in the sky. Everything's set. There's only one problem: now what do you do?

Your goal is clear—twenty minutes of 125 heartbeats per minute three times a week—but how do you get there? Some people simply decide, "I'll run a mile to start with." Well, assuming you're fit enough to run a mile—and many people are, at least the first time they try—how long will it take you? Eight minutes? Eighteen minutes? A half hour? Remember, in aerobic exercise it's not how far you run that counts but how long and at what heart rate. So you set off on your mile and, pride being what it is, you push hard the whole way. You arrive back home in fifteen minutes—not long enough for a good aerobic workout but a significant length of time nevertheless—with your tongue hanging out. No matter. At least you survived. The first day has been a success. And a few minutes later, shoes off, supine on the sofa, a cold glass in your hand, you're comfortable enough to wonder what the big deal about this exercise business is, anyhow. It wasn't so damn hard. One mile today, you'll push up to two tomorrow. Who said you weren't in good shape?

The next morning you can hardly get out of bed. And as the day wanes, so do you. You're too tired even to think about running. Best take a day off and get back to it tomorrow.

The next morning comes—you're worse. You hurt in places you didn't know existed. If you were simply too exhausted to move yesterday, today you're too sore to move. It hurts to climb out of bed, hurts to straighten up (you sort of shuffle into the shower, à la Groucho Marx), hurts to open the refrigerator door, hurts to bend into the car. And by the end of the day these general hurts have coalesced into specific hurts: your calves and Achilles tendons feel as though they're on fire, and your lower back undoubtedly was used for a punching bag when you weren't looking.

Finally, a week later, you've recovered enough to entertain the thought of moving again, maybe even running again, and a few days after that you once more pull on your running shoes and matching shorts. What have you gained? Nothing. Not only have you trashed your body, perhaps planted the seed of a problem that could persist and turn into something bigger, but you really haven't even started on the road to conditioning, because you've had to wait so long before you were able to go out again. Now, as you face setting off on your run, you're back where you started, perhaps even behind, and to make matters worse, after a couple of weeks of beautiful Indian summer the weather has turned. Today it's gray and drizzling, hardly running weather. Good Lord, you wonder, what's the big deal about this exercise business, anyway?

If a goodly portion of the income of sports medicine doctors comes from people who try to change their natural way of doing things, another sizable chunk comes from people who refuse to work into condition gradually. You simply have to start gently. So much so that it can almost seem ridiculous at first.

If twenty minutes of running is your goal, begin by working up to rapid *walking* for twenty minutes. Start with five minutes of walking the first day, two and a half minutes out, two and a half minutes back. (It's a good strategy for any aerobics activity. Distances really don't mean anything in aerobics; time does. If you split your time in half—half out, half in—at least you know you'll always make it home.) Then do seven minutes, and a couple of days later do nine. Go up a couple of minutes every other day, and in a couple of weeks you'll be walking for twenty minutes at a good, rapid pace, without hurting anything or suffering the next morning. At that point you've already begun to enjoy an aerobic workout.

Start exchanging running for some of your walking. Run the first five minutes of your workout and walk the last fifteen. A couple of days later run the first seven minutes and walk the last thirteen, then nine and eleven, and so on. Build up just as you did with your walking, and in a couple of weeks you'll be running the entire workout with no ill effects afterward.

Always remember to do the running at the *beginning* of the workout. Do your stretching and bending to warm up, and then get right to the running. Don't do what most people do, which is leave the tough stuff to last. There's no worse time to change your activity to one that's more stressful than when you're tired. It's hard enough for your body to have to worry about running instead of walking. Don't make it deal with fatigue at the same time.

The principle holds true for any stressful change. If you're training for the San Francisco Marathon, say, and you know you have to get used to running up and down hills, add the hills to your workout at the beginning, then run the flats. If you're going to add some sprints, do the fast stuff early in the workout rather than at the end. And so it goes. The less fatigued you are, the better able you'll be to handle change.

It's good to remember that you detrain at least twice as fast as you train. If you've been unable to work out for a few days, you shouldn't start right back in where you left off. Those few days of idleness have deconditioned your body twice as much as a comparable amount of exercise would have built it up. You don't have to start all over again, necessarily, but you should drop back to a level that's slightly less than that which you feel able to handle and then gradually increase to your normal speed. The good thing about such a step backward is that after a short layoff you'll be able to come back to top speed more quickly than it took to get you there in the first place.

If the reason you can't work out happens to be illness, then it's especially important to get back gradually. You've not only missed time and have suffered the deconditioning that mere lack of exercise brings about, but your body has been torn down by illness as well. You can really hurt yourself by starting back too hard. Being in bed for a week with the flu is much like being in space—you actually experience a decrease in muscle size and capability.

Remember also that the more fit you are, the more it takes to drive your pulse rate up high enough to be able to realize aerobic benefits. It's the bittersweet irony of aerobic training: as you become stronger, your heart is able to function more effectively with less effort, and the things you did yesterday to drive up your pulse don't necessarily do the trick anymore. You simply have to work harder to sustain the same benefits. Similarly, a fit body will readily relax. Your pulse rate will drop back to normal at the slightest break, rather than race to catch up, as it used to when you took a breather. So if you're involved in an activity that changes pace often during those twenty minutes, you may not be realizing twenty minutes of aerobic conditioning. During a significant amount of that time, your heart rate may have dropped back to nearly normal.

For most people, training every other day is enough. There's nothing wrong with working out every day, but you really don't need to—not for aerobic conditioning reasons, that is. Three to four days a week are enough to provide solid benefits. And, interestingly enough, after four times a week the increase in benefits doesn't keep pace with the increase in time and energy. Whereas working out four times a week may be 33 percent better for you than just three, training five times will not be 25 percent better than four. And training eight times won't be twice as good as just four. After a certain point, the rate of increase in the benefits of training flattens out. If you're a competitive athlete, then it may be worth it to grind out five, ten, or even more workouts a week for the relatively small increase in conditioning that extra effort gleans. But for those people who exercise for general fitness rather than with specific athletic goals in mind, the only real reason to do aerobic conditioning more than four times a week is that you enjoy it— which, all things considered, may be the best reason of all.

As for Carla French, she's back teaching, sort of. The isotope scan confirmed Garrick's suspicion that she had a stress fracture on her right leg, but it also turned up an incipient stress fracture on her other leg. That leg didn't hurt Carla—yet. It was only a matter of time.

So now Carla teaches the stretching and warm-up portion of her classes, and she supervises the cool-down. But to look at her you wouldn't suspect that she's pretty much been out of the studio for weeks. Now she swims and, by placing the pedals directly under her heels so as to reduce her ankle motion, she's even able to ride the stationary bicycle. She'll be back. But next time she'll work up to fifteen classes a week rather than throwing herself into it as though

she'd been doing it all her life. Her legs, and the rest of her body, will
last longer that way.

Weight Training

Aerobic conditioning is not the only valid kind of exercise, of
course. In fact, it can be a good idea to combine aerobic exercise with
other kinds, even alternate them day to day. A solid course of exercise
for just about anyone might include an aerobic workout every other day
and weight training every other day. Aerobic fitness is primarily
cardiovascular conditioning—weight training concentrates on the muscles themselves.

People usually go into weight training for two reasons. One is to
build strength. If you're a serious athlete, weight work can help you
perform better in your sport. If you're a skier, for example, you've got
to have rock-hard quadriceps. Weight training can help strengthen
those muscles. If you're a tennis player, you need strong legs and
shoulders. If you're a male dancer, you've got to have strong shoulders
and arms for lifting your partner. And it may be that you simply want to
be stronger for general, everyday reasons. You're tired of being exhausted for days after moving the furniture around. You want to be
stronger for yard work. Weight training can zero in on any particular
muscle group and help build strength.

The other reason is to look better. Muscle is better looking than fat.
You can work with muscle, tone and develop it. You can't tone fat. In
fact, one kind of fat, the infamous and dreaded cellulite, is much like
having an injection of lard under your skin. If you were rendered, that's
what it would be like. Weight training offers a way to attack these
areas, and if not eliminate them—you can't really spot reduce through
weight or aerobic training—at least firm them up. Any area of the body
will look better if the muscles underlying it are firm. You'll feel better
as well.

HOW SHOULD YOU APPROACH WEIGHT TRAINING?

Gradually. One of the real problems with fitness facilities is that
frequently they're run by people for whom lifting weights is a way of
life rather than simply a means to an end. For these people the idea is
to be as muscular as possible and *look* as muscular as possible—all of
which is fine, of course, but those may not be your goals. Yet often
these instructors create programs for you that are similar to the ones
they follow in order to look that way. These programs are geared to the

development of muscle bulk, and bulk may be the last thing you want. Runners don't want bulk. Tennis players don't want bulk. Certainly dancers don't want bulk. And often these programs emphasize rapid increases in weight-lifting capabilities. It's very impressive to pull your chart and see that in three months you've increased the weight you can lift 300 percent. Gives you a feeling of accomplishment.

But such huge percentage increases can be misleading. If you begin a free weight program able to bench press 50 pounds, say, and in a few months are hoisting 150 pounds, that's a 300 percent increase. But, as in anything, the easiest gains are the early ones. Another person, someone who's stronger to begin with, may begin at 150 pounds and during the same amount of time increase to 175 pounds. That's less than a 20 percent increase. Does that mean that the first program is better than the second or the first person is in better shape than the second? Nonsense. It all depends on where you start and what your goals are.

Similarly, weight training instructors often push you hard. The usual approach is that as soon as you can handle twelve repetitions at any given weight, add a plate. Well, if you're not very strong to begin with and you're lifting only thirty pounds on the knee-extension device, a full ten-pound plate represents a 33 percent increase. That's a big jump. A number of such increases, all of which are certainly possible in the beginning stages of a lifting program, look great on the progress chart. You'll probably notice some new muscle. You may also notice some new knee problems.

Our usual recommendation is that you shouldn't increase anything, ever, by more than 20 percent. And even that's a large increment. Ten percent might even be better. That rule of thumb pertains not only to lifting weights, but to distance and time as well. And it's wise to at least do twenty-four to thirty reps on the Nautilus machine before adding weight. That's asking a lot—people get bored doing too many reps— but it's even more boring being hurt. (A way to hedge the bet would be to do fewer reps and add only half a plate at a time.)

The better fitness facilities increasingly offer the services of exercise physiologists, and more and more the instructors have had some training in the area. So it's not as hard to get good training advice as it used to be. Still, the most important aspect of any fitness program is that you yourself know why you're doing it. Is it to bulk up or trim down? To prepare for a particular activity or to gain overall strength? To develop a particular muscle group or to keep in shape during the off season? The more you've thought about why you're exercising, the more accurately an instructor can tailor a program for you, and the more readily you'll attain your goals. The reason *why* you're there in large part determines *how* you should use the equipment.

HOW TO LIFT WEIGHTS

It's a discussion we probably wouldn't be having were it not for Nautilus equipment. Nautilus is as much responsible for the success of the fitness movement as anything else because it offered uniform equipment with uniform training programs. It took the weight room out of the smelly, boxing-style gym where women wouldn't go and transformed it into the shiny chromed and mirrored little palaces that are rapidly replacing singles bars as preferred places for the sexes to get together. The equipment is attractively and invitingly designed, and it actually offers a solid workout. Because of its eccentric cam, Nautilus was the first to offer equipment that loaded the muscle appropriately through the whole range of motion. It provided less resistance at the extremes of motion, where you're weaker, and more during the midrange, where you're stronger. Whereas people used to do the bulk of their lifting through the midrange only, because no one was strong enough to handle extremes, with Nautilus it was possible to lift uniformly through the entire range of motion. Moreover, if you used the equipment correctly it *forced* you to go through the entire range, and to stretch to get into the machine in the first place. Properly used, the equipment provided strengthening and stretching, so much so that with Nautilus equipment you may not need to stretch quite so much before beginning to lift. Still, stretching before any exercise is a good idea. It's one of the eight cardinal rules of lifting. They are:

1. *Stretch before and after lifting.* You'll feel much better afterward.
2. *Always lift weights that you can control.* If you start quivering when you lift, you're probably working with more weight than you can handle. A muscle that quivers is approaching its breaking point. And that's when the body begins to compensate by arching the back as well as performing other ill-advised tricks. Not good. Keep your lifting under control.
3. *Have somebody watch you.* Lifting weights with a friend is a good idea, because then someone can check on your technique and alert you to any bad habits. One of the problems with many fitness facilities is that they just don't have enough people (or the people don't have enough time—they're too busy trying to bring in new memberships) to properly supervise the weight room. If you lift weights incorrectly—arching the back is the primary offender (see Chapter 7, "The Back and Neck")—you might as well not lift at all. Partner up.
4. *Lift deliberately.* If you lift ballistically—that is, by bouncing into the weights—you're not going to gain the full benefit of the lifting because you're using momentum to help you. More than that, you can actually tear a muscle by beating into a weight that's too heavy.
But *deliberately* doesn't necessarily mean slowly. There's an advan-

tage to tailoring your training as closely as possible to the pace of the activity. if you do high-speed things like sprinting, swimming, dancing, gymnastics, then it can be a good idea to do high-speed reps. Slower, endurance activities like long-distance running may demand slower reps but more of them. But, in any case, lift deliberately and come down deliberately, always keeping your back pressed into the backrest. It's the coming down, the eccentric contraction, that is the most effective strengthening technique.

And go through the entire range of motion. Don't cheat yourself by using the cheater bar when you should be using your muscles.

5. *Work up to heavier weights in small increments.* A 20 percent increase is plenty. Ten percent may be even better. Sometimes it's impossible to increase this gradually, as facilities don't always have equipment with half increments, for example. But do the best you can within the limits of your particular facility. No matter the temptation, don't think that you can add two or three or even more plates each time you increase. Step up gradually.

6. *Find equipment that's the right size for you.* Smaller men, many women, and children have been the odd people out in many cases—the equipment simply has been too large for them. Now equipment designed for women is available, and the better nonspecialized brands are adjustable. Lifting with the wrong size equipment can lead to injury.

7. *Don't hurry through your workout.* When you race through a lifting program you start to do things wrong—you get tired, begin to arch your back, use less than the full range of motion—and the result can be diminished benefits at the least, injury at the worst, not to mention the fact that hurrying through is no fun. Give your workout the time and concentration it needs.

8. *Give yourself proper rest.* The ideal program might involve alternating lifting every other day with aerobic workouts every other day. Although it's often advertised as such, weight-circuit training usually isn't aerobic. When you're actually using the equipment, you're probably doing anaerobic training (pant, pant), and the breaks between stations can bring your heart rate down. So combining weight training with aerobic training is a solid way to go.

HOW TO DECIDE WHICH MUSCLES TO STRENGTHEN

First you have to know why you're exercising. Is it for a general tune-up or to get in shape for a specific activity? If the former, you may want to hit the entire circuit of stations. If the latter, then take your cue from the way you feel after doing the activity. For example, if you're working out to get—or stay—in shape for tennis, then simply remember how you felt last year when you went out and played for the first time *without* getting in shape first. What hurt? Where were you sore the next day? Those are the areas to work on.

With tennis, it's likely that your calves will hurt because you're using your soleus and gastrocnemius muscles to keep you up on your toes. Your back may hurt from all that bending and stretching. And your shoulder will most likely hurt, for obvious reasons. (And if you can't remember all this from last season, drag yourself out on the court for a refresher—it will come back quickly.) Armed with that information, simply find the equipment that works out the muscles in question and emphasize those stations in your workout. If in doubt, consult with a staff member. It's that easy. And other activities will just as clearly communicate their needs. Come the new season, you'll likely find yourself toned and ready to go.

FINDING YOUR LEVEL

Finding my level? What do you mean, finding my level? I just plan to get better and better.

Well, you may be in for a surprise: there *are* limits. Hard as it may be to accept, each of us has a point beyond which we can't do more. If that weren't true, people would be running two-minute miles and bench pressing 1,500 pounds. We just can't go on forever. But people assume that they can. If I can lift 150 pounds on the knee extender today, why can't I lift 175 pounds tomorrow? And 200 pounds soon thereafter? Why, it's just plain un-American to think that you can't; our society is always geared to do more. But the fact is that if you work at it, you'll arrive at a point where you're in good shape, and to go beyond that point probably means that you're going to get hurt, all the more so because after the age of twenty-five we probably get 1 percent weaker and 1 percent less flexible every year. Part of the reason for that is cultural—until the fitness boom we became much more sedentary as we became older—but for the most part it's just the way things are, one of the joys of aging. So if you want to keep doing what you've always been able to do, it'll take that much more effort just to hold your own.

But, you may ask, what about professional athletes? They're always trying to do more. They don't attain a certain level and stay there. True enough, but they pay a high price. To begin with, pushing the limits is a full-time job; you don't have time to do much of anything else. Second, successful athletes are a millimeter away from disaster all the time. They train to be always on the edge—push a little harder and they're liable to fall off. Top athletes constantly must deal with injuries. It's an occupational hazard for them, but not the happiest situation for the recreational athlete who's trying to get some fun out of his activity, hold down a job, and cultivate relationships with other people at the same time. You just can't do everything. Try and you'll be injured too much of the time.

So it's important to find a level that agrees with you and not worry because you aren't constantly doing more and better. Remember, the more fit you are, the more grudging your gains. At first your progress can be spectacular. It's easy to get used to 20 percent gains every week. But that kind of euphoria just doesn't last. If in the beginning you can almost measure improvements by the day, soon you're able to measure them only by the week, then by the month, and after a while you may not be able to measure them at all. The road to fitness looks something like this:

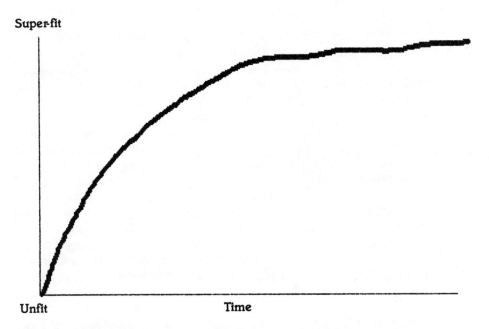

Super-fit

Unfit   **Time**

Spectacular gains at first and then the long, hard road. So stay with it, but don't expect improvement forever. Realize that what happens during the first two weeks will never happen again. Find a level that is satisfying and reasonably free of injury, and then best of luck in trying to stay there.

Warnings

Joint pain. If you hurt where you bend—in the knee, ankle, wrist, or elbow—then you may be in for trouble. These joints are pretty much devoid of muscle. Pain there is not a good sign.

If you hurt where you rotate—in the shoulder or hip—you're on somewhat safer ground. Both joints are embedded deep in muscle and other soft tissue. Pain here may well be muscular, something you might be able to stretch out and work through.

And if pain, no matter where it is, just doesn't go away, better think twice. Exercise can be terrific for someone who's healthy, but if you work out an injured body you invite real problems. And no matter how important it may seem to keep up your regimen, nothing is worth serious injury. See someone.

Stretching

Nobody thought very much about stretching until about twenty-five years ago. It was then that people in football (which is the origin of many of the things we do in conditioning) decided that weight training should be an integral part of getting in shape. In those days it was mostly free weights, and in order to maximize the amount of weight they could lift, people lifted only through the minimum range of motion. The result: muscle injuries. And the result of that was the stretching programs that we still see. These programs became popular not because football itself necessarily tore muscles, but because the weight programs, ill-conceived and sometimes ill-performed, developed substantial but tight muscles—thus the term "muscle-bound"—and these muscles readily tore. Stretching programs were an attempt to alleviate the problem. If muscles were well stretched beforehand, maybe they wouldn't become so tight and tear so easily during lifting.

In time, the fitness industry boomed and stretching became more than simply an attempt to prevent football players from injuring themselves during ill-advised weight sessions—it became a way to prevent any injuries and, more than that, an end in itself. Now we have stretching books, stretching TV shows, stretching classes. People go into stretching programs for stretching's sake. There's no goal, no end in mind. You just want to become more, and more, and more flexible. But when are you flexible enough? Certainly you'll never be as flexible as the instructor—she has been at it for years—but there she is, day after day, twisting her body into pretzels that you'll never come close to matching.

Still, you try, and the result can be an injury. We see lots of problems with these programs. You can only be so flexible. Like weight training, endurance training, and any other kind of training, there's a point beyond which you can't go without hurting yourself. Too much stretching can do more than stretch muscles and tendons—it can stretch ligaments and muck up joints. You have to decide how flexible is flexible enough, and stay at that level. And, for better or for worse, some of us are just not destined to be very flexible. Somehow or other we survive.

If you're in an activity that requires a certain degree of flexibility— that is, if your stretching is a means to an end—then it's a different story. Gymnasts have to stretch because they're going to put themselves into abnormal positions. Baseball pitchers have to stretch their shoulders because they pull way back before releasing the ball. Tennis players rear back before serving. Dancers likewise need a certain amount of flexibility—stretching is a way to attain it. And people who are simply going to jog around the block, swim a few laps, or lift a few weights can profit from stretching. It's a way to loosen up, get the blood flowing, tone the muscles. It's a good thing to do after exercise to keep your tired muscles from contracting and being sore the next day. And it can be important to rehabilitate a previously injured muscle or get it ready for exercise. But to approach stretching as a goal in itself, a way of dealing with other sins—no. There has never been anyone who has been able to document that a stretching program will prevent any injuries to muscles not injured before. It may be that the opposite is true: stretching for its own sake can cause more problems than it prevents.

Let your body be your guide. In any activity, listen to what it's telling you. It rarely lies. Rather than setting a goal and conforming to a schedule, it may be wiser—and safer—to proceed at a pace your body feels comfortable with. It never hurts to push a little, but when a body's shouting "Stop!" or "Slow down!" it doesn't pay to ignore it.

Rather, it *does* pay if your business is sports medicine.

12 Ballet

S tephanie Blau lies on her back on the operating table, her right ankle propped up while nurses clean it and prepare it for surgery. Her problem is almost unique to ballet: the bones and tissue at the front of her ankle joint have thickened to the point where she is unable to plié. Were she involved in almost any other activity, it would be no problem at all, but the plié is one of the foundations of ballet. All jumps begin and end in a plié, as do many turns. It is used at the barre to stretch the muscles and tendons. A ballerina who can't plié is like a springboard diver who can't spring—performance suffers athletically *and* aesthetically.

But a plié puts great pressure on the ankle joint. The skin and soft tissue over the bone must compress and wrinkle like an accordion. Sometimes, in reaction to this pressure, the bones grow ridges that lock against themselves, and the tissue swells, further reducing flexibility.

"These problems seem to surface when the dancers are at the highest level in the schools," Garrick says, "or during the preapprenticeship or apprenticeship years, when they're working very, very hard to make the company. There's no time to rest, so they get worse and worse. Virtually all the surgery we do for this kind of problem is on dancers between sixteen and twenty years old."

This describes Stephanie perfectly. A slim, blonde seventeen-year-old studying at the highest level of the San Francisco Ballet School, Stephanie first noticed the problem two years ago. "It started to hurt every time I did a plié," she explains. "Everything has to do with the plié, and I just couldn't do it. My heels would come off the floor, and the teachers would tell me to keep them down, and I'd try, and it would hurt more. It hurt a lot when I'd land after a jump, and it would hurt taking off and turning. And little by little it got worse. It's a bummer."

She has been working with Garrick for a month to see if there's a way to solve the problem without resorting to surgery. A physical therapist devised exercises for her, gave her hot and cold contrast baths. They tried ultrasound heat treatments, anti-inflammatory drugs.

Nothing worked. It's clear to Garrick now that nothing will work— nothing short of surgery, that is. So far as Stephanie is concerned, she'll try anything. At stake is a career in dance.

Now she lies quietly on the operating table as anesthesiologist Hugh Vincent gives her an injection of sodium pentothal, which will gently tranquilize her before the more powerful anesthetic puts her all the way out.

"All right, Stephanie," says one of the nurses. "Lift your leg so we can put clean linen under your ankle."

Groggy, drifting, perhaps dreaming that she is in the studio rather than on the operating table, Stephanie does as she is told. Up goes her leg, straight up, 90 degrees, toes nicely pointed, until it crashes against one of the overhead lights illuminating the table. The nurses dissolve in laughter. None of them has ever seen anything like this before. Just a reminder: this is a dancer you're dealing with.

Now they must prep Stephanie again, for the light casing may have contaminated her ankle. Scrub, sterilize, dry, and again they're ready to put clean linen under her leg. Anesthesiologist Vincent moves both overhead lights out of the way, retreats to his place behind Stephanie's head, and says, "Okay, Stephanie, this time you can lift your leg as high as you want."

Their second mistake. Stephanie groggily points her toes and transcribes a lovely arc, 180 degrees, interrupted only by Vincent's head. Her foot clips him in the face, almost stripping away his surgical mask.

After that, the surgery is almost an anticlimax. The nurses control their laughter and prep her one more time (this time carefully lifting her leg for her), Vincent rearranges his mask and replaces the overhead lights, and Garrick begins. It's what he calls "futzy surgery," involving the removal of some of the scar and swollen tissue in the ankle and then actually chiseling away the built-up bone hindering the movement of the joint. It's as though a sculptor were at work—if sculptors worked through tiny inch-long incisions on surfaces they can hardly see. And the sounds are those of a sculpture studio: scraping, scratching, knocking, the ping of hammer against the tiny chisel. "Orthopedic sounds," Garrick calls them.

There are no blueprints to go by, no ideal against which to measure progress. Everything is relative. Discolored tissue points to excessive rubbing, and a glimpse of pinkish rather than snow-white bone suggests an eroded area. "Interesting," Garrick says. "You can see evidence that someone this age has already begun chewing away at the cartilage in that part of the joint. She has a high arch, and I think that a high arch goes with this."

Garrick wants to take off enough bone to restore flexibility, but not enough to weaken the joint. "It's a little like shortening the legs of a coffee table," he says. "You take off a little here, a little there, but you don't want to be carried away by zeal."

Finally, a probe into the incision by his sterile-gloved little finger tells him that the joint feels right. "What do you think?" he says to the nurses. "Shall we pull up the tent and go home? Just don't tell her to lift her leg again, that's all."

The instant Vincent turns off the anesthesia Stephanie is awake. She'll spend the night in the hospital, start a muscle rehab program in a couple of days, and be back in the studio soon. The likelihood is that at the least she'll be able to plié without pain. At best she'll be more flexible than she was even before the problem began. And if, as a result of the surgery, she has the chance to find out if she'll be able to dance professionally, Garrick will consider the operation successful.

"It's what makes having to operate on a seventeen-year-old tolerable," he says. "That and the fact that it isn't an injury that will follow her through her life. You take athletes in some sports—their injuries are going to be a problem forever, regardless of what they do after they retire. Some linebacker who blows out two or three ligaments in his knee is going to suffer from that no matter what he does. Most dancers' injuries are so specific to dance that their residual in the real world is not very high."

Which may be a relief in one way but can complicate dancers' lives in another. Because so many dance injuries might not even be noticed in the outside world, it's hard to find someone to take care of them. You need someone who knows dance as well as medicine, and those people are few and far between, so much so that the sad fact is that medical care for dancers is almost a contradiction in terms. It's where medical care for football players was a good twenty-five years ago. The big companies attract people that take care of their dancers reasonably well, but that's about it. The rest of the dance population is forced to fend for itself, and, as anyone knows who has been forced to seek treatment for an athletic injury, fending for yourself may find you a competent doctor but not necessarily one who is used to dealing with sports injuries, much less dance injuries. All too often a dancer with what may be a routine injury in dance encounters a physician who has never dealt with the problem and whose advice is to stop dancing until the injury heals. Well, for a dancer to stop dancing is the kiss of death. You *can't* stop dancing. You may take a break from performing, take class in such a way that you don't risk making the problem worse, but you must stay active if at all physically possible. But the inexperienced doctor—inexperienced with dancers, that is—delivers the dictum: stop dancing. No wonder so many dancers seek help outside the mainstream of medicine—from herbalists, naturopaths, acupuncturists—often with useful results. At the least these people offer the dancer a sympathetic ear and attempt to set up treatments that allow her to continue dancing.

All that is changing, but slowly. For most doctors, there's little real inducement to direct a practice at dancers. Most dance problems are very specific overuse injuries that require a lot of time and knowledge of dance to sort out, whereas if you're dealing with contact sports, say, an anterior cruciate ligament tear is an anterior cruciate tear is an anterior cruciate tear. It doesn't matter much if it happens in football or while tripping over the family dog—the treatment is the same. And often that treatment involves surgery, which means big bucks. In contrast, taking forever to figure out that a dancer's lower back strain is the result of improper positioning of the hip due to overly tight quadriceps, and then devising specific exercise therapy that the dancer can do while continuing to dance, may be a great boon to the dancer, but it brings home neither the bacon nor spin-offs that can lead to other high-paying cases for the doctor. And often dancers have little money; billing becomes a problem. The only real rewards for the doctor are those gained from helping people in general and from dealing with the dancers themselves, who are among the most pleasant, grateful, and attractive people to step into the office. But, with rare exceptions, a doctor simply can't make a living by building a practice around dancers.

So it's important that dancers search out someone who knows dancing. You want to find someone who knows his stuff *and* tries to figure out ways to keep you dancing while helping you recover from your injury, which from the doctor's point of view may be a pretty tough trick but is good medicine. You're just buying trouble if you try to keep dancers out of the studio. They may pay lip service to you, but they're going to get back sooner rather than later no matter what. Then you'll simply see more problems later on. For certain problems the "doctor" to see may be another dancer. Dancers know how to take care of minimal common injuries like foot problems—corns, blisters, calluses, modification of shoes—better than anyone else. More serious problems, however, may require a physician. And now the dancer, or the dance parent, is faced with the biggest trick of all: finding a good one.

FINDING A DOCTOR

For the person new to dance it can be a daunting task. Often your family doctor's advice, while sound in other areas, may be off the mark when it comes to dance. Indeed, how may an uninformed doctor react when asked if a dancer should continue to take class? What does it mean to "take class"? Sitting at a desk while a teacher rattles on—that's the common interpretation of the term. Many doctors have never even seen a ballet class, and that lack of exposure doesn't always lead to the best medical advice. So how do you find someone who knows what's involved in dance?

If you're new to an area, or new to dance, a first step might be to comb the Yellow Pages for someone who advertises himself as a sports medicine doctor. At the least, such a person is probably used to dealing with active people who want to become active again. The first couple of minutes of the first interview should tell you if you've made a mistake. If a doctor doesn't respond to dance terminology, or gives little indication that he's interested in learning, it may be that you should look elsewhere.

Step two: you might call a local company for advice. Unfortunately, in some companies the official doctor may be a financial patron who likes ballet but has had little real interaction with dancers. Again, the initial interview should tell you a lot.

Step three: the head of the dance department at the local college might be able to recommend someone good. You might also ask your own teacher. People who deal with and are responsible for dancers should know what it takes to keep them going.

Step four: talk to other dancers. The best way by far. Dancers have an even better underground than runners do. At the very least, other dancers can point you toward someone who will listen to you rather than simply advise you to stay out of the studio. At best you may actually find someone who will suggest good treatment. And it never hurts to ask what it was that caused your dance friend to visit the doctor's office and what the treatment consisted of. If your friend's ailment is similar to yours and the treatment was successful, consider yourself lucky and on the right track.

Children in Ballet

It probably goes without saying that ballet is a world unto itself. For all its beauty, and the dedication it inspires from those involved, it can be a particularly demanding world, and even a forbidding one, especially to people entering it for the first time. And once the world begins to engulf you, it's difficult to retain a sense of perspective. Parents and their children who become hooked by ballet know the phenomenon all too well: the overriding imperative in life becomes dance. And as to how much, the answer is always "More!"

So, for parents and children just entering ballet, and those in various stages along the way, here are some suggestions from a sports medicine point of view.

BEGINNERS

Most kids begin ballet for recreational reasons. As in recreational gymnastics, a class a week rarely hurts anything. It's probably good, because it teaches kids a bit about their bodies and gives them something to do instead of sitting in front of the TV set. There are virtually no problems in recreational ballet.

GETTING SERIOUS

When kids start to become serious, it's usually for one of two reasons: they decide (or Mother and Father decide for them) that they really like ballet, or they start taking ballet to enhance their performance in other activities, notably gymnastics and figure skating. If the focus is ballet, then, the path is pretty straightforward. You start to advance and increase the number of classes at a rate consistent with your ability. You have to be able to trust your teacher in this regard. A tip-off as to whether you're progressing too quickly is how you feel. Your body will let you know if it's doing too much too soon. It speaks a pretty persuasive language—it's called injury.

If your interest in ballet is as a means to enhance other activities, however, you'd better watch out. Therein lies danger. It's hard to be semiserious about ballet. If your child takes class once a week just for the fun of it, fine. But if the motivation is more serious than that, one class just won't do—especially if the goal is to complement another sport. Once a week is simply not enough to make a difference. Moreover, the muscles and techniques involved in ballet are different enough from those in other activities that a casual exposure can actually hurt rather than help performance elsewhere. The experience of one nationally ranked skater is a case in point: she took a hard ballet class once a week, found that she was invariably stiff and aching the next day, yet still had to skate a five-hour workout. The day after that she would hurt so much that for the next couple of days she was unable to skate effectively at all. So she held back during workouts to nurse her body. By the time the next ballet class rolled around, she once again felt good, but then the class would make her stiff afterward, and the same cycle began again. She was taking just enough ballet to tear down her body, but not enough to condition it. Rather than attending class only once a week, she would have been much better off not taking ballet at all.

Similarly, a person who takes aerobic dance just once a week has a higher likelihood per hour of being injured than someone who takes at least three days a week, because the occasional dancer never reaps the conditioning benefits. If an athlete takes ballet as a complementary activity, she should take class three times a week and should start during a time when there's not much going on in the other sport. Later, after her muscles have become accustomed to the classes, she may be able to cut down to twice a week. Even then she may not be realizing all the benefits of the ballet training, but at least she'll avoid the hazards.

THE NUTCRACKER SYNDROME

Every year when early December rolls around, we brace ourselves for an onslaught of ballet injuries. The reason? *The Nutcracker.* Not that there's anything wrong with this old chestnut of a ballet, it's just that for many kids it offers a first chance to perform. Suddenly, a child who has been taking class once or twice a week is thrown into a rehearsal schedule that doubles or triples the amount of time she spends in ballet slippers. Even in the youngest children, that kind of rapid onset of activity can bring about problems, usually overuse injuries. They're not long-term problems, but they can assume an importance far beyond their seriousness because of the emotional involvement, especially that of the parents: *"My child* has been chosen for *The Nutcracker.* What do you *mean,* she might not be able to perform?" But the sad truth is that because the rehearsal period is often so contracted, sometimes no more than a couple of weeks, if a child is hurt badly enough to see a doctor there's a good chance she won't be able to make the show.

The way to get around the problem, of course, is to begin rehearsals earlier and gradually work up to the intensity of the last couple of weeks. Teachers also might integrate rehearsal work into classes, thereby avoiding the abrupt rush of work that can bring about overuse injuries, and students might simply take more classes as *Nutcracker* season approaches. But, given the need of most ballet schools to do the best they can with limited resources, both financial and human, such long-term solutions may not be realistic. Until then, parents and children simply may have to get used to some brand-new aches and pains come Christmastime.

RAPID GROWTH SPURTS

Dancers who attend summer workshops notice it a lot. The slim twelve-year-old ballerina, the shortest and lightest girl in class, comes back the next summer toting baggage she never had to deal with before—things like hips and thighs. Or the short, compact dynamo of a fifteen-year-old boy shows up a head taller, with arms and legs that seem to flop around like a rag doll's. The growth spurts of adolescents can cause them, and their teachers, to think that all of a sudden they've been handed a new body, one that just won't respond to their commands any longer.

And it's true, it might as well be a new body; during growth spurts things can change that much. Weight distribution changes as you grow, center of gravity changes, proportions of body parts change. Your head weighs pretty much the same throughout life, and the trunk doesn't change as much as the extremities—but, oh, those extremities. A couple of unfamiliar extra inches of leg or more flesh around the thigh and hips can make a big difference when you're trying to cut through space as gracefully and powerfully as possible. Coordination, that tenuous art based on precisely calibrated interrelationships, can fall apart pretty easily when new proportions are added.

Not only that, but the rapidly growing dancer runs a higher risk of injury than otherwise. Your skeleton outgrows the rest of your body at such times, making the muscles tight. And, as we've seen over and over in this book, tight muscles are readily injured muscles. Ballet is better-equipped than other activities to cope with this risk, however. It may be that there is no other athletic activity that offers a training regimen as thoughtfully designed as ballet. The slow, deliberate progression from stretching at the barre to practicing the same movements later in the center, then performing them onstage, develops strength and flexibility simultaneously. No other sports activity begins a student with the very same movements that she'll be using later when actually performing. And because by the time they enter their growth spurts serious students are in the studio a lot, stretching and practicing for hours at a time, the transition to awkwardness and increased injury risk may occur gradually.

One good thing that some gymnastic clubs do is keep growth charts on their kids and update them every month. When the young gymnasts start sprouting up, the instructors move them into a group of specific exercises that stretch the areas most frequently involved in muscle-tightness injuries like jumper's knee, Achilles tendinitis, and back problems caused by tight hamstrings. You can do the same thing at home. Put those family height measurements on the kitchen wall to good use. When your ballet student starts springing up the wall, start her on some stretching exercises. Stretch the quadriceps, hamstrings, and calf muscles. The exercises are easy (simply refer to the appropriate sections of this book to find some suggestions) and very effective. Most of the injuries attributable to tight muscles during growth spurts can be prevented if you keep the muscles stretched, strong, and flexible.

WHO CAN DANCE AND WHO CAN'T—SOME WAYS TO PREDICT TURNOUT

It's simply a harsh fact of ballet life that, whatever else you have going for you, if you don't have enough turnout, you're going to find it a long, difficult journey. Most ballet students begin training regardless of the suitability of their physical equipment. It's only later, if they become serious, or if they try to get into a professional school, that the amount of turnout can become a deciding factor.

Proper turnout comes from the hip. When a dancer turns out, there should be no rotation in the knee or ankle—it's the hip joint that must act as the swivel. Hip configuration is pretty well set by about eleven years of age. Some people are born with a lot of outside rotation, some people aren't. But after eleven years old or so, there's not much you can do about it one way or another. You can change soft tissues after that, develop what turnout you already have, but the bones are set.

So it can be a good idea to test turnout before you get too serious about this ballet business. That's exactly what the professional ballet schools do before they'll even admit a student. (They also look for a particular type of body—slim, with long limbs and a high instep—and a certain amount of native flexibility.) It can be horribly difficult for a fledgling dancer to find out at the start that she doesn't have the turnout necessary for ballet, but it may be less difficult than to discover it later on after investing so much in the effort. And it's not the end of the world. Other forms of dance—modern, jazz, and show dancing, for example—don't have the same kind of turnout demands as ballet. If a dancer knows early on that she doesn't have the physical equipment for ballet, she can point in another direction.

How do you go about measuring turnout? Most people have a similar amount of total hip rotation, in the neighborhood of 90 degrees. The crux is this: on which side of neutral—that is, when your leg is pointing straight ahead—does most of the rotation occur? If your leg rotates most of that 90 degrees to the inside, toward the other leg, that's perfectly fine so far as your general health is concerned, and actually may be better for some activities—the strongest kickers in swimming tend to be somewhat pigeon-toed—but it won't cut the mustard in ballet. If, on the other hand, most of the rotation is to the outside, you're probably in business. The physician for the Royal Ballet in London maintains that dancers must have at least 45 degree of external rotation; some people have more.

The way the Royal Ballet determines rotation is by having a dancer lie on her back on a table, with her knees bent and lower legs hanging off the edge. Then they actually turn out her legs and calibrate the amount of rotation. That's tough to do accurately at home, but there's a quick and easy way that's not as precise but will probably tell you all you need to know. The dancer should lie down on her stomach with her knees bent and one lower leg pointing to the ceiling. Keeping thighs together, let the leg flop to the outside. Then move it in the other direction, toward the other leg. If the leg bends out farther than it bends in, there isn't enough turnout. But if the leg flops more toward the inside, so much so that the other leg may get in the way, then you're in luck. (Don't be confused. In this position, turning the lower leg to the *inside* actually rotates the hip to the *outside*. Try it, and all will become clear.)

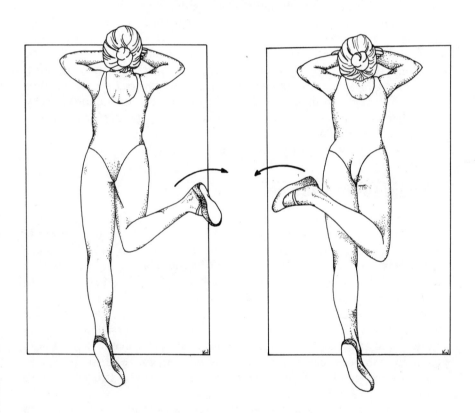

Test for Turnout

So if your child doesn't have sufficient turnout, then ballet can be fine in a nonserious way. Anything more than that is likely to be frustrating. It might be a good idea to start easing her into another kind of dance early on.

PROBLEMS OF TOO MUCH TURNOUT

Too much turnout? How in the world can a dancer have too much turnout? Well, it may be that too much is as bad as too little by the time a dancer reaches her late teens and the upper levels of her professional school. Dancers with ideal turnout tend to have more muscle injuries than other dancers once the going gets tough. It may be that they never became strong enough because it's all been so easy. They simply haven't had to develop their muscles fully over the years—they've always had more than enough turnout to get by—and once they find themselves swamped with classes and rehearsals and the pressure of vying for apprenticeships and corps positions, that God-given but underdeveloped equipment tends to break down.

It's nothing major, usually, nothing that can't be dealt with by stretching and exercise. But it's surprising to see hip injuries, for example, in girls with 70 to 80 degrees of turnout. That's the kind of problem you might expect to see in younger dancers who are overusing those muscles in an attempt to improve their turnout. Girls with an abundance of rotation should be able to sail through almost every obstacle that comes their way. But they don't; they get hurt. So dancers with a surfeit of turnout might be well advised to get some additional work so that they can fully develop their strength.

WHEN SHOULD YOU GO ON POINT?

It's the $64,000 question. There may be no other area that gives rise to so much controversy. Some teachers absolutely refuse to put a student on point until a certain age—twelve or thirteen, say. Others are more flexible, preferring to put a child on point according to her individual development and talent. And still others are somewhere in between, but no less vehement about their methods. For an outsider, a ballet parent first encountering this craziness, say, the question might be "Why *not* put a child on point whenever it's convenient? Why wait?" The answers are similarly diverse and passionately held: going on point too soon can cause deformity. It can cause arthritis. It can cause improper muscle development. It can harm the still-developing bone.

Well, all or any of that may be true, but we've never seen it. We've never seen any permanent problems resulting from going on point too soon. (Maybe people with those kinds of problems are no longer dancers and so limp off to somebody who's not in sports medicine.) It may cause a few aches and pains, bunions and blisters, and we sometimes see knee problems from being on point, but these are things that are associated with dancing in general. If for no other reason, young dancers who go on point aren't in toe shoes long enough to cause permanent damage. It's more likely that any long-term injuries will show up in the dancer's head rather than in her feet and legs. It's simply horribly frustrating for a child who may have been a reasonable dancer in technique shoes to go on point and not be able to do much of anything, and hurt all the time to boot. She may need a psychiatrist more than she does a sports medicine doctor, a sympathetic pat on the back more than a foot examination.

So when *is* a good time to go on point? The first thing to know is that you may or may not be able to rely on your teacher's judgment in this regard. The best instructors can simply look at a child at the barre and tell if she should be on point or not, but the best instructors are rare. Others, as we've suggested, simply set arbitrary rules—take it or leave it. And still others are so cowed by pressure from students—and their parents—that they may capitulate unwisely and put a child on point at the wrong time. (There are pressing economic reasons for such behavior as well. Ballet schools are in a very competitive business. If a student is unhappy at one school, no matter the reason, she may well go to another one across town.) It may be up to the parents to decide when it's best for their child to go on point. Here are a few suggestions to ease the burden.

1. The age that's most frequently given is twelve. It's more sensible to say that if a dancer is somewhere around the age of twelve and has had a minimum of three years of serious training, she's probably ready for point. It may be, however, that three years of serious training at ten years old, or eight years old, is enough. And it may be that eight years of serious training at age fifteen isn't nearly enough, and nothing ever will be. There are some dancers who should never go on point and some who take to it as though they were born in toe shoes. The bottom line is the strength of their training and their body.

2. If a student is able to do a solid passé on half-point, with a straight, pulled-up knee, she may be ready for point. It's a good test, demanding that she bear all her weight on one leg, with full knee extension and full relevé. If she's not pretty darn solid at that, it may be that she won't have the strength to handle point work.

3. If a dancer can go from a grand plié in the center to standing with knees straight, no wobbling, without altering foot position, it may be time for point.

4. If the teacher offers—or demands—to go with the dancer for her first toe shoes, it's a good sign. Toe shoes can be difficult to fit. That the teacher cares enough to offer her own time and expertise should bolster your confidence in her good judgment. If she doesn't, and simply says, "Go out and get some toe shoes," it may be time to

wonder. (In large schools, in which an entire level of students might go on point at the same time, it may be impractical for a teacher to thus offer her services. Still, it's something to look for.)

Again, there's no absolute answer. All else being equal, being able to trust the advice of your ballet instructor is by far the best way to go. Failing that, rest assured that it's highly unlikely that any lasting harm will come to your ballerina if she goes on point too soon. The saving grace of the whole business may be that toe shoes are so uncomfortable that only the best and strongest dancers are able to tolerate them long enough to risk real damage. And they're the ones who are least likely to suffer it.

Adult Beginners

It may be that the truest and kindest advice that one can give an adult beginning ballet student is, don't take it seriously. It's just too late to have lofty aspirations. The die—in this case, your body—is already cast. No matter how talented you may be, no matter how quickly you pick things up, if you haven't trained your body for a good ten years or so already, you will never be able to meet or survive the demands of the art.

The crux, as you may expect, involves turnout. For many dancers it's hard enough to develop adequate turnout after having worked on it since age eight, say. It's virtually impossible if you start at age eighteen. And too zealous an effort will only lead to injury. By that age, hip configuration is set for good; any extra turnout you may be able to squeeze out of your body must come from the knees and ankles, which simply aren't designed for such a thing.

Teachers usually realize the built-in inadequacies of adult beginners and don't stress the need for excessive turnout and flexibility, but sometimes the students themselves are hard to convince, especially the college student who takes a dance class for the first time (either because she's a P.E. major and dance is part of the curriculum, or it's her first opportunity to take nonrequired classes) and is swept away by the joy of moving to music. For that blissful innocent the limits of her own capabilities may be less glaring than they will be later on, and the result can be all sorts of problems.

At some point adult beginners come to realize their limitations and, if they want to continue dancing, find the kind of gentle, occasional arrangement that suits them. Until then teachers must be especially sensitive to their adult students' difficulties (is there anything more embarrassing than stepping into class in a leotard and tights for the first time?). Perhaps college dance classes should be considered more an introduction to movement than serious ballet training.

Professionals and Serious Preprofessionals

If one were to rank ballet injuries by their frequency, the list would go something like this:

1. Overuse knee problems, such as chrondromalacia, tendinitis, turnout-related kneecap injuries. (Here, as elsewhere, the chapters devoted to specific parts of the body contain discussions of these injuries. You can easily find the section that pertains to you in the cross-reference index.)

2. Overuse ankle problems.

3. Overuse hip problems.

4. Back problems (maybe 10 percent of all injuries, and more common in men).

5. Stress fractures, usually from big changes in activity levels.

It's obvious from the list that most injuries in ballet *aren't* cataclysms. They're nagging little things that, if ignored, can turn into nagging big things. More often than not, that's exactly what happens. By the time the dancer gets to the doctor, the little problem that might have been cleared up pretty easily has grown into something that threatens the dancer's ability to keep going. Of course, that's why she finally dragged herself to the doctor. Like anyone else, dancers tend to ignore problems that are ignorable, preferring to imagine that they will fade away on their own. What makes the situation worse is that, unlike most people, dancers are encouraged to do just that by the hierarchical structure of the dance world: at the top are directors and choreographers, who, even though they themselves were dancers, are often intolerant of injuries in their minions, and at the bottom are hordes of young dancers champing at the bit to step in and get their chance to perform. Caught in that kind of vise, it's no wonder that dancers are loath to own up to injuries.

This reluctance is strongest in high-level students, apprentices, and corps members. It's the most competitive time of a dancer's life, and it's also the time when any lack of proper training, any lack of strength or technique, will rear its ugly head. But who's going to admit it? Falter for an instant and there's an army of girls just waiting to nab your spot.

The tendency may be most pronounced, and most poignant, in the veteran corps dancer, the "old" trouper of twenty-five, say, who's beginning to realize that she's never going to break out of the corps, and that there are countless eighteen-year-olds who can do almost everything she can and are willing to abuse their bodies to do it. Of course, abusing one's body is nothing new to her—she's been at it for the seven or eight years she's been in the company—but now, only twenty-five years old, she doesn't heal as fast as she used to. The injuries are coming more frequently and lasting longer, and she can feel the breath of the younger dancers on her neck. So she says nothing, dances hurt, and then hurts more, until finally she simply hurts too much to go on.

It's easy enough to empathize with this dancer, even more so when you consider her options—there are none. There's no dancer's union strong enough to fight for her, and what can she look toward outside the dance world? It's a meaningless question, for her life has been so strongly directed and otherwise sheltered that there is no life outside dance. So she hurts.

Soloists and principals may suffer as many injuries—in some cases even more, because they dance longer and technically more demanding roles—but they're generally more willing to admit their problems and do something about them. They're much more likely than the corps dancer to say to the director, "I'm not going to do it because I hurt." And they're much more likely to get away with it. So, as a group, they're the healthiest dancers around. The smart ones won't risk themselves because they can look forward to five or ten years down the line. The corps dancer doesn't know if she can even look forward to next season.

But, if dancers and directors only knew, they could do themselves a great favor by admitting and dealing with injuries early on. Not only would dancers stay onstage more consistently, they might do so in reasonable health—a boon for everyone.

MALE DANCERS

The consensus is that men suffer more hip injuries than women. That may or may not be true—it's hard to know precisely—but if it's true, it may be a result of two factors: men usually start ballet later than women, and companies aren't nearly as selective when it comes to men as they are with women. There just aren't enough male dancers. Although things are beginning to change, schools and companies often take anyone who's willing. Forget the amount of turnout he may have; if he's a viable boy, take him.

So it may be that in the male dance population there is a higher proportion of people having problems with their hips than in the female. The men may not be as physically suited to ballet as the women in the first place, and because they usually start later, they have to force turnout even more than the women do. The result: hip problems.

Who knows what can be done about it? It may be that when men begin training as young as the women do, and when enough men go into ballet so that the companies and schools can be as selective as they are with the women (and that process is already beginning), then hip injuries will show up in men no more frequently than they do in women.

Male dancers also tend to have back problems. Here the cause is clear: lifting. Carrying all those women around all those years takes its toll. But even here the relative paucity of male dancers and their late development play a role. There simply aren't enough males to go around, and they're usually less advanced than girls of similar age. But the schools have to go ahead and train the girls to be lifted. So they use the boys on hand over and over until all the girls get their chance to be lifted. Well, the girls may be ready, but most likely the boys are not because up to now their training has built up solely the lower half of their bodies; their shoulders and arms are simply too weak, and after they do double and triple and quadruple duty lifting through all the girls, they're even weaker. Ideally they should do these lifts with their shoulders and arms, but as they tire they begin to use their backs. That usually means overarching the back, and, as any weight lifter will tell you, once you start overarching your back you're heading for trouble.

The problem is compounded because the girls are themselves beginners when it comes to partnering. Women who know how to be lifted do at least their share, if not more, of the lifting. They know when to jump, how to hold their body so it's light and alive rather than just dead weight, how to help in coming down. If a woman doesn't help out, even the strongest men have a hard time lifting. But, rather than knowing how to help the boys lift, these girls are just getting off the ground for the first time themselves. So it's the worst possible combination: inexperienced boys who aren't strong enough lifting inexperienced girls who don't know how to be lifted. And the boys bear the brunt of the consequences—in their backs.

This problem, at least, may have a solution—or perhaps a partial one. The boys should embark on an upper body strengthening program long before they start partnering. At least one large ballet school now incorporates a weight room for just that purpose. So by the time the partnering classes come around, the boys still may not be completely ready, but they'll be in much better shape than otherwise.

That's the part of the solution that's easily implemented. The other may be impossible, given the way things are in the ballet world. Why not teach the girls how to partner with the most advanced boys in the school, or company corps dancers, or even soloists? And vice versa with the boys. Let a boy learn to lift with a corps girl, someone who can help him rather than make things even harder. And only then, after both groups have learned basic techniques from experienced people and the boys have built up their strength, would it be time to put the beginning girls and boys together.

Sounds good, but even if there were time for such company-school interactions, what self-respecting soloist or corps dancer would risk herself in the grasp of a shaky beginning boy? And what working male dancer, who constantly battles fatigue and an aching back anyway, would make time to lift through a class of neophyte girls? It may be that building strength with weights is the only practical course of action, and that male dancers simply should expect back problems as one of the consequences of practicing their vocation—which, given the need constantly to support so much weight with such slow, seemingly effortless movements and to continue dancing and otherwise keep their own bodies under control in the meanwhile, may be one of the most difficult professions in athletics.

13 Snow Sports

I t was my first time skiing, ever. I took some lessons, and the next day I was going down the bunny slope, and I lost control and sat down. It was not the time to sit. I was in a snowplow, my legs just kept getting wider and wider, and I heard something snap. It was in Park City, Utah. It's beautiful, wonderful."

But not so wonderful when you tear the medial collateral and anterior cruciate ligaments of your right leg the second day out, the first time skiing, ever. On Thanksgiving, yet.

"I was so scared," Jo-Ann Cooper says. "I was alone, and I heard the pop, and I knew it was something bad, and I thought, 'What am I going to do?'"

What she did was make a reservation back to San Francisco for the next day, the Friday after Thanksgiving. At the airport she called her office, asked someone to set up an appointment at the Center for Sports Medicine, and hobbled onto the plane. When it landed in San Francisco, a friend from the office drove her straight to the Center. Garrick operated the next week.

"Your menisci are all right," he says. "We just put some stitches in your medial collateral ligament, so you don't have a very big incision. You look great. You didn't have very much fluid in your knee. Can you raise it?"

Jo-Ann gingerly elevates her knee a few degrees.

"Ah." Garrick smiles in appreciation. "You were doing that five hours after surgery. You're tough as a snake." He lifts his eyebrows. "Next time," he says, "if you don't want to hurt yourself skiing, don't fall down."

It's just about as simple as that. Between 85 and 90 percent of all ski injuries are the result of falls, and the kinds of injuries those falls produce can be serious and long-term. For example, skiing produces a higher percentage of fractures than any other sport. So, given that most skiers, especially beginners, are going to fall once in a while at least—a fact that Jo-Ann Cooper knows only too well—you want to do everything you can to keep those spills to a minimum. Here are a few suggestions.

Become a better skier. The better you are, the less chance you have of getting hurt. Studies have shown a strong correlation between increasing levels of skiing ability and decreasing levels of injury. Like the tennis player who takes a lesson to get rid of tennis elbow, take a ski lesson to avoid ski injuries. Despite Jo-Ann's experience, it's one of the best safety investments you can make.

Shorter skis are safer than longer skis. It used to be that anyone who was anyone used long skis. If your skis weren't taller than you were, there was obviously something wrong with you. Short skis, if available, were the sign of lack of ability, extreme youth, or some other unattractive ski-slope characteristic. Now that equation has turned around. Short skis are in, and available, and much easier to ski on. There may be some benefit from the short skis acting as smaller lever arms during falls, and transferring less force to your legs, knees, and ankles, but, most important, short skis lead to fewer falls in the first place. They require less energy and strength to manage, can be manipulated more readily, don't tire you as quickly. So if you're going to use your old skis for the first time in years, or are contemplating borrowing a pair from your parents, or older sibling, or aunt or uncle, you might be better off buying or renting a new, short pair. Your legs will thank you.

Proper binding tension is vitally important. The bindings are the link between you and your skis. Assuming that despite your lessons and good skis you're going to fall anyway (not a bad assumption) you'll want to be able to jettison your skis right away. Falling is the source of most ski injuries, and falling with your skis attached is the best way to make sure that the injury has a pretty good chance of being serious.

The most deadly fall for beginning and intermediate skiers—the bulk of people who ski—is a slow, twisting fall. When the people at the ski lodge set your bindings for you, however, they usually test the release by whacking the side of your boot. If the binding releases after such a blow, they send you off to the slopes. If you happen to fall with such an abrupt force, the binding will set you free. But that's not the fall that's going to injure you. It's the slow kind that's most dangerous, and it's likely that your binding will hold on tight during one of those, trapping your foot on the ski.

You should be able to snap your foot out of the bindings all by yourself. To test them, have somebody firmly hold the tip and tail of the ski as you stand on it. You should be able to twist the toe of the boot out of the binding simply by turning your foot to the inside. It should take some effort, but not so much that it hurts. If you can't get out, the bindings are too tight.

Once you've set your bindings, test them every day before you ski. Don't assume that setting them once will set them forever. Bindings are engineered precisely and can easily change their adjustment just by being jammed into a locker or strapped onto a car. A good thing to do is make sure you can twist out of them just before you step into the lift line each morning. And remember, you want to twist to the *inside*. Most falls will push your skis outward; you want your foot to be able to come free to the inside.

Some people object to having their bindings set too loose because they might let go inadvertently. It's no fun to be skiing along and have a binding come loose for no reason. Falls from inadvertent binding release can be traumatic—the binding comes loose, you know you're going to fall, and, as though it's all happening in slow motion, you have time to think about all the horrible possibilities. But few people are badly hurt by such falls—far fewer than those injured during falls in which the binding releases late, or not at all. If you're a beginner, you might just accept the fact that it may be your lot in life to spend a lot of time putting your skis back on. Better that than the six weeks or so you'd have to spend in a cast and the months of rehabilitation afterward. So if you've been falling a fair amount and your bindings are not coming loose, you'd better look out.

After you check your bindings, *warm up*. Slide over to the bottom of the slope and sidestep up about fifty feet. Then ski down, making a couple of turns on the way. Then turn around, sidestep up on the other side another fifty feet, and ski down again, turning along the way. Finally, herringbone up, make a turn, and come down. It'll take you about five minutes and is well worth the effort.

Most skiers don't do any such thng. They climb out into the cold from their cramped position in the car, put on their skis, get into the chair lift and assume another cramped position for the ten minutes or so of the ride, then suddenly unfold to ski down the ramp, which, for beginners, may be the steepest slope they see all day. Then, if they're still in one piece, they expect to be able to ski a mile back down to the bottom without hurting themselves. It's absurd. No one would attempt a few sets of tennis without stretching and hitting a few balls first; no one would set out to run a few miles without getting the blood flowing and muscles relaxed and stretched ahead of time. In fact, there's not another athlete in any other activity who would dream of doing anything so demanding, and with as high an injury potential, as skiing without any stretching or warming up exercises. But skiers do it all the time—simply ride up the lift, jump off, and expect to ski all day without doing a thing to warm up and prepare. Not smart. A disproportionate number of injuries occur in the first portion of the first run of the day.

When you do fall, try to *keep your legs together*. Most injuries occur when one leg splays away from the other—talk to Jo-Ann Cooper. Two legs held together splint each other, reducing the chance of harm. Sometimes you simply have to sit down in the snow while you're still in control rather than try to ski through an oncoming fall. Sometimes you have to hold back a bit, and better gauge your ability to stay upright. But sometimes you just don't have any choice. Even if you follow every suggestion we've made, you might be injured. Injuries will attack the best-prepared, smartest, and best-conditioned people. It's the nature of the sport.

PROBLEMS YOU MIGHT NOT THINK ABOUT

A less dramatic and virtually entirely preventable ski problem is *sunburn*. Snow is an almost perfect reflector of ultraviolet light, especially for those wavelengths that burn. And the light is not significantly altered by cloud cover. You can get burned badly on cloudy days.

Novices sometimes say, "How bad a burn can it be when there isn't much of me exposed?" The answer is "Very bad." The part that is exposed, your face, is the most critical part. People come from the city, from having been inside for weeks or months, and suddenly find themselves on the slopes in bright sunshine. They can burn so badly that their eyes swell shut. Sometimes people can't eat because their lips are grotesquely swollen and blistered from the sun. You can burn the corneas of your eyes as well. They swell at night, while you're trying to sleep. They can feel as though someone has poured broken glass inside. And, once burned, your eyes can become overly sensitive to sunlight for the rest of your life.

These are problems not lightly shrugged away. Good-quality sunglasses and sunblocks are very important, and it's best to expose yourself to the sun gradually (no matter how hard it is to do when you have only a few days on the slopes).

Frostbite and *exposure* can be problems as well. Remember that you create your own wind when you ski, to the tune of ten to fifteen miles per hour. That extra breeze must be added to any existing wind chill factor when you're judging weather conditions. So even if you've reserved your ski week months before, it pays to be wise concerning the weather. A day inside to acclimate and wait for better conditions might save a lot of grief.

Some ski areas have problems with injuries and *alcohol*. Most people ski at an altitude much higher than that at which they live. A couple of beers at sea level may do nothing to you; at eight thousand feet, especially when you're a little tired, you may find that it doesn't take many sips to affect your coordination.

Drinking and skiing can be a problem even if you're not the one drinking. Collisions on the slopes are not uncommon no matter what the reason, and the person causing the impact usually comes away in better shape than the victim. Twice as many people who have been hit seek medical help than those doing the hitting.

SOME GENERAL TIPS

Some serious ski injuries are not terribly painful. About half the people with medial collateral knee ligament tears ski down the slope by themselves. If you're hurting badly, you should see someone who can help you, obviously; if a joint feels no more than loose, you should still get help. It might be fully as serious an injury, if not more serious, than one that is more painful.

If you hurt your leg, *don't take your boot off.* The boot provides compression to minimize swelling, and if your leg is broken the boot can be a handy tether for a splint or traction device.

And *never ski alone.* That admonition may seem unnecessary on jam-packed alpine slopes, but be cautious about wandering off onto little-used trails, especially late in the day. In any activity in which the environment is not hospitable, and which requires special means to get about, it's always wise to have a friend around for help if the conditions get the better of you.

Cross-country Skiing

Skiing began as ski touring—what we now call cross-country skiing. For years, during the growth and peak popularity of alpine skiing, cross-country skiing was a sport reserved for the true enthusiast, the person who hiked and camped and donned skis for something other than simply whizzing down a slope at top speed. Recently, though, as the costs of ski equipment and lift tickets and lodging have gone through the roof, alpine skiers have begun to look elsewhere for things to do in the snow. Many of them have discovered cross-country skiing, a much more economical sport. So now there are a number of people who are not woods-wise setting off on mountain trails. For these people, a couple of words of caution:

Don't ski too long or too far. Especially early in the year, as you're rounding into condition, it's much better to go out and come back twice than it is to go out and not be able to come back at all. The alpine skier is used to skiing until tired and then just sliding downhill and home.

Ski touring doesn't work that way. You can't simply go on until you're tired—you still have to make it back, a task that can include navigating uphill slopes and difficult terrain. Instead, pick a specific distance, or a time, and then turn around. Go out for forty minutes, say, then come back. As you grow stronger and begin to learn your body's limitations, you can increase the length of your excursions. Until then, frostbite, exposure, and just plain fatigue can be very real problems.

Be careful when using cross-country skis on alpine slopes. It used to be that most ski areas wouldn't let people with cross-country skis onto lifts, as they figured—rightly—that cross-country skiers were a hazard on the slopes. Now, perhaps for economic reasons, that policy has changed in a number of areas, and as a result the injuries are beginning to roll in—serious injuries, fractures and the like.

Cross-country skis are designed to go in straight lines, primarily, and not to make the quick, sharp turns demanded by alpine courses. Turning in a cross-country ski demands technical expertise and a lot of room. If you're zipping down an alpine slope and are suddenly confronted with a little ravine, or a grove of trees, or another skier, you'd better be a ski touring expert, or in luck. So if you want to practice with your cross-country skis on alpine slopes, pick a slope that's gentle, relatively unpopulated, and open, so that if you don't execute a turn you won't end up off a cliff or into the trees or tangled up with another skier.

A less dramatic problem in ski touring is *muscle strains,* and not just in the legs. People forget that, in contrast to alpine skiing, cross-country skiing is a lower *and* upper body sport. You use your arms to pull and push as much as you do your legs. It's important to condition the entire body for this sport. A rowing machine in combination with bicycling might be an effective off-season conditioner. Better yet is a ski touring trainer, a treadmill device that requires you to use your arms and legs in working out. These are terrific exercise devices, and not just for ski touring. We've used them to help rehabilitate knee-surgery patients. They're commercially available.

Ice Skating

Like alpine skiers, the major injury problems recreational ice skaters face are the result of falls. There the similarity ends. For although ice skating, like alpine skiing, is a lower body sport, skating injuries tend to be in the upper part of the body—a fractured wrist, a dislocated elbow or shoulder. The reason is clear when you think about it: when people fall they thrust out their arms for protection and so absorb the brunt of the fall in the upper body. Competitive skaters learn to collapse and let the meaty parts of the body, the buttocks and thighs, take the force. Recreational skaters continue to land on their outstretched arms. It's a problem for which there's no ready answer. Again, it pays to become a better skater so you'll fall less frequently. (See Chapter 14, "Figure Skating," for more on skating injuries.)

Snowmobiling and Other Vehicular Winter Sports

The rule of thumb here is that *snow vehicles don't mix well with other man-made objects,* especially if the object is bigger than the vehicle. The number of people injured and even killed in highway collisions between snowmobiles and road vehicles is astonishing. If you're driving a snow vehicle, look out for roads and moving objects.

Also look out for stationary objects. Telephone-pole guy wires and fence links can be invisible to a snowmobile driver whizzing by at thirty-five miles an hour. You're much safer in areas where there's nothing man-made, because nature doesn't string invisible, immovable things from one point to another. You may run into a tree limb, but odds are that if it's big enough to do any damage you'll be able to see it.

And, as with cross-country skiing, it's important to be able to return from your excursion. Snowmobiles allow you to get to places from which you can't return if anything happens to the vehicle. Never go snowmobiling alone, make sure you have enough gas, and know where you are and how you might get out if something should go wrong.

Tobogganing

Tobogganing has a higher proportion of spinal injuries than any other sport. The culprit is the constant pounding and jarring the spine undergoes in a toboggan. These are not paralyzing injuries, for the most part, but they are significant.

A second problem in tobogganing is injury to the medial collateral ligament in the knee. What do people do when they want to stop? Right—they stick out a leg to the side of the toboggan. The leg catches in the snow and stays there while you and the toboggan go by.

What can be done about the first problem? Not much, probably, short of somehow padding the toboggan or the clothing of the people riding it. In the second case, people might be well advised to *keep their limbs inside the toboggan.*

(A related suggestion: kids sledding on rolled plastic sheets should never do so around roads. The sheets are impossible to stop.)

14 Figure Skating

Jennifer Verili looks down at her right ankle. On the inside front, round and swollen as an egg, is a fluid-filled bursa. It really doesn't hurt that much; she can run around all day if she wants to. But Jennifer is a figure skater, and it's getting so that she can hardly lace up her boot. At the ripe old age of ten she is facing the primary occupational hazard of her sport, one that is not dangerous in itself but can lead to more serious problems by causing her to overcompensate for the lump filling her boot.

"How serious are you about skating?" Garrick asks.

"Very," Jennifer answers.

"Really serious?"

"Really!" Jennifer nods vigorously, her long brown ponytails bobbing up and down.

"Well"—Garrick peers over his half glasses—"you've had it aspirated three times, and it just isn't working. I don't think it's a good idea to have that lump in there anymore." He turns to Jennifer's mother. "And if we keep sticking needles in, one of these days it's going to get infected. We've tried everything we can to get it to go down, but it hasn't gone down. So I think that either you have to take a deep breath and live with it, or you have to get it removed surgically."

Jennifer looks from Garrick to her mother and back to Garrick. "If you take it off, do I have to stay off the ice?"

"Yes. For a while."

"I'll live with it."

Garrick sighs. "Well, that's up to you. What you have to be careful about if you're going to live with it is that it doesn't compromise what you're doing. You don't want to wind up with tendinitis somewhere else in your ankle or with your knee hurting or your hip hurting. You have to figure out how much it's screwing up your skating."

Garrick knows the answer to that: the bursa is screwing up Jennifer's skating quite a lot. But although bursitis in the ankle is the single biggest problem in figure skating, most skaters don't encounter it so young. Jennifer is the youngest by a good five years of anyone Garrick has seen with the problem. And now she's faced with the prospect of surgery and, what's worse, three weeks off the ice and another three weeks after that before she can get back to spinning and jumping. Jennifer's eyes fill with tears. The idea of surgery doesn't scare her so much as being off the ice that long. For a ten-year-old, six weeks is a lifetime.

Garrick pats her on the shoulder "I wish I could tell you that you could be back in five days," he says, "but I'd be lying to you. But you don't have to decide right now. There's no rush. It doesn't matter if we do it today, or tomorrow, or next year. You just have to figure out what you want to do."

Jennifer's swollen bursa almost certainly formed as a protective device. Football players get them on the elbow, for example, to provide a cushion against the constant pounding on the ground (they're especially common on unyielding artificial turf). But the body works against itself. The fluid begets more fluid, which stretches and irritates the skin, producing more fluid. World champion Brian Boitano's bursa was as hard and swollen as a Ping-Pong ball. The process goes like this:

BOOTS AND BURSITIS

Bursas are small, moist envelopes that form in and around joints, wherever things slide over each other. They're the body's friction reducers, its ball bearings. The walls of the bursa slip back and forth against each other, allowing things on top of the bursa—soft tissue—to slide easily over things beneath—bone. Sometimes the bursas can become irritated and inflamed. When that happens, they can swell and fill with fluid. The problem is called bursitis.

Bursitis in the ankle of figure skaters is a function—or rather, a *lack* of function—of the way boots fit. When you skate, your stroking foot rotates to the outside. Keep it up long enough and eventually the tongue of the boot will inch to the outside as well. In time the tongue will move almost wholly to the outside of the boot. So, rather than functioning as a buffer between your foot and the lacing gap at the front of the boot, the tongue now provides a *double* thickness of padding to the outside, where you don't need it, and *nothing* to the inside, where you do.

When the tongue is in place and doing what it should be doing, your skin (often figure skaters don't wear socks inside their boots but for a precise fit wear leotards or tights, which are too thin to offer the skin any real protection) actually sticks to the tongue, which itself slides back and forth against the boot. So even though you may be bending and rotating your foot inside the boot, the leather never actually encounters the front of your ankle. The tongue functions as a surrogate skin, absorbing all that friction. Once the tongue has rotated out of place, however, all bets are off. Now it's virtually naked skin against naked boot, and, rather than *sliding* against the boot, your skin *sticks* to the boot just as it used to stick to the tongue.

So here's the scenario: skater skates, ankle bends and rotates, stiff leather boot resists bending and rotation, skin sticks to boot—something's got to give. And what gives is the bursa. Since your skin doesn't slide against the boot, it actually slides against itself, and the poor bursa is just plain overwhelmed. True, it's the bursa's job to facilitate such slipping and sliding, but this is ridiculous. My mother didn't raise me to put up with all *this,* the bursa says, and promptly begins to swell and fill with fluid. Most serious figure skaters eventually have to deal with some degree or another of bursitis.

And it can be a bear to deal with. Once they're well along, there's little to do about swollen bursas except remove them. They can be drained, but often they'll just fill up again. The trick is to prevent them from swelling in the first place.

It's a pretty tough trick, as the legions of beswelled figure skaters can testify, but here's an approach that might work: since it's the movement of the tongue that causes the bursitis, it pays to keep the tongue in place. You can do that by tearing a page from the runners' book and *lacing* the tongue in place. With a razor, cut two ¼-inch-long parallel slits in the tongue and thread the laces through the slits, crossing them at the center. The cross in the laces will always try to find the center of the boot; that will make the tongue stay put in the center and protect your ankle as it's designed to do. Pretty simple stuff, but it might save you a great deal of trouble.

In general, there are more equipment-related problems in figure skating than in most other sports. And *equipment* means *boots.* But it's not that skating boots are particularly ill-designed or -manufactured, it's just that skaters demand a great deal from their boots, demands that are becoming even greater as skating grows technically more difficult and dangerous. Skating boots must be flexible enough to allow extensive ankle rotation and almost as much forward and backward motion as ballet requires. Skaters must be able to drop down into a grand plié as well as rotate and point their feet in jumps and arabesques. But the boots must be stiff enough to prevent all side-to-side motion—few skaters' ankles are strong enough to be able to manage the variety and quantity of jumps required these days without the support of their boots. And the boots must be light enough so as not to slow down the skaters.

It's a large order. How can a boot be light, strong, flexible, and rigid all at the same time? The answer is, it can't. Too firm a boot—great stability but not enough flexibility. Too flexible—you slop all over the place. And no matter how successful a compromise they are, when you bend forward the boots buckle and become ill-fitting on the sides. It's just the nature of the beast. The more you're on the ice, the more waterlogged, and therefore heavy, the leather becomes. And you can't solve problems by putting things inside the boot; unless custom-made in advance for just that purpose, an expensive and involved process, boots just won't tolerate orthotics.

So skaters must constantly battle their boots. And there's little likelihood that things will change very much. The two major skating boot manufacturers are both mom-and-pop operations. They may make as many as three thousand pairs a year. Compare that to the millions of pairs of footwear the large shoe companies manufacture for other sports, and it's understandable why these small firms are simply not able to spend a great deal of time developing and producing new designs or to invest a great deal of money—there are too few skaters to pay for that kind of R & D. It's enough just to keep up with the cost of boots as they are. If a large footwear manufacturer became interested in making skating boots, perhaps some of these problems might be solved. But perhaps not. It may be that struggling with boots is simply a skater's lot in life. The variety of demands may be too great for the most ingenious engineering to solve.

STRENGTHENING SKATERS' ANKLES

The stronger your ankles, the better your boot will fit. The less external support you need, the less reinforcement the boot will have to provide, and so the more flexible it can be. Thus, a better and closer fit.

One good way for skaters to strengthen their ankles is to stroke with successively fewer hooks laced together. For example, try stroking daily for ten to fifteen minutes, twice the amount of time forward as backward (forward is more work). During the first week, don't run the laces through the top hook of your boots. During the second week, don't use the top two hooks. During the third week, don't use the top three hooks, the fourth week the top four hooks, and so on until you get down to the eyelets. Then lace only through the eyelets for all your stroking.

Your ankles will strengthen noticeably because you'll no longer be able to depend on the boot for support. When you jump and turn and do other things that might be dangerous to attempt with only half a boot, lace all the way up. Then, when you go back to stroking, lace down again. It's an easy exercise that skaters can do on their own so as to be able to use class and private instruction time to work on technique.

WEIGHT TRAINING FOR SKATERS

It's probably a good idea. Certainly for men some work on the arms and torso can be a help, as male skaters are more and more required to lift their partners. Lifts often look bad if the man isn't strong enough to let the woman down slowly; injuries can be the result of such lack of strength. As with male dancers, back problems are common among male skaters, and the women can suffer stress fractures in the lower leg if they're consistently let down too quickly or too hard. (See Chapter 11, "Exercising to Stay Fit—Aerobics and Weight Training," for some suggestions on how to approach weight training.)

DANCE TRAINING FOR SKATERS

Also a good idea. Not so much for conditioning purposes—ballet really doesn't give skaters a great deal of conditioning—as much as for reasons of artistic quality. One of the important things dance can teach skaters is what to do with their arms. Leg movement is pretty much dictated by the maneuvers skaters must accomplish, but not arm movement, and it's the arms that can do so much to make or break a performance. Ballet in particular is good for arm movement as well as for control from the waist up and overall presence.

But if skaters are going to take ballet, they should take it consistently. If a high-level skater takes ballet class only once a week, she may be letting herself in for more problems than benefits. The flexibility demands in ballet are greater than those of skating, so different muscles are exercised. After a substantial ballet class a skater may find herself hurting for a good day or two. If you take ballet on a Monday, it may be Thursday before you're fit enough to give it your all in skating class. And by the time you're feeling all the way back to snuff, here comes ballet again. So three classes a week is a reasonable minimum for skaters.

Of course, it's hard to fit in so many classes during much of the skating season. An alternative is to take three months or so of ballet at the end of the competitive season, work on your arms and upper torso, and when the skating again becomes hot and heavy drop out of ballet until things slow down. That way, you may be able to have the best of both worlds.

Other Problems in Skating

Skating injuries are overuse injuries for the most part, similar to the things dancers have to put up with: back problems from backbends and partnering, hip problems from turnout, chondromalacia from weak quadriceps, stress fractures from repeated landings (skaters practice jumps off the ice as well, more often than not on the hard concrete floor of the rink's changing area—a prime cause of stress fractures). And, as elsewhere, students' growth spurts can cause problems in skating.

There really should be stretching programs for skaters, weight training programs, conditioning programs, all built into the regular training. Especially these days, as skating has become more gymnastic and less balletic, there should be integrated conditioning programs. But there are none. It's up to individual skaters to become involved in these extra activities on their own. Some do; most don't. It's tough— besides the extra financial burden of such supplemental activities (skating is a particularly expensive sport, but skaters are not wealthy— about 70 percent of them come from blue-collar families in which the mother must work to finance the skating), there's little time and even less left-over energy. Skaters are at the mercy of the rinks, not a lot of them to begin with, which can't survive by depending on serious figure skaters. It's open skating that provides the rinks with their livelihood, so the serious skater must find ice time during the odd hours when the general public is not around—4:00 or 5:00 A.M., for example. After a day that begins in the dark, after school and homework and meals and then crashing into bed to get a few hours of sleep before the next morning's workout, few skaters find themselves dying to set aside time for working out at the gym.

And you're certainly not going to waste time stretching at the rink. Ice time is precious. You pay for it whether you use it or not. In fact, coaches who emphasize conditioning often get complaints from parents who must pay for ice time that their kid is frittering away by stretching at the side of the rink. Under that kind of duress, even the most committed coach quickly abandons such tactics.

The workouts themselves are intensive. With ice time at such a premium, and the technical demands of the sport ever increasing, the sessions are crammed full with activity. Forty-five minutes for figures, forty-five minutes for freestyle, and precious little time to catch your breath or perfect techniques. As in gymnastics, you spend so much time putting your performance program together that there's relatively little time to learn basic skills. And through it all you're growing— growing out of boots, growing out of costumes, growing out of your own body. No wonder injuries in figure skating are increasing.

And what happened to Jennifer Verili? It didn't take her long to figure out how much her inflamed bursa was screwing up her skating. A week after her examination she made a trip to the operating room.

The bursa turned out to be the biggest Garrick had ever seen. It ran all the way from her Achilles tendon to the midline of her ankle, measuring close to two and a half inches in diameter. Garrick removed all of it.

"Makes you feel pretty good," he says, "because that one sure as hell wasn't going to go away by itself." Jennifer earns his highest accolade: "She's tough as a snake."

Three hours after the operation Garrick goes up to Jennifer's hospital room to find her sitting on the side of her bed, eating and wondering why he hasn't gotten there sooner so she can go home.

"How do you feel?" Garrick asks.

"Great," Jennifer answers. "When can I get back on the ice?"

15 Swimming

It's a terrific sport. Buoyant, stretched out, gliding through cool water—what could be better? For millions the answer is, *nothing* could be. Swimming is the country's most popular athletic activity, by far. From jumpers and splashers to competitors of all ages, to rough-water swimmers, to people rehabilitating injuries, the water offers an environment that is at once refreshing, supportive (no gravity to fight against here), and safe—once you learn to swim, that is. It may be that no one is as devoted to an activity as a swimmer.

But don't ask age-group competitive swimmers about the joys of their sport. They're too busy to answer you—busy staggering around trying to catch up with homework, trying to catch up with meals, trying to catch up with sleep. Too busy trying to keep up with a regimen more tyrannical than that of almost any other activity. The little league baseball player works out a few afternoons a week during the season. Ditto the soccer player. Ditto the member of the high-school tennis team. The really heavy stuff comes later. The college football player, certainly a participant in a sport more intense than most, goes through a pretty demanding season, shows up for spring workout, and tries to stay in shape between time. But even he doesn't get up at five in the morning—every morning, all year—for a couple of hours of weights and workout. He doesn't return for a couple more hours in the afternoon—every afternoon—for another workout. And he doesn't fill those hours with the intensity and sheer quantity of work that a swimmer does. It may be that dance is the only activity that rivals competitive swimming in the devotion and single-mindedness required. But, even so, the physical demands of dance come nowhere near those the swimmer must constantly face.

And this isn't only a college swimmer, a nineteen- or twenty-year-old with an adult body, a scholarship in hand, and the end in sight. This is a reasonably serious fourteen- or fifteen-year-old (or, especially in the case of girls, even younger—a look at the ages of world-class female swimmers tells you that). We're talking double workouts—ten thousand, fifteen thousand, twenty thousand yards a day (that's eight hundred laps of a twenty-five-yard pool). We're talking weight training three to five times a week. We're talking up to five hours a day of virtually nonstop stroking and kicking and gliding and turning. For what? For the privilege of racing a few minutes once or twice a month. For the ability to swim fifty to four hundred yards flat out (there are longer races, of course, up to fifteen hundred yards, but the bulk of competitive swimmers don't swim those). Nowhere else in sports is the discrepancy between performance demands and training methods more dramatic. The equivalent in track would be for Carl Lewis to run fifteen miles a day to stay in shape for his occasional hundreds and two hundreds. He'd tear himself apart in three or four weeks.

Yet swimmers carry on this way day in and day out, year in and year out. No wonder so many of them burn out (for example, Mark Spitz never wanted to see a pool again after his last Olympic race), and no wonder so many have shoulder problems. It may be that well over half of all serious swimmers have had shoulder problems at one time or another. They're mostly overuse things—tendinitis, inflammation, rotator cuff tears, a condition called swimmer's shoulder—and they're probaby the result of the length and frequency of workouts. Whereas in most sports overuse injuries usually come from some kind of change—new shoes, new track, new racket, new training regimen, new floor, new teacher—in swimming they come from simply wearing out the joint.

It's the endless miles and miles slogged in the pool, the endless rotations the shoulder performs, against the resistance of the water, dragging the entire body weight, never letting up even when fatigued, and, after a respite of a few hours during the day or night, going back to the same thing again. If you subject any joint to that kind of repetitive abuse, you're going to have difficulties. And what's more, in swimming, in contrast to most repetitive activities, you're using the joint's entire range of motion. Cycling involves only partial range of motion of the hip and knee, running the same, although your ankle might reach its limits if you're sprinting. But swimmers go through the entire 360 degrees, over and over and over. The larger the range of motion, the more quickly the joint fatigues.

The only way to treat such injuries is to back down to a level of activity that no longer hurts, give the joint some rest, and carefully begin to stretch and strengthen the muscles involved (see Chapter 8, "The Shoulder," for more detailed suggestions). But do that in swimming and before you know it you're thousands and thousands of yards behind in your training and, what can be more devastating to the young, competitive swimmer, thousands of yards behind the others on the team. For members of big, high-powered clubs, in which there's lots of competition for berths on relay teams and traveling squads, an enforced break can wipe out a big part of the reason you're there.

It may be that the only long-term way to prevent these injuries is to take a more thoughtful approach to workouts. In an effort to manage swimming injuries, just about everything has been investigated except the length of the workout itself. Perhaps coaches should lean more toward the quality of the workout rather than the quantity. Toward more stroke work and less yardage. More tapering and less building up. Swimming fresh rather than tired. Taking time off rather than adding time on. The recent success of world-record holder Matt Biondi has caused a number of people to take a serious look in this direction. Biondi, a strong water polo player, began swimming seriously only a few years ago. His performance gives the lie to the notion that you need years and years and miles and miles behind you to compete successfully. And even now he ascribes much of his success to the fact that he alternates swimming and polo and so comes fresh to each. It's an approach that swim coaches are beginning to look into. In any case, so far as preventing injuries is concerned, it's just about the only thing left to try.

That and taking a look at stretching. Swimmers are great ones for stretching, maybe as a result of the notion that swimmers need long, flexible muscles. And not only do they stretch themselves before workouts and meets, they stretch each other. A common sight is one swimmer twisting and extending the arms of another. But swimmers never use these extremes of flexibility in the water. There's no stroke that demands that kind of range of motion. The stretching serves no functional purpose (if any group would need that kind of flexibility it would be gymnasts, and they don't stretch like that). Still, swimmers do it anyway, with the result that they injure themselves by stretching before they even jump into the water.

Again, a more reasonable approach to workouts may be the answer, so that coaches can be sure that they're strengthening and preparing their swimmers for their chosen activity, rather than tearing them down and burning them out.

16 So You're Going to Have an Operation

Garrick concentrates on a large TV screen about six feet away from him. So does everyone else in the room. Everyone, that is, except Michael Renker, who is in a deep, anesthetized sleep on the operating table. Garrick and his team are performing an operation, but not just any operation. This is the high-tech glamour event of sports surgery: arthroscopy.

The technique involves slipping a thin probe directly into the knee and then attaching a fiber optics-illuminated camera that projects the scene onto a large TV screen nearby. Like magic, the inside of the knee appears on the screen, in living color, and Garrick is able to explore the terrain in detail. Here's the kneecap, here the end of the femur, there the anterior cruciate ligament—what's left of it. Quickly it becomes apparent that this knee is not in good shape.

"That scarring is probably the remnants of the ligament," Garrick says. "See, it should be a nice, tight band, but even when I test it, it really doesn't tighten up. It just kind of floats around."

Scar tissue that looks like floating white elastic bands clogs the screen. The bottom of the kneecap, which should be smooth, rains strands of decomposing bone. That stuff that looks like the frayed end of a nylon rope is what's left of the meniscus.

"All this wispy stuff in front of the screen is swollen joint lining," Garrick says. "Over there is an area where he's worn all the way through, down to the bone. These are changes that occur over long periods of time, and that's not so good, obviously. It sure explains some of his pain."

All this congestion is the product of an initial soccer injury and a couple of subsequent surgeries. The patient, Michael Renker, is twenty-nine years old. He had his first surgery when he was twenty-two. He can't walk without limping, and his right ankle splays out to the side, the result of a previous removal of an ankle tendon to use to reconstruct a ligament in his knee, and the fact that he's been overcompensating for his knee problems all these years. Now his ankle is swollen and inflamed—an operation on that is next.

Garrick decides that the most he can do for Renker's knee is clean it up. He can't provide any more stability—it's pretty much shot in that regard—but he can help get rid of some of the pain Renker is suffering. He flushes the knee with a sterile saline solution that simply washes away much of the debris and then inserts a tiny scissorslike instrument to snip away the rest. The instrument is only ⅛ inch in diameter, but on the screen, magnified about forty times, it looks like nothing less than *Jaws*. Snip! Off goes part of the frayed cartilage. Snip! Away with another. By the time Garrick flushes the knee clear, it looks like a brand-new landscape—clean, neat, everything in its place. Renker's only lasting surgical mementos will be two tiny puncture wounds, each covered by a Band-Aid.

Sounds like magic? Not quite. But it *is* slick, so slick that arthroscopy has heralded a new attitude toward surgery found few places outside the world of athletics. In fact, we might have called this chapter "So You *Want* to Have an Operation," because when it comes to athletic activities, people sometimes do strange things. One of those things is to dive into surgery with the eagerness of a skier diving into a hot tub. An injured athlete often will do anything—*anything*—to get back to an athletic activity as soon as possible, and if that "anything" involves surgery, so be it. In fact, maybe all the better. There seems to be among some athletic types a pecking order based on experience in the operating room. A red badge of courage complete with impressive scars. And if it's arthroscopic surgery ... well, you just can't do any better than that. The scars are even more impressive for being tiny, and the company is terrific. After all, Olympic marathon champion Joan Benoit did it. So did Mikhail Baryshnikov—twice. What's more, you'll be good as new in a few weeks.

Wrong. We're not out to scare anyone, for there are good reasons for surgery—we've been talking about them all the way through the book—but the reality is that surgery not only entails risks, it rarely makes things as good as they were to start with. And in those rare cases when it does, it may be that all the time and effort spent in rehabilitation—and any surgery involves extensive rehabilitation—may not be worth the end result. It all depends on why you had the surgery in the first place. If it's to enable you to run, or walk, again, that's one thing. If it's to enable you again to be the star of the noon pickup basketball game, that might be another. The point is that surgery should not be rushed into without real thought. Short-term impatience is not the best reason to have a long-term operation, nor is the desire to stand out in your social set. There is much to consider before you decide to bare yourself to the surgeon's knife.

Surgery for Sports Injuries

In general, there are two kinds of operations in sports. One involves *repair*, the other *removal*. For the most part the removal operations work best, because you're taking out something that doesn't belong there. It may be a torn piece of meniscus that's jamming up a runner's knee, a bone spur in the back of a dancer's ankle that prevents her from going on point, a gob of bone and gristle in the front of the ankle that prevents a gymnast from beginning or landing jumps. These are things, like bone spurs, that shouldn't be there in the first place, or things that are in the wrong place—torn cartilage, for example. Once they're gone, the body is able to resume its usual activity. The knee and ankle bend and flex as though nothing was ever the matter—or pretty nearly so. And, as a number of these procedures can be done with the arthroscope, the period of recovery is often shorter than with other surgery.

Repair operations are never this successful. These are attempts to repair things that have been torn or stretched or otherwise put out of commission—ligaments and tendons mostly. Once you tear a ligament, it's never going to be as tight as before. And it's not the fault of the operation. Whether you treat these injuries surgically or not, they simply don't come back all the way. It's just the nature of the beast. The best the surgeon can do is try to improve a situation that without his help might be much worse. Gains are relative, and there are no guarantees.

But what about all the well known athletes who come back from major operations? For example, Magic Johnson and Joe Montana had knee surgery (and the knee is involved in 75 percent of all athletic-related surgery), and they continue to play, and star, afterward.

The answer is that sometimes major repair surgery can be successful because few athletes, even the best ones, operate at 100 percent efficiency anyway. So they may lose 10 percent of their ability after surgery but with more diligence and harder work afterward might actually approach their previous level. Still, you always lose something, and the people who come back strongly from big operations probably fall into one of two categories: like Johnson and Montana, they're either so much better than anyone else to start with that they can afford to give away 10 to 15 percent of their ability, or they're willing to ignore bad news. Many athletes fall into this latter category—they get back to their activity in record time, but they really shouldn't. Not only are they no longer performing anywhere near their former level, they're going to pay the price later on. Ask any number of retired footballers how their knees feel now.

Many athletes are aware of this trade-off and consider it an equitable one, especially if they make their living with their bodies. A few more years of prime earning power—even if you can do no more than perform at 75 percent on a team that just can't find anyone else to do 76 percent—are worth all the problems that are sure to follow. But most athletes are not professionals. Not only do they not depend on their bodies for their livelihood, but they don't have available the same round-the-clock medical care that professionals enjoy (more on that in a moment). Nevertheless, their thinking—or lack of it—ignores these differences. A skier hobbles into the doctor's office, leans the crutches against the wall, struggles onto the examining table, and announces, "I've got to ski again next season. Do whatever is necessary, Doc." Well, this skier, flushed with the stories he's heard of professional athletes returning to action after all sorts of horrendous injuries, and ready, as many people are, to lie back and let the doctor work his medical magic to make him well, should be apprised of a few interesting bits of information.

First, no matter how successful the treatment, no matter what ingenious things the doctor does, some people are simply not going to get back to skiing—or running, handball, tennis, dance, or whatever their favorite activity might be. *There are certain injuries that just don't get better,* or enough better, anyway, to allow a return to the activity that caused them. In such cases, you must modify your life to accommodate your injury, not the other way around.

Second, and often the opera*tor* doesn't bother to tell the opera*tee* about this, *you're going to play a larger role in recovering from your injury than does the operation.* Often people ask, "How long am I going to be in the hospital?" Well, you may be in the hospital for only three days, but that's the least of your worries. With some of the more involved operations, what you'd better be ready to face is six months of daily hour-and-a-half supervised rehabilitation sessions. That's what professional athletes do, and if you want similar results you have to play the game.

But the pro athlete has nothing better to do than work to get back into action—it's part of the life. In the real world, an hour and a half of daily rehab translates into nothing less than a part-time job. By the time you get yourself to the physical therapy facility, park, change clothes, do the exercises, take a shower, change clothes, climb into your car and get back to work, half the day is gone. And the exercises themselves are *tough.* There are many more enjoyable things in life than pitting your slowly recovering knee against the Cybex machine. So there are more things to consider than the size of the scar and the number of days in the hospital.

Third, *sometimes the operations just don't work.* The most reliable surgical procedures are successful no more than 90 percent of the time—pretty good odds but no guarantee—and for others the rates are considerably lower. Once the doctor opens you up he may discover that the injury is more extensive than he first thought, or that you've developed secondary problems as a result of trying to compensate for the injury. Even in the most successful removal operations this can be the case. A dancer may have a bone spur in the ankle removed, for example, theoretically allowing her to flex and extend to a degree she hasn't experienced in years. But just because she hasn't been able to use that full range of motion in so long, her body may have tightened up to the point where it could take her another full year to stretch out enough to be able to enjoy the benefits of the operation.

And fourth, *people die during surgery.* It doesn't happen often in sports-related operations, but it *does* happen. Surgery, no matter how minor, entails risk.

So approach surgery with your eyes open. Guard against the "if I have an operation, all my problems will be solved" type of thinking. They won't. Surgery should be considered a last resort. If possible, explore every nonsurgical means of treatment before considering it. In most cases you can wait on surgery until the problem simply can't be dealt with otherwise, but you certainly can't undo an operation once it has been performed. And even if it does come to surgery, and your operation is a complete success, you'll be faced with the need to rehabilitate your injured part. Don't let anyone tell you otherwise.

Some Questions to Ask Your Doctor When Considering an Operation

Are there any nonsurgical alternatives?
Yes. There always are alternatives. What you have to decide is if the alternatives are more or less palatable than the surgery itself.

It may be that an alternative to surgery is for you to give up tennis, for example, or dance. And it may be that giving it up is simply out of the question. Or it may be that you can live without tennis more readily than you can live with a difficult operation and a long rehab period, during which you won't be able to do much of anything anyhow, and after which the odds of getting back to your previous level are not very good. If you have a knee problem that prevents you from playing in the noon basketball league, say, then it may be that an alternative to surgery is to take up racketball. Or it may be that the alternative to surgery is the pain and disability of continuing to have your knee lock up on you, whereas a relatively simple operation could relieve you of all that. It all depends on why you're considering surgery.

In all these cases, it's important that your doctor think along the same lines as you. He should know why it is that you may want an operation. He should present you with the alternatives and ask you what your priorities are. And he should offer a recommendation one way or the other. But remember that orthopedic surgeons make their living by performing operations. The more operations, the better the living. If your doctor seems too eager to put you under the knife, or doesn't explain the alternatives, or, at the least, doesn't advise caution, it may be time for a second opinion.

So a good reason for surgery may *not* be that you can't dunk the basketball any longer or hit a 90 mph serve. Instability in your knee, yes. Inability to dunk, no.

Why don't we try the alternatives first?

When it comes to athletics, surgery is often an elective procedure. There's seldom any life-or-death issues involved. At stake is performance in a certain athletic activity, or, it may be, pain and disability. So if the alternative to surgery is an exercise program that only works in 10 percent of the cases, what's the disadvantage in giving it a try? You might be among those 10 percent.

In any case, it's important that your doctor make you understand how urgent any possible operation might be. Again, in most cases you can give surgery a try if all else fails. But you can't undo the consequences of the knife.

What are the odds that the operation will work?

And to what degree will it work? Will it allow me to go back to the same high level of activity? Can I work out daily? Do I have to take any special precautions? You want the answers beforehand. You want to go into surgery knowing as much about the likely results as possible.

A good way of judging the success of any operation is by talking to someone who's had it. We make a point of contacting people at least a year afterward. "Now that you've gone through all this," we ask, "now that you've been to the hospital, had to leave work or school, gone through all the rehabilitation, made all these visits to the doctor—knowing what you know now, would you have the operation again?" If the answer is "yes," that's one thing. But—stability during examination, muscle size, X-rays, arthrograms, calibrated strength, and all the other clinical determinations to the contrary—if the answer is "I sure wouldn't go through all that again," then you've got to think long and hard about the worth of it all.

Operations are simply no fun. And despite all the publicity about arthroscopy, they aren't glamorous in the least, especially if something goes wrong.

Can the operation make me worse?

Yes. There's always a chance. *How much* of a chance is the issue. What are the odds? And what, *exactly,* could go wrong? These are the kinds of questions people rarely ask. They don't like to hear bad news, even if it's only potential bad news. But these are the kinds of things you need to know.

Again, here's where getting a second opinion can make sense. And if your doctor throws a tantrum when you mention a second opinion, then you should be even more determined to get one. No doctor should get upset at the thought of a second opinion, not these days. Besides, more and more insurance companies are beginning to require them.

How extensive will rehabilitation be?

If someone tells you that you won't have to do any rehab work, look for a second opinion. Some kinds of operations require less rehab than others, but all require *something* on your part. Anyone who says otherwise is simply not being realistic.

And along with this question should come others: How long will I be in the hospital? How long before I can go back to work? How long before I can take a shower? How long before I'm back to my athletic activity? Will I be able to rehab at home, or do I have to come to the physical therapy facility all the time? And will my insurance pay for physical therapy? It can be more expensive than the surgery itself.

What about a second operation?

Sometimes it takes a long time to realize benefits from an operation, even a simple one. And sometimes patients and doctors become impatient. If you're looking at an *unplanned* second operation (sometimes two-part operations are planned in advance—that's a different story) for the same problem within three to six months after the first one, you might well get a second opinion. It simply may be that not enough time has elapsed to find out if the first operation worked or not.

If enough time has gone by so that it's clear that the first operation didn't work, be aware that it's even less likely that the second one will do the job. The surgeon would have done the second procedure the first time if it were more likely to be successful. It may be that there's something else going on, a problem that neither you nor your doctor yet understands.

If the person who's going to operate on you is unwilling to answer your questions, for whatever reason, then you'd better look elsewhere. When you pay $3,000 or so for surgery, you're not just paying a surgeon for his two hours in the operating room—you're paying for him to answer your questions before surgery and afterward, for return visits, and for him to supervise your rehab program. If he's not prepared to do all of these things, you might think twice about having him do any of them.

And don't depend on your infallible memory to hold on to the surgeon's responses forever. *Write down the answers to your questions.*

Arthroscopic Surgery

Back to arthroscopy. It may not be magic, but the first time you see the inside of a knee in full color on a twenty-four-inch television screen, you might think so. *See* is the crucial word here. The most important thing about arthroscopy is that it has allowed surgeons to *see* what they're doing. If you can see what's going on inside the knee (or elsewhere—arthroscopy is increasingly used in other joints as well), then you can figure out *precisely* what the problems are and do the right operations. No more surmising from external evidence and digging into the interior of the knee through a two-inch incision not quite knowing what you're going to find there. With arthroscopy, the proof of the pudding is right before your eyes, in living color. And you can even make a video tape of the whole business for consultation afterward.

The technology for this not-quite-magic instrument is sophisticated in the execution but pretty straightforward in conception. Why not make a tiny telescope, attach its own light source, add a miniature TV camera, and connect the whole package to a neeedlelike probe that you can slip into the knee through a ¼-inch incision? *Voilà,* the arthroscope. It took the technologies of miniaturization, fiber optics, and video to make this idea work, and now it's fast becoming a staple of orthopedic surgery. It may be that as many as 30 percent of all orthopedic operations are now done by arthroscopy.

That may be too many. Often arthroscopy is just not necessary; you can determine what the problem is with a good physical exam. If examining the knee convinces you that someone has torn an anterior cruciate ligament, say, there's no point in documenting it by poking an arthroscope into the knee, especially when surgery probably won't be necessary to treat the problem. But sometimes that's just what is done. Be careful. If your surgeon suggests that you don't need an operation but he'd like to use the arthroscope to find out exactly what the problem is, here's one more question to ask: *will my treatment be the same whether I have the operation or not?* If the answer is that the treatment will vary depending on what the arthroscope turns up, then there may be good reason for going ahead with it. But often no matter what the result of the diagnostic surgery may be, you'll have to do the same rehabilitation exercises anyway. In that case, such a precise diagnosis may not be necessary, especially as you're the one who has to undergo the surgery.

A case in point is the shoulder. In the shoulder there are few problems caused by something being where it shouldn't (unless it's the entire shoulder being where it shouldn't, as in a dislocation, and you're certainly not going to remove the entire shoulder—not through the arthroscope or any other way), so in the shoulder the primary value of arthroscopy is to diagnose problems. You can look at the underside of the rotator cuff, for example, and you can look for possible weaknesses from recurrent dislocations. But no matter what you may find, there's not as much you can do about it through the arthroscope as you can in the knee. (There are studies under way to develop new arthroscopic techniques to deal with dislocations, but they're all in the beginning stages.) And there may be little to be done about it in any case—except rehabilitate it, that is.

Ironically, one of the effects of arthroscopy has been to make people less wary of having surgery. People come in *demanding* the operation and get angry if you tell them that they're not going to need it. You may say to them, "We're as sure as we can be what's wrong with your knee. Even if you were arthroscoped it wouldn't change the rehabilitation treatment we've set up for you."

"I don't care," they answer. "I want you to arthroscope my knee."

Well, TV pictures, fiber optics, and high tech to the contrary, arthroscopic surgery *is* surgery. Someone gives you an anesthetic, makes an incision, no matter how tiny, inserts a foreign body into your knee, and swaps around in there, often taking something out.

Complications are not very frequent with arthroscopy, but, as with any surgery, they're always a risk. Infection can be a problem; instruments break. Yet some people have the impression that it's just like getting an immunization shot—you come in, have your arthroscopy, then go back to volleyball the next day. Not so. Joan Benoit to the contrary, most people take four to six weeks to get back to where they were. Plus, it will cost you or your insurance company (which ultimately means you) anywhere from $3,000 to $5,000 for your "shot." Even if you're only paying 20 percent, that's still a lot of money. So it makes economic sense at least to have an orthopedist who prefers to make as many decisions as possible *without* going into your knee. Almost magic it may be, but arthroscopy is not a cure-all. That you can remove a torn cartilage through the arthroscope is nice, but studies have shown that six months down the road it doesn't make any difference whether your cartilage was removed through two ¼-inch incisions or one 2-inch incision. Once you've been through a rehabilitation program, it just doesn't matter.

That said, it's clear that the arthroscope is a handy tool. It's so tiny that you can put it into corners that are too remote for a light and your naked eye. And you can do surgery through it. You can take out loose bodies and torn cartilage; you can sew some cartilage back together, and people are even doing some ligament surgery with it. All this through a couple of ¼-inch incisions. Few stitches are required to close things up, and, compared to the 2-inch-long scar produced by other surgical techniques, the mementos of being arthroscoped are negligible. Pretty slick. But still, the most important benefit of the arthroscope is that it allows you to plan precisely what you need to do to the knee, because you're able to see everything as clearly as though you'd slipped in there yourself.

Arthrography

People sometimes confuse *arthrography* and *arthroscopy*. Arthrography is *not* surgery. Arthrography is an X-ray technique in which you inject into the knee, or any joint, a dye that X-rays will not penetrate. Since most problems in the knee don't involve bones, which *do* show up in X-rays, but rather soft tissue such as cartilage, ligaments, and tendons, which *don't,* X-rays are limited as to what they can tell you about knee injuries. The idea behind injecting dye into the knee (it's called a contrast medium) is that it colors the soft tissue so that it can be visible in X-rays. (Sometimes a combination of dye and air is used.)

It's a common technique for figuring out what's wrong with your knee, and an effective one. And it involves little more than a shot and an X-ray—often a good alternative to exploratory arthroscopic surgery. In time your body will simply absorb the injected stuff, and you'll be no worse for wear. Except, of course, for the knee problem that forced the arthrogram in the first place. But because you had it done, you may be well on the way to repair.

17 Kids and Sports Injuries

A ndrea Ignoffo has a problem. A strong, spunky thirteen-year-old gymnast, Andrea was flying through her normal routine on the uneven parallel bars when an unfortunate thing happened: she went through the bars but her knee didn't. Now, two weeks later, the knee is still swollen and stiff. The diagnosis: hyperextension, possibly cartilage damage. Andrea has been on crutches and has had to wear an orthopedic sleeve. And, worst of all, she has not been able to return to the gym.

"Been wearing the sleeve?" Garrick asks.

"Yeah," Andrea says. *"Seriously"*—she catches Garrick's skeptical look—"until the swelling went down. I didn't wear it to school today, but I wore it all weekend and all last week."

Sleeve or no, today Andrea looks better. She's able to bend the knee again, the swelling is down, and although the knee seems loose, Garrick suspects that it's a function of being thirteen as much as the injury. Growing kids have loose ligaments, as though their bodies are preparing for more growth. He calls for a therapist to instruct Andrea in how to build up her quadriceps muscle to take pressure off the knee. Then comes the crunch: he wants her to stay out of the gym.

"How much longer?" Andrea asks, defeated.

"Ten days."

"Ten days?" Andrea looks ready to break into tears.

"All right," Garrick says. "I'll make a deal with you. I'll see you in a week. If it looks like the other knee, with no more swelling ..."

"Oh." A quick comparison of one knee with the other. "I've got a long ways to go."

"... and if you build up as much muscle on the good side, then maybe ..."

"Do I still ice and do all these *things*?"

"Yep. Can't do too many of these things. If you don't get your strength back, then you're going to get hurt more easily. And you don't need any help in that department. Even when you *weren't* going to get hurt easily, you got hurt. So instead of going to workout, you just go build back your strength. I know it's horrible." Garrick pats her on the shoulder. "I know it's horrible."

And so it goes. Dealing with kids is like ... well, dealing with kids. But as anyone who's read through the rest of the book can see by now, it isn't all *that* different from dealing with adults. When it comes to most sports injuries, kids are miniature adults. The same problems attack them that afflict bigger and older people. And for the same reasons. Overuse and abuse are the major causes, and an occasional acute injury strikes children just as it does adults. For most of these problems, the suggestions we offer throughout the book will help kids as readily as adults. Look for your child's ailment in the text (we make special note if the treatment is any different for children than it is for adults). And the general injury tip-offs discussed in Chapter 1 are as true for kids as they are for grownups:

1. Joint pain
2. Tenderness at a specific point
3. Swelling
4. Reduced range of motion
5. Weakness
6. Numbness and tingling

If any of these symptoms show up in your child, better do something about it.

But, as any parent knows, kids are much, much more—and less— than little adults. They have special talents and problems that adults just don't have. When it comes to sports injuries, those special problems are almost always a result of their size, or lack of it, and the fact that they're constantly making up for that lack—that is, growing.

Think about it. We adults become used to our bodies. The changes that active people experience usually result from concentrated effort to increase skill and conditioning, injury, or that inexorable process that we know only too well: aging. But most of these are gradual changes, subtle and in the long run relatively minor. We hold on to the general shape and size of our body from our late teens to the day we die. We become used to walking with the same size feet, reaching to the same high shelves, squeezing through the same tight places. In sports that familiarity translates into a confidence in our bodies that allows us to perform on a roughly consistent level day after day, year after year. If you're an adult, chances are that living in your body is pretty darn comfortable.

Not so for kids. Especially during rapid growth spurts, kids have to contend with a new body virtually every six months, a body that's different in size, shape, center of gravity, flexibility. You just get used to one body, more or less discover your angles and leverages, more or less figure out how much push comes to how much shove, and all of a sudden you're hit with an entirely new one. And the changes don't have to be all that dramatic to throw off the best-laid plans. A sudden extra inch of height is enough to foul up the best coordination. A few new pounds in an unaccustomed spot will cause the most steady balance to waver. And then, just as you're finally figuring out this new body, wham!—here comes another one. You can't win.

So pity the poor child athlete. But not too much. That same energy that fuels their growth gives kids a resilience and flexibility that adults just don't have. Kids catch on quicker than adults. They usually bounce back from injuries far faster than adults. They need less time to prepare for athletic activities than do adults, less time to recover afterward, and less care to keep going in the meanwhile. And for kids, the performance curve just keeps going up. None of this leveling-off business that adults constantly contend with. Kids continue to run faster, jump higher, balance better, and grow stronger until ... well, until they're no longer kids.

SOFT BONES

One consequence of this tendency toward more and bigger and stronger is what some people call "soft bones," or "growing bones." Much has been made of the fact that kids' bones have spots called growth centers. These are areas that produce new bone for growth and, as such, are softer than the rest of the bone—so soft, some people say, that the growth centers are not as strong as ligaments. So if a kid turns his ankle, for example, the bone will break more readily than the ligaments will stretch or tear. Instead of spraining the ankle, the child will fracture it. If so, the child can have a real problem, because not only are fractures in general more troublesome than sprains, but fractures of growth centers can sometimes lead to deformities as the child continues to grow. So if growth centers present an especially high risk of fractures, it may be wise to keep kids out of sports. So goes this line of thinking.

It's a big "if." Although kids *are* subject to certain problems because of growth centers (see the discussion of Osgood-Schlatter's disease in Chapter 5, "The Knee"), and although it may be true that if you take bones and joints in a lab and subject them to testing, ligaments are stronger than growth centers, the fact of the matter is that when you look at large numbers of injuries in sports, you just don't see kids getting fractures rather than sprains. As with adults, the ligaments tend to go before the bones do. Kids do suffer growth center fractures more often than adults, true—adults don't have growth centers—but they don't suffer an inordinate number of them. And, other than skiing, there aren't that many activities that produce fractures anyway. So "soft bones" really *aren't* a problem for children in sports, and certainly are no reason to keep them away from these activities.

Weight Training

For years it was thought that weight training for kids was useless, an exercise in futility. Kids are growing, changing, the reasoning went. Their bodies just don't respond to weight work the way an adult's does. Better to wait until the growth spurts are done with and the child is settling into an adult body. Then pile on the weights.

Not so. Kids *can* benefit from weight training, especially in the trunk muscles. Good back and abdominal muscle strengthening programs can produce some long-lasting results, more so than working on the arms and legs.

But there are problems with weight training for kids. One is that the equipment just isn't made for small people. Kids don't fit into the lifting devices very well, and the weight increments are often too large. Ten pounds, the usual increment, can be too much of an increase for a little person to manage. So kids often work with weights that are simply too heavy for them and develop bad training habits in order to compensate. (Misusing the back is a common consequence—see Chapter 7, "The Back and Neck," for a detailed discussion of the proper use of the back in weight training.)

Compounding the problem is the fact that kids require a lot more supervision than adults. Kids tend to play with the equipment, which can be dangerous. They drop things on each other, compete with each other, often don't have much common sense. The supervision has to be careful and constant, and most fitness centers simply don't offer that level of attention. They expect to take an adult through the circuit once and let it go at that. But you can't deal with kids that way.

So it's not that weight training is bad for kids, it's just hard to create a situation that's beneficial *and* safe. If you can solve that problem, the weights can do some good.

There are a number of techniques involving small weights attached to the body that purport to make kids better athletes. You improve your basketball skills by playing with ankle weights, improve your hitting by swinging a heavy leaded bat, learn to jump with weights strapped to your shoulders. Be careful. Whenever the weight involved in any activity changes—your weight or the weight of the equipment—you change your technique accordingly. You don't swing a leaded bat the same way you swing a normal bat. You don't jump with weights the same way you do without them. And the added weight can cause problems, forcing your body to compensate so as to deal with the increase. The result can be injury rather than increased ability.

So if you want to jump higher, practice jumping. If you want to hit a ball better, practice batting. There aren't any shortcuts, and those that claim to be are frequently hazardous.

Shoes

Ah, yes, shoes. Growing feet and the cost of shoes are the bane of any parent's existence, especially if your child is involved in athletics. It can be a full-time job just to keep your kid in soccer shoes, or skating boots, or toe shoes, or just plain all-purpose sneakers, and it sometimes seems as though it takes another full-time job just to pay for them. You want to buy the shoes big because in no time your kid will have grown out of them, but if they're too big they won't work at all. So you buy them a little too big, which means that they'll be a bit uncomfortable at first, then just right, then too small. And in the seasonal sports it means that invariably they're too small toward the end, when your child is involved in the play-offs. But who wants to buy a brand-new pair of shoes for the last two weeks when you know they'll be much too small at the beginning of next year's season?

It's a quandary. Would that we had a ready solution. When the shoes are too small, they're simply too small—nothing to do about it except grin and bear it, or get a new pair. When they're too big you can tighten things up a bit by inserting insoles—that might help. But if there's little you can do about the size of the shoes (except keep buying more of them), there *is* something you can do about the shape. A real problem with kids' outdoor athletic shoes is that they have negative heels—that is, the heel is lower than the rest of the shoe. In and of itself, a negative heel presents no problem. In fact, take a walk on the beach, or on soft ground, and your heel naturally sinks lower than the rest of your foot. But most of the shoes that we wear—kids and adults—have raised heels. Therein lies the rub. The raised heel tends to shorten our Achilles tendons, which would be okay if we wore nothing but raised-heel shoes. But we don't. The minute we pull on soccer shoes, say, our Achilles tendons suddenly have to stretch to accommodate the negative heel. Often the result is Achilles tendinitis.

With kids the problem is compounded because, shoes or no shoes, kids are prey to Achilles tendinitis anyway. Bones grow faster than muscles, so the calf muscles of rapidly growing kids tend to be short, making their Achilles tendons tight even before they put on their everyday raised-heel shoes. Still, so far so good—maybe. But once they get into their negative-heeled athletic shoes, which is always during their most physically active time of day, and the tendon stretches out even tighter than before, look out. Something's got to give, and that something is usually the Achilles tendon.

Shoe companies pay lip service to raising heels by making the heel cleats a bit longer than the rest, so at least the shoes look good sitting on the display shelf. But if you use them on a halfway-decent field, the heel cleats sink farther into the ground than the others, and you're right back to the negative heel. So much for cosmetic solutions. The trick is to build up the heel yourself. A pair of good heel pads will do it. But don't buy the ones that look soft and comfortable. They'll only smoosh down under pressure and won't accomplish anything. Buy either felt or cork heel pads, or ones made of hard rubber, and place them under the insole of the shoe. They may seem hard and uncomfortable to the touch, but they'll feel fine once they're in your child's shoe. And they may help prevent Achilles tendon problems.

A Few Other Suggestions
WATCH PRACTICE

Parents should go and watch their kids work out from time to time. Many parents never miss a competition or performance, but they should watch practice sessions as well. You'd never think of leaving your eight-year-old child with an unknown baby-sitter, but when it comes to athletics people think nothing at all about turning over their kids to some football or basketball or soccer coach whom they've never met and know nothing about, and who coaches only on a part-time basis at that. Kids are on their best behavior during games and performances. Go catch a practice to see what's really going on.

That said, we must also say that most coaches genuinely care about kids. They do their coaching after work, during their spare time, with little or no pay, out of real commitment. They would not knowingly hurt any child. But some do because they simply don't know any better. It pays to drop in on practice once in a while.

DON'T IGNORE JOINT PAIN

We've said it before, but it bears repeating, especially with kids: if joint pain lasts more than a couple of days, especially pain in the "naked" joints—the elbow, knee, ankle, wrist; those not covered by muscle—better do something about it. Muscle pain is usually no problem. So long as it doesn't show up all of a sudden—as with a muscle tear—the muscle is probably sore from being overused and can for the most part be ignored. Not so joints. Pain there can mean real problems, especially with kids. Because they're growing, kids' joints are looser than those of adults. Just as bones grow faster than muscles, so do joints. In fact, it sometimes seems that muscles are the last to know when anything important is happening. They are the simpletons in the family. Joints are much smarter than muscles; so are ligaments. They anticipate rapid growth spurts and loosen up in preparation. Meanwhile, the muscles go merrily on their way, tight as ever, oblivious to the whole thing. You have to loosen up your own muscles; joints loosen up by themselves.

No one has been able to document that there's an increase in injuries due to that looseness, and certainly if there is, it's not substantial, but prolonged pain in these loosened joints still should make you suspicious. Don't let it persist in your child without trying to find out why it's there.

P.E. CLASSES

Dedicated child athletes probably *don't* belong in P.E. classes. If a kid is grooming himself for a particular activity, let's say ballet, he certainly is getting enough exercise without taking a P.E. class. Most likely he's getting everything P.E. is supposed to give him and more, except perhaps social contact with his classmates. And by not taking P.E. he reduces his risk of injury.

There are two major problems with P.E. classes. One is that, like the rest of school, they're geared for the widest possible student population—a little something for everyone. That approach may not be right for a child who specializes in a particular activity. The training simply may not be appropriate for him. And the other is that P.E. classes change activities too abruptly. For one quarter they concentrate on volleyball, say, or basketball, two court-oriented jumping games. Then, wham! it's up and down the field playing soccer, with all the running and kicking that sport demands. Then it's a sudden change of pace to softball—throwing, sliding, twisting while swinging the bat. Well, for kids who aren't in particularly good shape, the change won't matter much. They can slop around safely enough in just about any sport. But for a kid who's fine-tuned for one particular activity or another, such an abrupt change can bring on problems. As we've seen so often in this book, it's the abrupt changes that cause injuries. When a body is used to one kind of activity, a quick change forces it to reeducate itself too quickly. The body just doesn't like suddden, unexpected demands; it breaks down.

For example, the ballet dancer's muscles are stretched for extreme flexibility. He's geared for sudden bursts of activity separated by slow movements and a great deal of posing. To subject that body to the constant running and jumping and contact of basketball, say, simply because the school calendar demands it, is to invite problems. (The opposite is true as well, by the way. If a basketball player were suddenly forced to achieve the extreme flexibility and quick movements of ballet, he too would quickly find himself hurting.) Yet that's just what many schools demand. P.E. is held sacrosanct, as though bypassing it meant somehow tampering with an entire institution rather than simply dealing with the needs of any particular kid most effectively.

We even see injuries as a result of the tests sponsored by the President's Council for Fitness. Suddenly kids are forced to see how far and fast they can run, how many push-ups they can do, how many sit-ups, and so on. Interestingly, it's usually the best athletes, those kids who score best on the tests, who suffer the most injuries from them. As in other things, it's the most finely tuned instrument that breaks down most readily when asked to perform unfamiliar tasks. When that instrument is your child's body, it may be wise to think about the need for P.E.

SPORTS PARENTS

They go by various names—ballet mother, little league father, to name just two—and in this case the stereotype is alive and well. The ballet mother hangs around the studio almost as much as her offspring does, constantly nagging the instructors for promotions for her child, for better parts in productions, for more attention and more praise. She knows all the gossip about everyone, most of it derogatory, and is almost always sure that her child is getting a raw deal. The little league father is the one screaming from the stands, berating the coach for not playing his kid enough, berating the officials for calls that go against his kid, even berating his kid for not playing up to family standards. He makes his child practice after school and on the weekends whether the kid wants to or not; he regales him with stories of his own prowess in years gone by.

These are the parents who push their children to be something that the parent wants them to be, rather than helping them to be themselves. These are the parents who have a far stronger personal stake in their children's activities than do the children themselves. These are the parents who push, cajole, and bludgeon their way along, *forcing* their kids to do well in their activities rather than merely *facilitating* their achievement. For these parents, athletics are not games—they're serious business.

True, the world might be poorer without them, as there would undoubtedly be fewer dancers and baseball and football and tennis players around, but from a sports medicine standpoint they might not be missed too much. In fact, when it comes to injuries one of the major problems kids have is their parents.

Kids who are involved in their activities, who are deeply committed *on their own,* can be treated as adults. They listen to suggestions for treatment, they act on them, they care. And they get well. Children who are involved in athletics because of their parents tend to remain children. They often ignore advice, disregard treatment, and remain hurt much longer. Age has nothing to do with it, really. There are adult children and childish adults. What counts is the level of commitment. Kids who care about what they do *for themselves* are the kids who will most readily recover from injuries. They're the mature ones.

Garrick puffs on a corncob pipe in his office. He looks at Andrea Ignoffo's chart.

"She's a tough kid. Gymnasts are tough as snakes." He laughs. "You know, they're all kids. Everyone we take care of is really a kid. They look at a rehabilitation program as 'Jesus, is this something I'm going to have to do the rest of my life?' But the whole idea of this business is to get them back doing what they want to do, which is probably more strenuous than the rehab program anyway, as quickly as possible."

A knock on the door. Andrea hobbles in.

"Do I still have to wear the sleeve?"

Garrick shrugs. "If you can walk comfortably without it, go to school comfortably without it, then that's cool. Okay?"

"Okay!" A delighted smile.

"Hey!" Garrick shouts to her departing back. *"Stay out of the gym!"*

18 How to Choose a Sports Medicine Doctor

A bout a year ago I did a really bad thing," says James Wisner, a fifty-two-year-old San Francisco attorney. "I was sitting in a restaurant, on a low chair, with my leg locked underneath. And when I got up I could hardly stand. It felt as though the knee was out. I used to be able to press it against the floor and it would pop back in, but this time it wouldn't pop in. In fact, I'm never aware of it having popped back from that episode."

Wisner's knee problems began years ago while he was rock climbing. He fell and slammed the knee into the side of the cliff. Since then it has gradually gotten worse, finally locking at the restaurant, and now he has lost some mobility, he feels a burning sensation inside the joint, and he can't go up and down stairs without the knee grinding. Worst of all, it threatens to interfere with the upcoming ski season.

"I'll tell you why I'm here," Wisner says. "I went to a very fine orthopedic surgeon for the knee, and he said, 'Well, Jim, after fifty it's patch, patch, patch.' Well, even though we may have to patch, patch, patch, I don't want to call it that and get into that mood. I don't like to go into my declining years that way."

"Don't say anything about declining years," Garrick says. "We're almost the same age."

"So I said to myself," Wisner goes on, "you know what, I'm learning things from my new young lawyers. I'm going to talk to the guys at Sports Medicine, because I think they have a different approach to these things."

It's true, those two extra words—*sports medicine*—make a difference. A doctor who may be perfectly able to treat all manner of life-threatening problems might *not* be the one to best deal with your bum knee. Or your swimmer's shoulder. Or your tennis elbow. Although one body resembles another, and an aching elbow may look much the same whether it's the result of tennis or carpentry, the treatment afforded that elbow may vary a lot. One doctor may accurately diagnose the injury as tendinitis of the elbow and suggest, rightly, that the problem will disappear in time if you quit tennis. But you don't want to quit tennis. Athletes go to sports medicine doctors to find ways to recover from their injuries *and* continue to perform their athletic activity.

Sometimes that's simply impossible, neither practical nor good medicine. But most often you *can* get back to your sport, if the treatment is based on not only a thorough understanding of the way the body works but a no less thorough understanding of the activity that caused the problem in the first place. In sports medicine, the injury and the activity are forever wedded. You can't treat one without understanding the other.

Better, then, that your doctor should say, "You have tendinitis of your elbow because your backhand is lousy. You'll never get rid of the problem until you improve your backhand. Go take some lessons. Meanwhile, you've got to regain strength and flexibility. Here are some specific exercises to start you on that road."

Contained therein are all the ingredients that characterize a good sports medicine doctor: someone who gives you a precise diagnosis, looks for the cause of the injury, suggests precisely how to get rid of the injury and keep it from happening again, and gets you safely back to your athletic activity as soon as possible—in other words, someone who not only treats your tennis elbow but helps you get back onto the court. Let's look at them one at a time.

What to Look for in a Sports Medicine Doctor

A sports medicine doctor should offer a *precise diagnosis*. It's not enough simply to say "You've hurt your elbow." *You* know you've hurt your elbow; what you want to hear is what precisely is wrong with it. It's true that some people aren't really interested in what goes on inside the body; they just want to get well. And it's also true that medical terminology can be forbidding to anyone outside of medicine—a little bit of "tendinitis at the lateral humeral epicondyle" can go a long way. But your doctor should at least make an effort to explain to you what it is you've done to yourself, accompanied by definitions of terms (just what is "tendinitis," anyway?) and a guided tour of the body, if necessary (the lateral humeral epicondyle is that bump on the outside of your elbow, the one that hurts).

If your doctor doesn't explain your problem to you, ask questions. He may have not have had much practice in having to explain himself, as often people become cowed and meek when they enter a doctor's office. The same person who won't drive his car away from the mechanic without finding out what was wrong, or who demands a precise accounting from her child's teacher as to what's been going on in the classroom, suddenly turns mute in the doctor's office so as not to seem a bother. It's your body at risk, and your money—ask questions.

A hint: write down the answers. It's too easy to nod your head in understanding in the heat of the moment and later on forget everything that was said. Another hint: don't go in with a written list of questions. In these days of malpractice suits, a written list might make any doctor very nervous. Memorize your questions ahead of time; then write down the answers. Your doctor should answer all your questions. If he doesn't, it might be time to look for another doctor.

The doctor should *look for the cause of the injury.* In sports medicine, the cause is critical—it plays a large role in determining the treatment. Not so much in the case of acute injuries. If you break your leg or blow out a knee ligament, managing the injury isn't going to be much different whether you did it skiing, playing football, or tripping over the family cat. But most sports injuries are not acute; between 65 and 75 percent are overuse problems, the kinds that sneak up on you. With these, the cause is not obvious. But unless you know how it happened, you won't know how to treat it so that it won't happen again.

And that takes time. It takes time for a doctor to talk it over with you, to ask the questions that lead back to what caused the injury in the first place. It can be tricky. A dancer's back problem can be the end result of a chain of difficulties that started with overly tight hamstring muscles. Treating the back pain may get rid of the problem for a time, but unless you go on and do something about the hamstrings, it won't be long before you're hurting again—and finding yourself right back in the doctor's office.

The two-minute office consultation just doesn't work in sports medicine. Unless your doctor is prepared to spend time with you and get to the heart of your problem, you might well be advised to spend time finding another doctor.

The doctor should tell you, *precisely, how to get rid of the injury and keep it from happening again.* How many people with sprained ankles have been told "Wrap the ankle, ice it, and stay off it?" Period. Not how to wrap it so it doesn't end up looking like a sausage, how to ice it so it receives the benefit of the cold everywhere, and how to keep the muscles strong in the meanwhile so they don't simply waste away. Yes, you can recover from a sprained ankle—more or less—if you wrap it, ice it, and stay off it, but you can recover sooner, more thoroughly, and with less chance of spraining it again if you receive some instructions as to how to go about it effectively. And if such is the case with an obvious injury like a sprained ankle, how much more important it is to deal precisely with a more obscure injury, an injury, say, that may have its roots elsewhere in the body. A large number of sports injuries are like that. Don't shortchange yourself with anything less than a precise course of treatment.

And it's the physician's responsibility to set you up with a rehabilitation program as well. If you've had a severe injury, if you're involved in any kind of reasonably high-intensity athletic activity, or if your injury has nagged you for at least a couple of weeks (making it virtually certain that you've been favoring something for those two weeks, forcing other parts of your body to perform inappropriate functions to compensate), you're going to have to rehabilitate yourself, restrengthen yourself, regain your flexibility. Your doctor may have a physical therapist in his office actually devise the program for you, or he may send you to someone else, but it's his responsibility to set something up. If no such rehab program is forthcoming, it might be another strong hint to look elsewhere.

The doctor should get you *safely back to your activity as soon as possible*. Otherwise, why bother? Rest, staying away from what hurts, will cure many problems, but you can rest on your own. Besides, if you're willing to stay away, much of what we've been talking about doesn't apply to you. Athletes, from pros to recreational types like most of us, are often characterized by an almost fanatical devotion to their activity. If they can't do it, they suffer. You can't tell a swimmer, "Don't swim. Run instead. You'll derive the same cardiovascular benefits." It won't work. Swimmers like to be in the water. By the same token, runners feel cheated unless they feel their feet pounding on the ground, tennis players like to wield rackets, skiers want to slide down slopes, dancers immediately look for a barre. For these people, recovering from injury is only half the battle. The rest is being able to get back to their favorite activity quickly.

Facilitating all that can be quite a trick. And it must be done safely as well. If not, you're right back where you started, at the least, and probably even worse off. It can take a great deal of ingenuity on the part of the doctor, combined with a thorough understanding of the body and the activity involved. It's not easy. Still, it's what you look for in a sports medicine doctor. There may be no reason to settle for less.

A few more suggestions:

Beware of the instant cure. With many injuries—in particular overuse problems that involve inflammation and swelling—a cortisone injection or some other kind of dramatic medication can effect a seemingly miraculous cure. Suddenly you're well—for about forty-eight hours, anyway. Then it's right back to where you were.

In some cases there may be a good reason for such treatment. A professional tennis player on the eve of an important match may opt for this kind of temporary solution, ditto the dancer who doesn't want to bow out of a performance—always with the understanding that long-lasting treatment must come later. But if there's no overriding reason to temporarily eliminate symptoms this way, and for most of us there really isn't, people would be well advised not to go this route. It does no good in the long run and can even do some harm. At best it's a highly calculated risk. When it comes to sports injuries, the true instant cure is exceedingly rare. Usually all you're doing is putting off any real treatment of the problem in exchange for a temporary, and risky, elimination of symptoms.

Most injuries don't require surgery. And of those that do, only a few require urgent surgery. So if your doctor announces that you have to undergo an operation, you should always ask whether there are alternatives.

There *are* alternatives, almost always. They may not be what you want to hear, however. An alternative to knee surgery may be to give up skiing, or running. An alternative to shoulder surgery may be to give up tennis. An alternative to ankle surgery may be to give up dancing. Or worse. Or, in many cases, much better. But the point is that if someone tells you there's absolutely no choice in the matter, except in the rarest of instances, that's simply not the case. It's at times like this that a second opinion may be just what the doctor ordered.

You want a doctor to schedule a follow-up visit. Medical fees being what they are, a return visit may seem something of an extravagance. Who wants to pay more than is absolutely necessary? But in this case a return visit—and the fee that it entails—may be a good investment. You want your doctor to stay involved with your injury until you're well. That is, you want to know what to do if things *don't* go as planned. Who's going to offer that information? It should be the doctor who treated the injury in the first place, and a return visit indicates his willingness to do just that.

If there is no follow-up visit scheduled, at the very least your doctor should offer to make himself available if things go wrong. Any indication that your doctor is involved with you and your problem is good. With today's increasing demands on sports medicine facilities, it's all too easy to encounter just the opposite.

A sports medicine doctor doesn't have to be an orthopedic surgeon. Most sports medicine doctors probably are orthopedic surgeons, but it's not necessary. What is necessary is that the doctor have as solid an understanding of musculoskeletal anatomy as an orthopedic surgeon, and a solid understanding of athletic activities—which orthopedic surgeons may or may not have—as well. Of course, a nonorthopedist won't be able to do surgery, but maybe only one in twenty people needs surgery anyhow. Besides, what's important in surgery is that the doctor be competent and experienced, rather than strictly a sports medicine surgeon. Doing an operation well is a function of how often you've done it, not whether the reason for it is sports-related. How the injury is managed afterward, what kind of rehabilitation is involved, and even whether or not to do the operation in the first place—all that is sports medicine stuff more than the actual operation. And your sports medicine doctor, whether or not he actually performs the surgery, can be involved in those decisions. The important thing is finding a good sports medicine doctor, no matter what his specialty.

But if you're lost, or just starting your search for a sports medicine doctor, and you don't have anywhere else to go, it can be a good idea to start with an orthopedic surgeon. Orthopedists deal with the anatomy of the musculoskeletal system all the time. At least you'll have someone who knows intimately how the body moves.

Physical therapists should not passively make you well. That is, if a therapist wants you to come in every afternoon for an hour of ultrasound, or galvanic stimulation, or hot packs, or ice massage, or any of the other tricks of the trade (all of which, when applied appropriately, can be very effective), and doesn't give you a rehab program to do at home, ask for one. If the therapist refuses, it might be time to go elsewhere.

You *can't* get over your injury without actively working at it. True, you may recover well enough to go back to work or school, but you aren't going to be able to get back onto the court or the track, or into the gym or studio. Without an active involvement on your part, you'll never get all the way back.

But it's so comforting to have someone else take care of you. Kind of like crawling back into the womb. So nice just to lie there and have someone massage and knead you and bathe you with all sorts of relaxing unguents. As a supplement to the hard work you're doing on your own, these ministrations can help you along. But by themselves they're simply not enough.

Why then are some therapists so reluctant to set up home rehab programs? For a number of reasons. It takes time to set up such a program, time to instruct you, time to make up handouts and written instructions, and in a busy therapy center time is at a premium. And the more you do at home, the less often you come to the therapy center—therapists are in business, after all. The irony there is that although it may seem bad business to have people do things at home, it's really the smartest approach therapists can take. People get well that way, and the more people you help back to health, the more people recommend you and come back to you. After all, it's better business to see fifteen people for five visits each than it is to see one person twenty times.

The moral of the story: rehab therapy should be active, centered in the home and supplemented at the therapy center.

Finding a Doctor

So, all that said, how do you go about finding the kind of sports medicine doctor you want? Where do you begin?

The best place to start is with other athletes. Legitimate athletes, serious athletes, not just someone who works out once in a while and has been hurt occasionally. Ask another athlete to recommend a good doctor. The athletes' underground is usually a pretty good source of information.

Failing that, you might look to various sports medicine societies. There's a society for almost every discipline—orthopedic surgeons, podiatrists, physical therapists, and so on—and at the least the doctors who belong to these groups have been interested enough to pay dues, go to some meetings, subscribe to a journal. Probably the most reliable of the groups for the purpose of finding a sports medicine doctor is the American Orthopedic Society for Sports Medicine (70 West Hubbard, Suite 202, Chicago, IL 60610; [312] 644-2623), as orthopedists are more involved with being team physicians and the like than other doctors.

The American College of Sports Medicine (401 West Michigan Street, Box 1440, Indianapolis, IN 46206-1440; [317] 637-9200), even though it consists of a number of physician members, may not be the best place to go for a recommendation. Many of the members are Ph.D.s and exercise physiologists who don't deal with injuries. If you want to find out how fit you are, then this group can most likely locate someone to measure your physical condition, but it might be wise to look elsewhere for someone to take care of your injury.

Simply going to a facility that calls itself a sports medicine clinic might be better than going elsewhere—or it might not. There are no regulations where such designations are concerned. There are some physicians who have had a great deal of experience in dealing with sports injuries and so legitimately call themselves sports medicine doctors; there are others who are trying to attract athletes and so label themselves sports medicine doctors regardless of their expertise and experience. So in a way you just have to pay your money and take your chances. But at the least the title, sports medicine doctor, is something to look for rather than just going to someone cold.

Going to a doctor who is himself a runner, say, or who regularly attends the ballet, doesn't necessarily mean that the person knows anything about how to treat ballet injuries, or how to treat any running injuries other than his own, if that. Seeking out a physician who happens to be an athlete, or enjoys athletic events, is no guarantee that you're going to find a sports medicine doctor. Again, experience with sports injuries is what counts. That and the ability to make a precise diagnosis, the readiness to look for a cause, explain to you what you're supposed to do and what to do if the treatment doesn't work, and help you safely back to your activity as soon as possible.

There's no foolproof way to find such a doctor. Perhaps the best way is to talk to other athletes who have been happy with their medical care. Nothing beats word of mouth.

That was precisely how James Wisner found his way to the Center for Sports Medicine. Two of his fellow lawyers, athletes, had been there before.

"Well, you might have displaced a fragment of the meniscus into the center of the joint," Garrick says, "and it's far enough displaced so that it will never go back. It might be something called a bucket-handle tear. A part of the meniscus actually flips over into the joint, just like the handle of a bucket flipping from one side to the other. The result is that you've subtly lost some extension."

The news does not sit well with Wisner. "I just don't want to say at my age that I'm going to have a lousy knee, that it's just going to be weak. I want to give it a little bit of a go."

"Well," Garrick says, "it may be that you *do* have a lousy knee and there's nothing to do about it, but I don't think we know that right now. It looks as though it's a problem we can do something about."

That something is to remove the piece of meniscus that's in the way. It's likely that sooner or later it'll come to that. What makes the prospect less daunting than it might be is the fact that the surgery can be performed through the arthroscope.

"I'm inclined to opt for a look at it," Wisner says. "It's nice, I guess, that I've waited all this time so that now you have a procedure that's less intrusive."

Garrick laughs. "Good of you," he says.

"But," Wisner says, "I'm wondering how this relates to the current ski season. What would happen if I waited until April?"

Garrick knew it was coming sometime. It's what separates sports medicine patients from all others: these people want to stay active.

"If you stay away from those things that cause you problems," Garrick says, "and if you're able to remain comfortable, I suspect nothing will happen. Your knee isn't going to turn brown just like that. You'll know it. But you have to make a pact with yourself: 'I'll try the skiing, but if it starts giving me problems, I won't ignore it.' Okay?"

"Okay," Wisner says.

"Good. See you after the snow melts."

Glossary

Achilles tendon: the large tendon in the back of the leg that connects the muscles of the calf to the heel bone. The largest tendon in the body.

acromion: a bony shelf that juts up from the shoulder blade to provide a kind of protective roof over the shoulder joint. It connects to the collarbone, or clavicle, at a small joint called the acromioclavicular—or AC—joint.

adductors: any muscles that move one part of the body toward another or toward the midline of the body. In particular, the groin muscles.

aerobic exercise: exercise involving breathing, the utilization of oxygen (as opposed to anaerobic exercise).

anaerobic exercise: exercise involving the utilization of stored energy sources (as opposed to aerobic exercise).

arabesque: in ballet, the pose in which the body is supported by one leg while the other leg is extended behind and at a right angle to the supporting leg.

arthrography: an X-ray technique for examining joints. A dye opaque to X-rays is injected into the joint, allowing its outline and contents to be traced accurately.

arthroscopy: a surgical technique that involves inserting into a joint a small telescope that projects the scene onto a television screen. Arthroscopy is used most frequently in knee surgery.

Baker's cyst: a large, fluid-filled swelling in the back of the knee.

baseball finger: tearing of the tendon that attaches near the fingernail. The result is the finger won't straighten. Also called mallet finger.

biceps: a muscle with two heads of origin. Particularly, the biceps muscle in the front of the upper arm from the shoulder joint to the elbow. This muscle flexes the elbow.

black toenail: the result of bleeding under the nail.

blister: a swelling containing watery fluid and sometimes blood. A blister is simply a callus that hasn't been given enough time to form.

bruise: an area of skin discoloration caused by bleeding from blood vessels rupturing underneath the skin. The cause is usually a blow. Also called a contusion.

bunion: swelling of the joint between the great toe and the first metatarsal bone.

bursa: a small, moist fibrous envelope that occurs where body parts move against each other. A bursa helps to reduce friction.

bursitis: inflammation of a bursa.

calcific tendinitis: calcium deposits in an area of tendinitis. In the shoulder, it is one of the most painful injuries possible.

callus: a hard, thick area of skin occurring in parts of the body subject to pressure or friction.

cardiovascular conditioning: exercise that increases the heart's ability to circulate blood through the body.

carpal tunnel: a tunnel in the wrist and palm that protects the tendons that connect the fingers to the muscles in the forearm. The median nerve that supplies sensation to part of the palm runs in the carpal tunnel as well.

carpus: the oblong wedge of eight small bones in the wrist. They afford the wrist its flexibility.

carrying angle: the elbow's tendency to cause the forearm to veer out to the side when extended. Especially prominent in women.

cartilage: dense tissue that usually provides cushioning at the meeting of bony surfaces.

cheerleader's hip: the result of sudden demands on the muscles of the hip that pulls muscle away from the bone, popping off a piece of bone in the process. Bouncing into splits can do it.

chondromalacia: wear and tear of the cartilage in a joint. Used to describe problems of the kneecap not tracking effectively. Chondromalacia patella is a roughening of the inner surface of the kneecap.

chymopapain: a substance derived from papaya fruit, used to dissolve the center of ruptured disks.

clavicle: the collarbone.

coccyx: the tailbone.

collateral ligaments: ligaments that run along the side of a joint. In the knee there is one on each side (lateral collateral ligament on the outside, medial collateral ligament on the inside). They connect the femur to the tibia and prevent the knee from moving sideways.

compartment syndrome: a condition, usually in the shin area of the lower leg, in which a muscle swells, sometimes up to a third more than its usual size, but the fascia compartment surrounding the muscle does not. The result can be serious, a reduced blood supply to the muscle.

constriction tendinitis: tendinitis caused by the pressure of constricting clothing, especially in the foot.

contrast baths: alternating warm and cold baths to reduce swelling and promote healing.

contusion: an area of skin discoloration caused by bleeding of blood vessels rupturing underneath the skin. The cause is usually a blow. Also called a bruise.

corn: a callus that often occurs between or on top of the toes. Between the toes it is called a soft corn.

cruciate ligaments: ligaments that cross within the knee, from the middle of the tibia to the middle of the femur. The anterior cruciate ligament, the forward of the two, restrains the shin from moving forward. The posterior cruciate ligament, the one toward the back of the knee, prevents the shin from moving backward.

cyst: a sac filled with fluid.

deltoid: the thick triangle of muscle that slopes over the shoulder onto the upper arm. It is responsible for raising the arm away from the body. The muscle separates into three leaves. The most apparent is the anterior deltoid.

De Quervain's disease: a common tendinitis of the wrist, affecting the tendons that connect the thumb to the muscles in the forearm.

disk: a fibrous spacer between vertebrae.

dislocation: the displacement from their normal position of bones meeting at a joint. For example, a shoulder dislocation involves the separation of the ball of the shoulder joint from its seat in the socket of the scapula.

dorsiflex: to flex the foot or hand or fingers backward.

epiphyses: growth centers near the ends of bones.

extensor mechanism: the drive train from the quadriceps to the shinbone that allows extension of the lower leg.

facet joints: bony hinges connecting the vertebrae to each other.

fascia: a tough, gristlelike envelope that encloses muscles.

fascial hernia: tiny balloonlike bulges or defects under the skin, often in the lower outside shin area, just above the ankle.

femur: the large bone in the thigh. The body's largest bone.

fibula: the long, thin outer bone of the lower leg.

foramina: small holes in the vertebrae through which protrude nerves from the spinal cord.

fracture: breakage of a bone, either complete or partial.

funny bone: the ulnar nerve, which runs in a groove behind the elbow and down into the forearm and the outside of the hand. Also called crazy bone.

gamekeeper's thumb: sprain of the ligaments at the base of the thumb, where the web between the thumb and index finger begins. The result is a loss of ability to pinch.

ganglion: a small fluid-filled cyst that grows from a joint, often on the back of the wrist.

gastrocnemius: the large muscle in the calf that attaches in the lower thigh, runs behind the knee about two thirds of the way down the lower leg, and connects to the Achilles tendon.

gelling: stiff, painful movement of a joint, especially the knee.

gluteal muscles: the large muscles in the buttocks, responsible for extending and rotating the hip and leg—primarily the gluteus maximus, gluteus medius, and gluteus minimus.

grand jeté: in ballet a great jump from one leg to the other in which the leading leg appears to be thrown into the air.

greater trochanter: the protruding knob at the upper outside end of the femur.

hamstrings: large muscles in the back of the thigh.

heel spur: a spike of bone up to ¾ inch long extending from the heel bone.

hip pointer: a blow to the bony ridge of the pelvis. One of the most painful athletic injuries.

humeral epicondyle: the lateral humeral epicondyle is the bump on the outside of the elbow, the location of tennis elbow. The medial humeral epicondyle is the bump on the inside of the elbow, the location of little league elbow.

humerus: the upper arm bone.

iliotibial band: a long, thick, rigid tendon that runs from the upper part of the hip along the outside of the thigh and across the knee and connects to the shinbone.

impingement: buildup of bone and soft tissue, primarily in the ankle and wrist, blocking movement.

ingrown toenail: a toenail that curls at the edges and grows into the fleshy part of the toe.

isotope scan: a diagnostic technique involving injecting into the body a radioactive-isotope solution that searches out the healing process in bone.

joint mice: loose bodies in a joint—for example, bone chips in the elbow.

jumper's knee: tendinitis of the tendon attached to the kneecap. It usually occurs at the bottom of the kneecap, where the tendon from the shinbone connects. Also called patellar tendinitis.

lactic acid: a simple sugar that's the end product of anaerobic exercise. It can accumulate in the muscles and cause burning or cramping.

laminectomy: surgery involving removing at least part of a ruptured disk.

ligaments: tough bands of fibers that connect bone to bone.

little league elbow: tendinitis of the inside of the elbow, at the medial humeral epicondyle. Also called medial tennis elbow.

menisci: thick rings of cartilage that cushion the knee and provide shock absorption. Also called fibrocartilage.

meniscus cyst: a fluid-filled sac attached to a torn meniscus.

meralgia paresthetica: irritation of the lateral cutaneous nerve, which crosses the bony ridge of the pelvis. The problem can cause pain down the upper front of the thigh.

metacarpus: the five bones of the hand that connect the carpus, or wristbones, to the phalanges, or finger bones.

metatarsal bones: the small bones between the toes and the top of the foot.

myositis ossificans: the result of a blow against a muscle that not only ruptures blood vessels but pulls the muscle away from the bone, taking periosteum with it and resulting in bone forming within the muscle.

navicular: a boat-shaped bone in the foot and hand. In the hand it lies at the base of the thumb; in the foot it rests against the lower ankle bone, the talus. In the hand it's also called the scaphoid.

olecranon process: the large end of the ulna, which extends behind the elbow joint.

orthopedic sleeve: a tight, pullover neoprene bandage, often used for the knee.

orthotic: a custom-made shoe insert.

Osgood-Schlatter's disease: a form of tendinitis at the end of the patellar tendon, where it goes into the shinbone. It affects growing people, primarily between ten and sixteen years old.

osteochondritis dissecans: a condition in which a piece of bone and overlying cartilage loses its blood supply and flakes away into a joint, often the knee or ankle.

osteoporosis: a loss of bone strength affecting primarily postmenopausal women. Symptoms include stooped and rounded shoulders.

paraspinous muscles: the strong ropes of muscles that run along either side of the spine.

passé: in ballet, a movement in which the foot of the working leg passes the knee of the supporting leg.

patella: the kneecap.

pectoral muscles; the chest muscles. The pectoralis major is a large fan-shaped muscle that draws the arm forward across the chest. The smaller pectoralis minor draws the shoulder blade downward.

pelvis: the bony ringlike structure to which the bones of the legs are attached. Also called pelvic girdle or hip girdle.

periosteum: a layer of dense tissue that covers the surface of bone. In children the periosteum is especially thick and rich with blood to promote growth.

peroneal muscles: muscles that run along the outside of the lower calf. They enable one to pull the foot to the outside.

peroneal tendons: tendons that connect the peroneal muscles, which run along the outside of the lower leg, to the bones of the foot.

phalanges: the bones of the fingers and toes.

piriformis syndrome: irritation of the piriformis muscle, a small muscle that lies in the buttocks underneath the gluteals and assists them in rotating and extending the hip.

plantar fascia: a ligamentlike rope of fibrous tissue that runs along the inside of the sole of the foot from the heel to the base of the toes. Among other functions, it maintains the arch.

plantar fasciitis: inflammation of a stretched, torn plantar fascia.

plantar neuroma: a pinched nerve usually between the third and fourth toes. Sometimes called Morton's neuroma.

plié: in ballet, bending the knee over the ankle.

popliteus: a tiny muscle in the back of the knee that helps to flex the knee.

pronation: the act of turning the hand so that the palm faces downward.

quadriceps: the muscle group in the front part of the thigh. The body's largest and most powerful muscles.

quadriplegia: paralysis of the arms and legs.

radial head: the head of the radius, convex in shape, which rotates against the humerus.

radius: the outer and shorter bone of the forearm.

rectus femoris: the portion of the quadriceps muscle that connects to the pelvis.

reduction: restoring a displaced part of the body to its normal position by manipulation or surgery. For example, a dislocated shoulder is reduced by centering the ball of the shoulder joint against its seat in the scapula once again.

relevé: in ballet, raising the body onto the toes or half-point.

rhomboid muscles: muscles in the center of the back that attach the edge of the shoulder blade to the spine. They help to pull the shoulder blade upward and toward the spine.

rotator cuff muscles: the group of small muscles in the shoulder joint below the deltoids. These muscles hold the joint in the proper position and are responsible for subtle, precise shoulder movements. They are frequently torn.

rupture: tissue that bursts apart or open. For example, an Achilles tendon can rupture. So can the biceps muscle.

sacrum: the fused portion of the backbone at the level of the pelvis.

scapula: the shoulder blade.

Scheuerman's disease: abnormal growth of the vertebrae, causing a forward curve of the backbone.

sciatica: irritation of the sciatic nerve, the large nerve that supplies sensation to much of the body from the hips downward. The result can be pain that runs down the back of the thigh and calf all the way to the foot.

scoliosis: a side-to-side curve of the backbone.

sesamoid bones: tiny bones in the feet within the tendons that run to the big toe.

sesamoiditis: any irritation of the sesamoid bones.

shin splints: all-purpose category describing pain in the lower leg.

shoulder separation: dislocation of the acromioclavicular joint, thereby separating the collarbone from the shoulder.

snapping hip: popping in the hip joint, sometimes for unknown reasons.

snowball crepitation: squeaking caused by inflammation of the tendon and its sheath. As the tendon moves within the sheath, it squeaks, sounding like the noise made by squeezing a handful of snow.

soleus: the muscle in the lower part of the calf.

spondylolisthesis: a severe stress fracture of the vertebrae that causes one vertebra to slip forward on another.

spondylolysis: a stress fracture of the vertebrae.

spinal column: the flexible bony column extending from the base of the skull to the small of the back. It encloses and protects the spinal cord, articulates with the skull, ribs, and hip girdle, and provides attachment for the muscles of the back. It consists of three parts: the cervical spine, thoracic spine, and lumbar spine.

spinous processes: small bumps of the backbone, just under the skin, an inch to an inch and a half long, that function as muscle attachments.

sprain: an injury to a ligament caused by sudden overstretching or tearing.

sternum: the breastbone.

stress fracture: a hairline fracture, often too fine to show up on X-rays, caused by stress on the bone just to the point of breaking.

subluxation: partial dislocation of a joint, so that the bone ends are misaligned but still in contact.

supination: the act of turning the hand so that the palm faces upward.

synovial membrane: the fluid-producing lining that surrounds joints.

talus: the lower of the ankle bones.

tendinitis: inflammation of a tendon.

tendon: the tough cords that attach muscle to bone.

tennis elbow: tendinitis in the elbow, at the point of the bump on the outside of the elbow, the lateral humeral epicondyle.

tennis leg: the ripping away of part of the calf muscle from the Achilles tendon. Also called calf strain.

tensor fascia lata: a small fist-shaped muscle in the hip, under the bony ridge of the pelvis.

thoracic outlet syndrome: irritation of the nerves that begin in the neck and run into the shoulder and down the arm. The result can be pain in the arms and hands, far from the point of irritation.

tibia: the shinbone.

trapezius: the huge, flat, triangular muscle that covers the back of the neck and shoulder. It moves the head backward to either side and is important in movements of the shoulder blade.

triceps: a muscle with three heads of origin. Particularly, the triceps muscle in the back of the upper arm. It contracts to extend the elbow.

ulna: the inner and longer bone of the forearm.

vastus medialis: a tiny section of the quadriceps muscle located just above and to the inside of the kneecap. This muscle is very important in keeping the kneecap tracking properly.

vertebrae: the small bones that comprise the spinal column.

Cross-Reference— Injuries Listed By Sport

Index